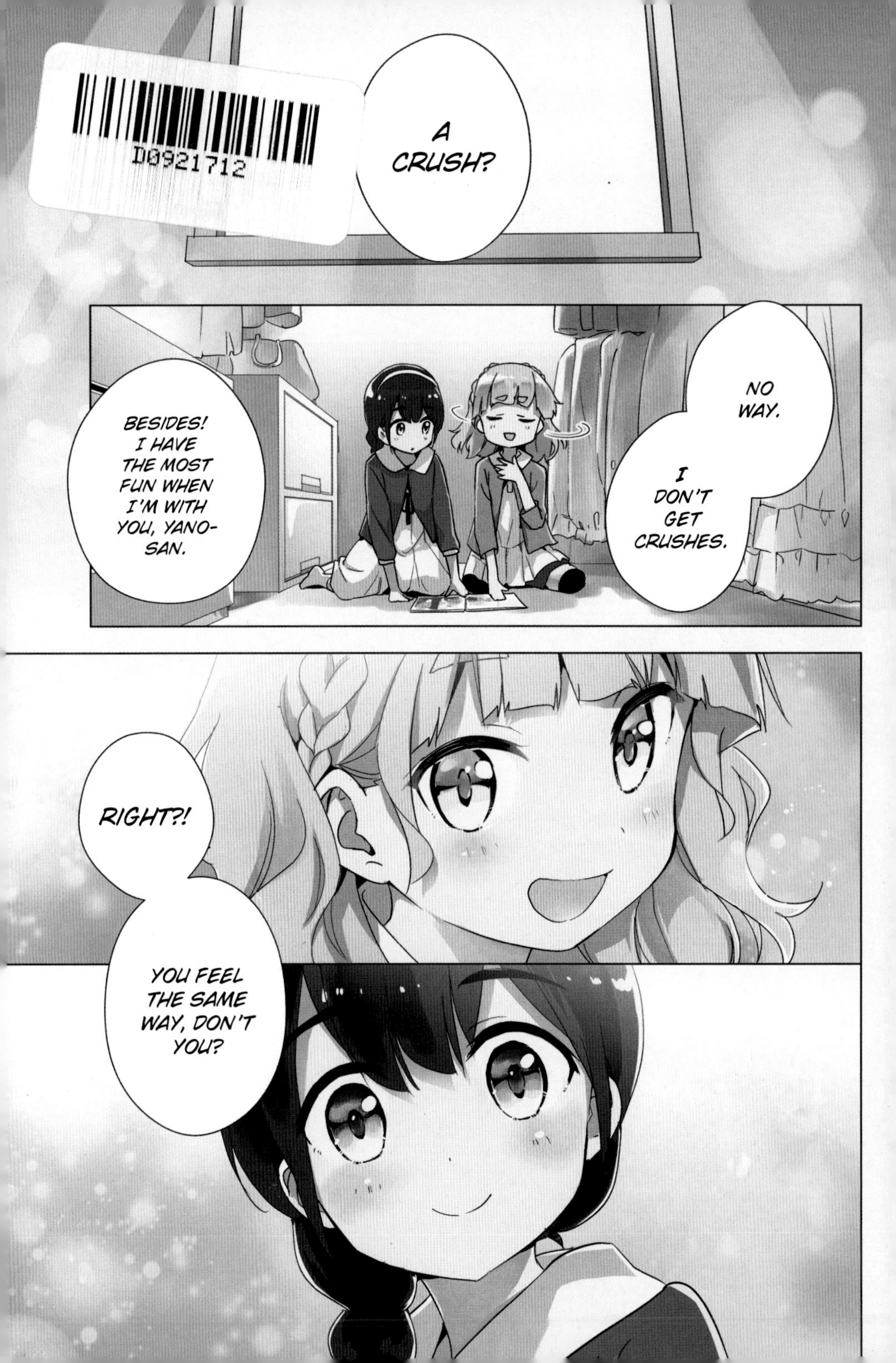
A CRUSH?
NO WAY.
I DON'T GET CRUSHES.
BESIDES! I HAVE THE MOST FUN WHEN I'M WITH YOU, YANO-SAN.
RIGHT?!
YOU FEEL THE SAME WAY, DON'T YOU?

Shift 27 Onee-sama's Absence

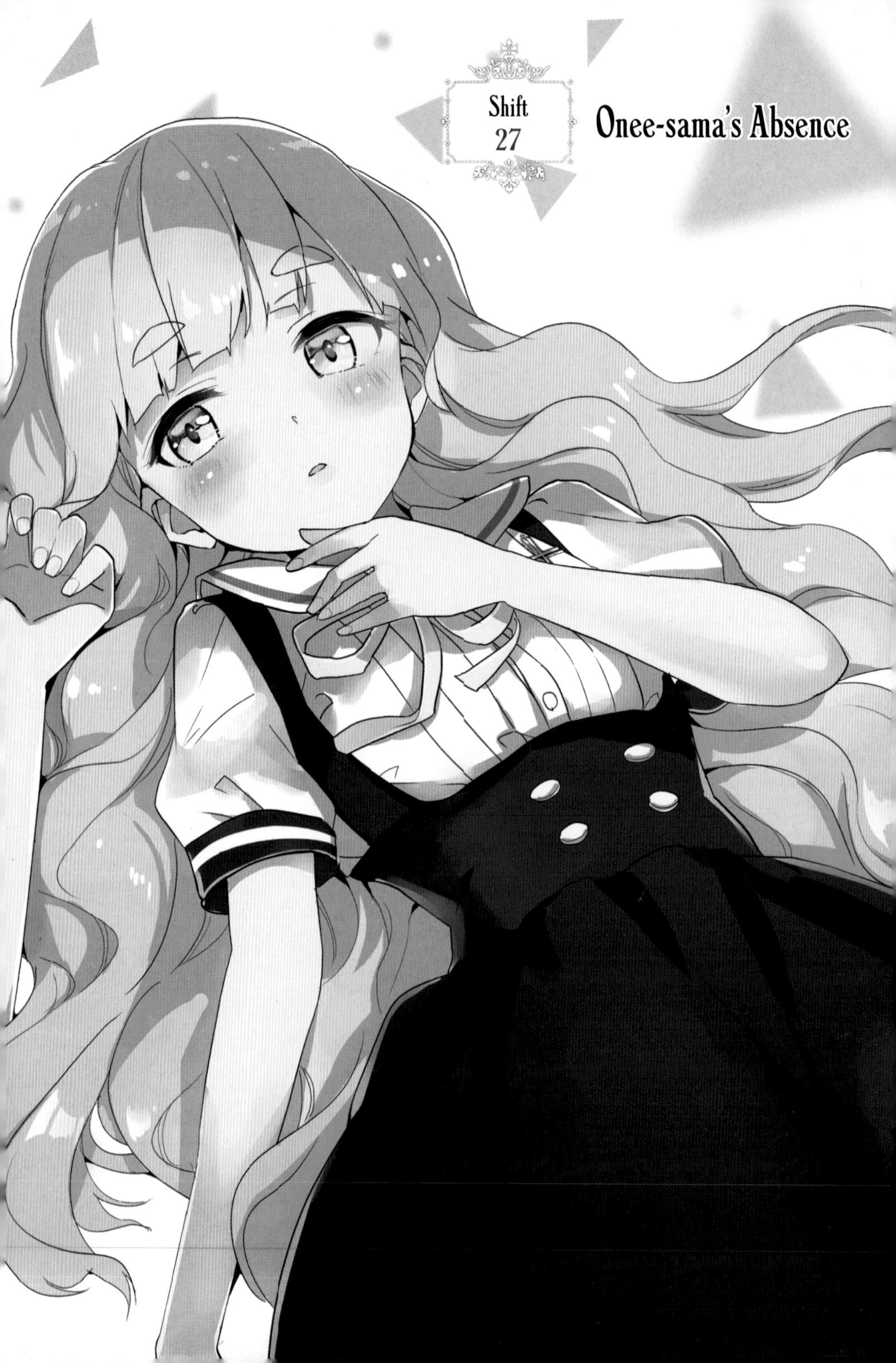

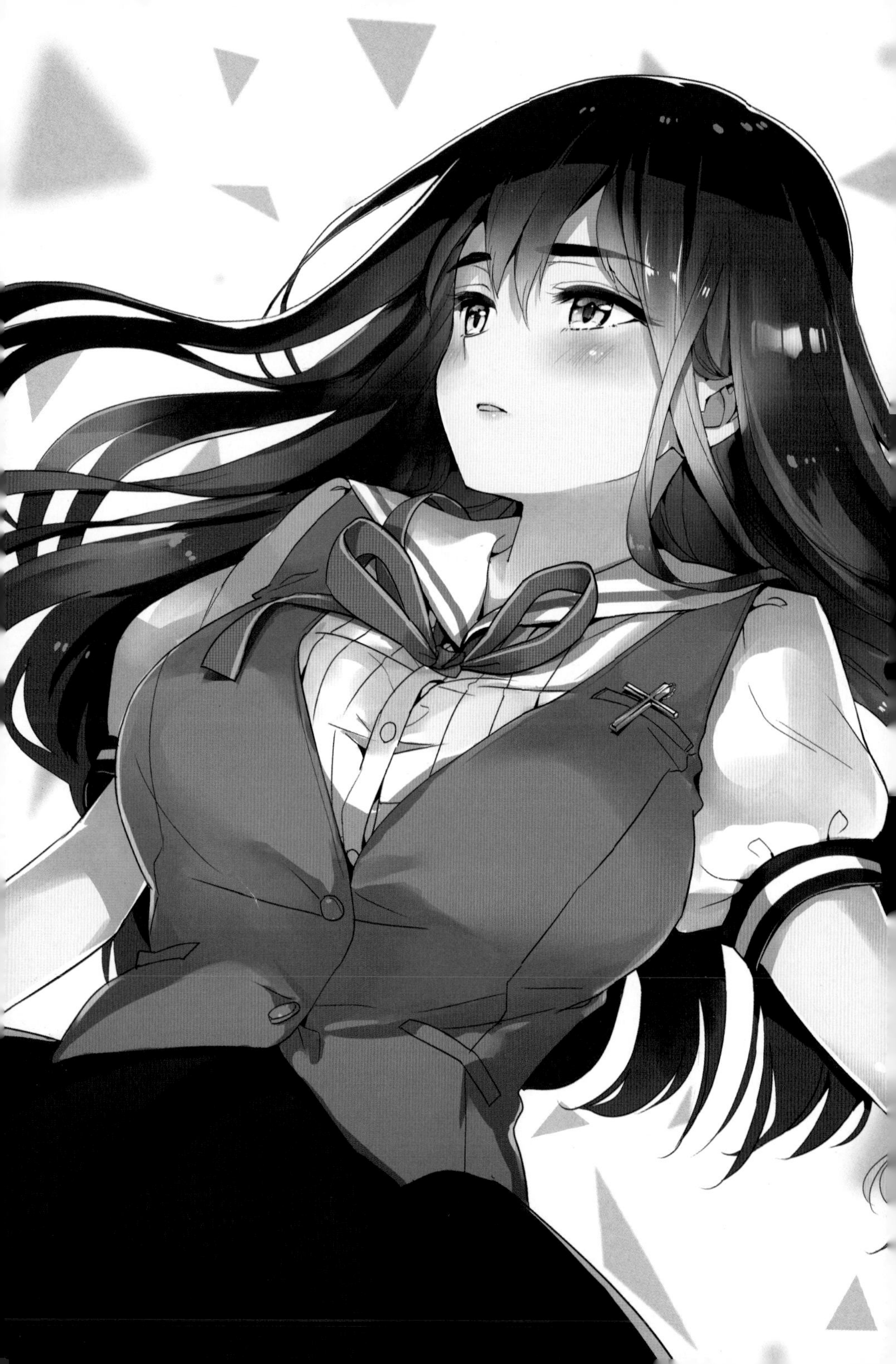

CONTENTS

6

Schwestern
in
Liebe!

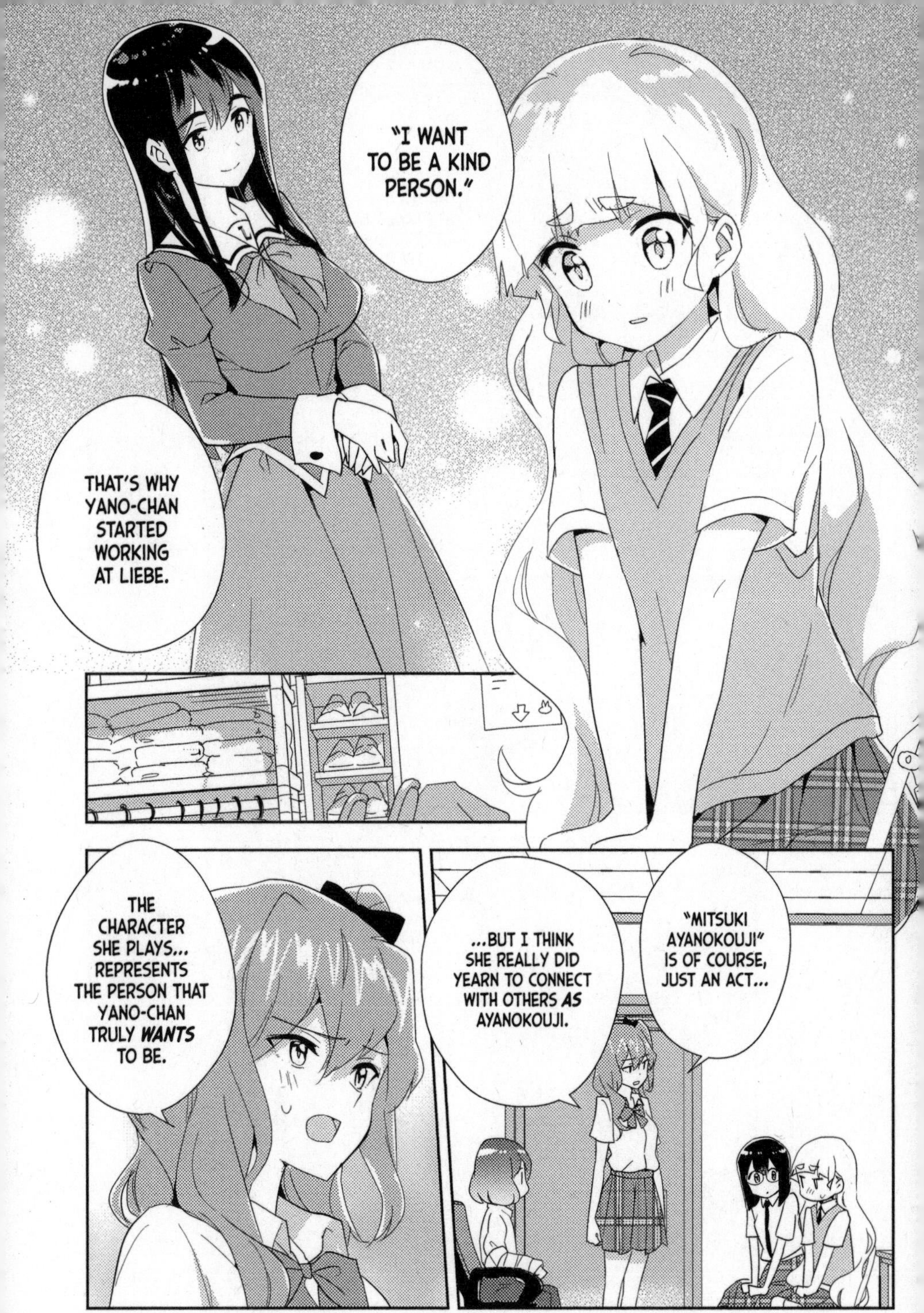
"I WANT TO BE A KIND PERSON."
THAT'S WHY YANO-CHAN STARTED WORKING AT LIEBE.
"MITSUKI AYANOKOUJI" IS OF COURSE, JUST AN ACT...
...BUT I THINK SHE REALLY DID YEARN TO CONNECT WITH OTHERS *AS* AYANOKOUJI.
THE CHARACTER SHE PLAYS... REPRESENTS THE PERSON THAT YANO-CHAN TRULY *WANTS* TO BE.

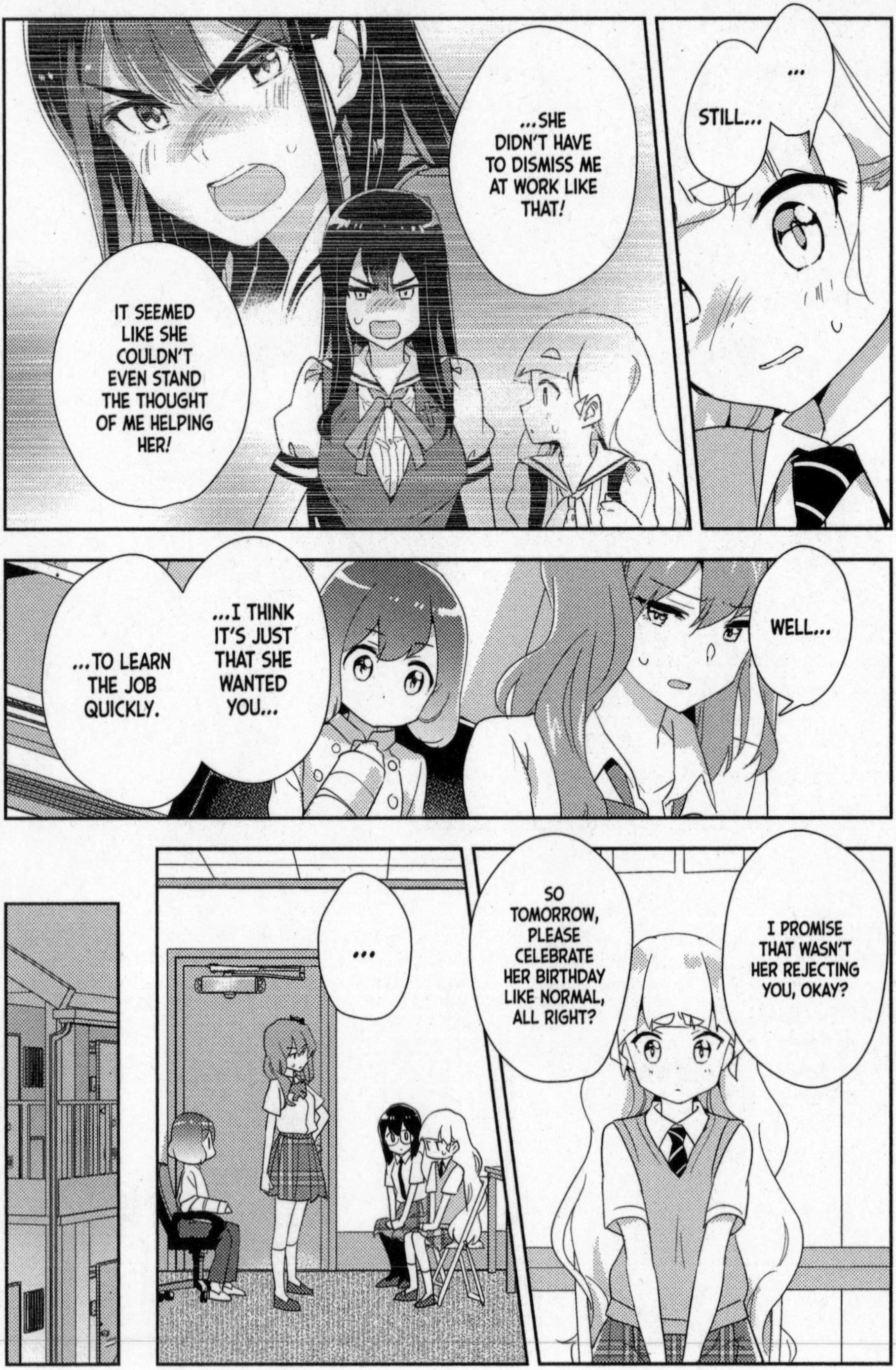
...
STILL...
...SHE DIDN'T HAVE TO DISMISS ME AT WORK LIKE THAT!
IT SEEMED LIKE SHE COULDN'T EVEN STAND THE THOUGHT OF ME HELPING HER!
WELL...
...I THINK IT'S JUST THAT SHE WANTED YOU...
...TO LEARN THE JOB QUICKLY.
I PROMISE THAT WASN'T HER REJECTING YOU, OKAY?
SO TOMORROW, PLEASE CELEBRATE HER BIRTHDAY LIKE NORMAL, ALL RIGHT?
...

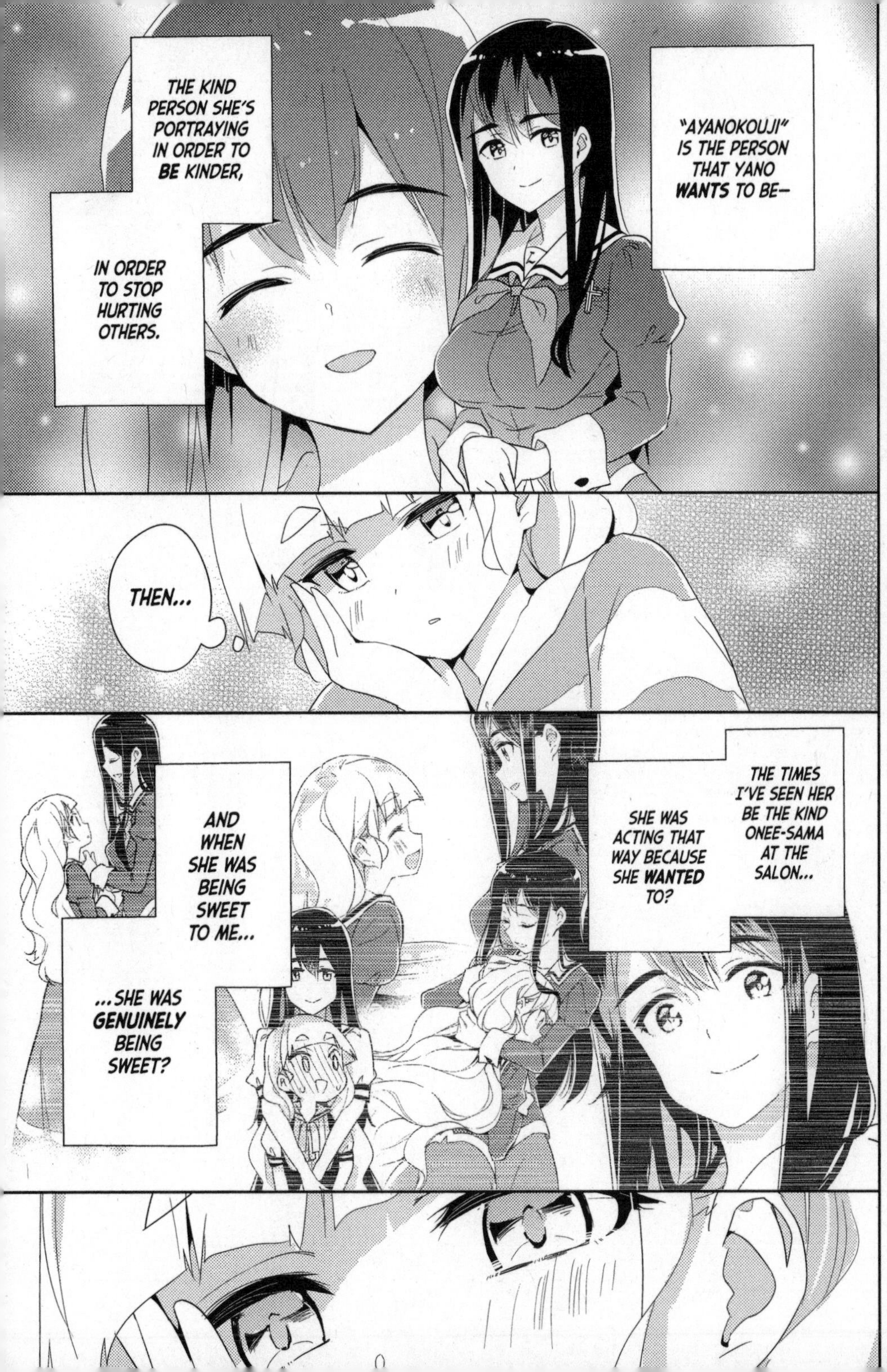
"AYANOKOUJI" IS THE PERSON THAT YANO WANTS TO BE—
THE KIND PERSON SHE'S PORTRAYING IN ORDER TO BE KINDER,
IN ORDER TO STOP HURTING OTHERS.
THEN...
THE TIMES I'VE SEEN HER BE THE KIND ONEE-SAMA AT THE SALON...
SHE WAS ACTING THAT WAY BECAUSE SHE WANTED TO?
AND WHEN SHE WAS BEING SWEET TO ME...
...SHE WAS GENUINELY BEING SWEET?

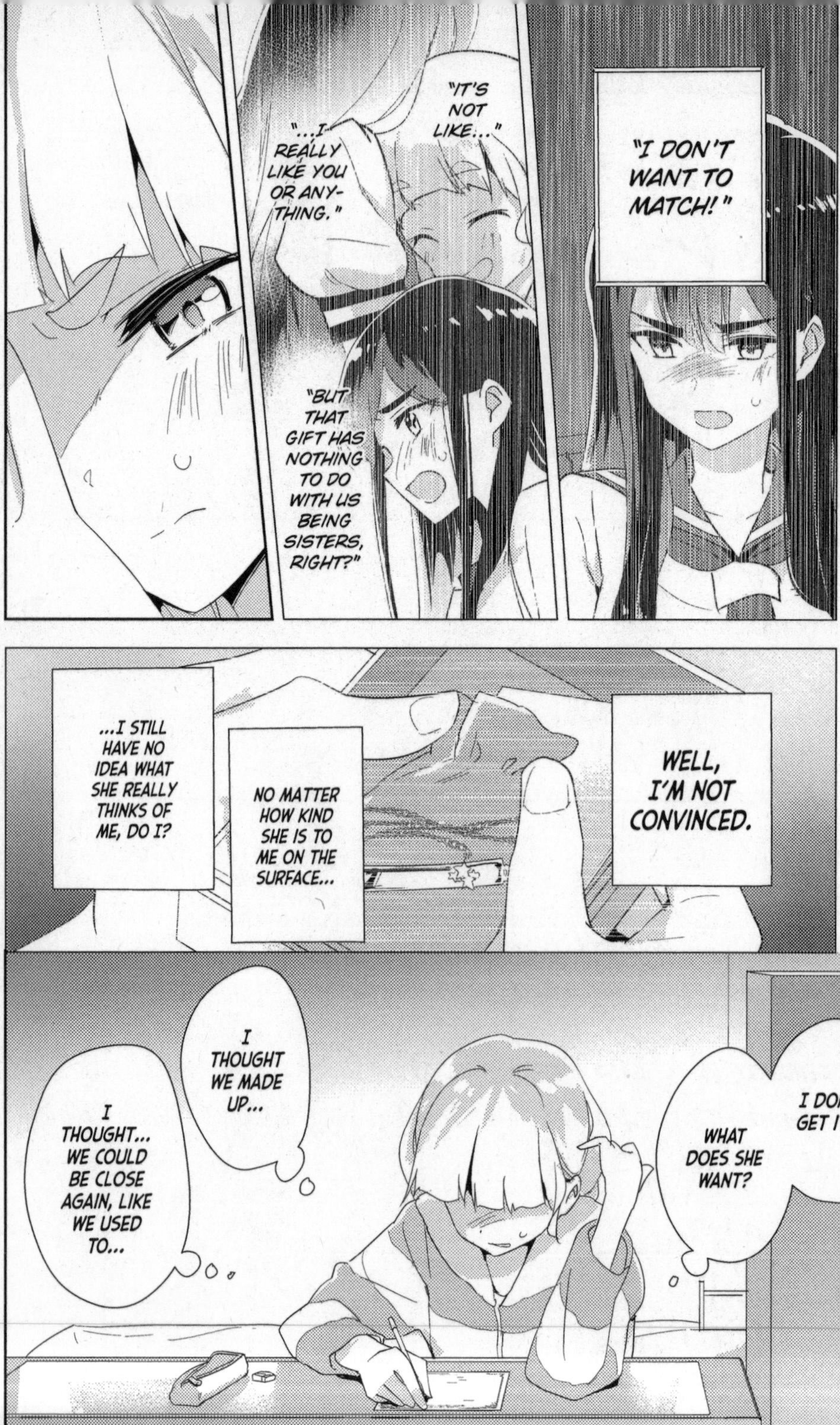
"I DON'T WANT TO MATCH!"
"IT'S NOT LIKE..."
"...I REALLY LIKE YOU OR ANY-THING."
"BUT THAT GIFT HAS NOTHING TO DO WITH US BEING SISTERS, RIGHT?"
WELL, I'M NOT CONVINCED.
NO MATTER HOW KIND SHE IS TO ME ON THE SURFACE...
...I STILL HAVE NO IDEA WHAT SHE REALLY THINKS OF ME, DO I?
I DON'T GET IT...
WHAT DOES SHE WANT?
I THOUGHT WE MADE UP...
I THOUGHT... WE COULD BE CLOSE AGAIN, LIKE WE USED TO...

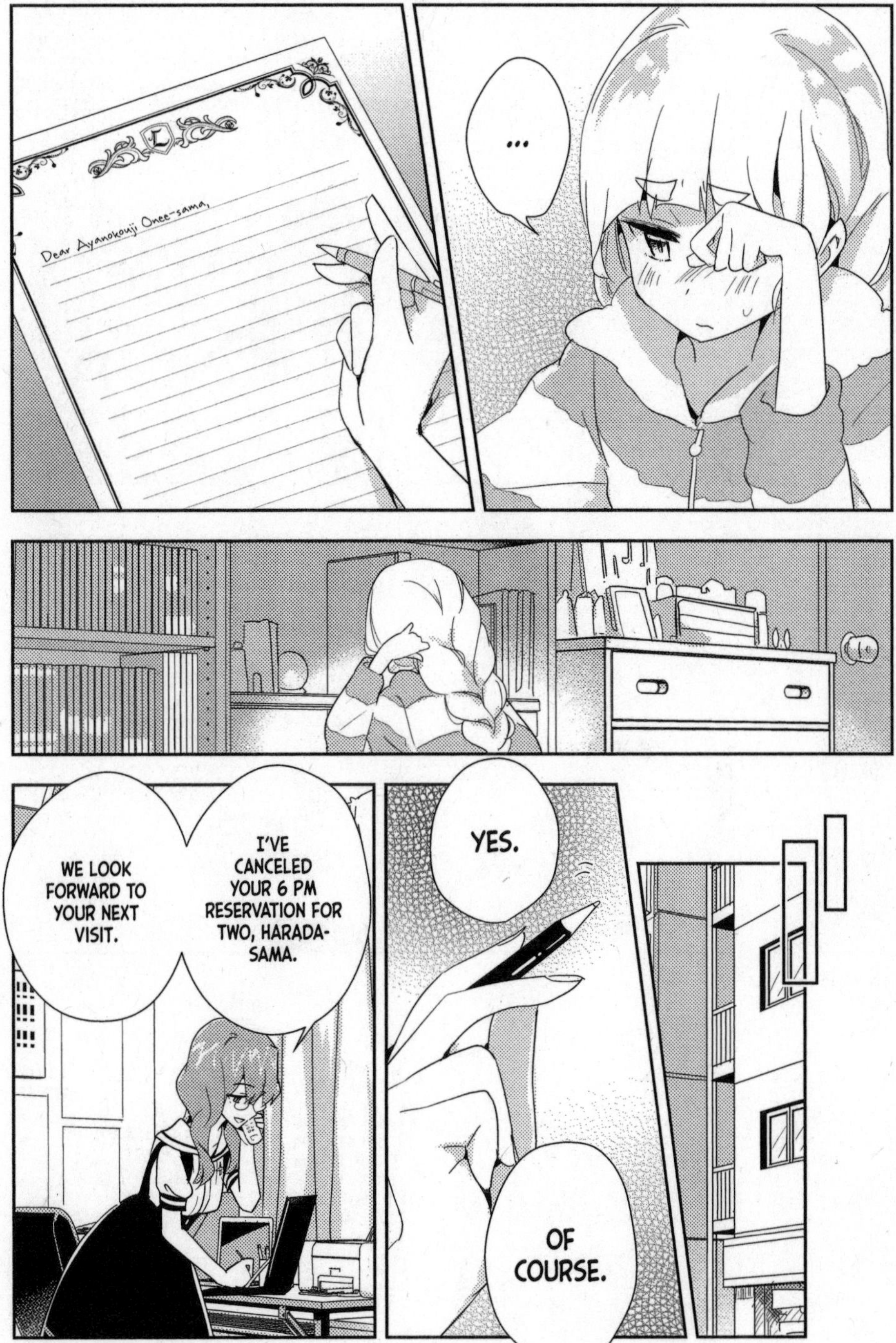
...
Dear Ayanokouji Onee-sama,
YES.
OF COURSE.
I'VE CANCELED YOUR 6 PM RESERVATION FOR TWO, HARADA-SAMA.
WE LOOK FORWARD TO YOUR NEXT VISIT.

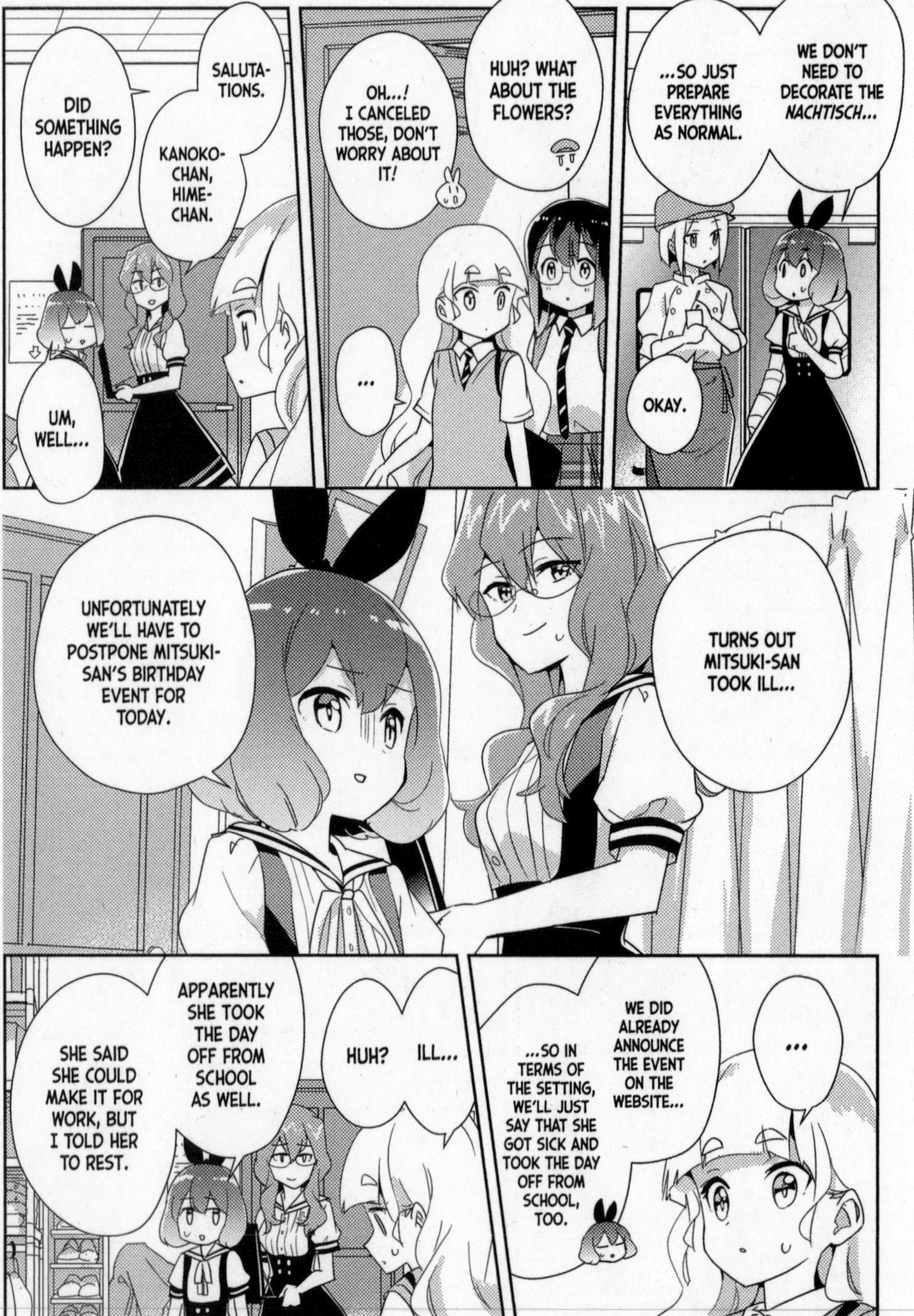
WE DON'T NEED TO DECORATE THE *NACHTISCH*...
...SO JUST PREPARE EVERYTHING AS NORMAL.
OKAY.
HUH? WHAT ABOUT THE FLOWERS?
OH...! I CANCELED THOSE, DON'T WORRY ABOUT IT!
...
SALUTATIONS.
KANOKO-CHAN, HIME-CHAN.
DID SOMETHING HAPPEN?
UM, WELL...
TURNS OUT MITSUKI-SAN TOOK ILL...
UNFORTUNATELY WE'LL HAVE TO POSTPONE MITSUKI-SAN'S BIRTHDAY EVENT FOR TODAY.
...
WE DID ALREADY ANNOUNCE THE EVENT ON THE WEBSITE...
...SO IN TERMS OF THE SETTING, WE'LL JUST SAY THAT SHE GOT SICK AND TOOK THE DAY OFF FROM SCHOOL, TOO.
ILL...
HUH?
APPARENTLY SHE TOOK THE DAY OFF FROM SCHOOL AS WELL.
SHE SAID SHE COULD MAKE IT FOR WORK, BUT I TOLD HER TO REST.

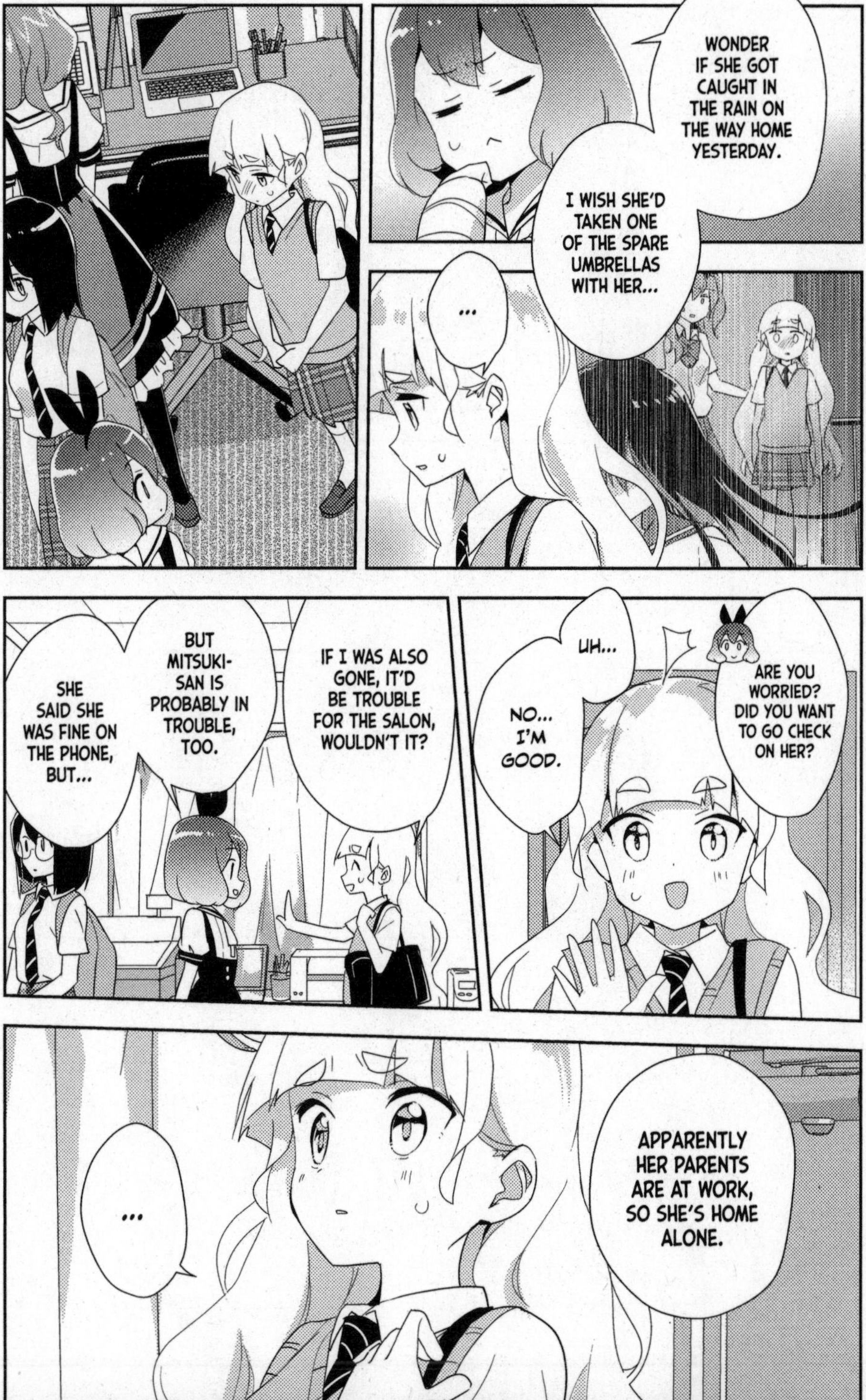
WONDER IF SHE GOT CAUGHT IN THE RAIN ON THE WAY HOME YESTERDAY.
I WISH SHE'D TAKEN ONE OF THE SPARE UMBRELLAS WITH HER...
...
ARE YOU WORRIED? DID YOU WANT TO GO CHECK ON HER?
UH...
NO... I'M GOOD.
IF I WAS ALSO GONE, IT'D BE TROUBLE FOR THE SALON, WOULDN'T IT?
BUT MITSUKI-SAN IS PROBABLY IN TROUBLE, TOO.
SHE SAID SHE WAS FINE ON THE PHONE, BUT...
APPARENTLY HER PARENTS ARE AT WORK, SO SHE'S HOME ALONE.
...

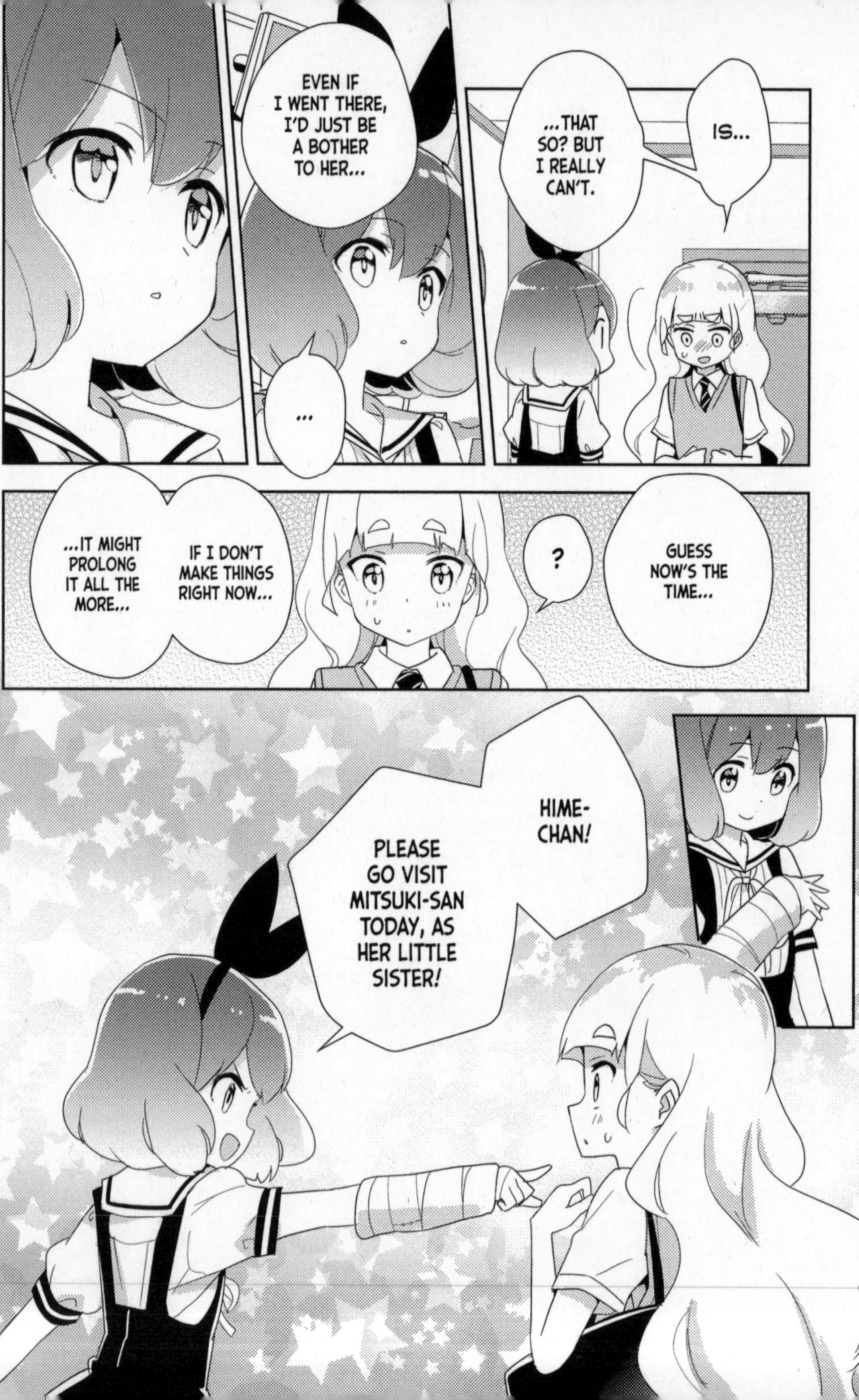
IS...
...THAT SO? BUT I REALLY CAN'T.
EVEN IF I WENT THERE, I'D JUST BE A BOTHER TO HER...
...
GUESS NOW'S THE TIME...
?
IF I DON'T MAKE THINGS RIGHT NOW...
...IT MIGHT PROLONG IT ALL THE MORE...
HIME-CHAN!
PLEASE GO VISIT MITSUKI-SAN TODAY, AS HER LITTLE SISTER!

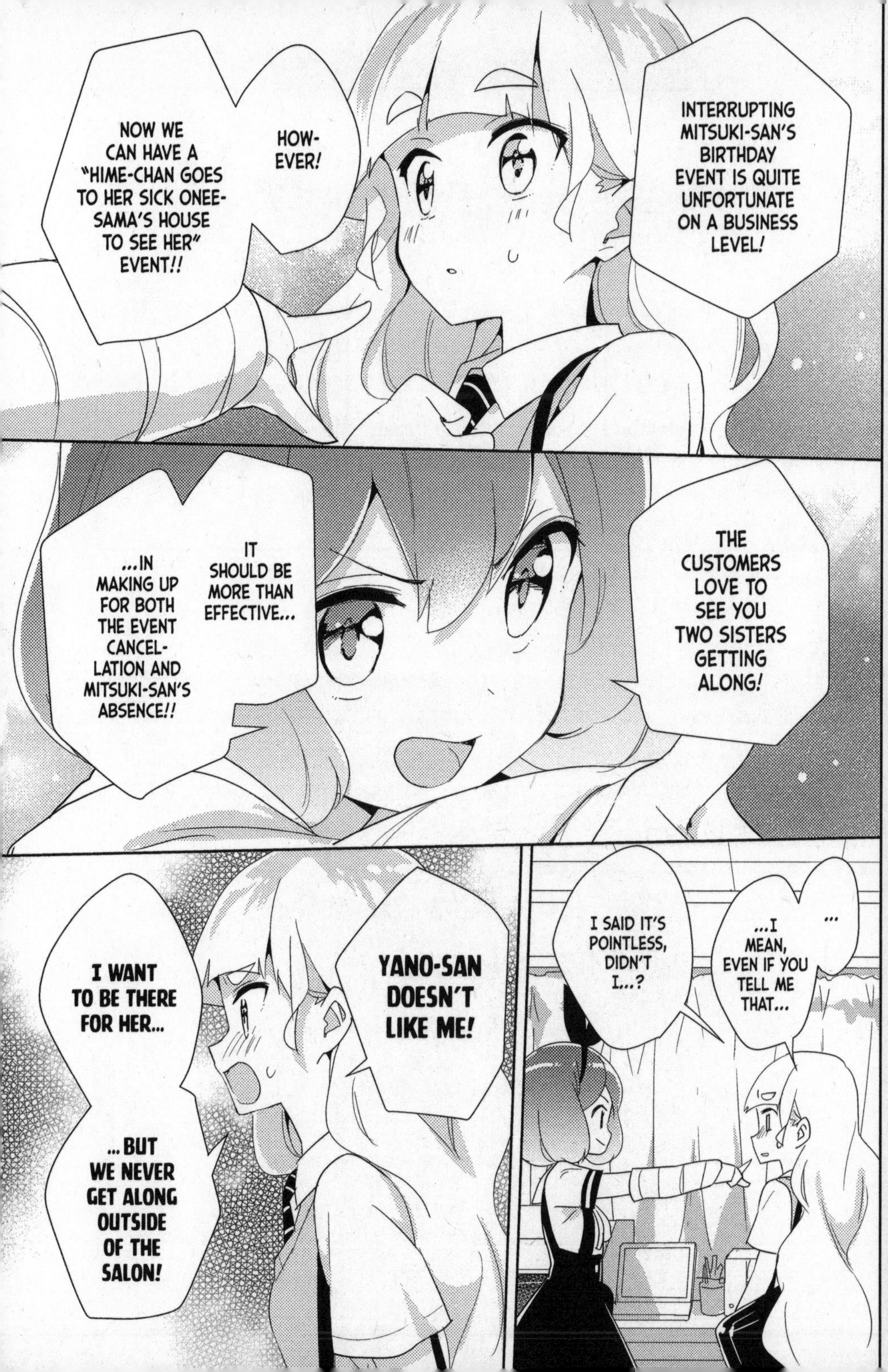

INTERRUPTING MITSUKI-SAN'S BIRTHDAY EVENT IS QUITE UNFORTUNATE ON A BUSINESS LEVEL!
HOW-EVER!
NOW WE CAN HAVE A "HIME-CHAN GOES TO HER SICK ONEE-SAMA'S HOUSE TO SEE HER" EVENT!!
THE CUSTOMERS LOVE TO SEE YOU TWO SISTERS GETTING ALONG!
IT SHOULD BE MORE THAN EFFECTIVE...
...IN MAKING UP FOR BOTH THE EVENT CANCEL-LATION AND MITSUKI-SAN'S ABSENCE!!
...
...I MEAN, EVEN IF YOU TELL ME THAT...
I SAID IT'S POINTLESS, DIDN'T I...?
YANO-SAN DOESN'T LIKE ME!
I WANT TO BE THERE FOR HER...
...BUT WE NEVER GET ALONG OUTSIDE OF THE SALON!

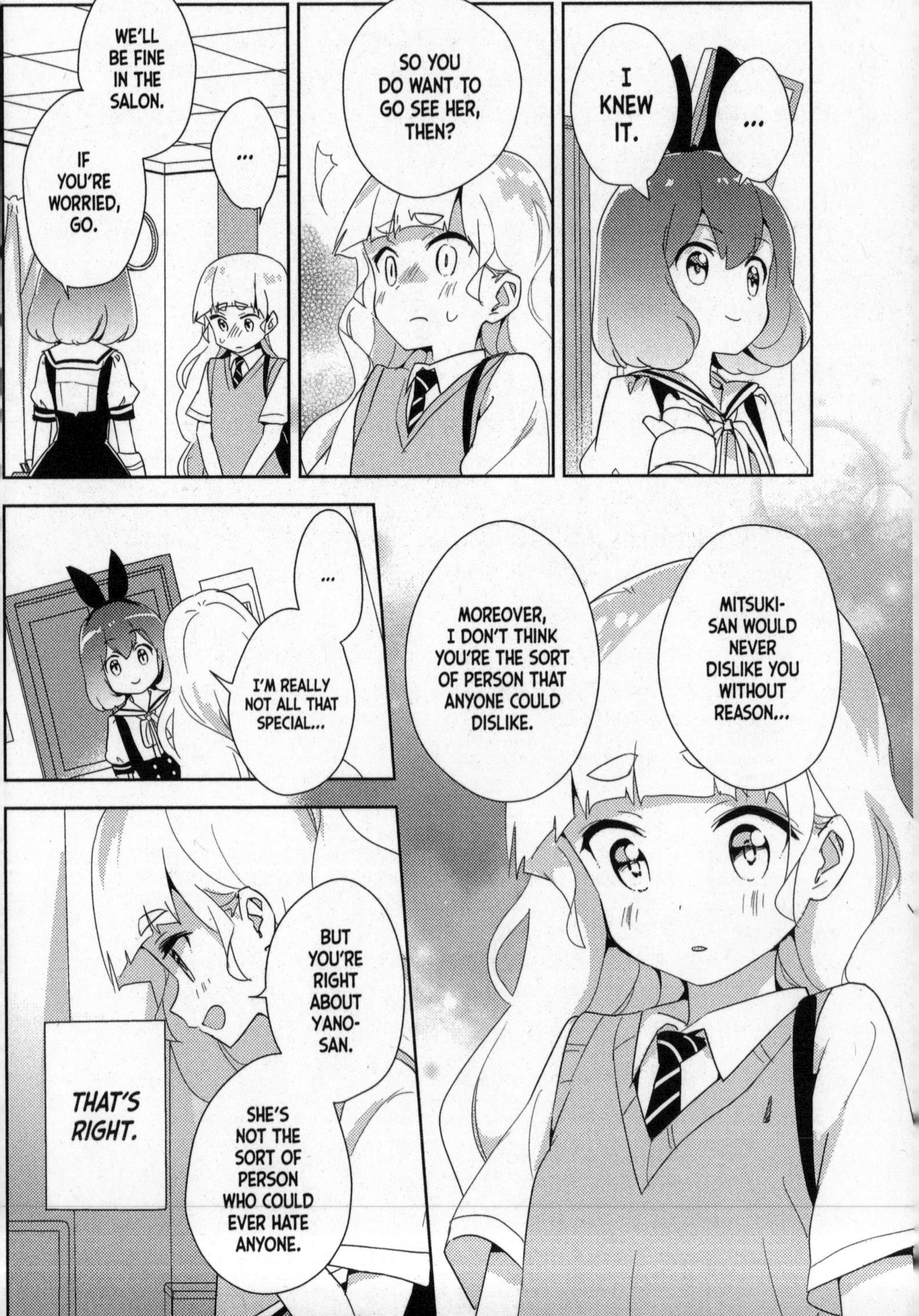
I KNEW IT.
...
SO YOU DO WANT TO GO SEE HER, THEN?
WE'LL BE FINE IN THE SALON.
IF YOU'RE WORRIED, GO.
...
MITSUKI-SAN WOULD NEVER DISLIKE YOU WITHOUT REASON...
MOREOVER, I DON'T THINK YOU'RE THE SORT OF PERSON THAT ANYONE COULD DISLIKE.
...
I'M REALLY NOT ALL THAT SPECIAL...
BUT YOU'RE RIGHT ABOUT YANO-SAN.
SHE'S NOT THE SORT OF PERSON WHO COULD EVER HATE ANYONE.
THAT'S RIGHT.

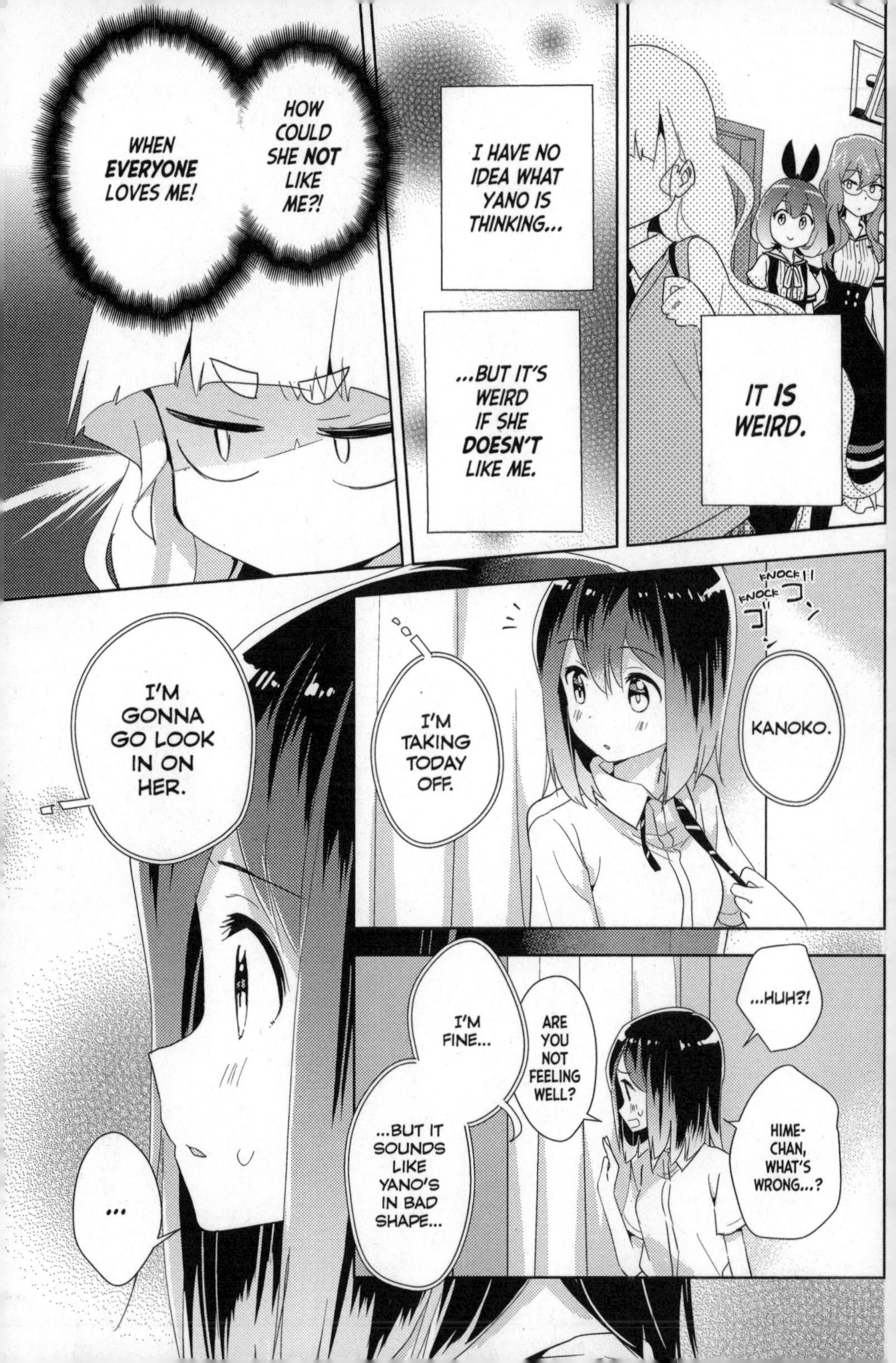
IT IS WEIRD.
I HAVE NO IDEA WHAT YANO IS THINKING...
...BUT IT'S WEIRD IF SHE DOESN'T LIKE ME.
HOW COULD SHE NOT LIKE ME?!
WHEN EVERYONE LOVES ME!
KNOCK KNOCK
KANOKO.
I'M TAKING TODAY OFF.
...HUH?!
HIME-CHAN, WHAT'S WRONG...?
ARE YOU NOT FEELING WELL?
I'M FINE...
...BUT IT SOUNDS LIKE YANO'S IN BAD SHAPE...
I'M GONNA GO LOOK IN ON HER.
...

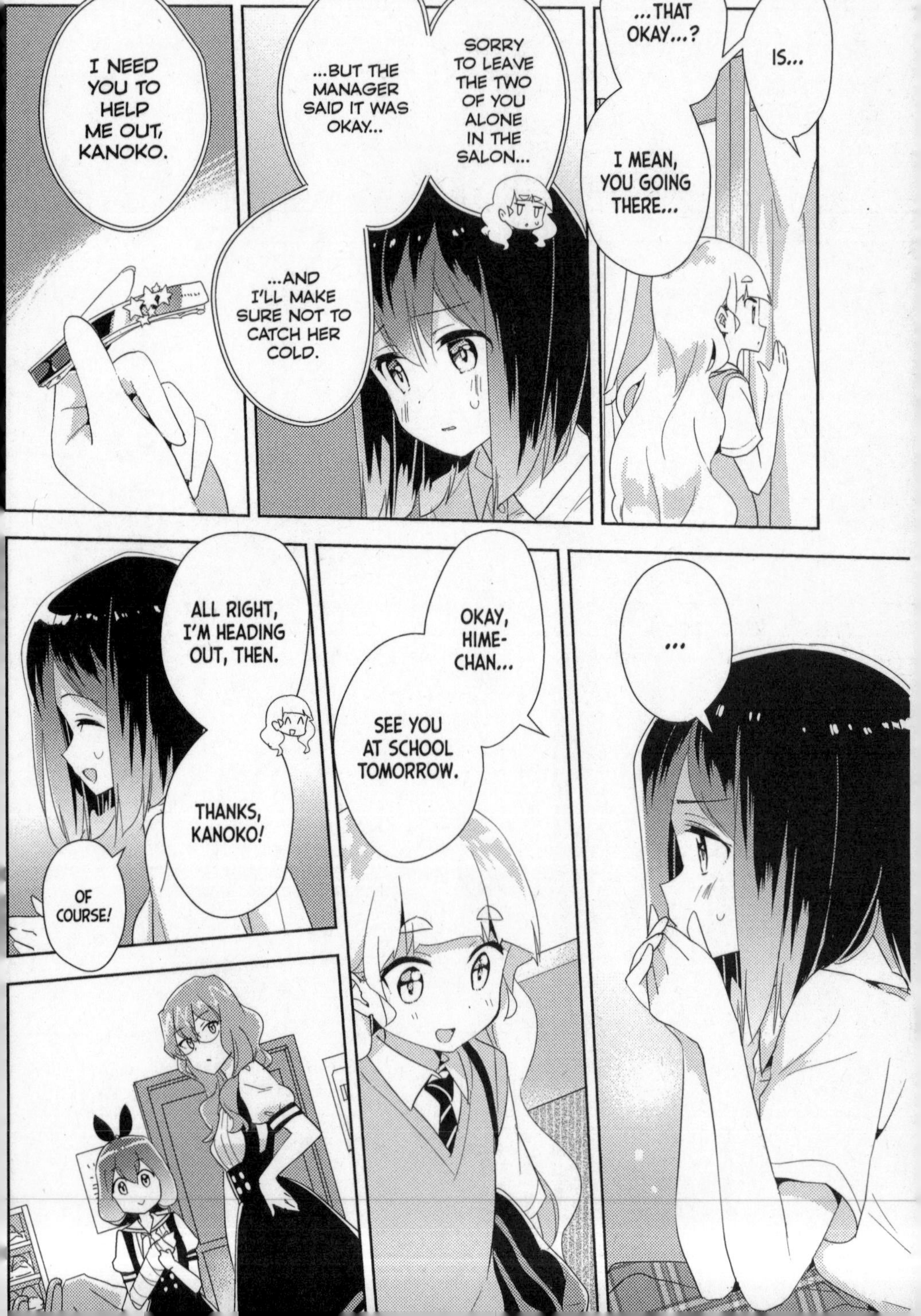
IS...
...THAT OKAY...?
I MEAN, YOU GOING THERE...
SORRY TO LEAVE THE TWO OF YOU ALONE IN THE SALON...
...BUT THE MANAGER SAID IT WAS OKAY...
...AND I'LL MAKE SURE NOT TO CATCH HER COLD.
I NEED YOU TO HELP ME OUT, KANOKO.
...
OKAY, HIME-CHAN...
SEE YOU AT SCHOOL TOMORROW.
ALL RIGHT, I'M HEADING OUT, THEN.
THANKS, KANOKO!
OF COURSE!

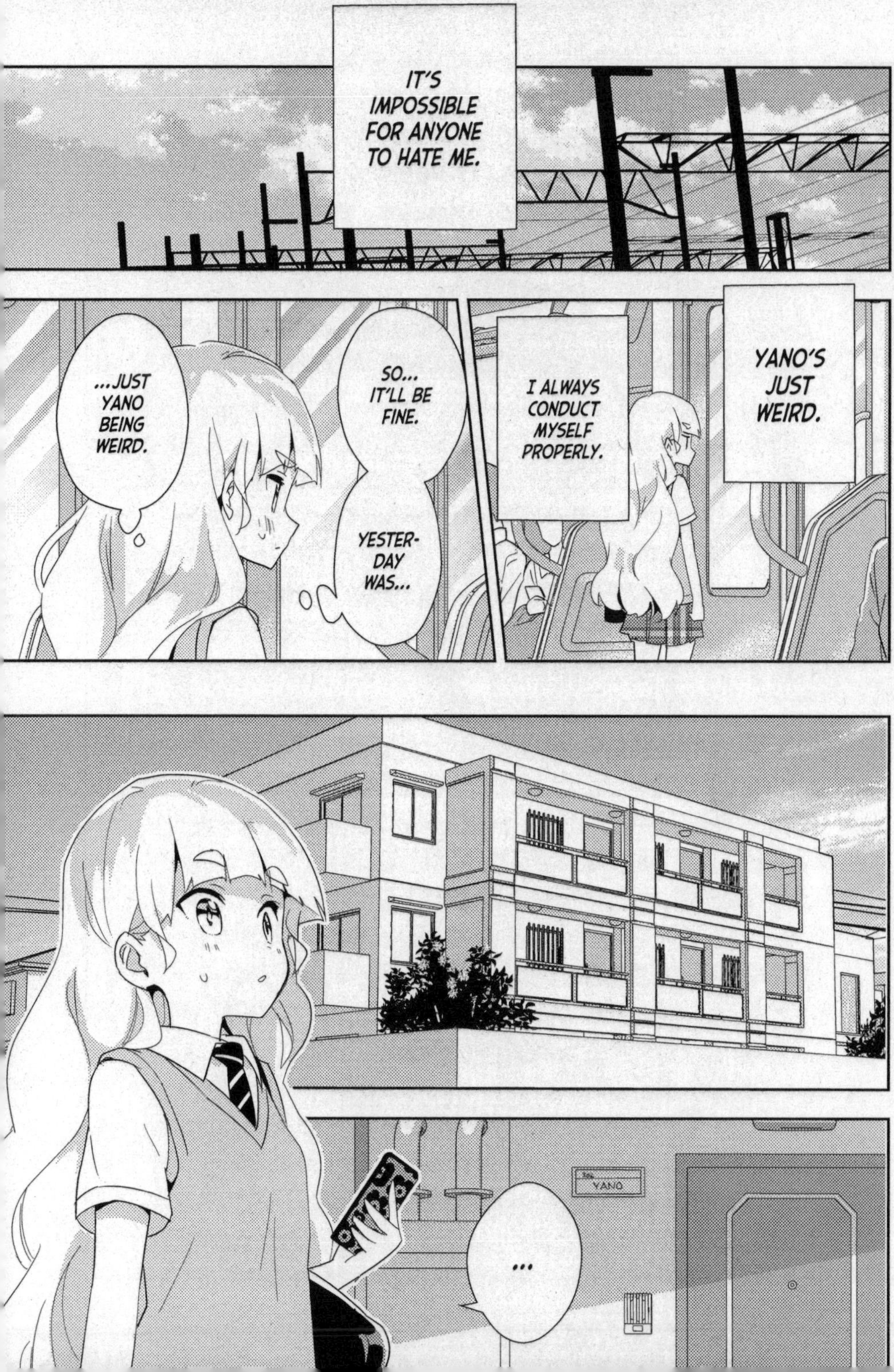
IT'S IMPOSSIBLE FOR ANYONE TO HATE ME.
YANO'S JUST WEIRD.
I ALWAYS CONDUCT MYSELF PROPERLY.
SO... IT'LL BE FINE.
YESTER-DAY WAS...
...JUST YANO BEING WEIRD.
YANO
...

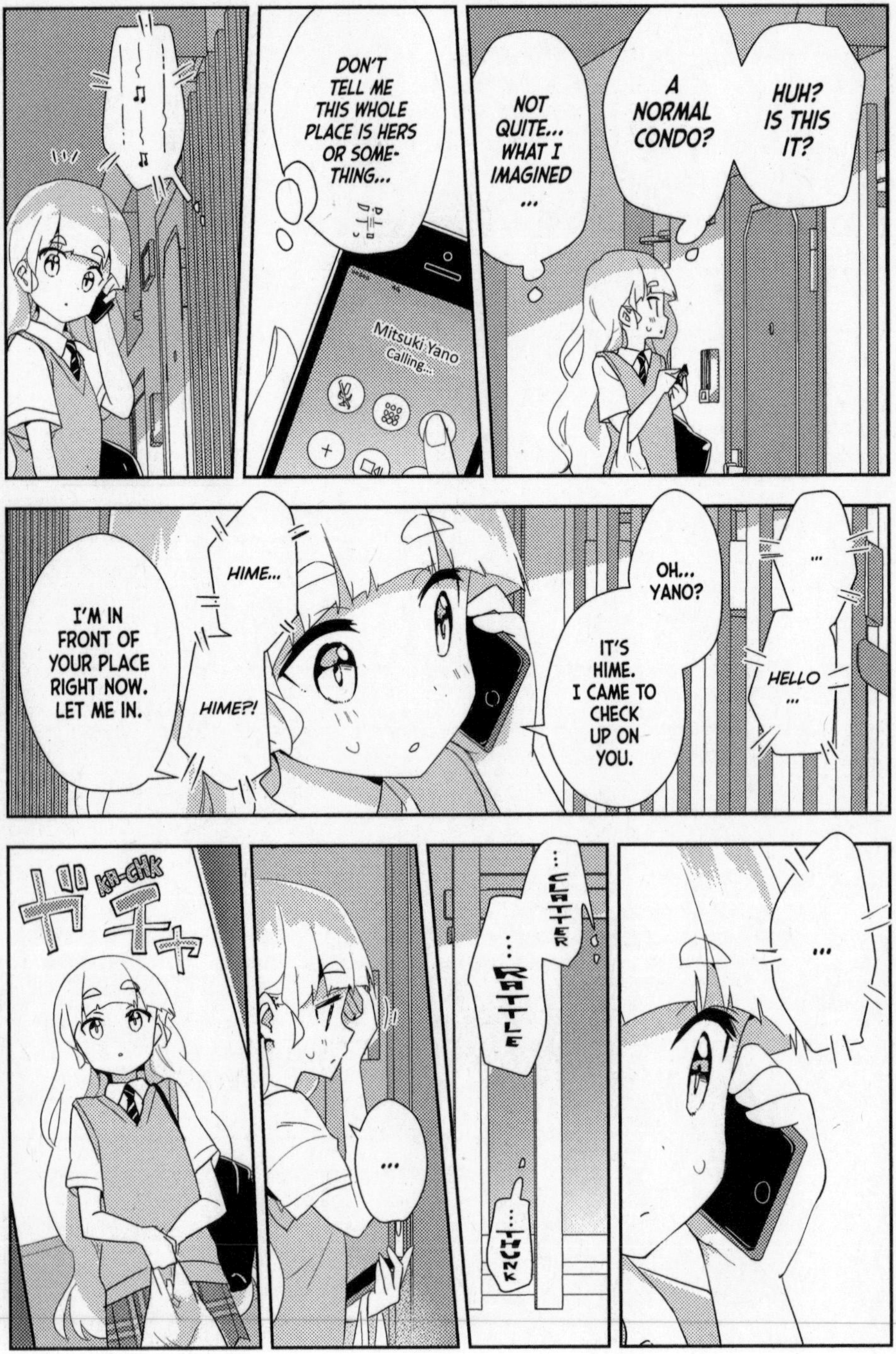
HUH? IS THIS IT?
A NORMAL CONDO?
NOT QUITE... WHAT I IMAGINED ...
DON'T TELL ME THIS WHOLE PLACE IS HERS OR SOME-THING...
Mitsuki Yano
Calling...
...
HELLO ...
OH... YANO?
IT'S HIME. I CAME TO CHECK UP ON YOU.
HIME?!
HIME...
I'M IN FRONT OF YOUR PLACE RIGHT NOW. LET ME IN.
...
...CLATTER
...RATTLE
...THUNK
...
ガチャ
KA-CHK

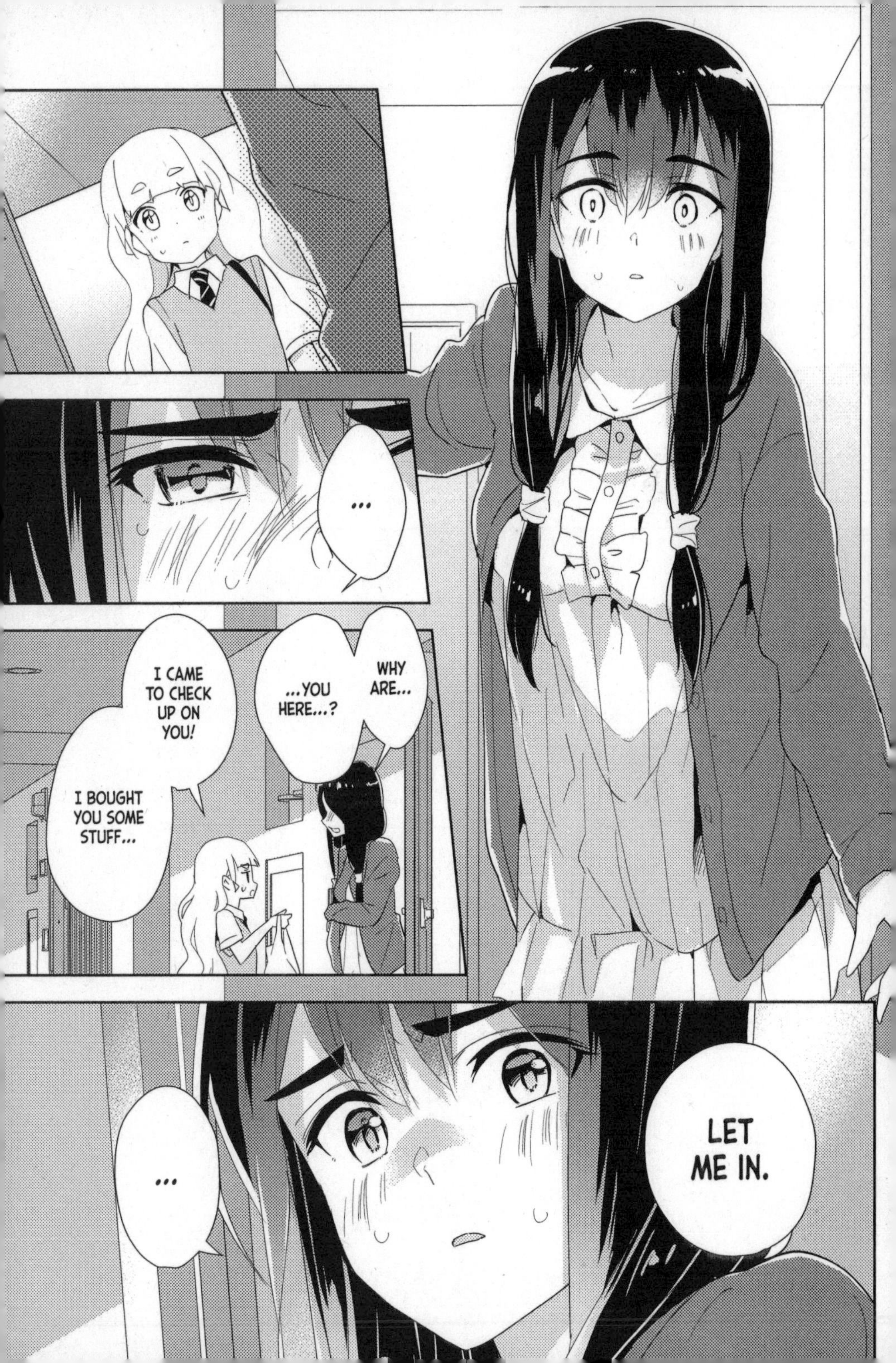
...
WHY ARE...
...YOU HERE...?
I CAME TO CHECK UP ON YOU!
I BOUGHT YOU SOME STUFF...
LET ME IN.
...

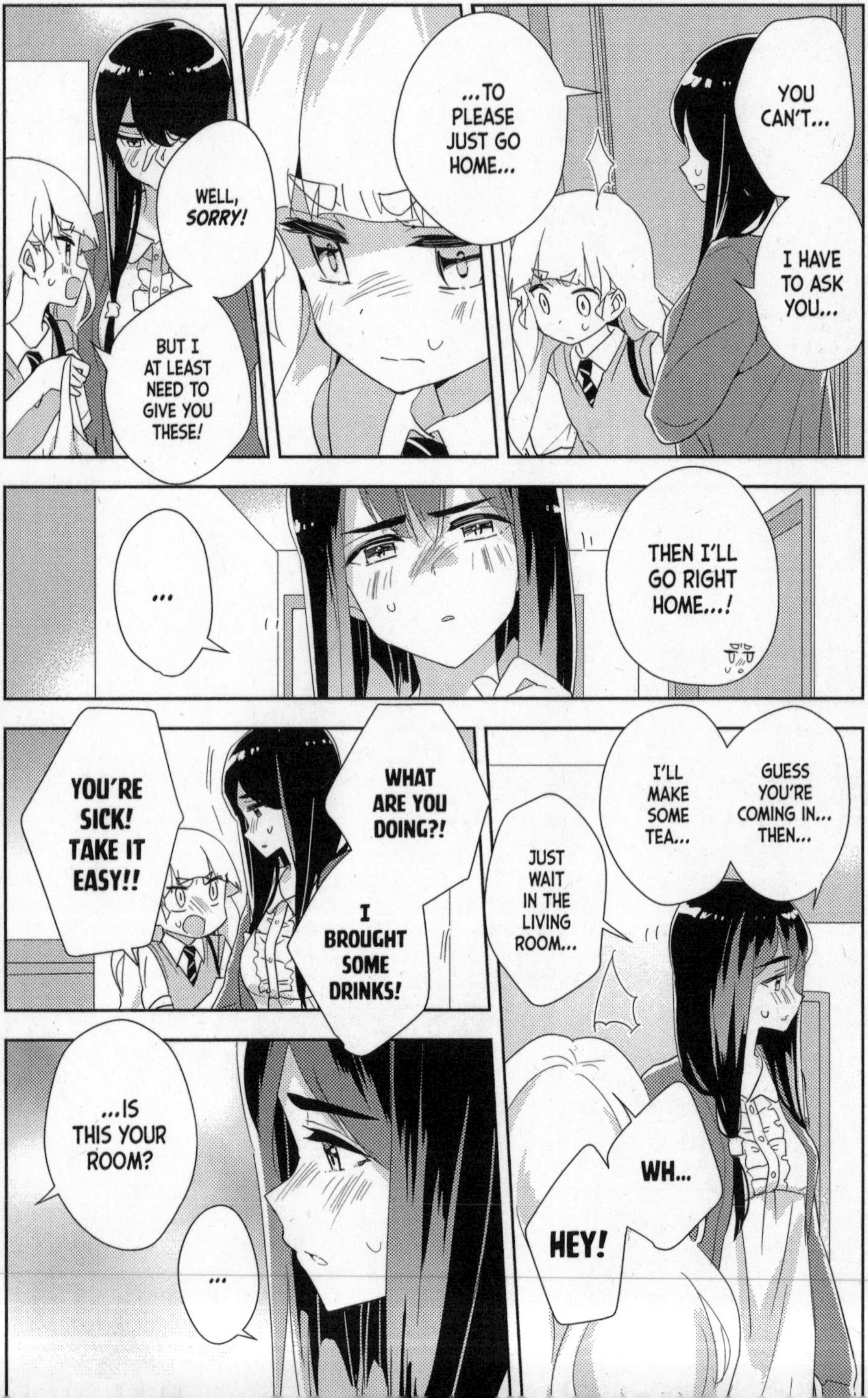
YOU CAN'T...
I HAVE TO ASK YOU...
...TO PLEASE JUST GO HOME...
WELL, *SORRY!*
BUT I AT LEAST NEED TO GIVE YOU *THESE!*
THEN I'LL GO RIGHT HOME...!
...
GUESS YOU'RE COMING IN... THEN...
I'LL MAKE SOME TEA...
JUST WAIT IN THE LIVING ROOM...
WH...
HEY!
WHAT ARE YOU DOING?!
YOU'RE SICK! TAKE IT EASY!!
I BROUGHT SOME DRINKS!
...IS THIS YOUR ROOM?
...

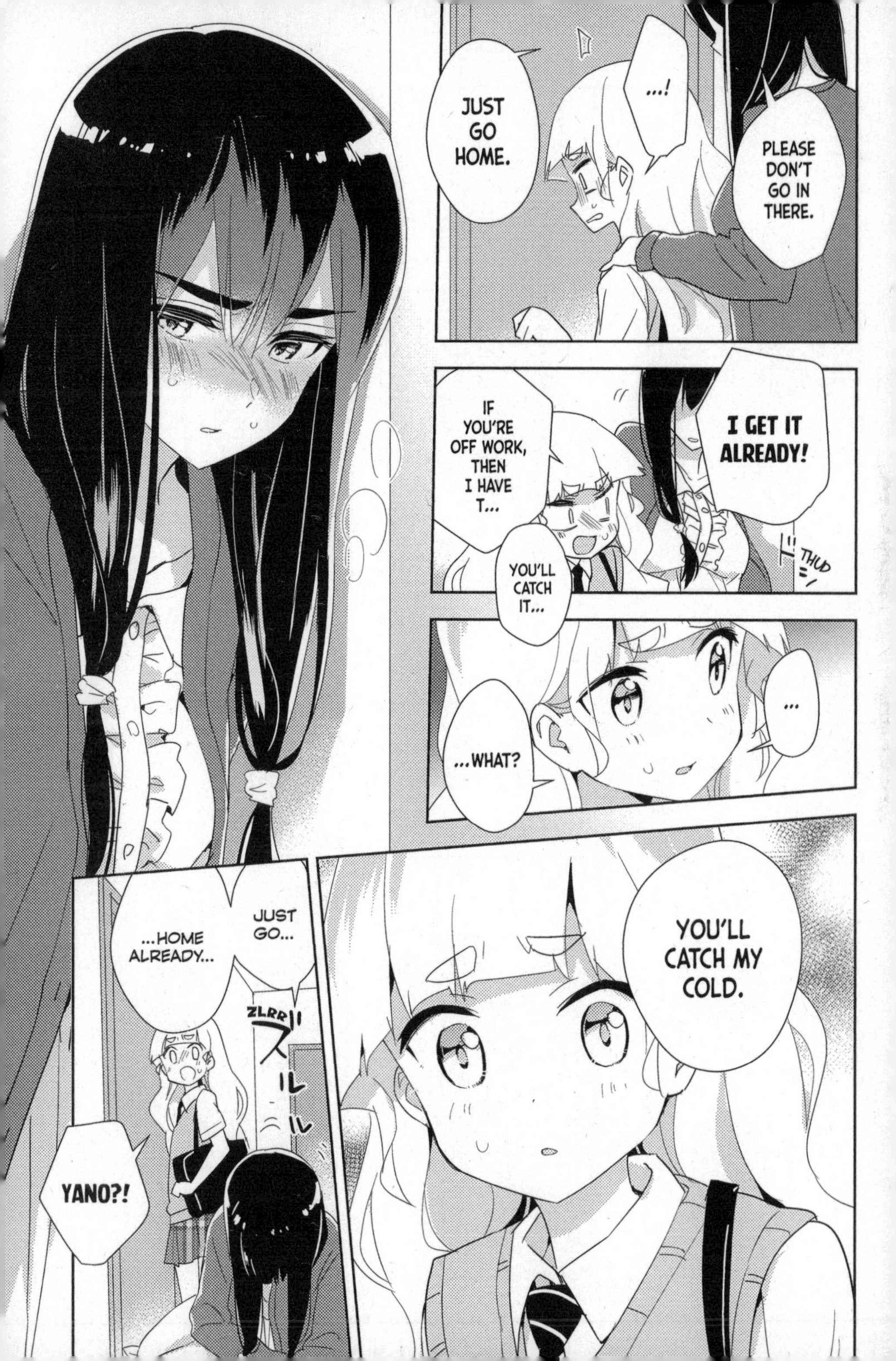
PLEASE DON'T GO IN THERE.
...!
JUST GO HOME.
I GET IT ALREADY!
THUD
IF YOU'RE OFF WORK, THEN I HAVE T...
YOU'LL CATCH IT...
...
...WHAT?
YOU'LL CATCH MY COLD.
JUST GO...
...HOME ALREADY...
ZLRR
YANO?!

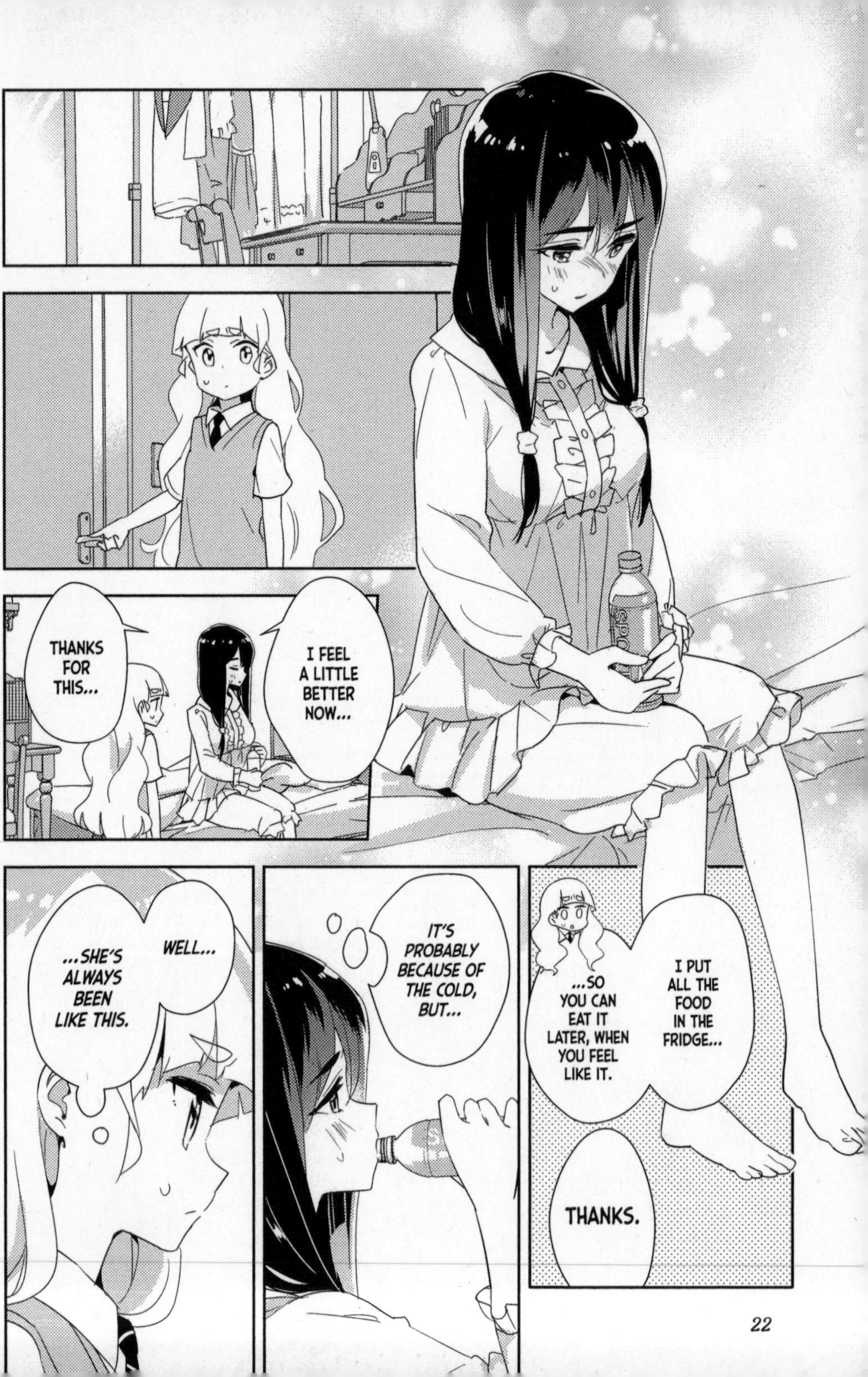
I FEEL A LITTLE BETTER NOW...
THANKS FOR THIS...
I PUT ALL THE FOOD IN THE FRIDGE...
...SO YOU CAN EAT IT LATER, WHEN YOU FEEL LIKE IT.
THANKS.
IT'S PROBABLY BECAUSE OF THE COLD, BUT...
WELL...
...SHE'S ALWAYS BEEN LIKE THIS.

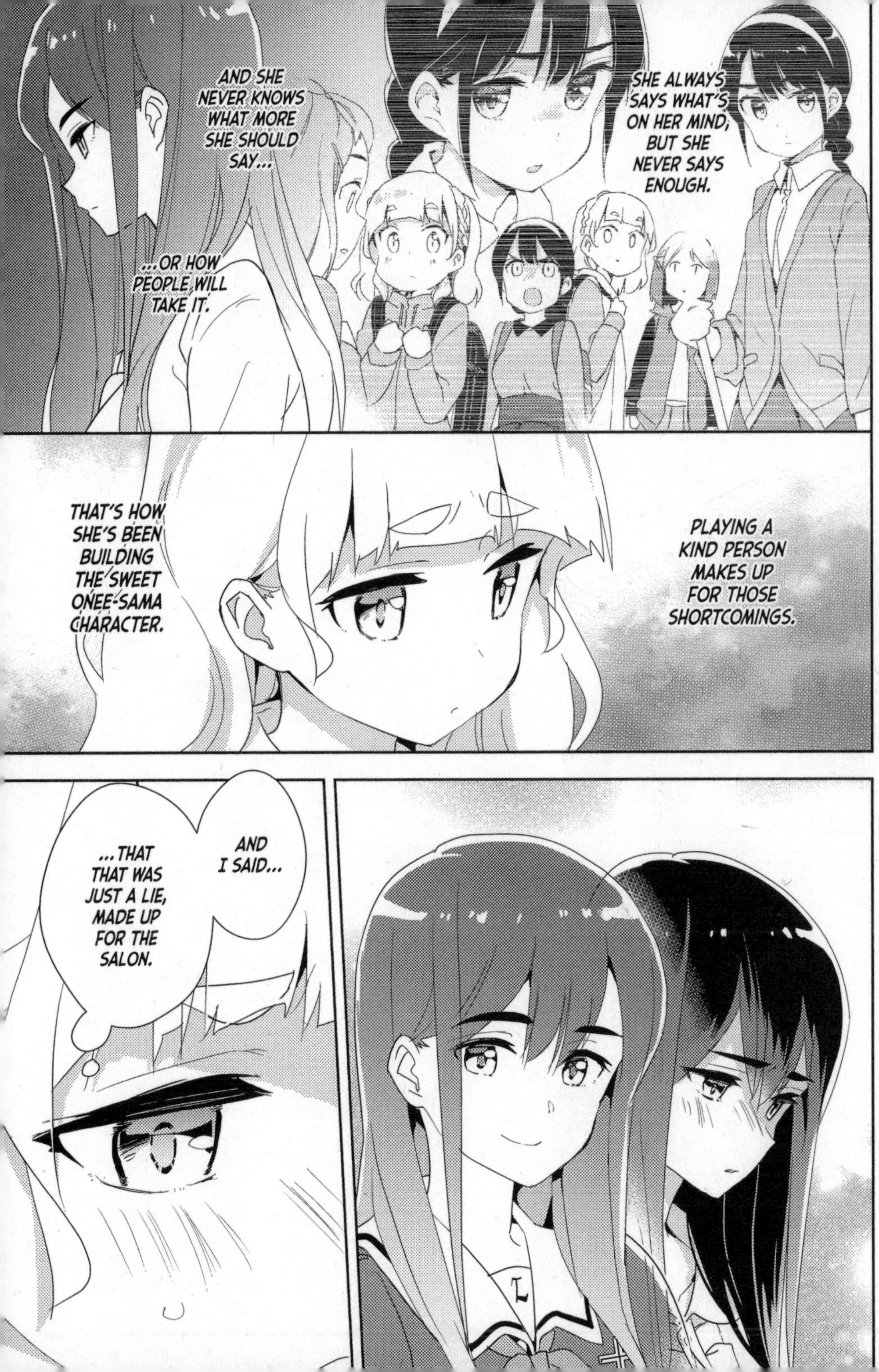
SHE ALWAYS SAYS WHAT'S ON HER MIND, BUT SHE NEVER SAYS ENOUGH.
AND SHE NEVER KNOWS WHAT MORE SHE SHOULD SAY...
...OR HOW PEOPLE WILL TAKE IT.
PLAYING A KIND PERSON MAKES UP FOR THOSE SHORTCOMINGS.
THAT'S HOW SHE'S BEEN BUILDING THE SWEET ONEE-SAMA CHARACTER.
AND I SAID...
...THAT THAT WAS JUST A LIE, MADE UP FOR THE SALON.

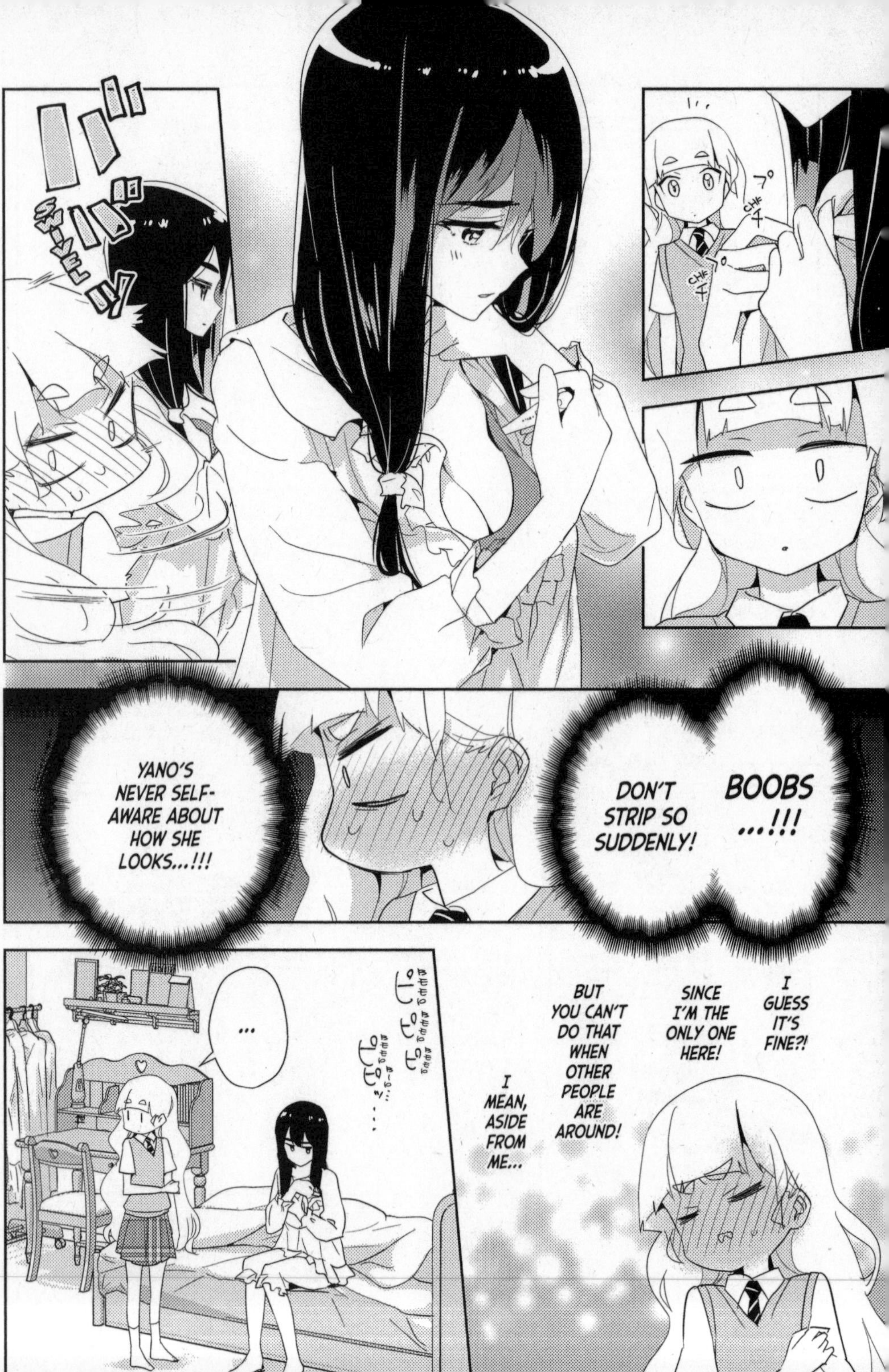

CHE
CHE
SWIVEL!!
BOOBS...!!!
DON'T STRIP SO SUDDENLY!
YANO'S NEVER SELF-AWARE ABOUT HOW SHE LOOKS...!!!
I GUESS IT'S FINE?!
SINCE I'M THE ONLY ONE HERE!
BUT YOU CAN'T DO THAT WHEN OTHER PEOPLE ARE AROUND!
I MEAN, ASIDE FROM ME...
...

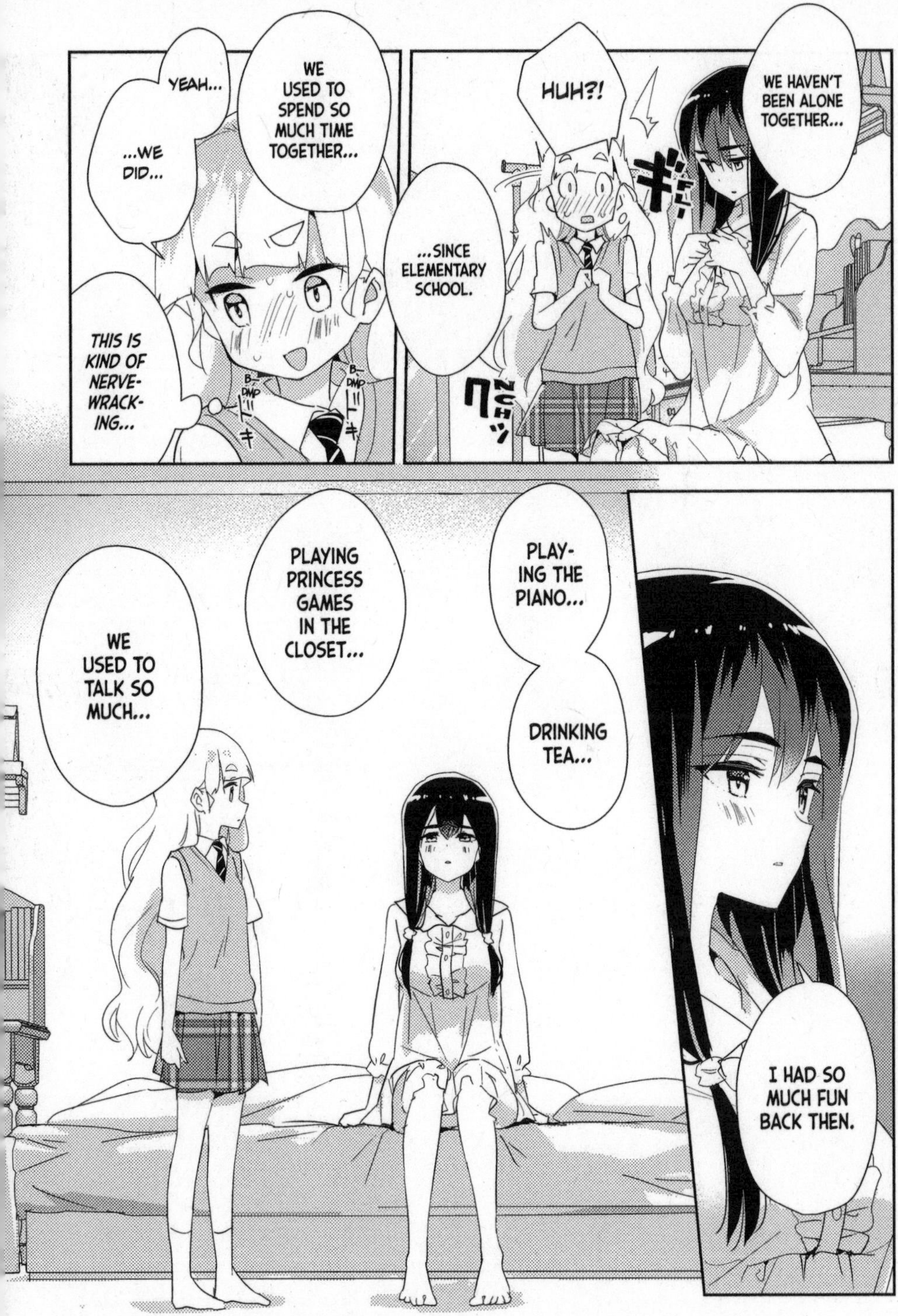
WE HAVEN'T BEEN ALONE TOGETHER...
HUH?!
...SINCE ELEMENTARY SCHOOL.
NCHU
WE USED TO SPEND SO MUCH TIME TOGETHER...
YEAH... ...WE DID...
THIS IS KIND OF NERVE-WRACKING...
B-DMP
B-DMP
I HAD SO MUCH FUN BACK THEN.
PLAYING THE PIANO...
DRINKING TEA...
PLAYING PRINCESS GAMES IN THE CLOSET...
WE USED TO TALK SO MUCH...

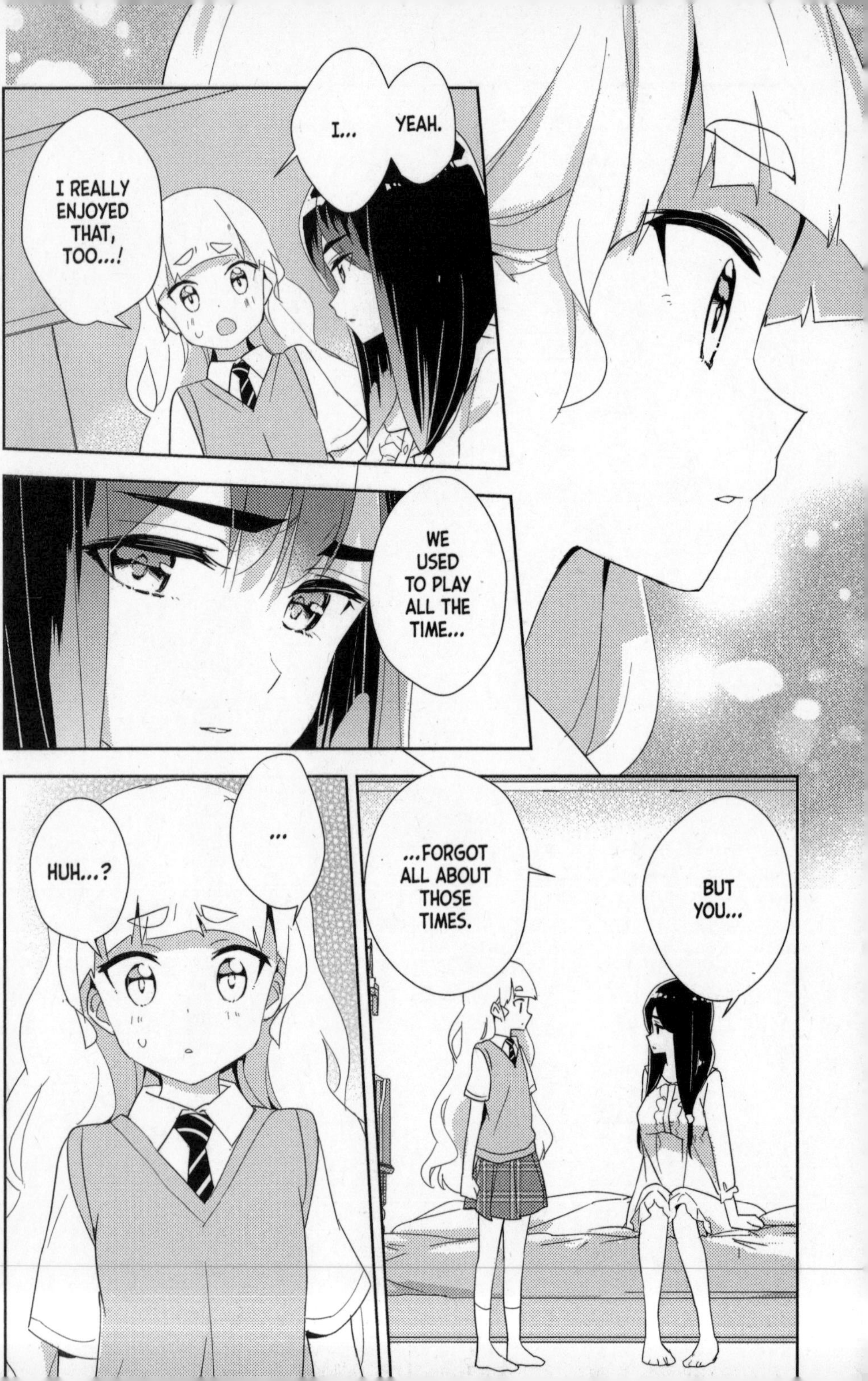
I... YEAH.
I REALLY ENJOYED THAT, TOO...!
WE USED TO PLAY ALL THE TIME...
BUT YOU...
...FORGOT ALL ABOUT THOSE TIMES.
...
HUH...?

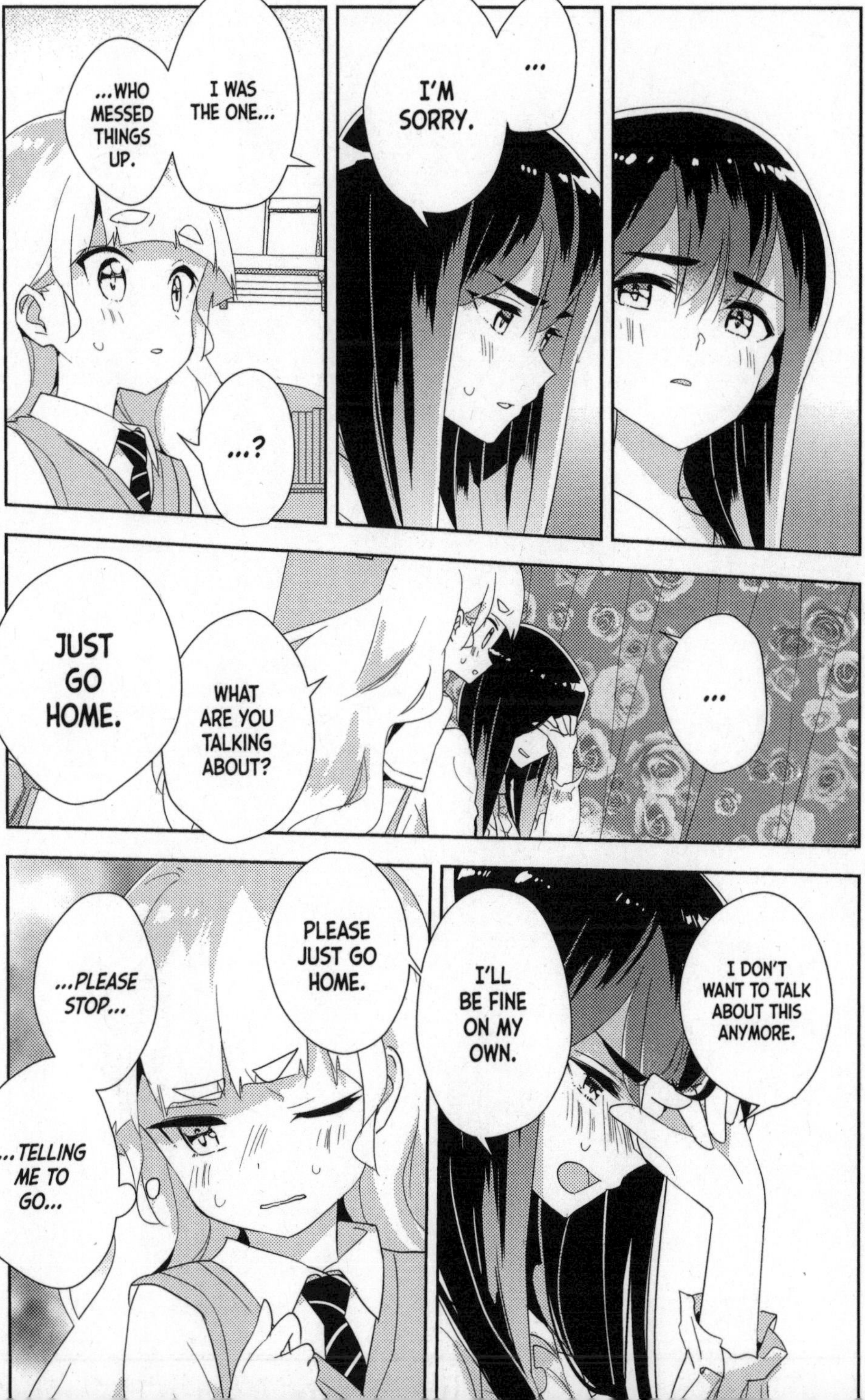
...
I'M SORRY.
I WAS THE ONE...
...WHO MESSED THINGS UP.
...?
...
WHAT ARE YOU TALKING ABOUT?
JUST GO HOME.
I DON'T WANT TO TALK ABOUT THIS ANYMORE.
I'LL BE FINE ON MY OWN.
PLEASE JUST GO HOME.
...PLEASE STOP...
...TELLING ME TO GO...

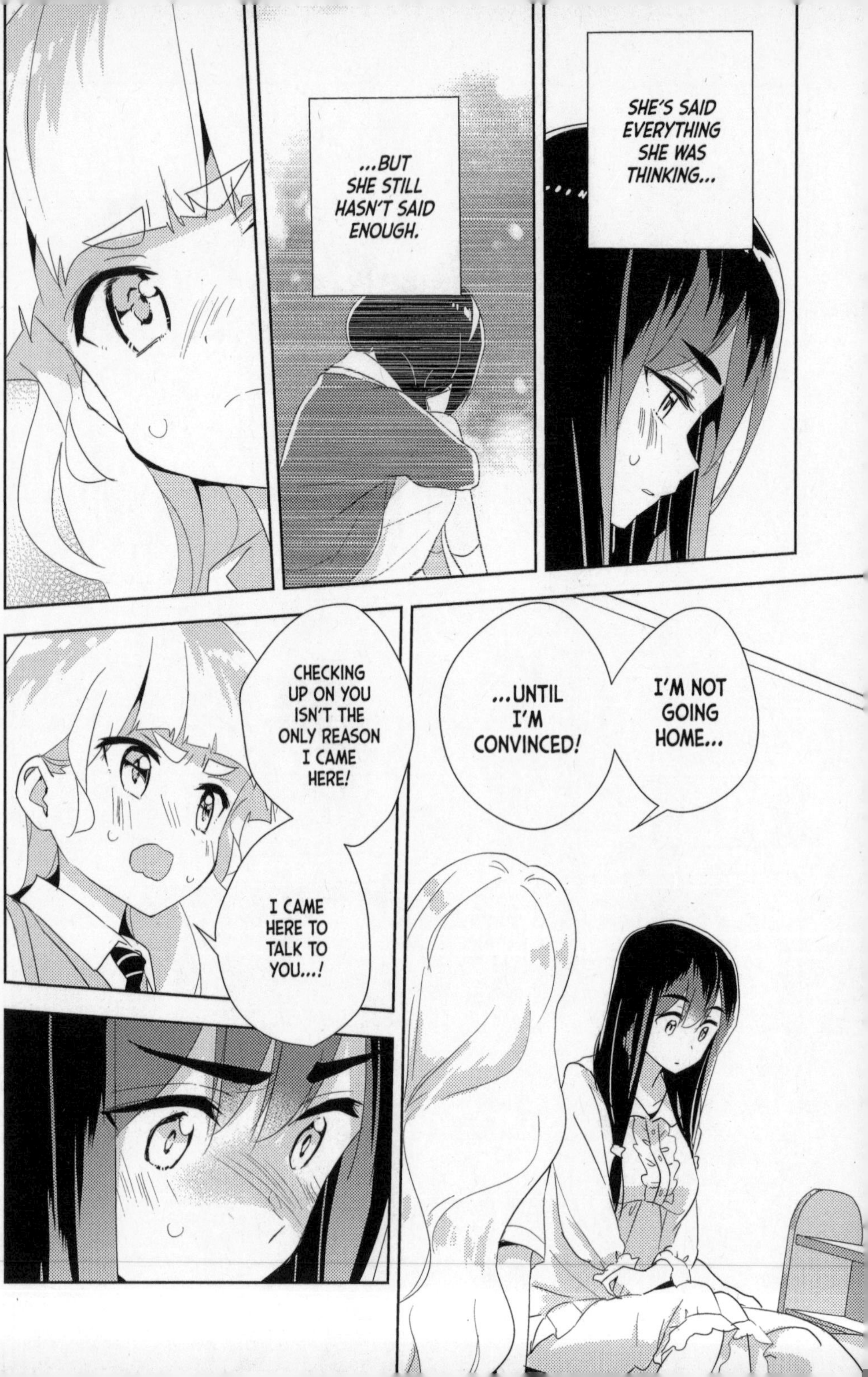
SHE'S SAID EVERYTHING SHE WAS THINKING...
...BUT SHE STILL HASN'T SAID ENOUGH.
I'M NOT GOING HOME...
...UNTIL I'M CONVINCED!
CHECKING UP ON YOU ISN'T THE ONLY REASON I CAME HERE!
I CAME HERE TO TALK TO YOU...!

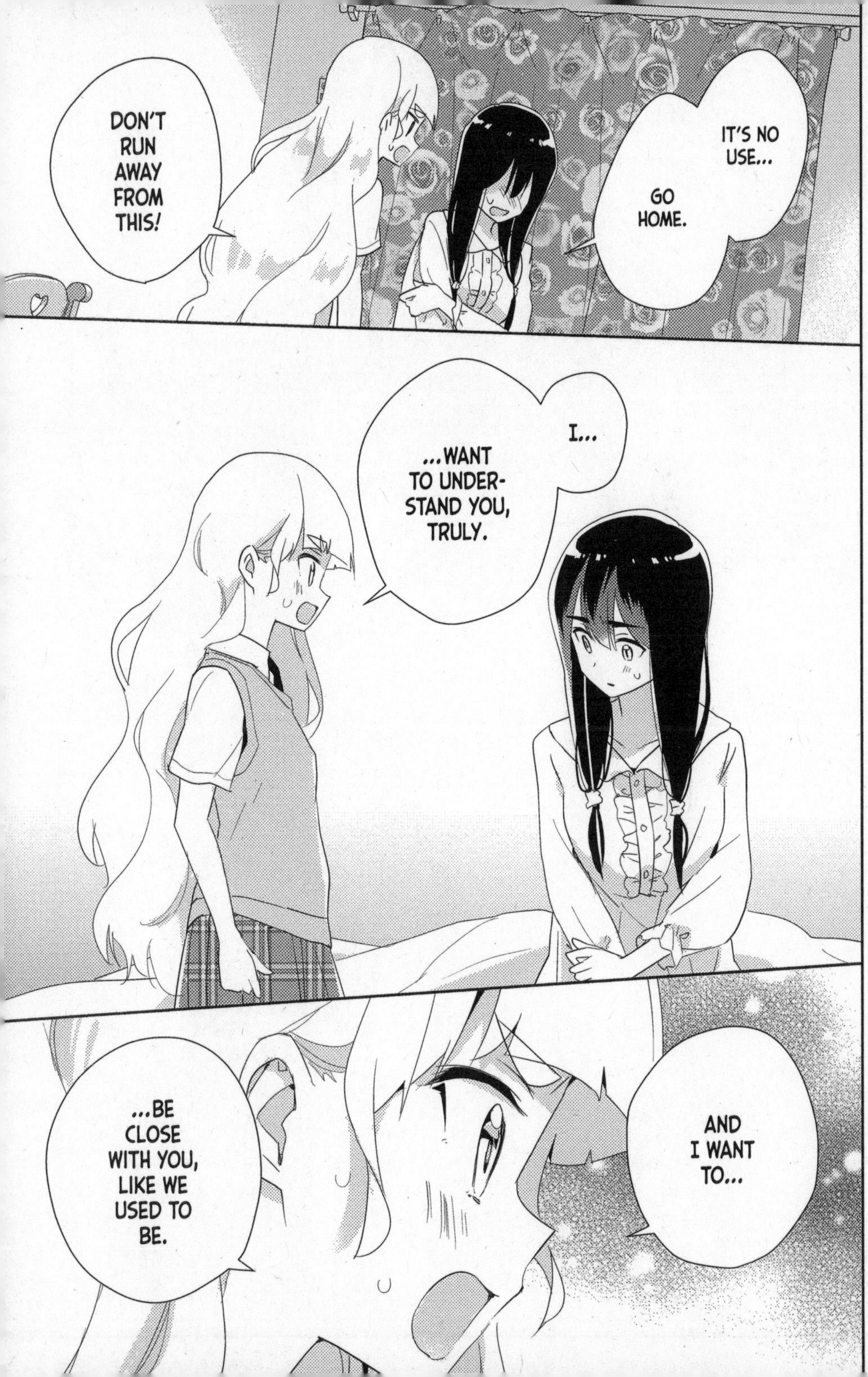
IT'S NO USE... GO HOME.
DON'T RUN AWAY FROM THIS!
I... ...WANT TO UNDER-STAND YOU, TRULY.
AND I WANT TO...
...BE CLOSE WITH YOU, LIKE WE USED TO BE.

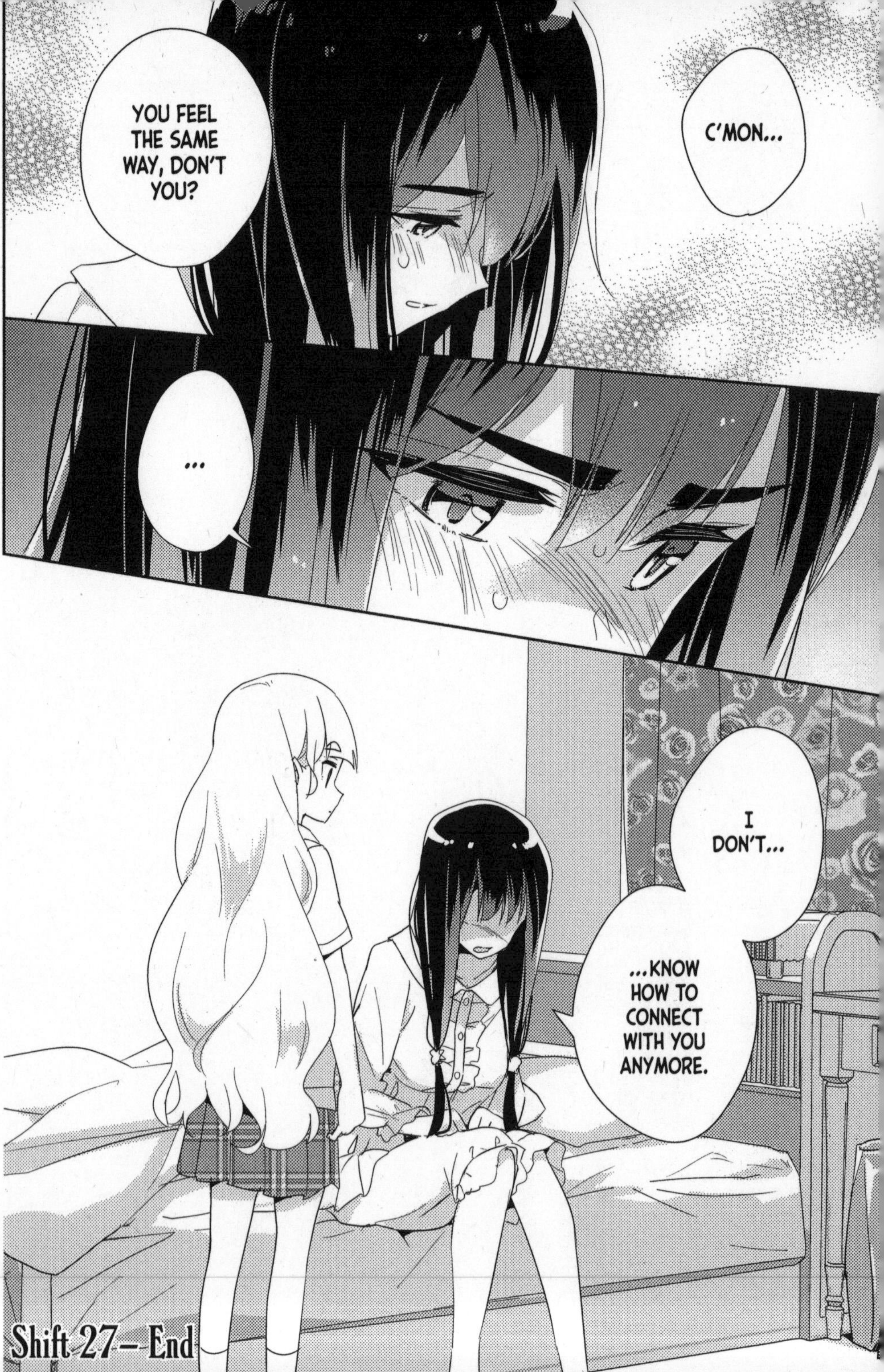
C'MON...
YOU FEEL THE SAME WAY, DON'T YOU?
...
I DON'T...
...KNOW HOW TO CONNECT WITH YOU ANYMORE.
Shift 27 – End

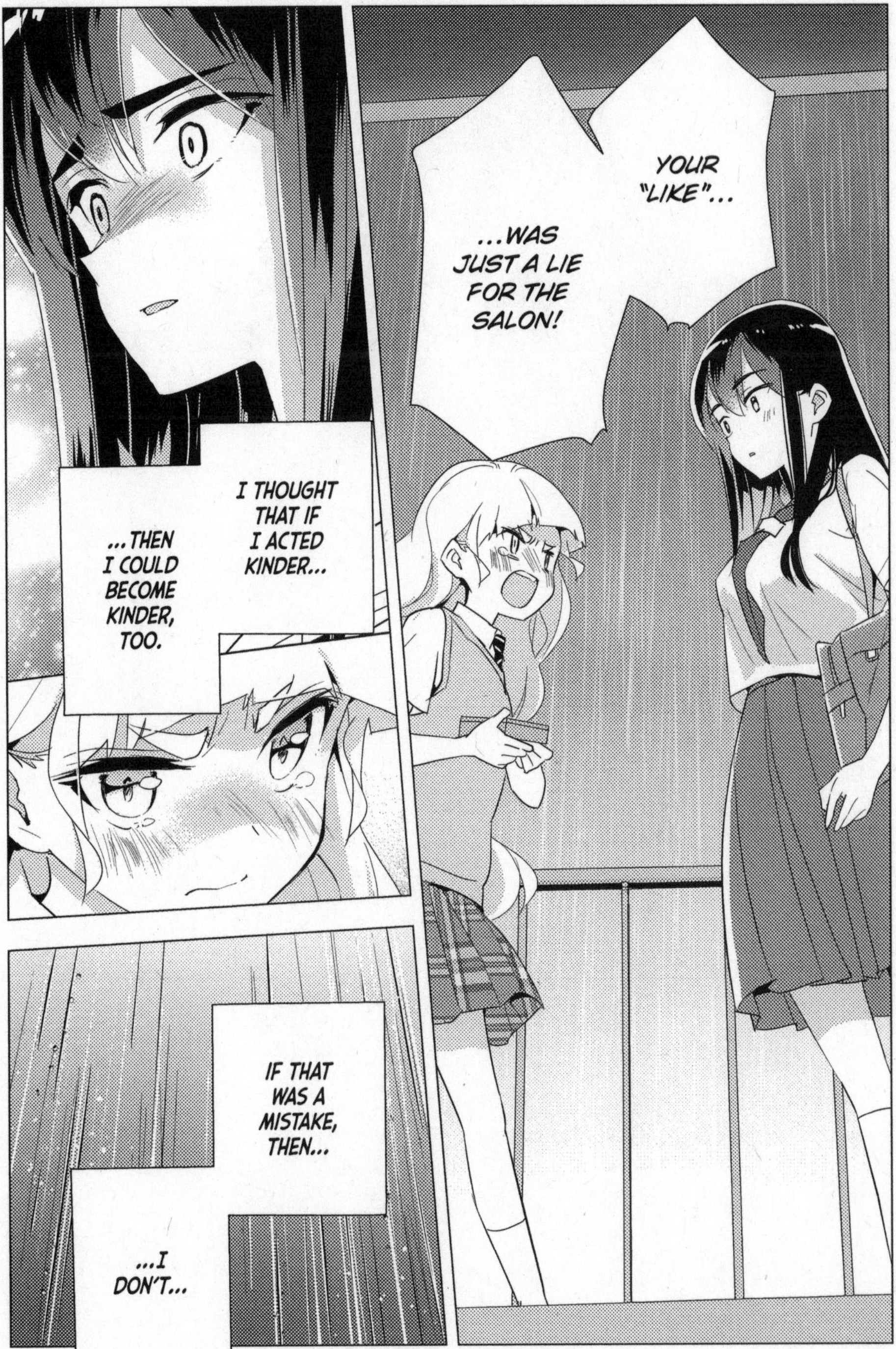
YOUR "LIKE"...
...WAS JUST A LIE FOR THE SALON!
I THOUGHT THAT IF I ACTED KINDER...
...THEN I COULD BECOME KINDER, TOO.
IF THAT WAS A MISTAKE, THEN...
...I DON'T...

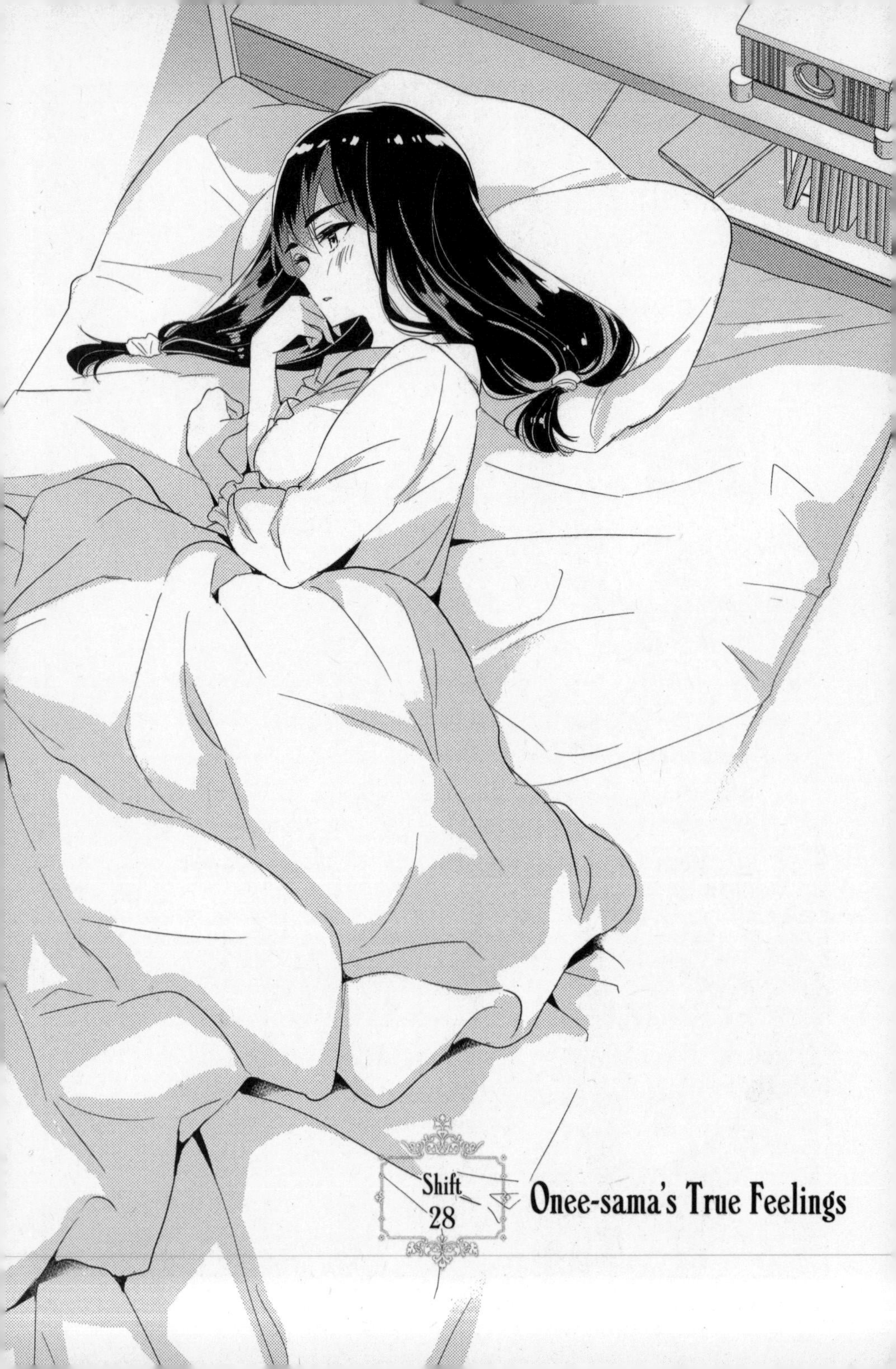
Shift 28
Onee-sama's True Feelings

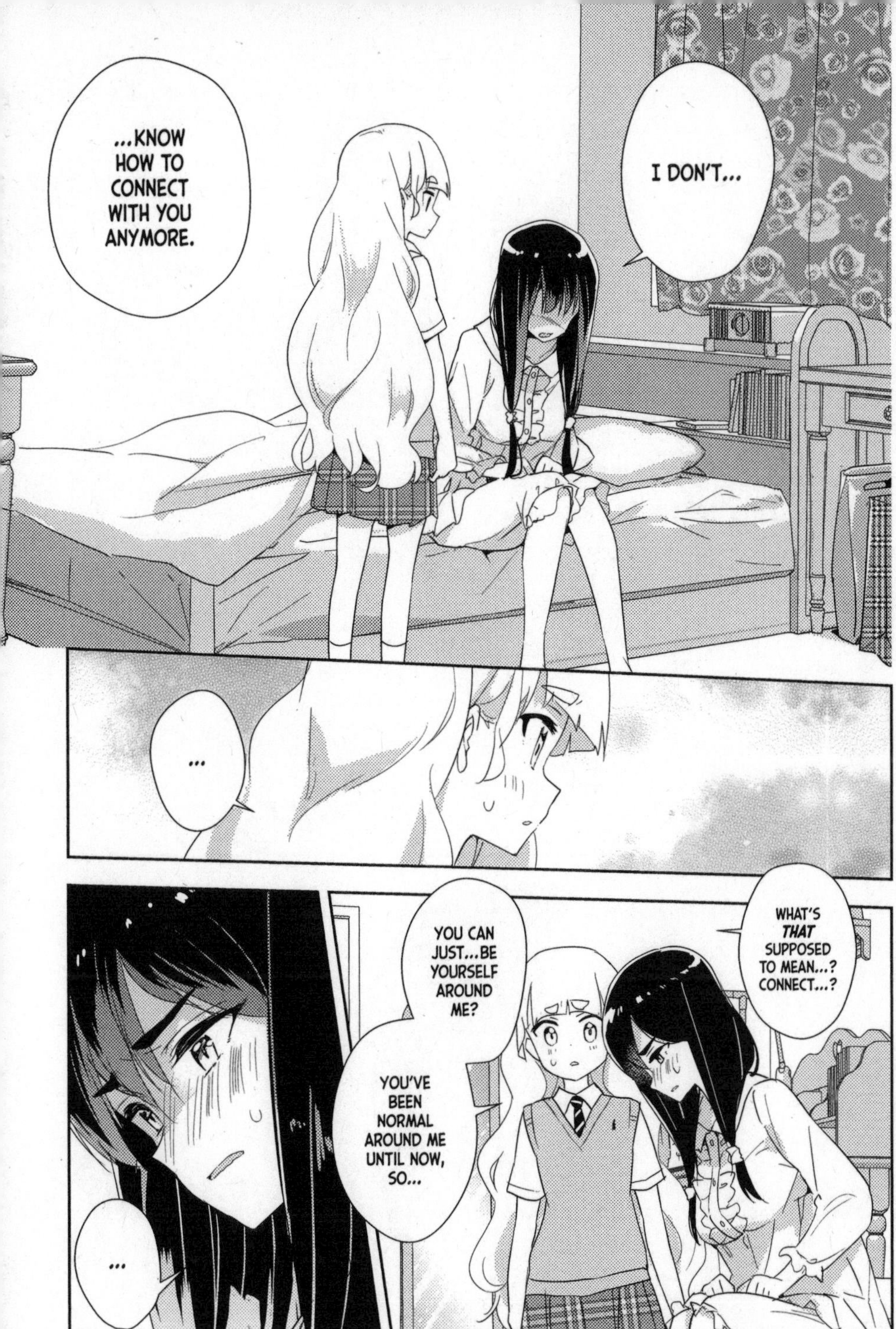
I DON'T...
...KNOW HOW TO CONNECT WITH YOU ANYMORE.
...
WHAT'S *THAT* SUPPOSED TO MEAN...? CONNECT...?
YOU CAN JUST...BE YOURSELF AROUND ME?
YOU'VE BEEN NORMAL AROUND ME UNTIL NOW, SO...
...

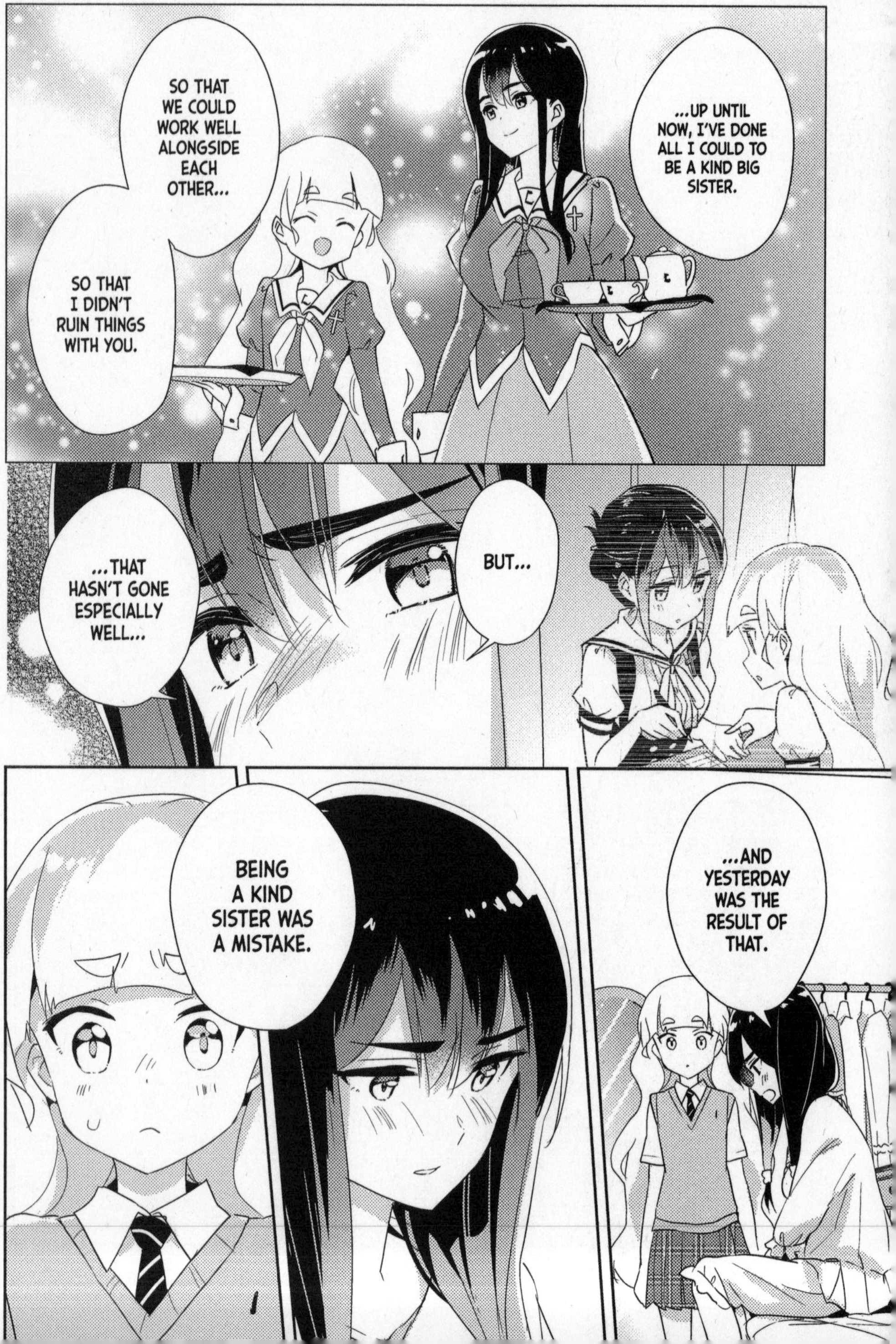
...UP UNTIL NOW, I'VE DONE ALL I COULD TO BE A KIND BIG SISTER.
SO THAT WE COULD WORK WELL ALONGSIDE EACH OTHER...
SO THAT I DIDN'T RUIN THINGS WITH YOU.
BUT...
...THAT HASN'T GONE ESPECIALLY WELL...
...AND YESTERDAY WAS THE RESULT OF THAT.
BEING A KIND SISTER WAS A MISTAKE.

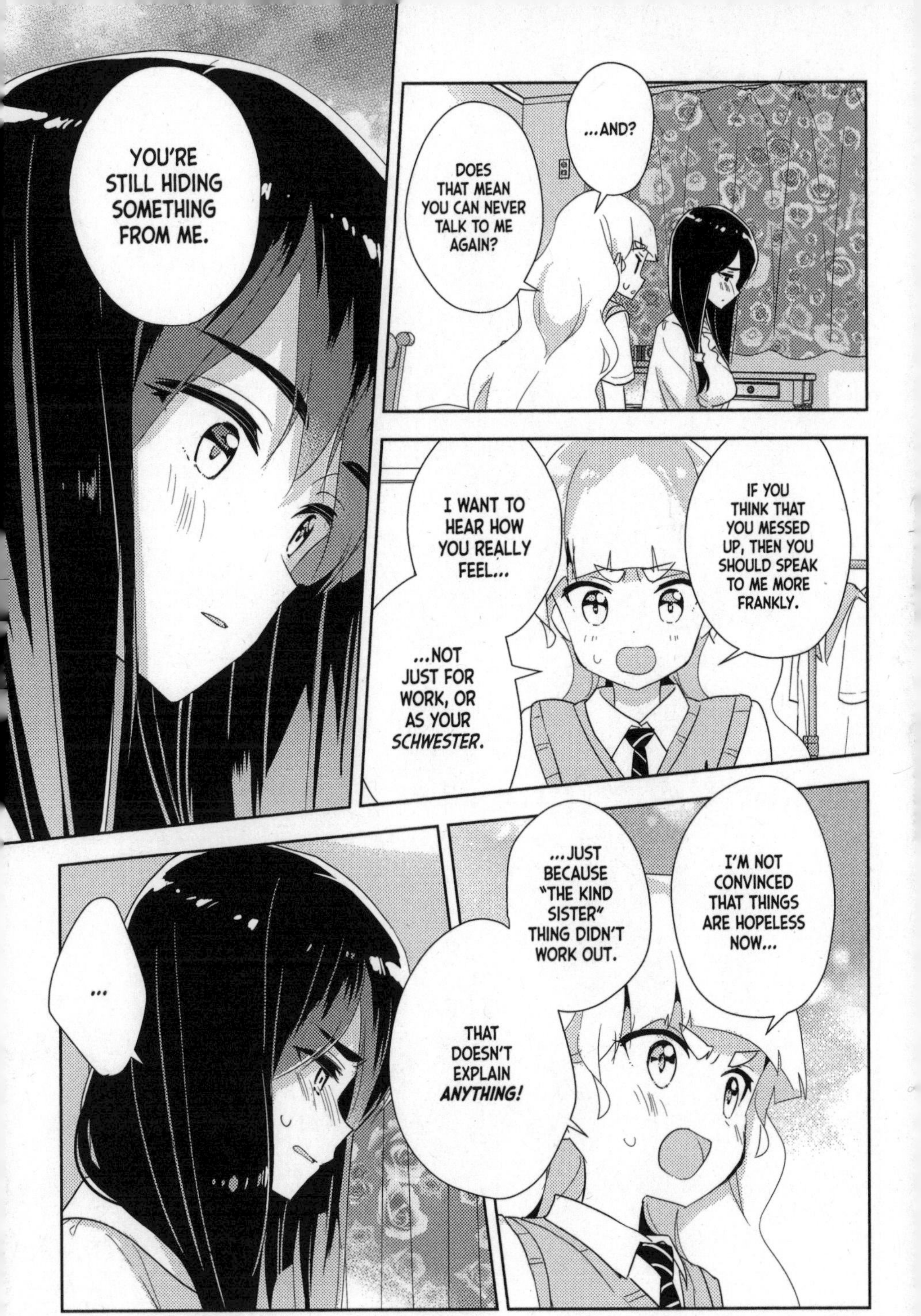
...AND?
DOES THAT MEAN YOU CAN NEVER TALK TO ME AGAIN?
IF YOU THINK THAT YOU MESSED UP, THEN YOU SHOULD SPEAK TO ME MORE FRANKLY.
I WANT TO HEAR HOW YOU REALLY FEEL...
...NOT JUST FOR WORK, OR AS YOUR *SCHWESTER*.
YOU'RE STILL HIDING SOMETHING FROM ME.
I'M NOT CONVINCED THAT THINGS ARE HOPELESS NOW...
...JUST BECAUSE "THE KIND SISTER" THING DIDN'T WORK OUT.
THAT DOESN'T EXPLAIN ***ANYTHING!***
...

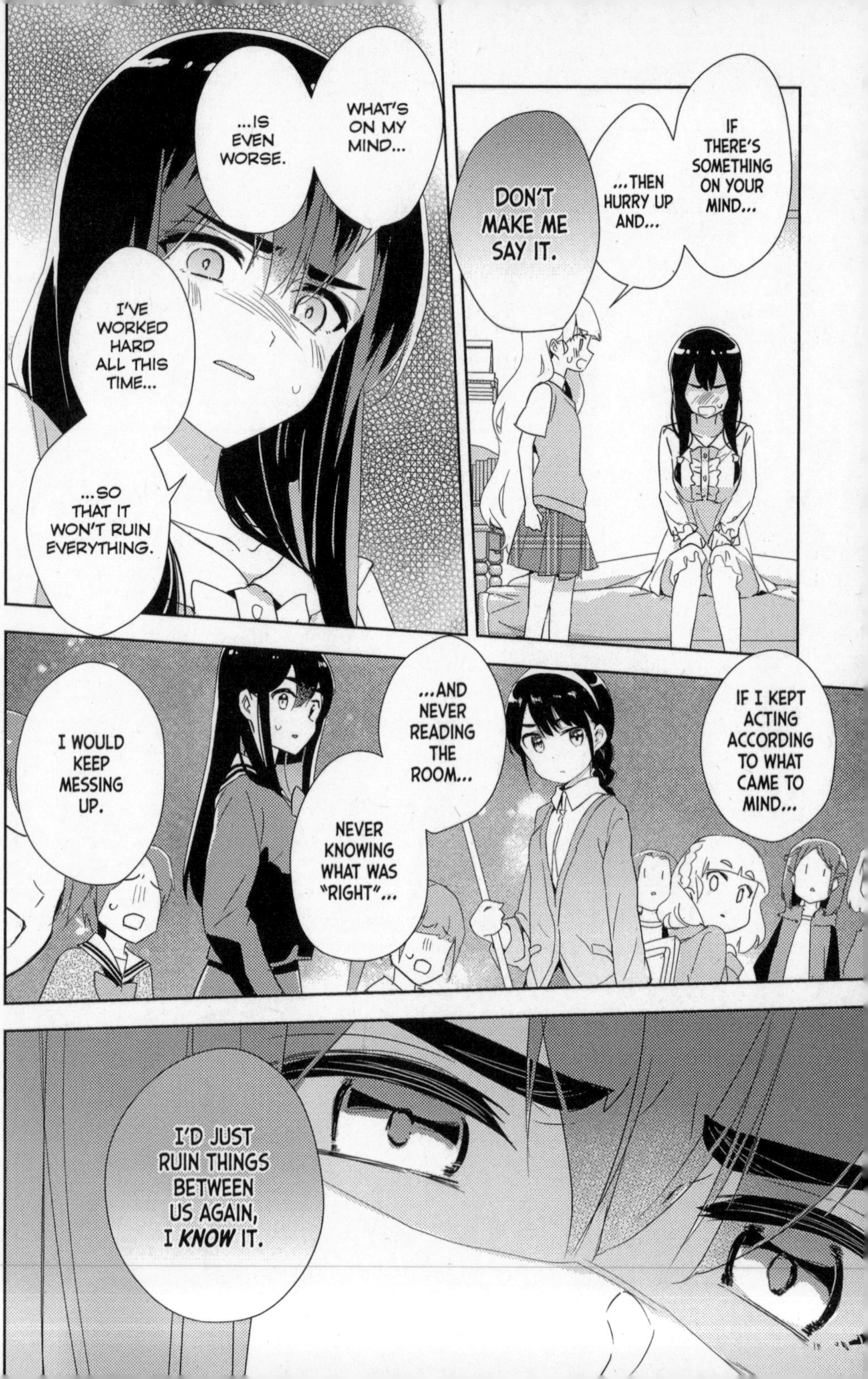
IF THERE'S SOMETHING ON YOUR MIND...
...THEN HURRY UP AND...
DON'T MAKE ME SAY IT.
WHAT'S ON MY MIND...
...IS EVEN WORSE.
I'VE WORKED HARD ALL THIS TIME...
...SO THAT IT WON'T RUIN EVERYTHING.
IF I KEPT ACTING ACCORDING TO WHAT CAME TO MIND...
...AND NEVER READING THE ROOM...
NEVER KNOWING WHAT WAS "RIGHT"...
I WOULD KEEP MESSING UP.
I'D JUST RUIN THINGS BETWEEN US AGAIN, I *KNOW* IT.

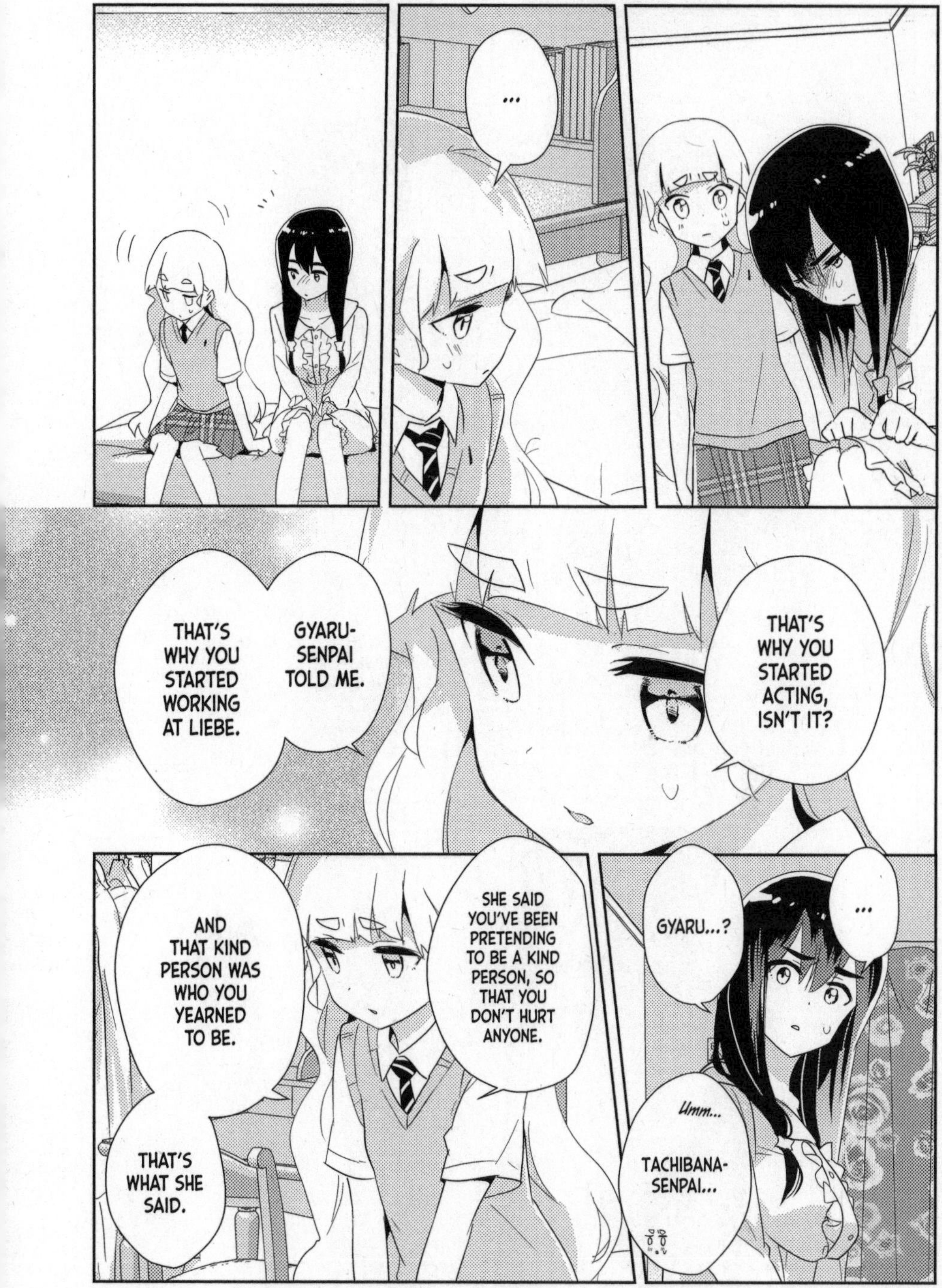
...
THAT'S WHY YOU STARTED ACTING, ISN'T IT?
GYARU-SENPAI TOLD ME.
THAT'S WHY YOU STARTED WORKING AT LIEBE.
...
GYARU...?
Umm...
TACHIBANA-SENPAI...
SHE SAID YOU'VE BEEN PRETENDING TO BE A KIND PERSON, SO THAT YOU DON'T HURT ANYONE.
AND THAT KIND PERSON WAS WHO YOU YEARNED TO BE.
THAT'S WHAT SHE SAID.

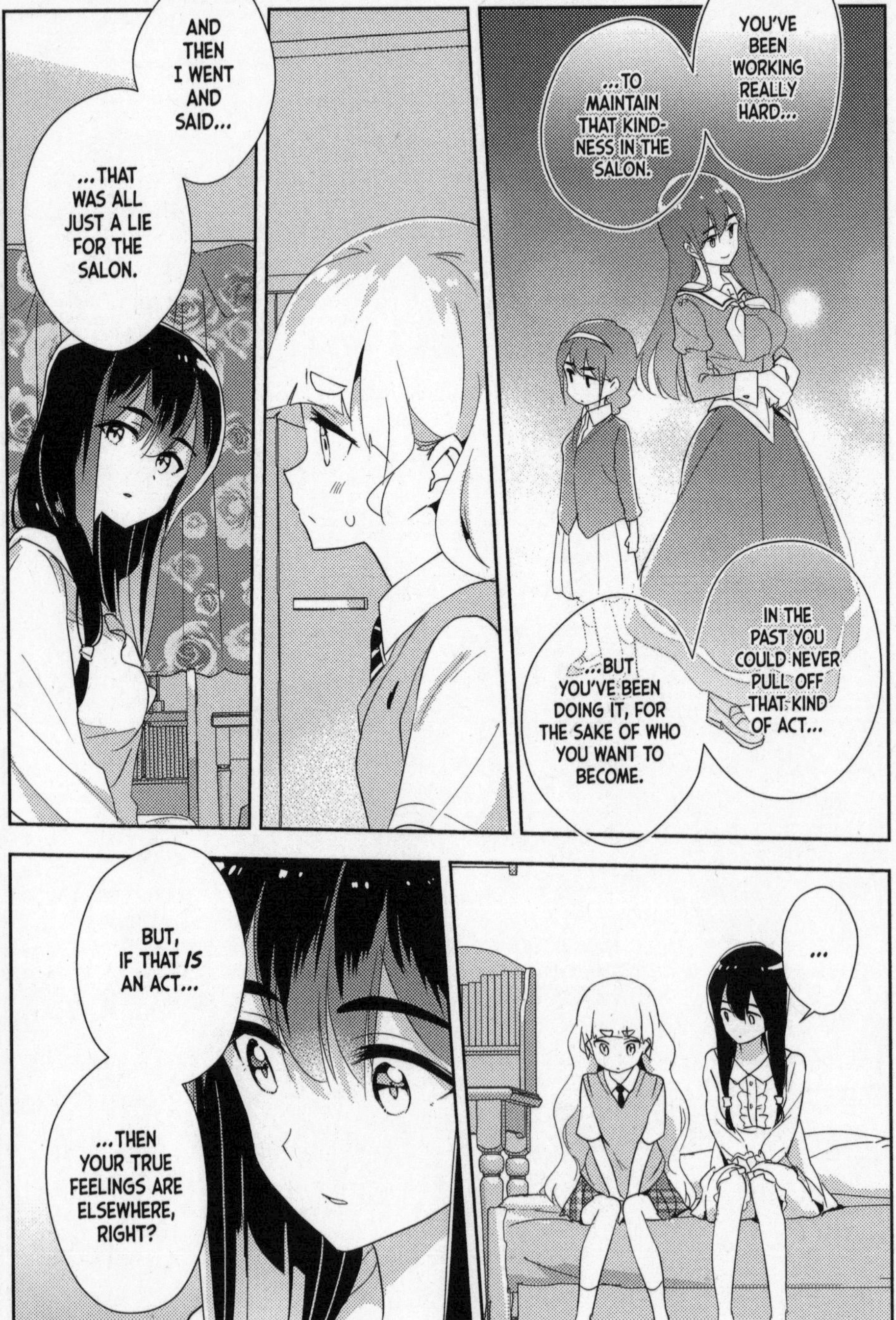
YOU'VE BEEN WORKING REALLY HARD...
...TO MAINTAIN THAT KIND-NESS IN THE SALON.
IN THE PAST YOU COULD NEVER PULL OFF THAT KIND OF ACT...
...BUT YOU'VE BEEN DOING IT, FOR THE SAKE OF WHO YOU WANT TO BECOME.
AND THEN I WENT AND SAID...
...THAT WAS ALL JUST A LIE FOR THE SALON.
...
BUT, IF THAT *IS* AN ACT...
...THEN YOUR TRUE FEELINGS ARE ELSEWHERE, RIGHT?

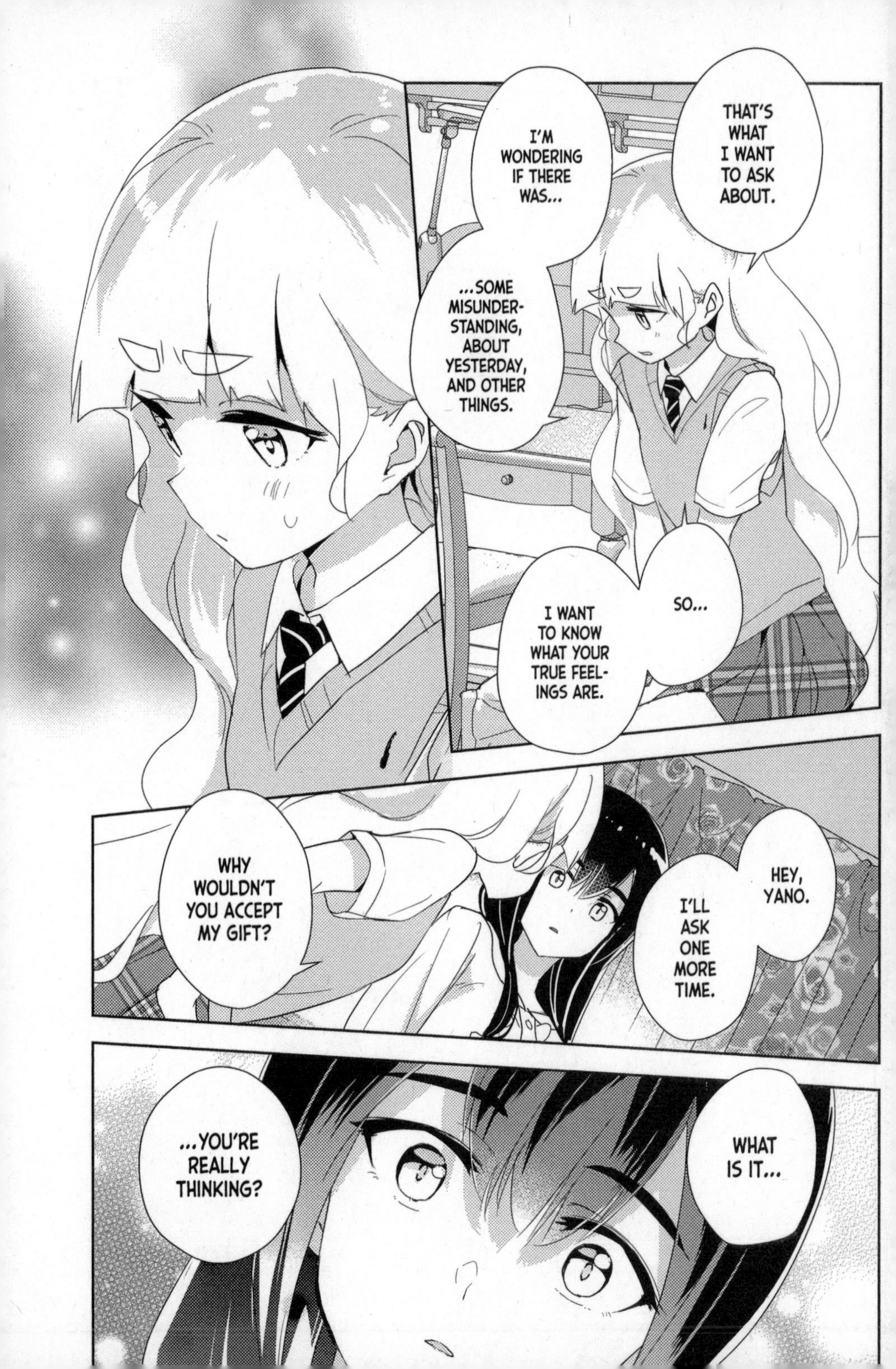
THAT'S WHAT I WANT TO ASK ABOUT.
I'M WONDERING IF THERE WAS...
...SOME MISUNDER-STANDING, ABOUT YESTERDAY, AND OTHER THINGS.
SO...
I WANT TO KNOW WHAT YOUR TRUE FEEL-INGS ARE.
HEY, YANO.
I'LL ASK ONE MORE TIME.
WHY WOULDN'T YOU ACCEPT MY GIFT?
WHAT IS IT...
...YOU'RE REALLY THINKING?

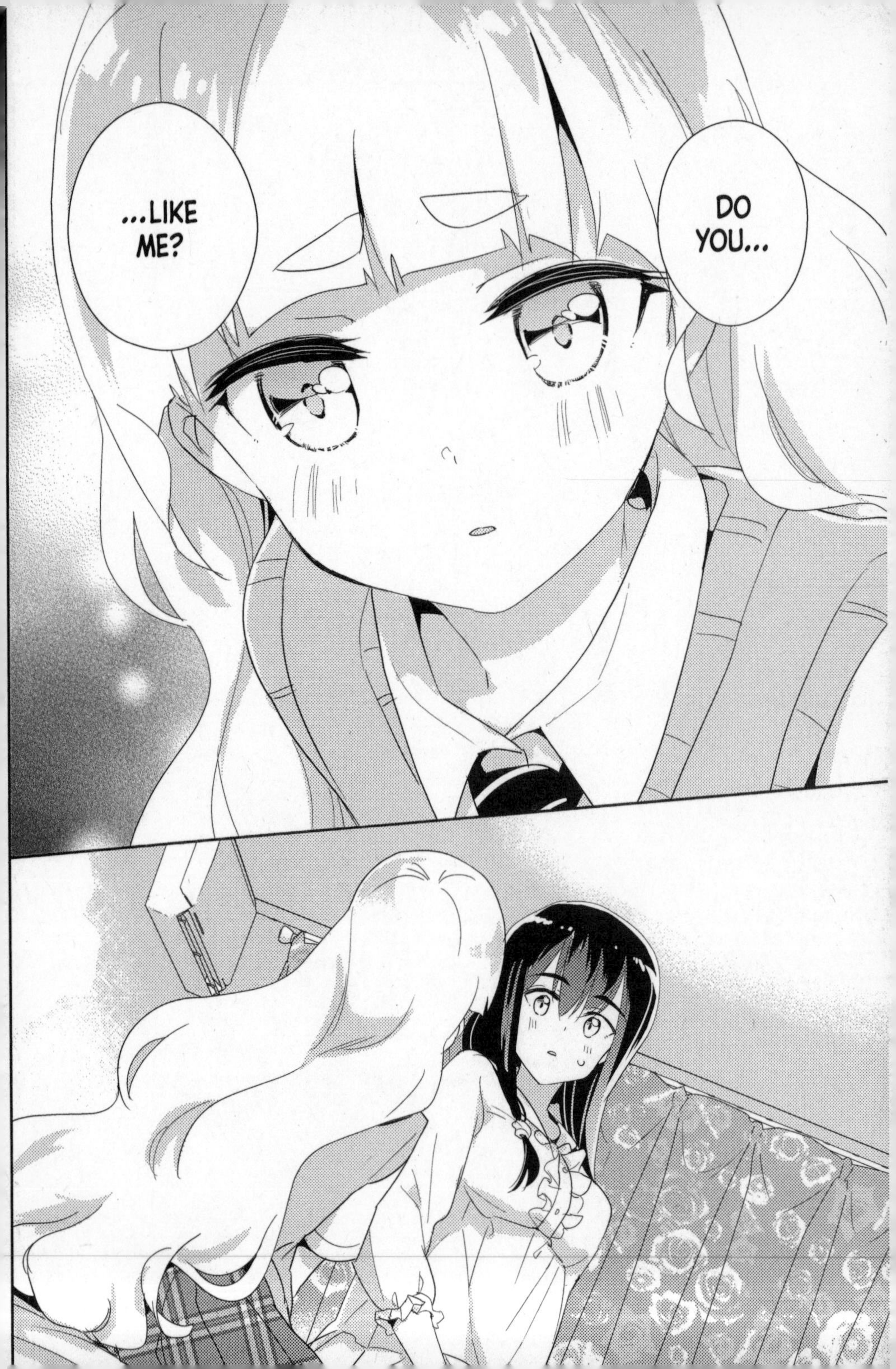
DO YOU...
...LIKE ME?

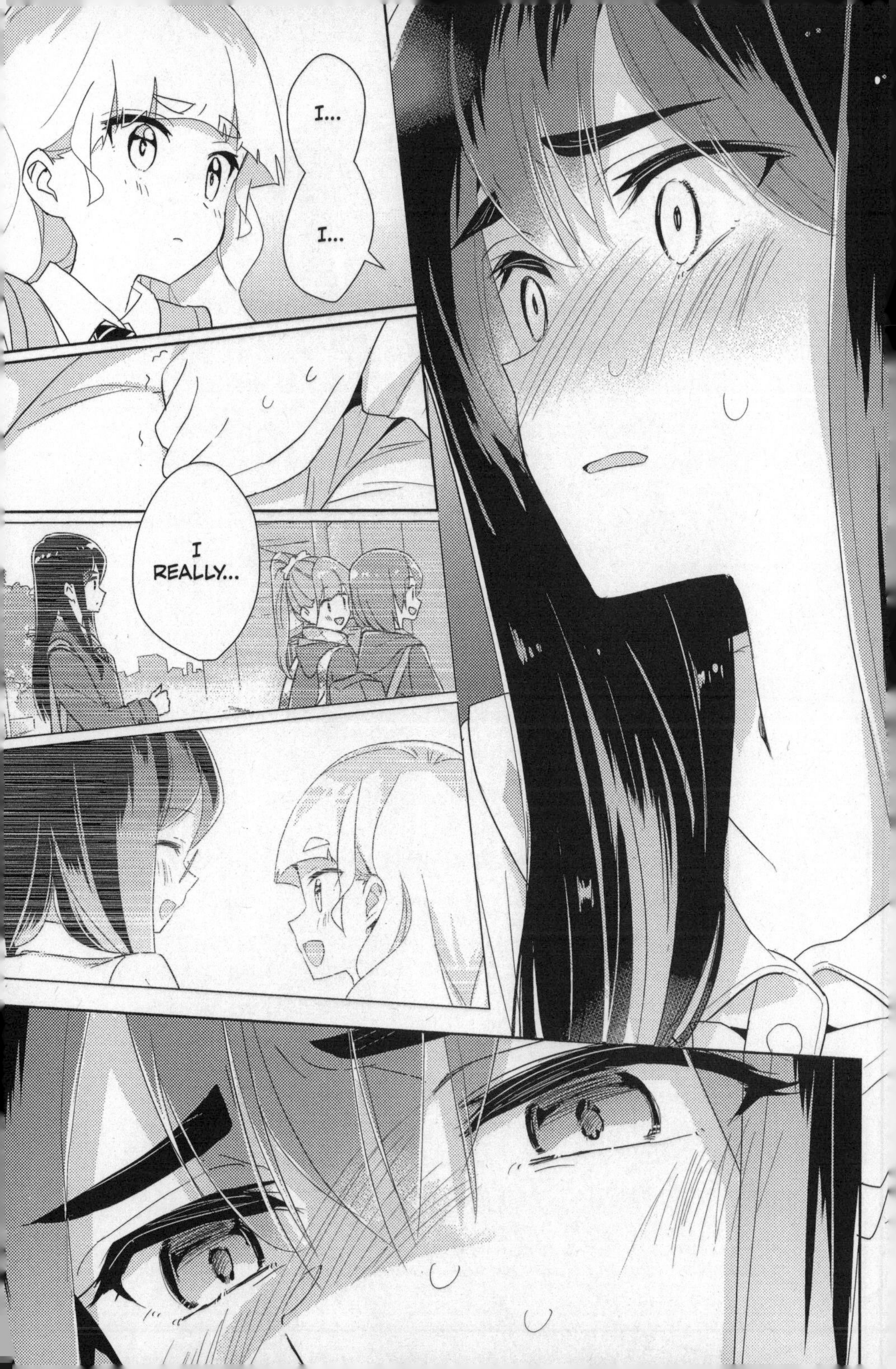
I... I...
I REALLY...

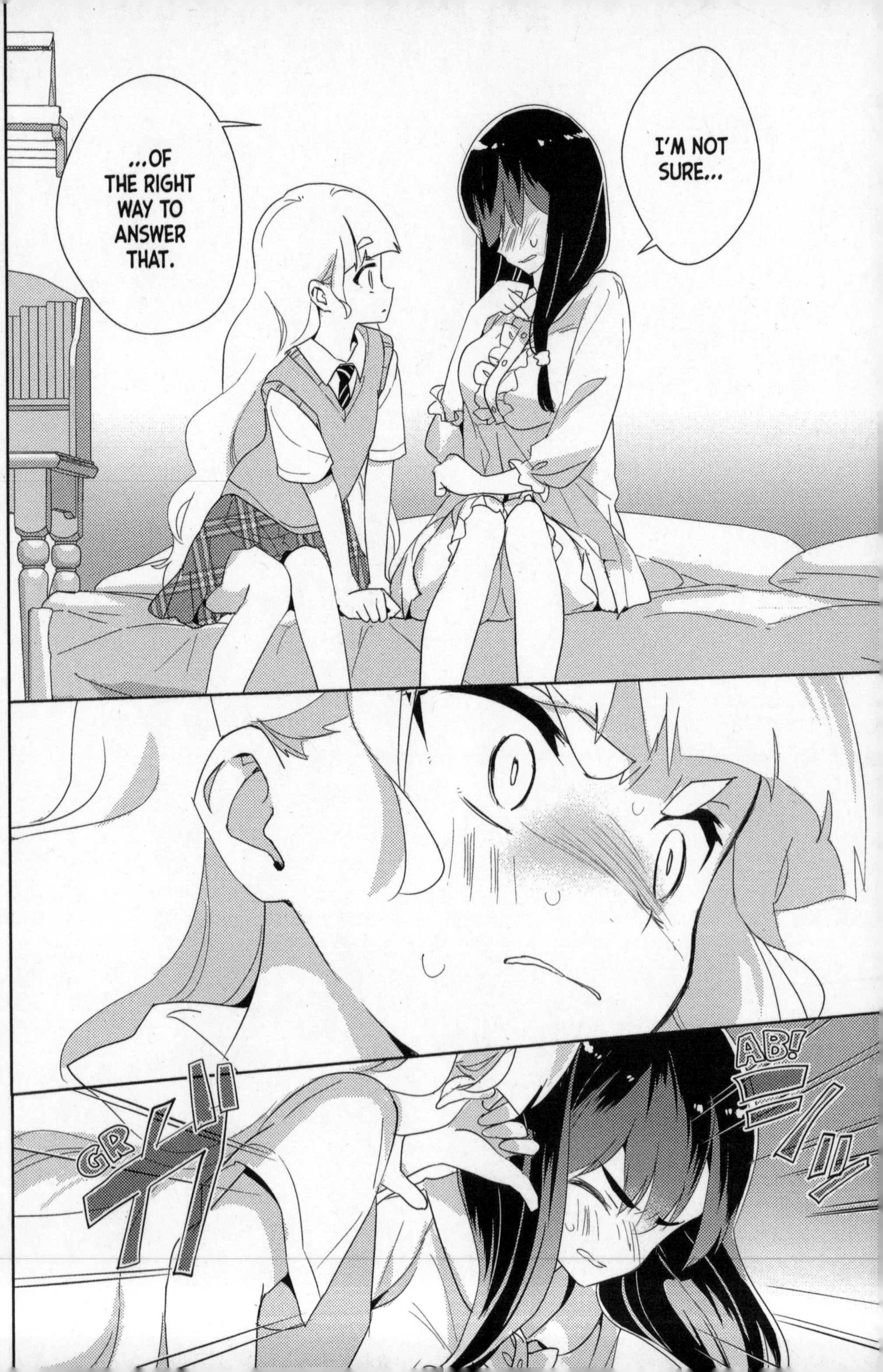
I'M NOT SURE...
...OF THE RIGHT WAY TO ANSWER THAT.
AB!
GR

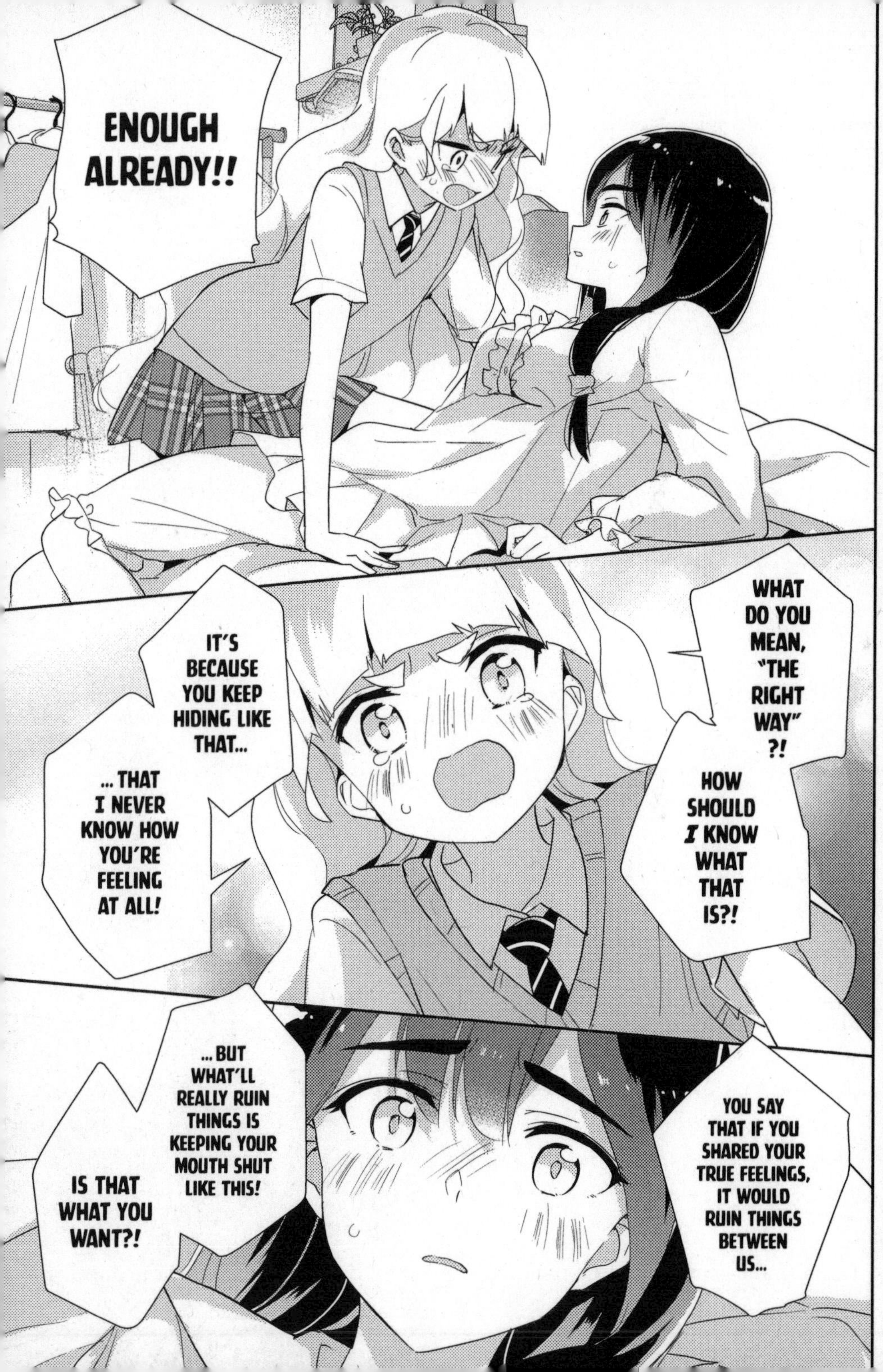
ENOUGH ALREADY!!
WHAT DO YOU MEAN, "THE RIGHT WAY"?!
HOW SHOULD *I* KNOW WHAT THAT IS?!
IT'S BECAUSE YOU KEEP HIDING LIKE THAT...
...THAT I NEVER KNOW HOW YOU'RE FEELING AT ALL!
YOU SAY THAT IF YOU SHARED YOUR TRUE FEELINGS, IT WOULD RUIN THINGS BETWEEN US...
...BUT WHAT'LL REALLY RUIN THINGS IS KEEPING YOUR MOUTH SHUT LIKE THIS!
IS THAT WHAT YOU WANT?!

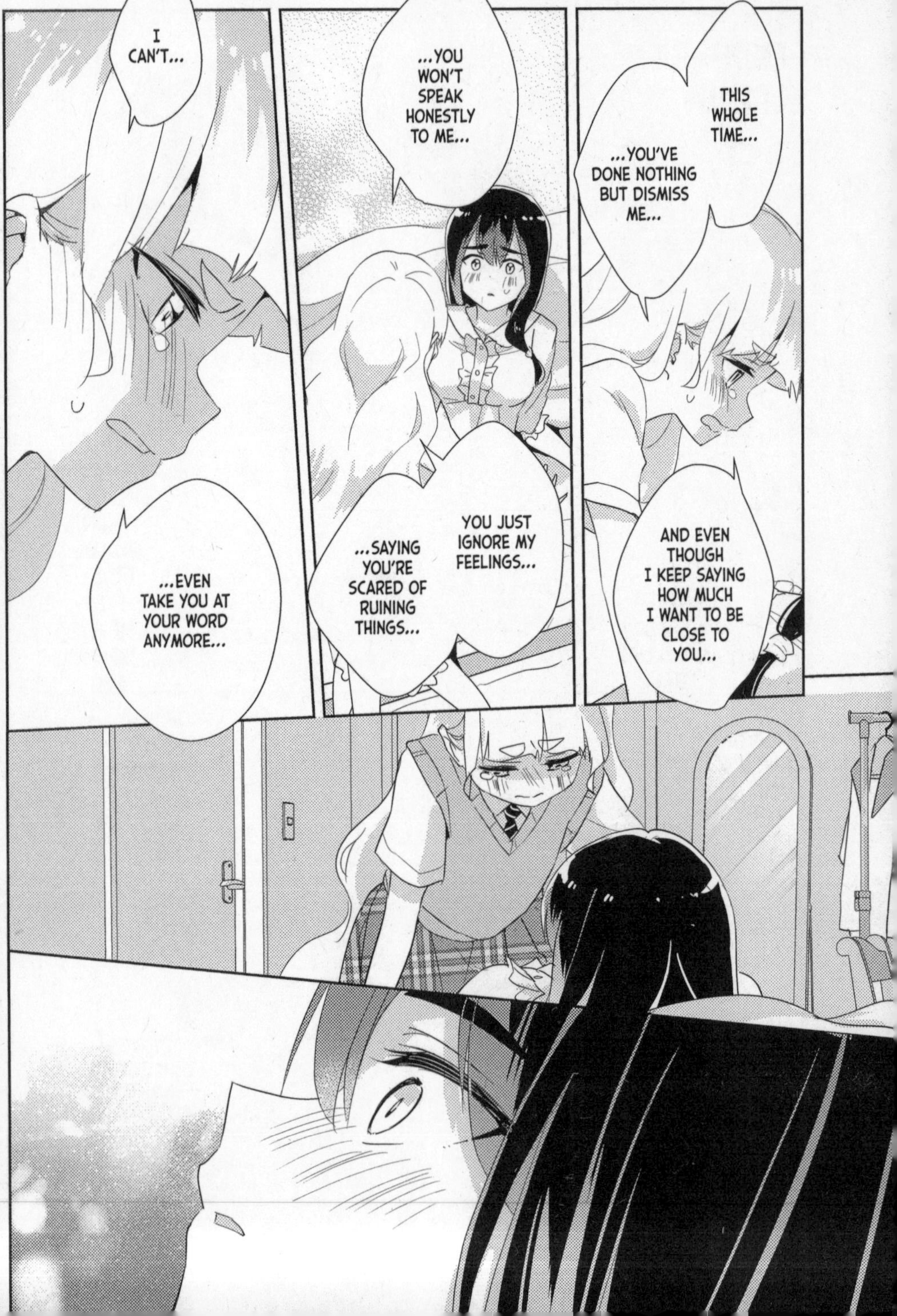
THIS WHOLE TIME...
...YOU'VE DONE NOTHING BUT DISMISS ME...
AND EVEN THOUGH I KEEP SAYING HOW MUCH I WANT TO BE CLOSE TO YOU...
...YOU WON'T SPEAK HONESTLY TO ME...
YOU JUST IGNORE MY FEELINGS...
...SAYING YOU'RE SCARED OF RUINING THINGS...
I CAN'T...
...EVEN TAKE YOU AT YOUR WORD ANYMORE...

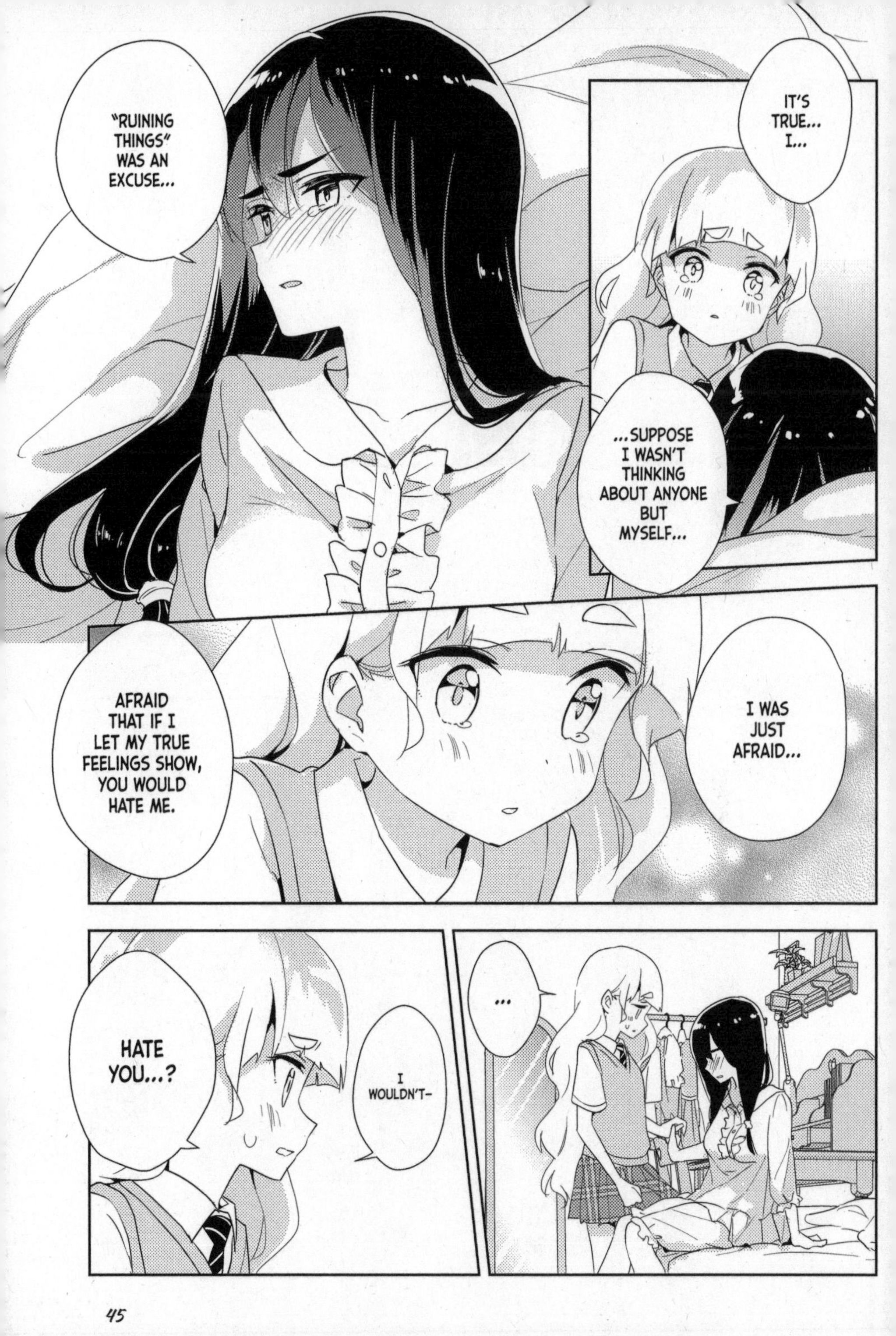
IT'S TRUE... I...
...SUPPOSE I WASN'T THINKING ABOUT ANYONE BUT MYSELF...
"RUINING THINGS" WAS AN EXCUSE...
I WAS JUST AFRAID...
AFRAID THAT IF I LET MY TRUE FEELINGS SHOW, YOU WOULD HATE ME.
...
HATE YOU...?
I WOULDN'T-

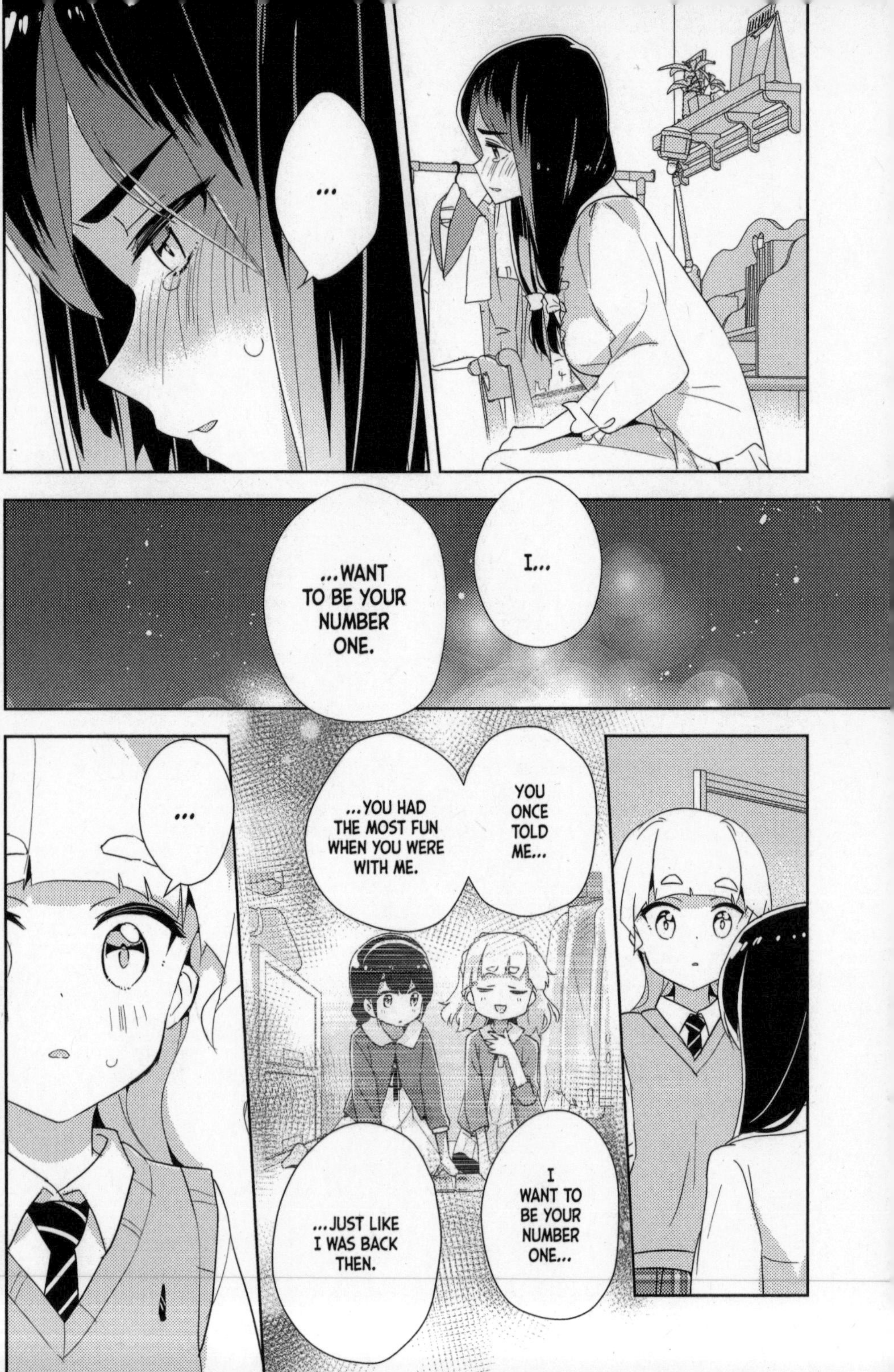
...
I...
...WANT TO BE YOUR NUMBER ONE.
YOU ONCE TOLD ME...
...YOU HAD THE MOST FUN WHEN YOU WERE WITH ME.
I WANT TO BE YOUR NUMBER ONE...
...JUST LIKE I WAS BACK THEN.
...

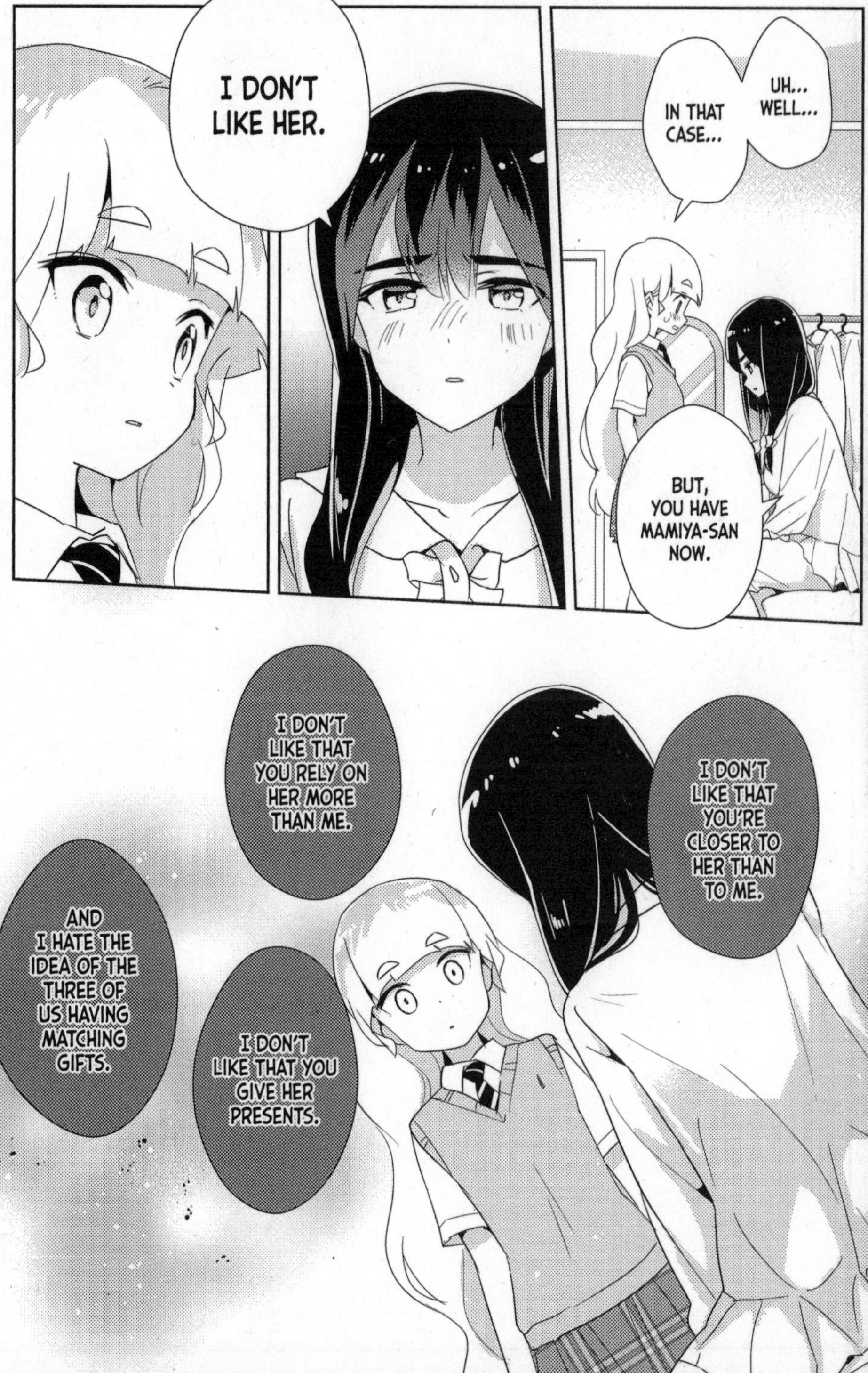
UH... WELL...
IN THAT CASE...
BUT, YOU HAVE MAMIYA-SAN NOW.
I DON'T LIKE HER.
I DON'T LIKE THAT YOU'RE CLOSER TO HER THAN TO ME.
I DON'T LIKE THAT YOU RELY ON HER MORE THAN ME.
I DON'T LIKE THAT YOU GIVE HER PRESENTS.
AND I HATE THE IDEA OF THE THREE OF US HAVING MATCHING GIFTS.

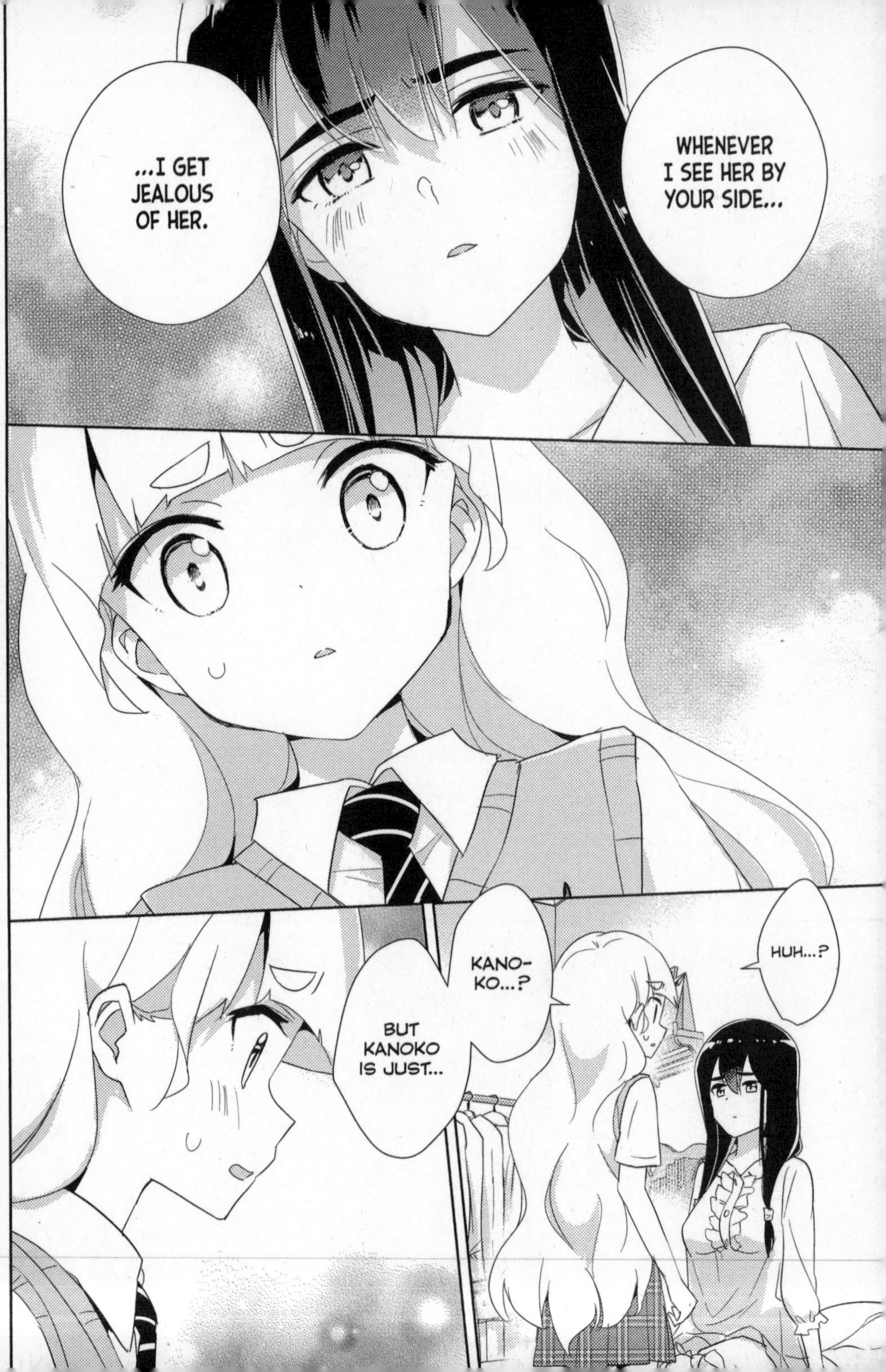
WHENEVER I SEE HER BY YOUR SIDE...
...I GET JEALOUS OF HER.
HUH...?
KANO-KO...?
BUT KANOKO IS JUST...

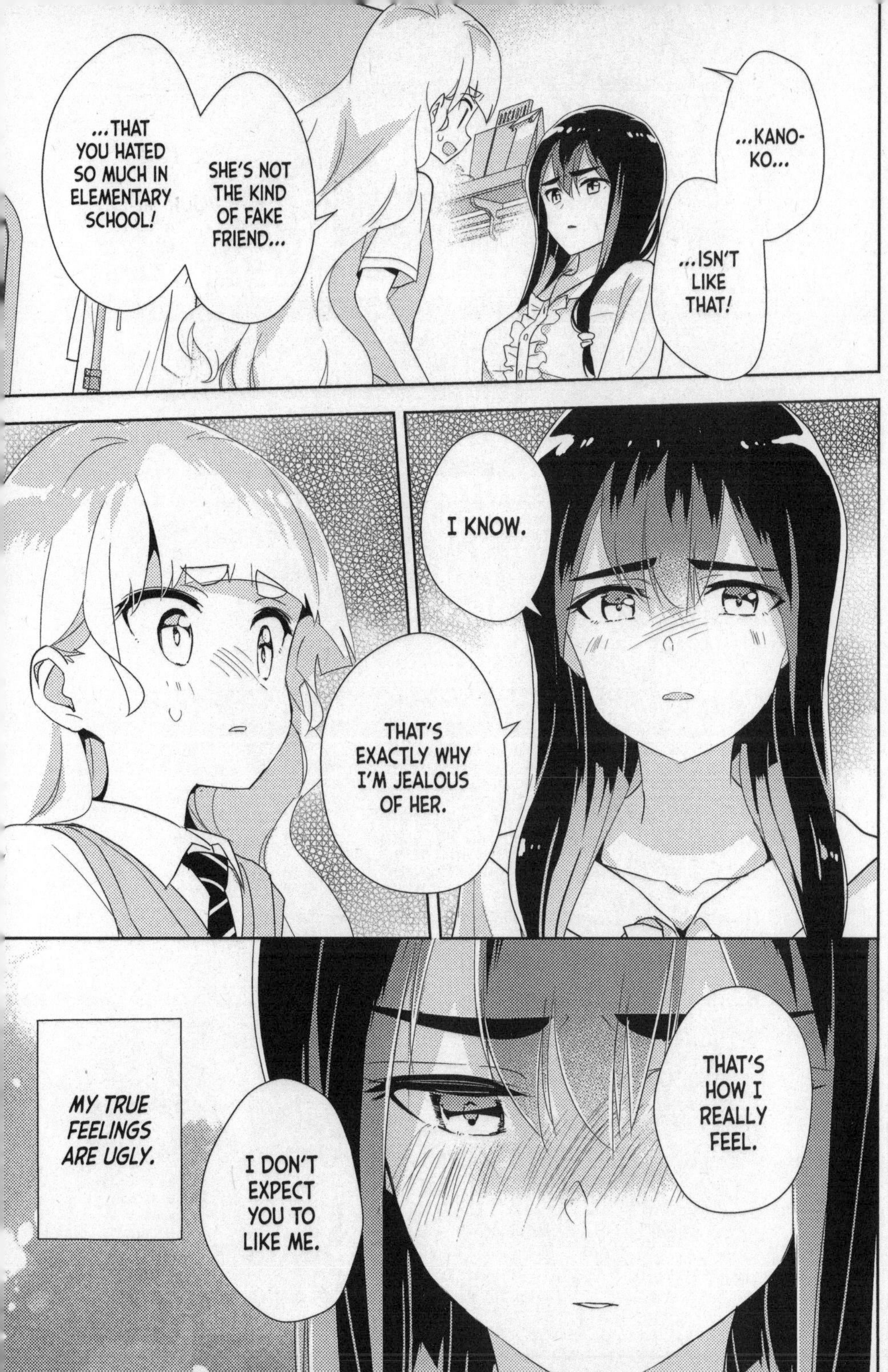
...KANO-KO...
...ISN'T LIKE THAT!
SHE'S NOT THE KIND OF FAKE FRIEND...
...THAT YOU HATED SO MUCH IN ELEMENTARY SCHOOL!
I KNOW.
THAT'S EXACTLY WHY I'M JEALOUS OF HER.
THAT'S HOW I REALLY FEEL.
I DON'T EXPECT YOU TO LIKE ME.
MY TRUE FEELINGS ARE UGLY.

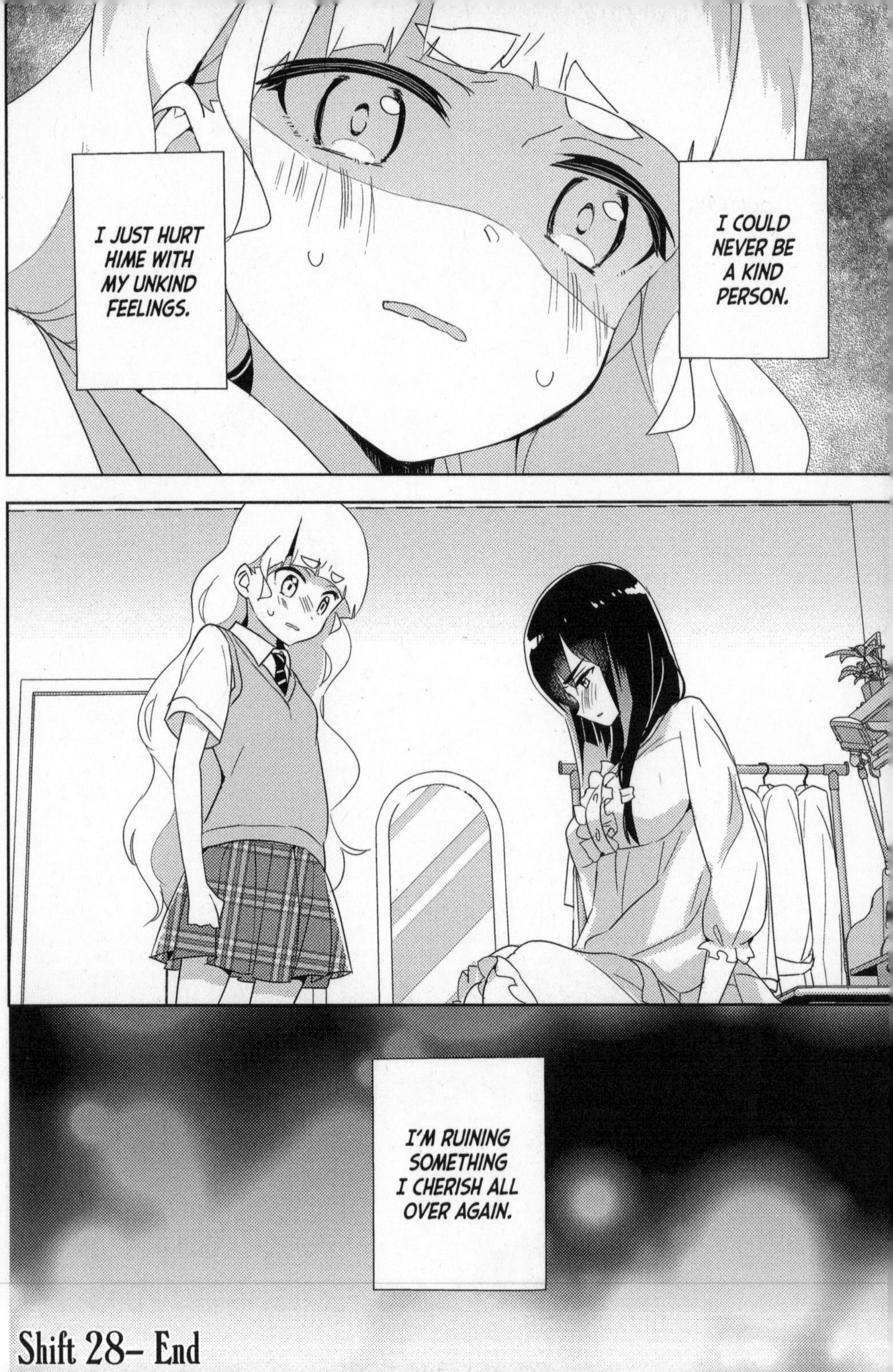
I COULD NEVER BE A KIND PERSON.
I JUST HURT HIME WITH MY UNKIND FEELINGS.
I'M RUINING SOMETHING I CHERISH ALL OVER AGAIN.
Shift 28– End

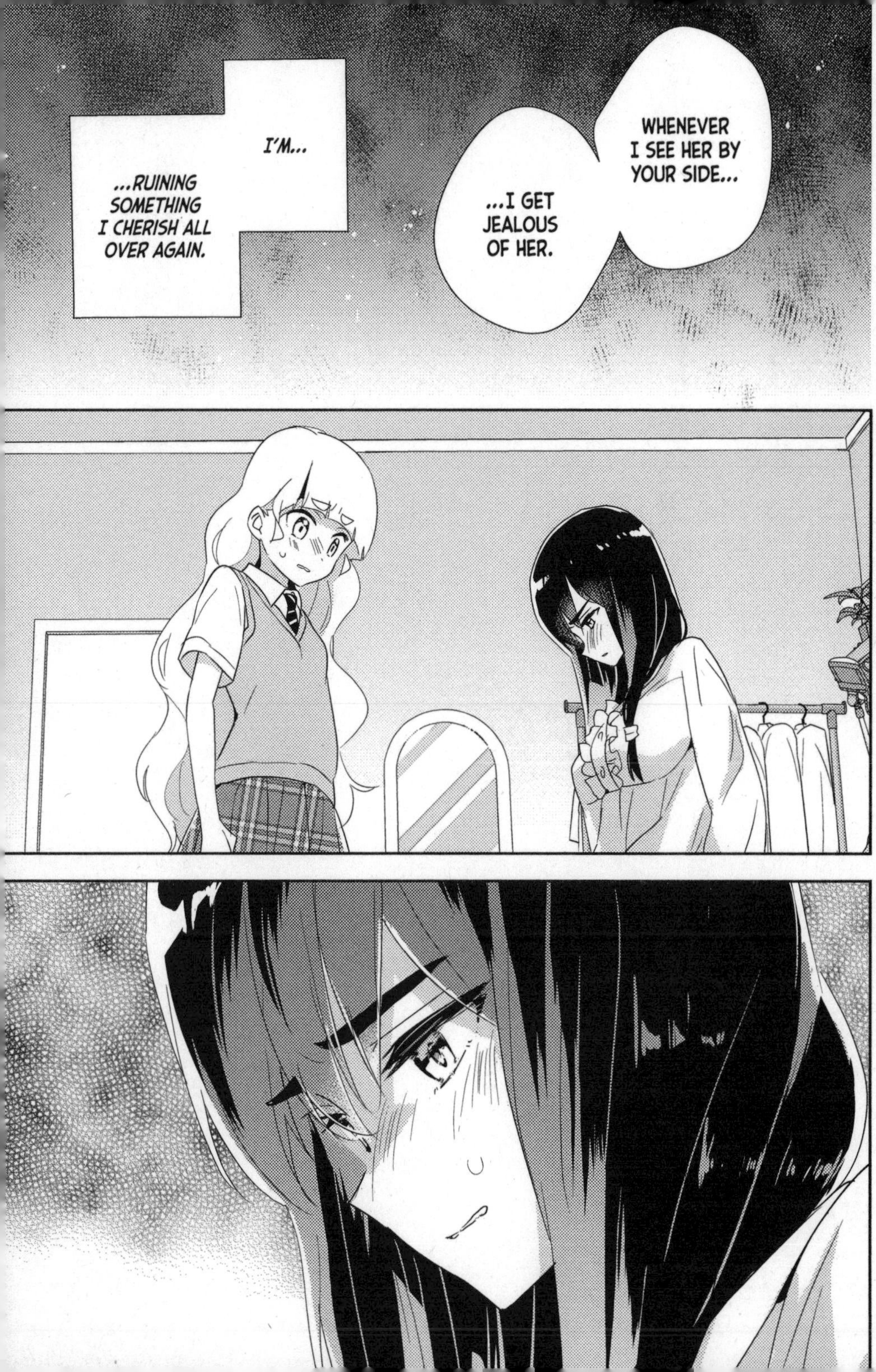
WHENEVER I SEE HER BY YOUR SIDE...
...I GET JEALOUS OF HER.
I'M...
...RUINING SOMETHING I CHERISH ALL OVER AGAIN.

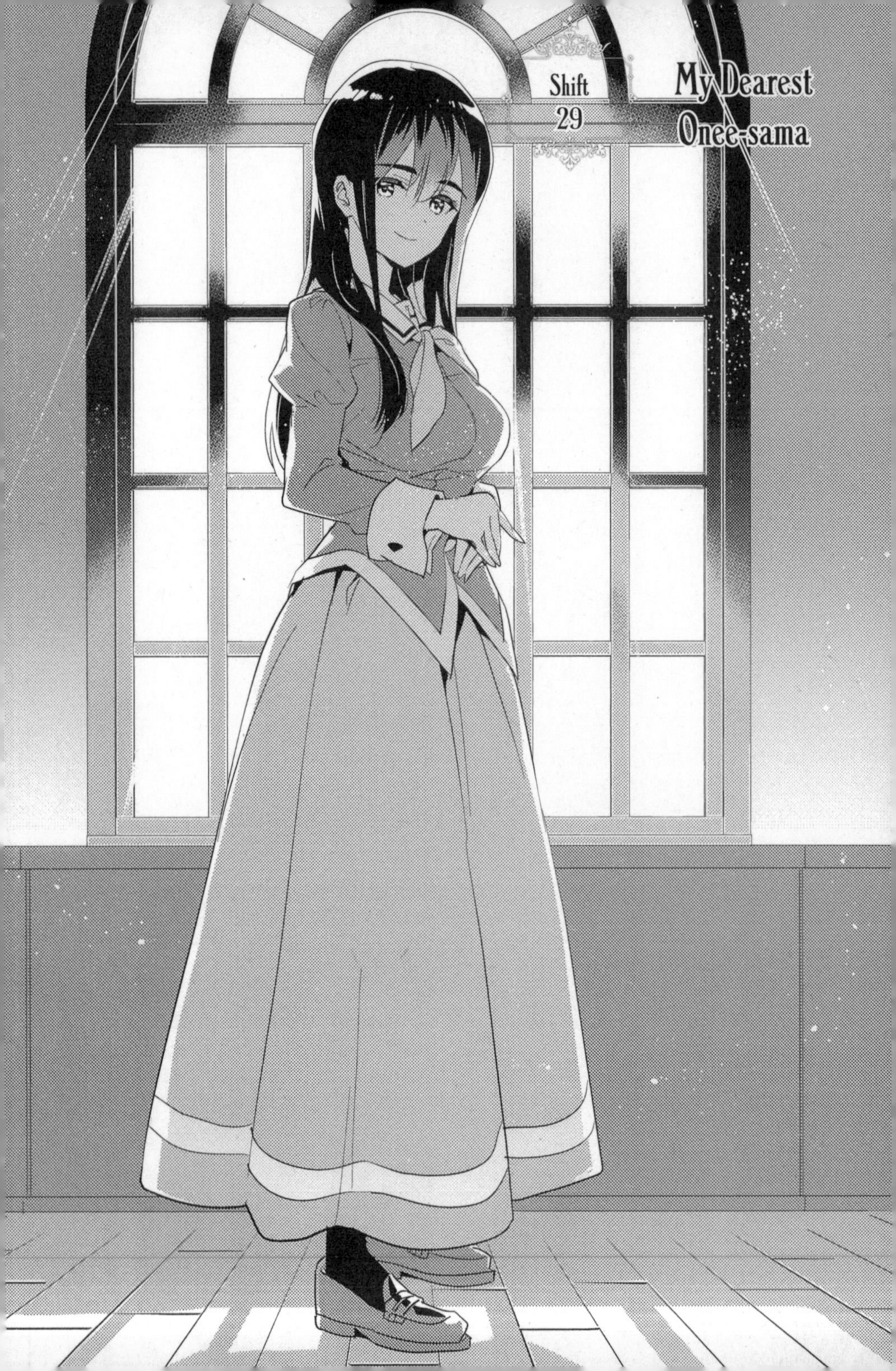
Shift 29
My Dearest Onee-sama

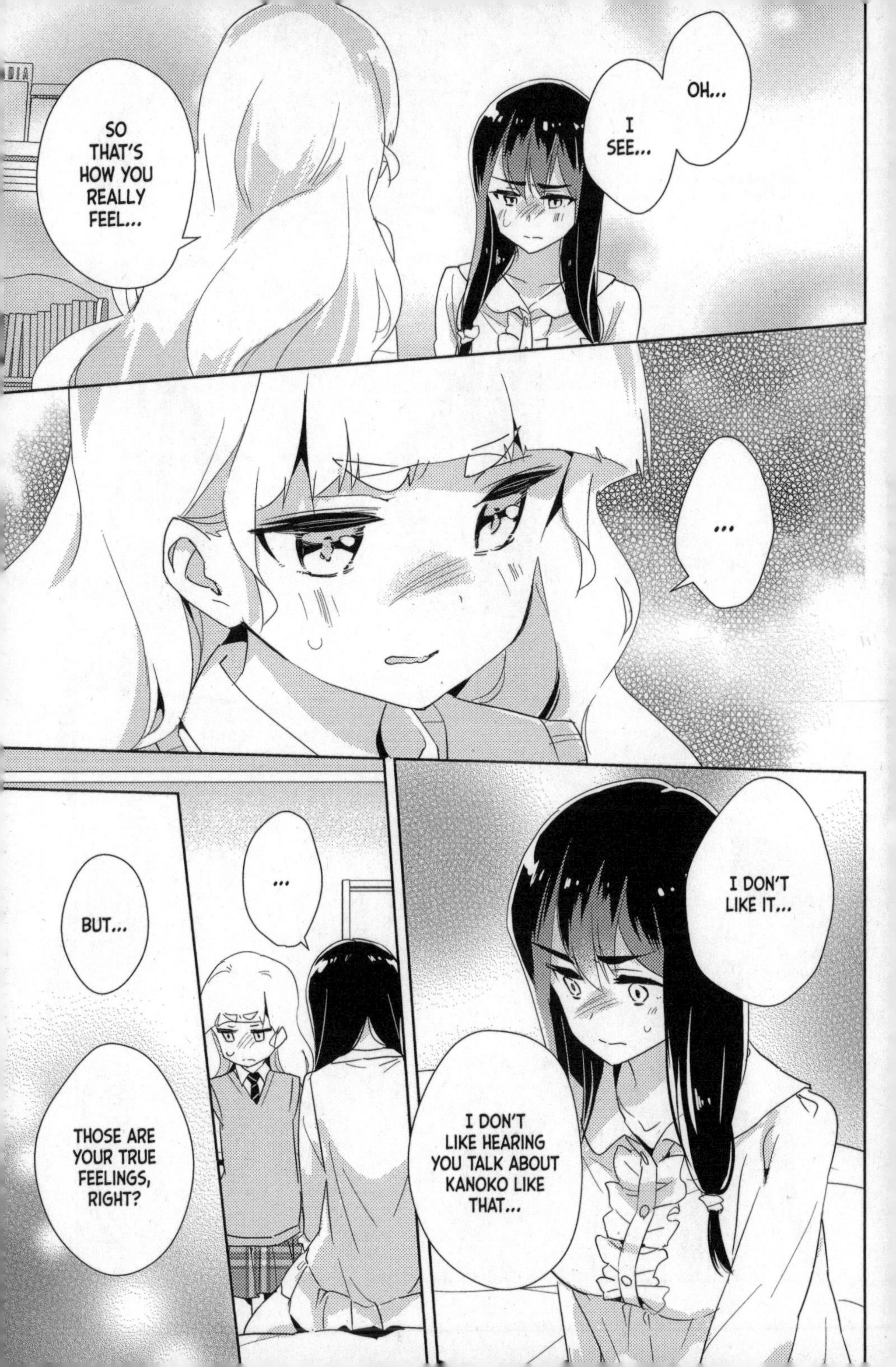
OH... I SEE...
SO THAT'S HOW YOU REALLY FEEL...
...
I DON'T LIKE IT...
I DON'T LIKE HEARING YOU TALK ABOUT KANOKO LIKE THAT...
...
BUT...
THOSE ARE YOUR TRUE FEELINGS, RIGHT?

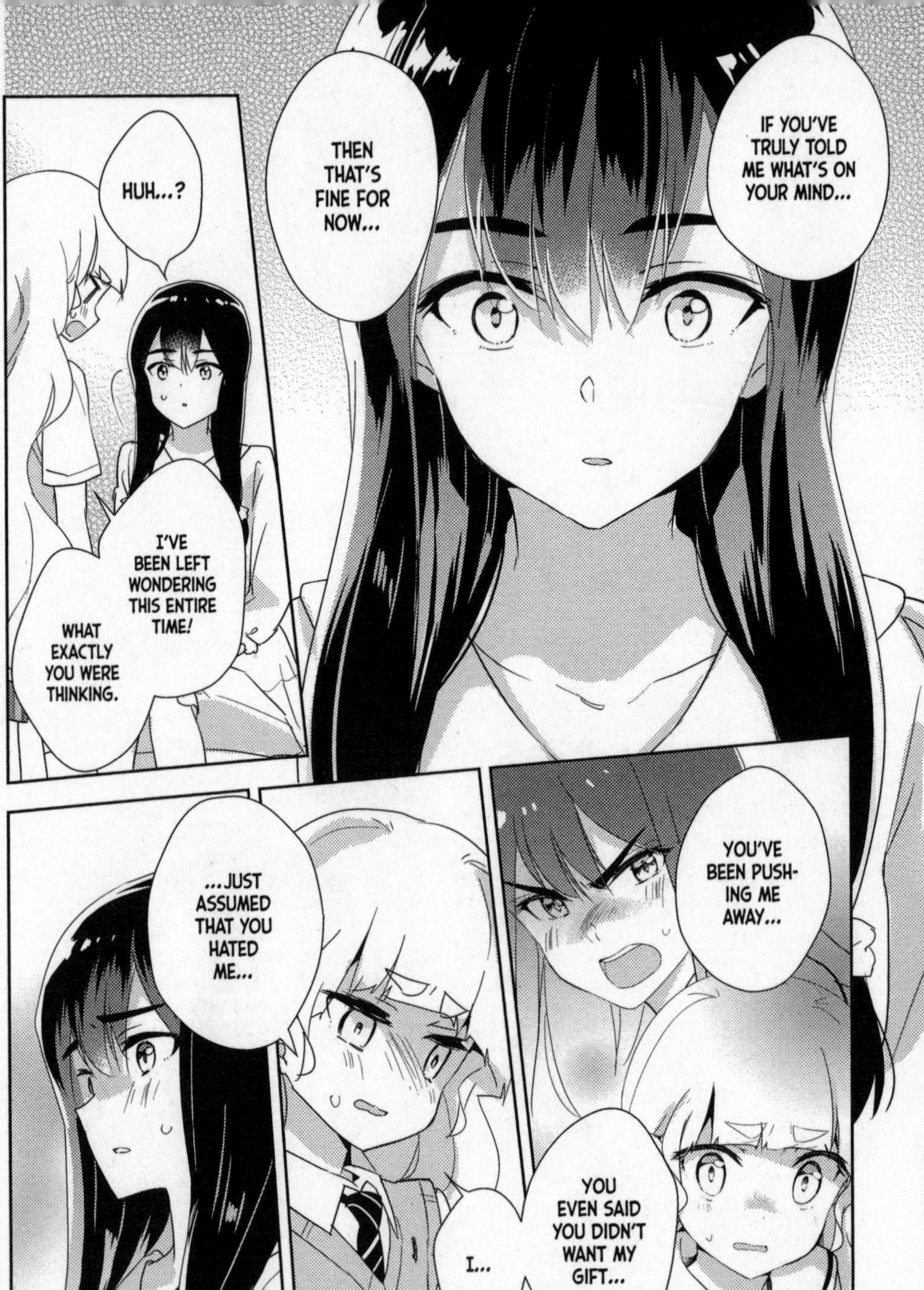
IF YOU'VE TRULY TOLD ME WHAT'S ON YOUR MIND...
THEN THAT'S FINE FOR NOW...
HUH...?
I'VE BEEN LEFT WONDERING THIS ENTIRE TIME!
WHAT EXACTLY YOU WERE THINKING.
YOU'VE BEEN PUSH-ING ME AWAY...
YOU EVEN SAID YOU DIDN'T WANT MY GIFT...
I...
...JUST ASSUMED THAT YOU HATED ME...

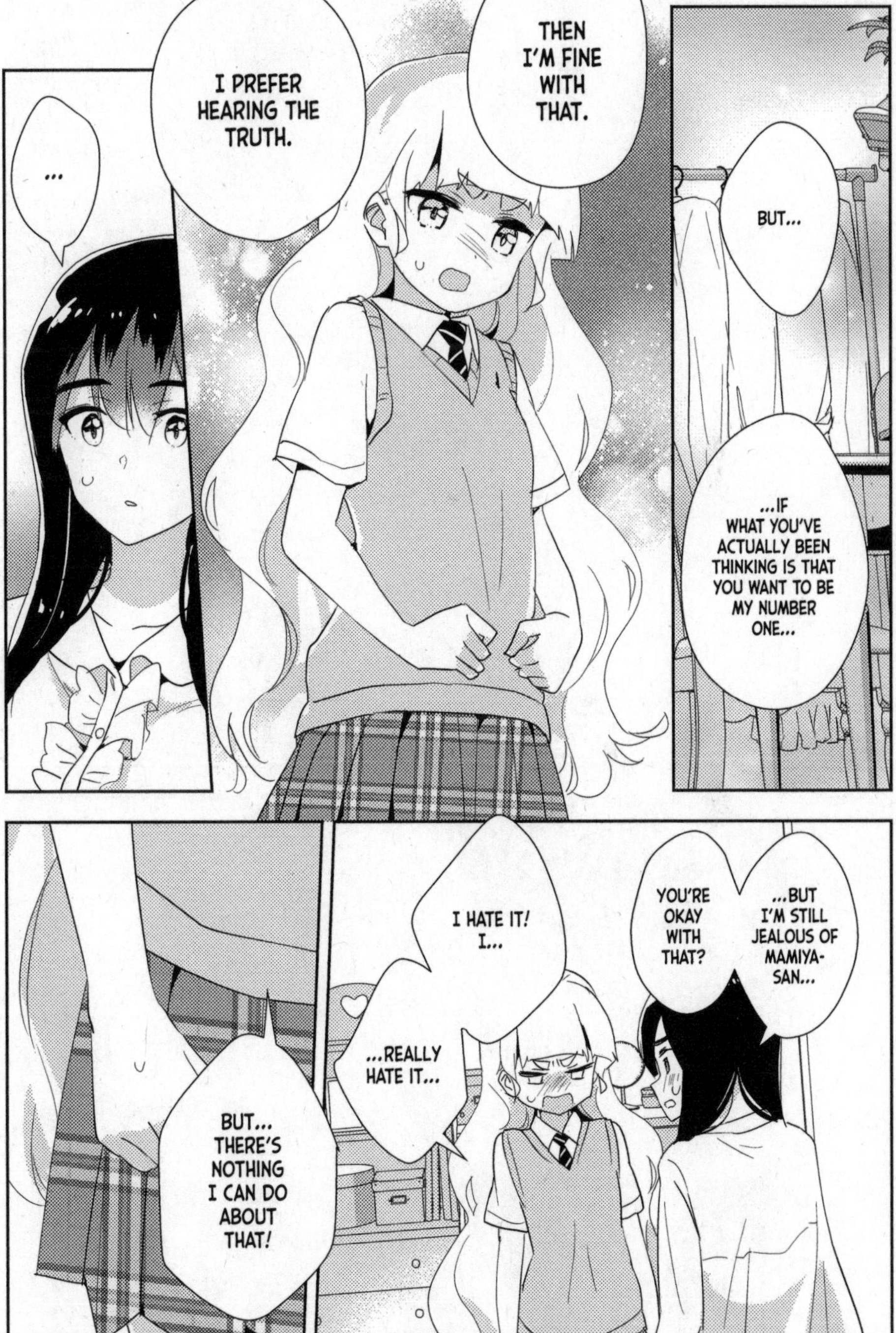
BUT...
...IF WHAT YOU'VE ACTUALLY BEEN THINKING IS THAT YOU WANT TO BE MY NUMBER ONE...
THEN I'M FINE WITH THAT.
I PREFER HEARING THE TRUTH.
...
...BUT I'M STILL JEALOUS OF MAMIYA-SAN...
YOU'RE OKAY WITH THAT?
I HATE IT! I...
...REALLY HATE IT...
BUT... THERE'S NOTHING I CAN DO ABOUT THAT!

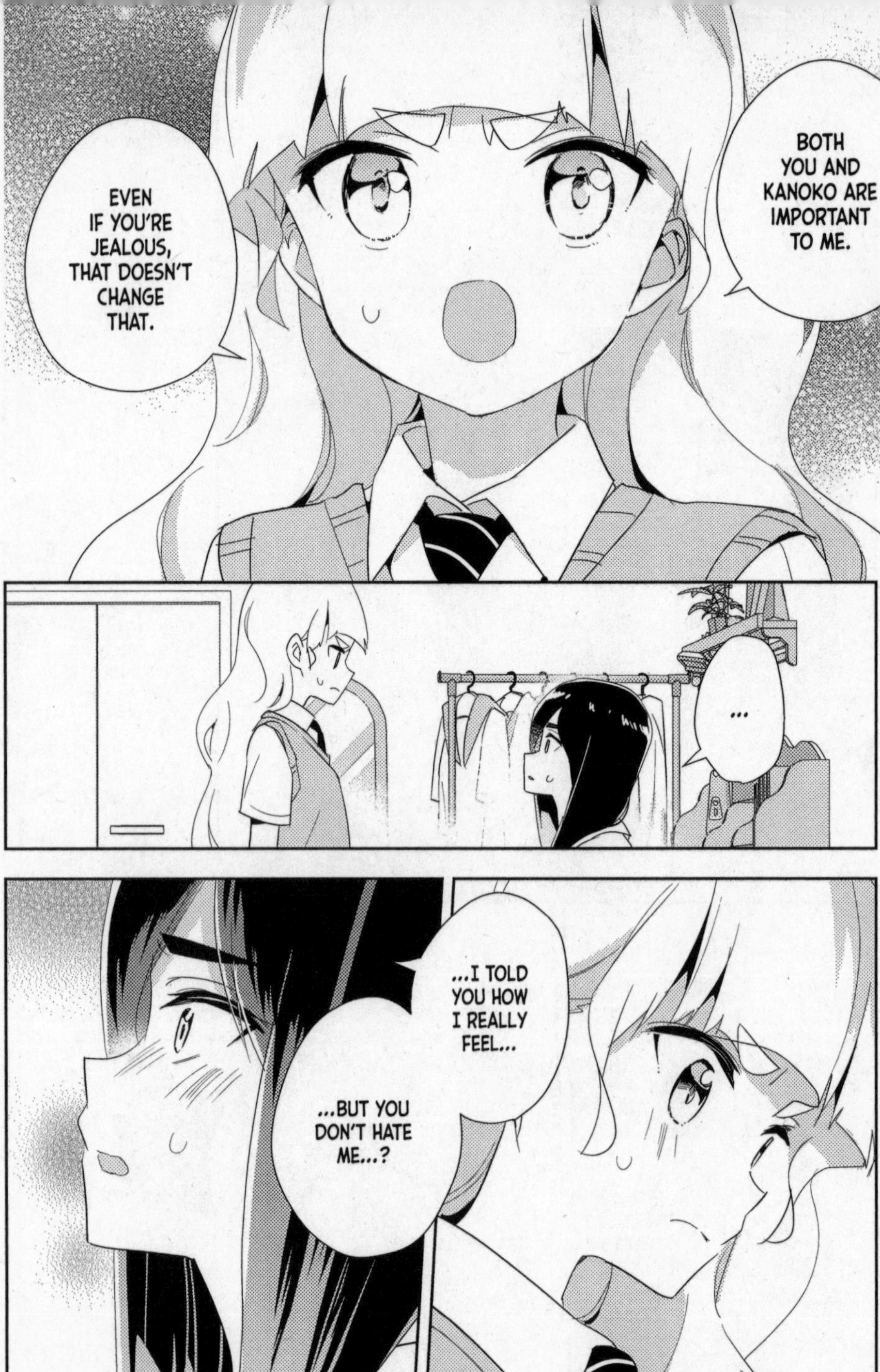
BOTH YOU AND KANOKO ARE IMPORTANT TO ME.
EVEN IF YOU'RE JEALOUS, THAT DOESN'T CHANGE THAT.
...
...I TOLD YOU HOW I REALLY FEEL...
...BUT YOU DON'T HATE ME...?

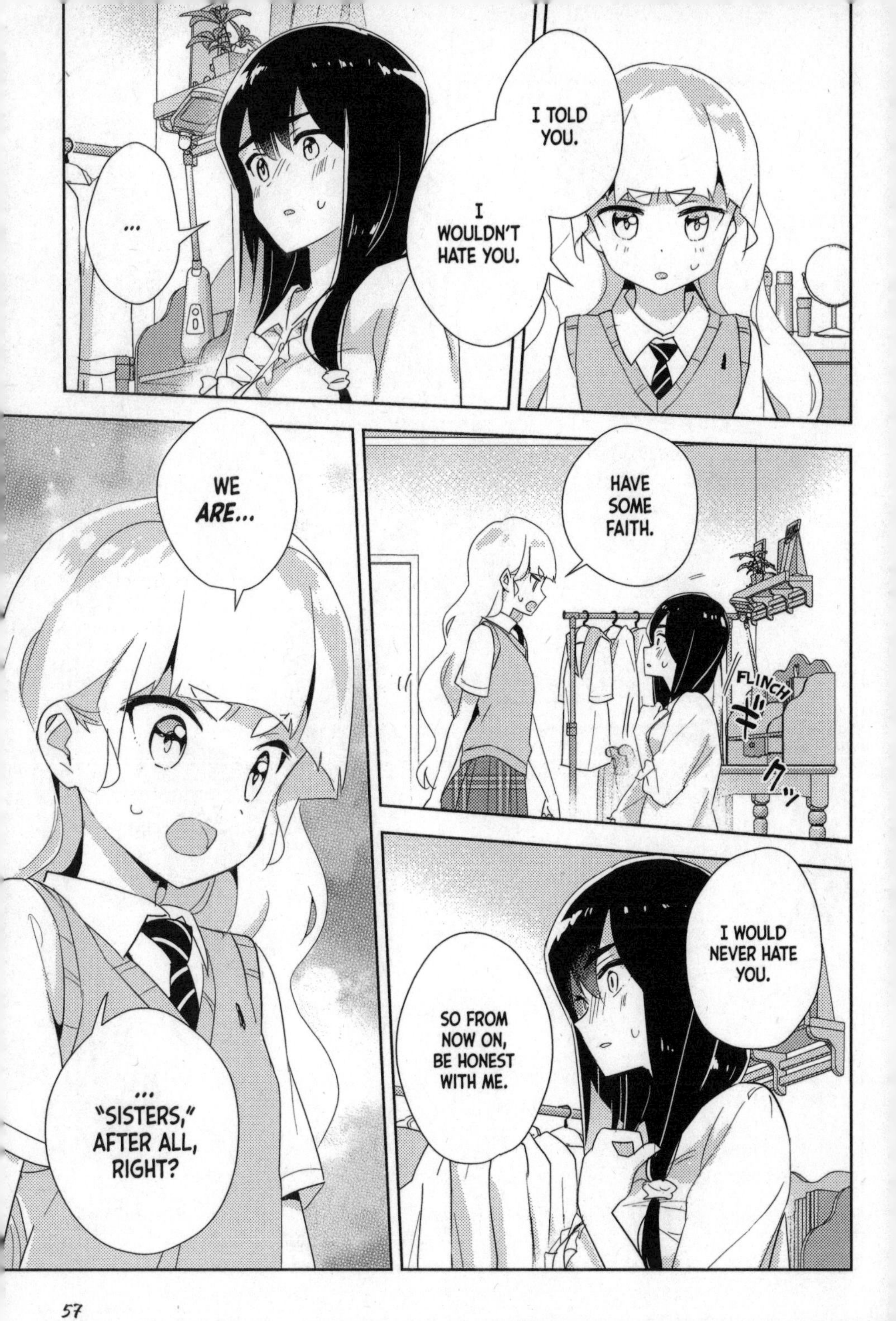
I TOLD YOU.
I WOULDN'T HATE YOU.
...
HAVE SOME FAITH.
FLINCH
I WOULD NEVER HATE YOU.
SO FROM NOW ON, BE HONEST WITH ME.
WE *ARE*...
... "SISTERS," AFTER ALL, RIGHT?

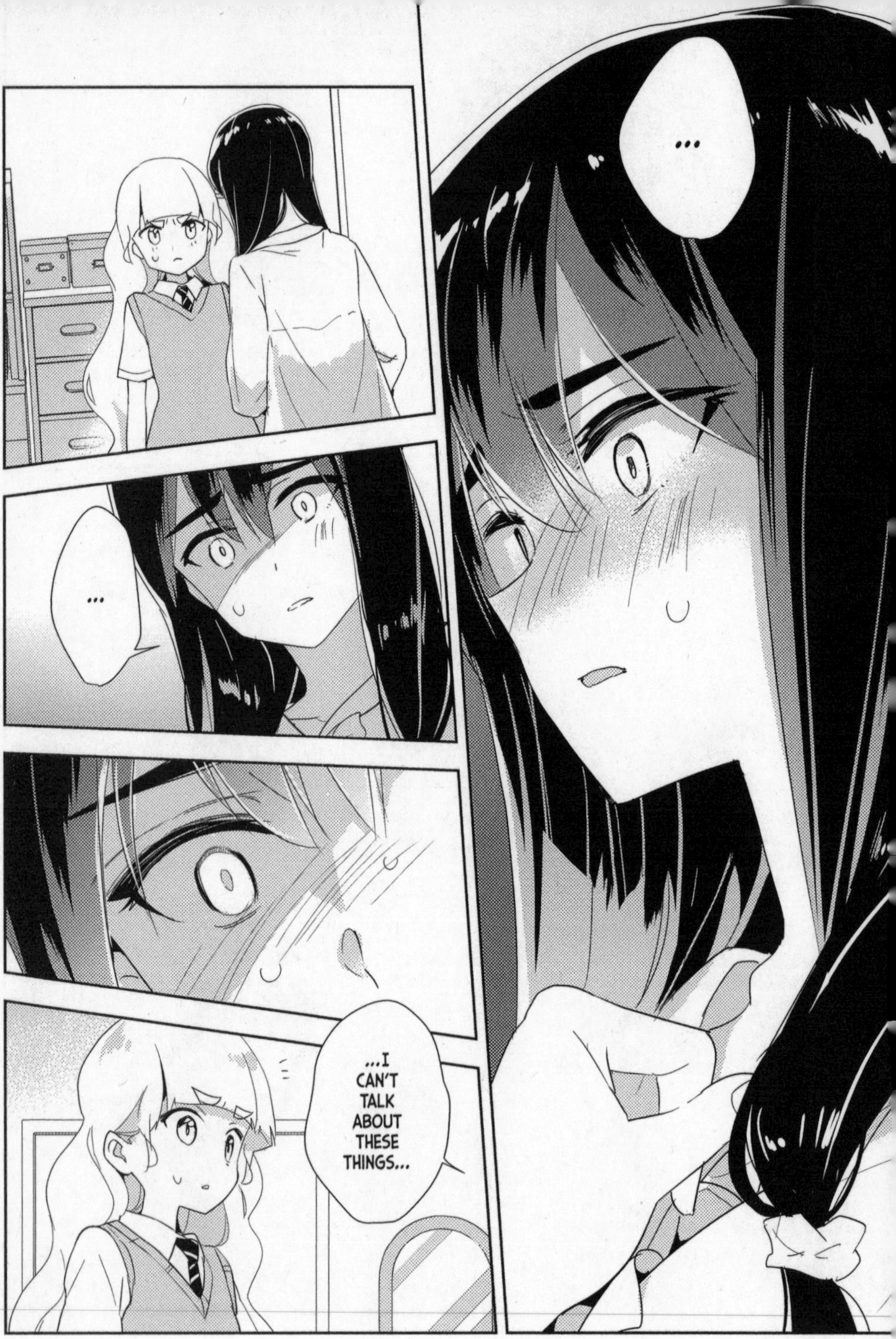
...
...
...I CAN'T TALK ABOUT THESE THINGS...

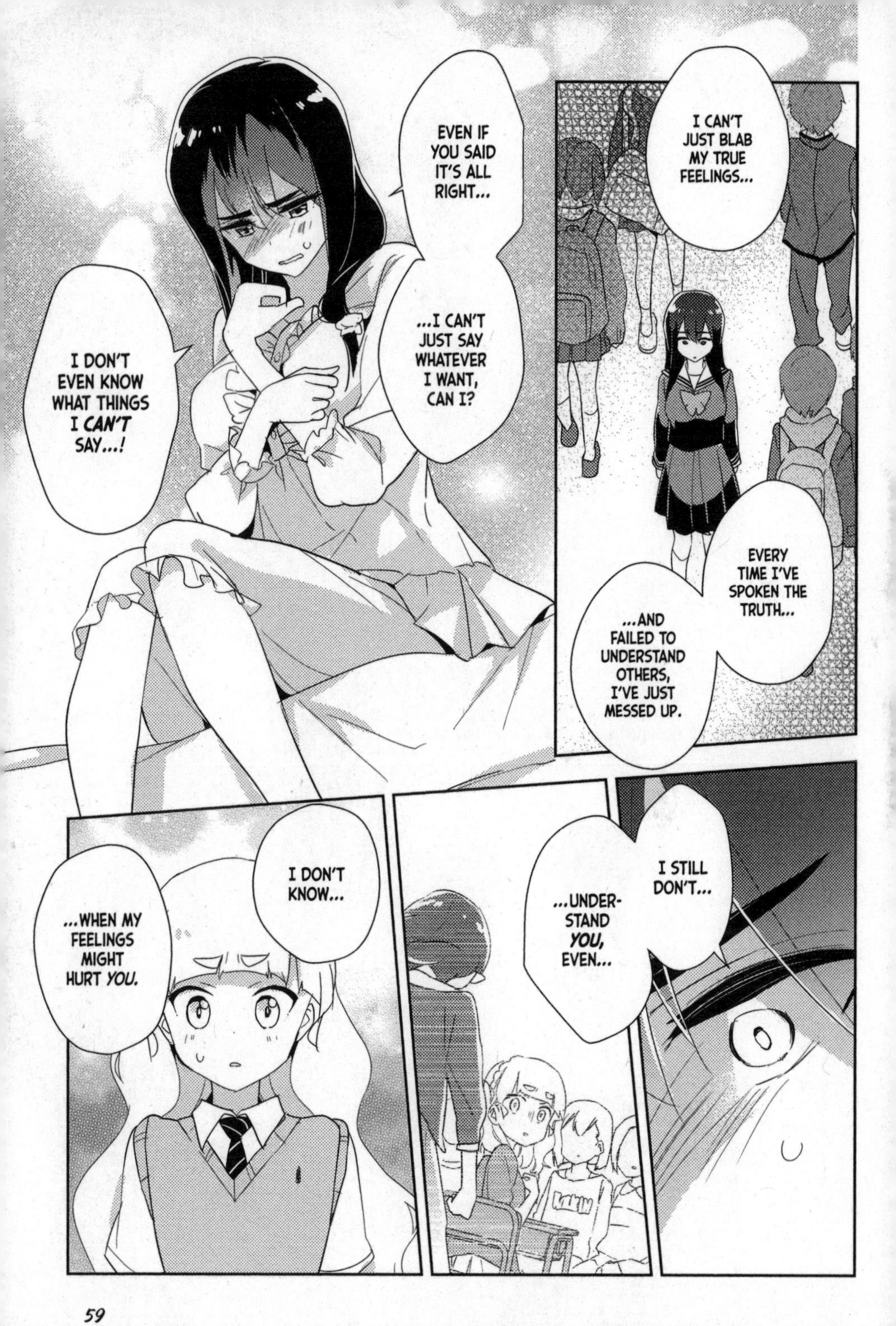
I CAN'T JUST BLAB MY TRUE FEELINGS...
EVERY TIME I'VE SPOKEN THE TRUTH...
...AND FAILED TO UNDERSTAND OTHERS, I'VE JUST MESSED UP.
EVEN IF YOU SAID IT'S ALL RIGHT...
...I CAN'T JUST SAY WHATEVER I WANT, CAN I?
I DON'T EVEN KNOW WHAT THINGS I *CAN'T* SAY...!
I STILL DON'T...
...UNDER-STAND *YOU,* EVEN...
I DON'T KNOW...
...WHEN MY FEELINGS MIGHT HURT *YOU.*

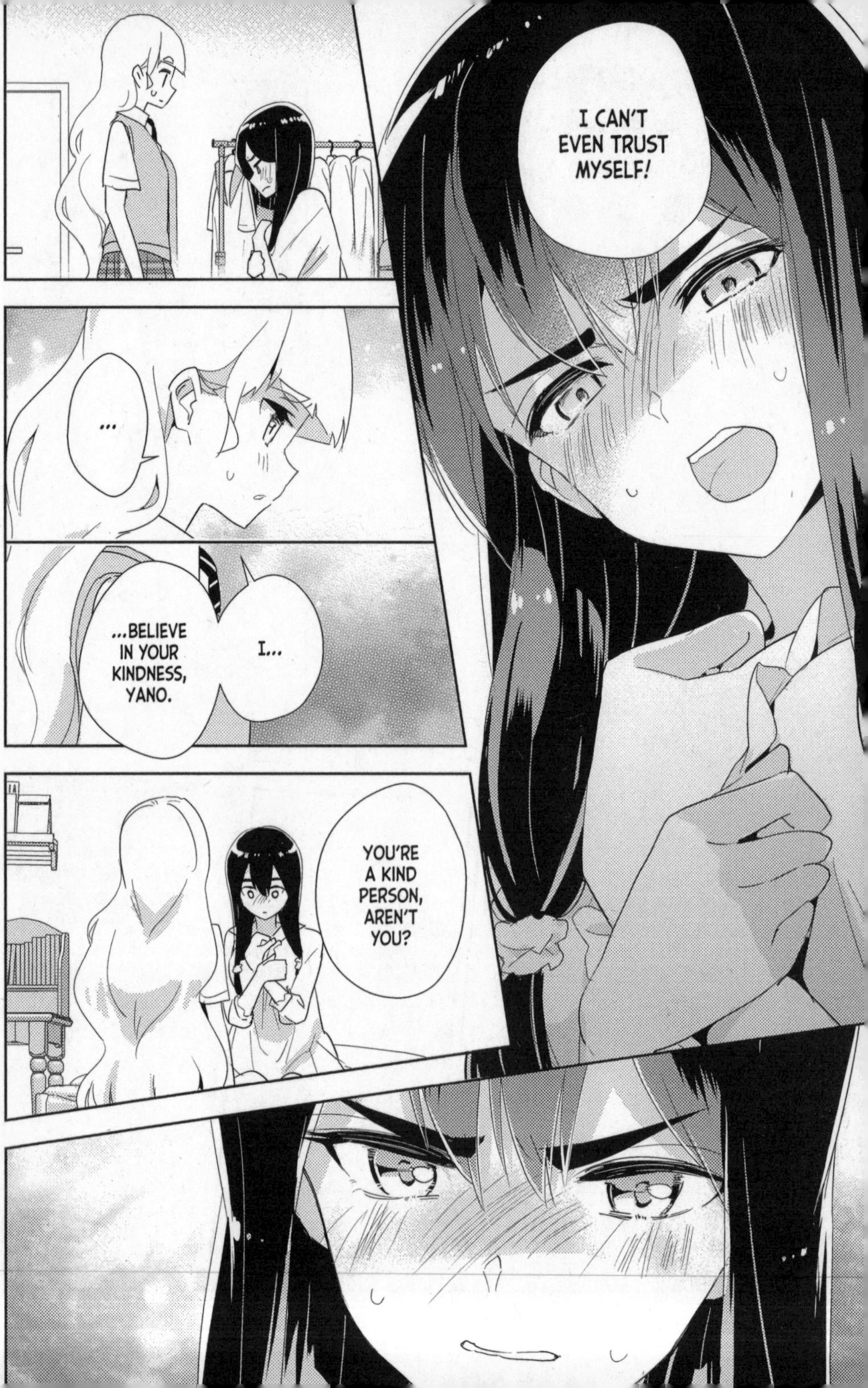

I CAN'T EVEN TRUST MYSELF!
...
I...
...BELIEVE IN YOUR KINDNESS, YANO.
YOU'RE A KIND PERSON, AREN'T YOU?

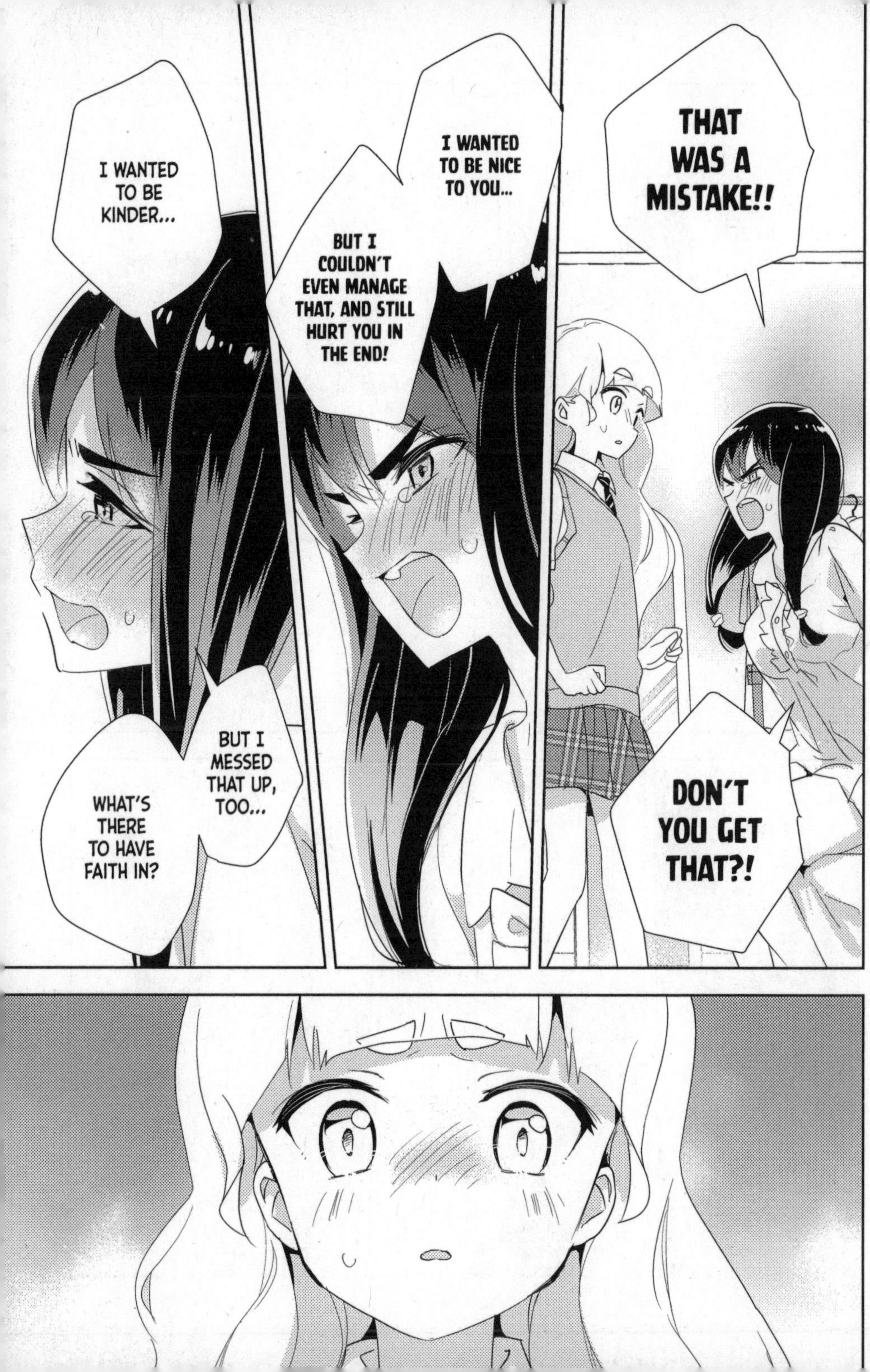
THAT WAS A MISTAKE!!
DON'T YOU GET THAT?!
I WANTED TO BE NICE TO YOU...
BUT I COULDN'T EVEN MANAGE THAT, AND STILL HURT YOU IN THE END!
I WANTED TO BE KINDER...
BUT I MESSED THAT UP, TOO...
WHAT'S THERE TO HAVE FAITH IN?

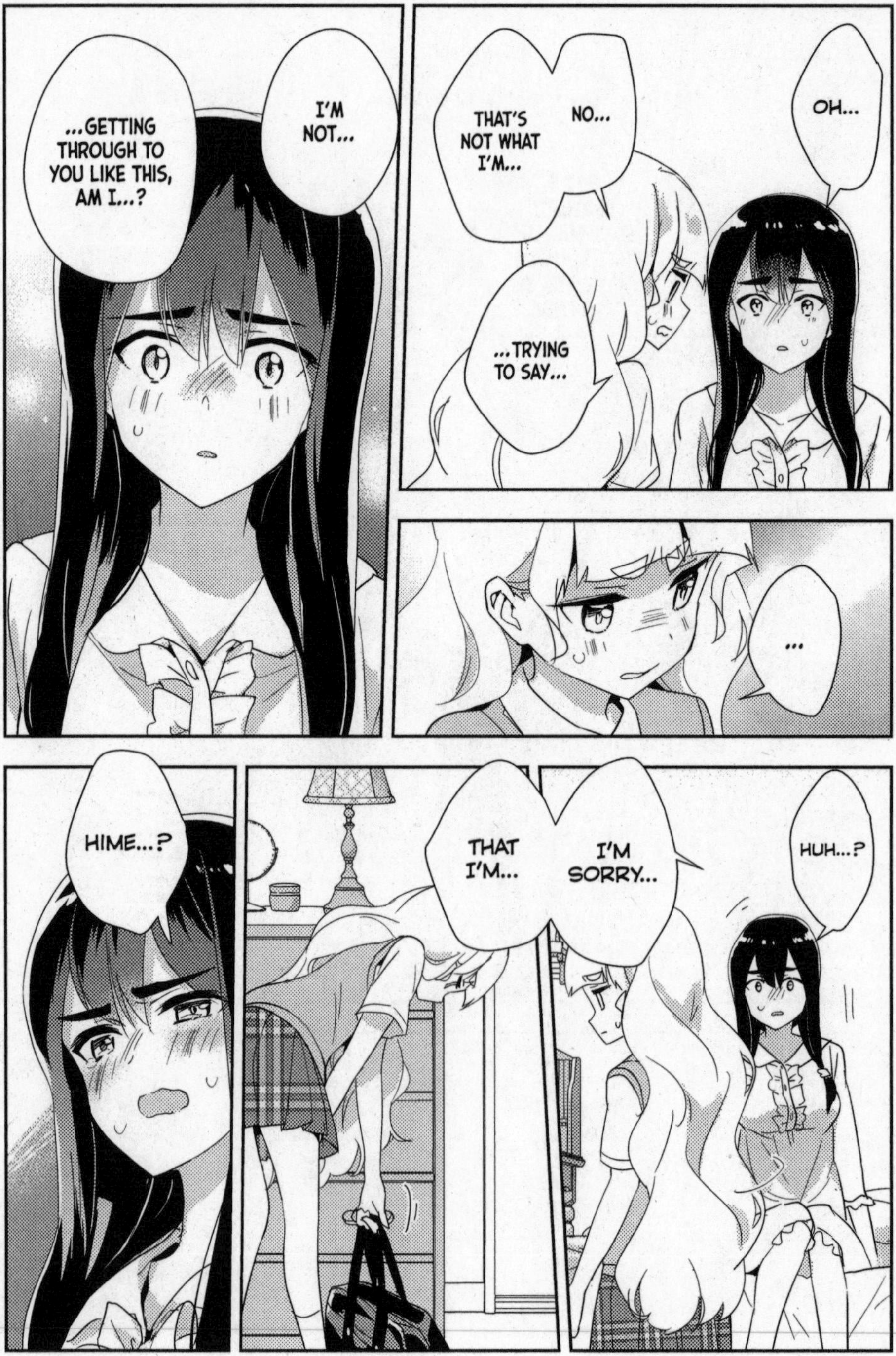
OH...
NO...
THAT'S NOT WHAT I'M...
...TRYING TO SAY...
...
I'M NOT...
...GETTING THROUGH TO YOU LIKE THIS, AM I...?
HUH...?
I'M SORRY...
THAT I'M...
HIME...?

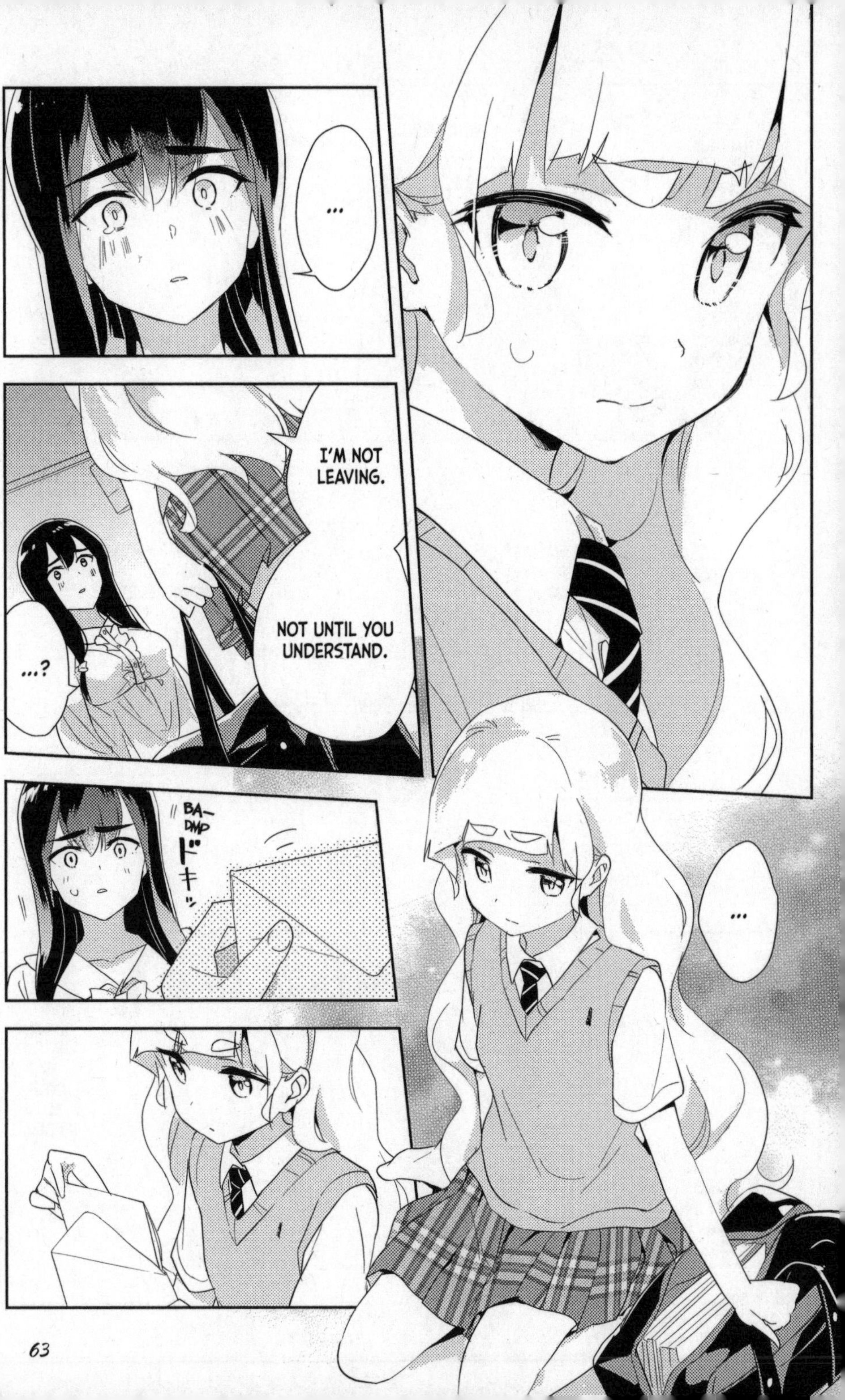
...
I'M NOT LEAVING.
NOT UNTIL YOU UNDERSTAND.
...?
BA-DMP
ドキッ
...

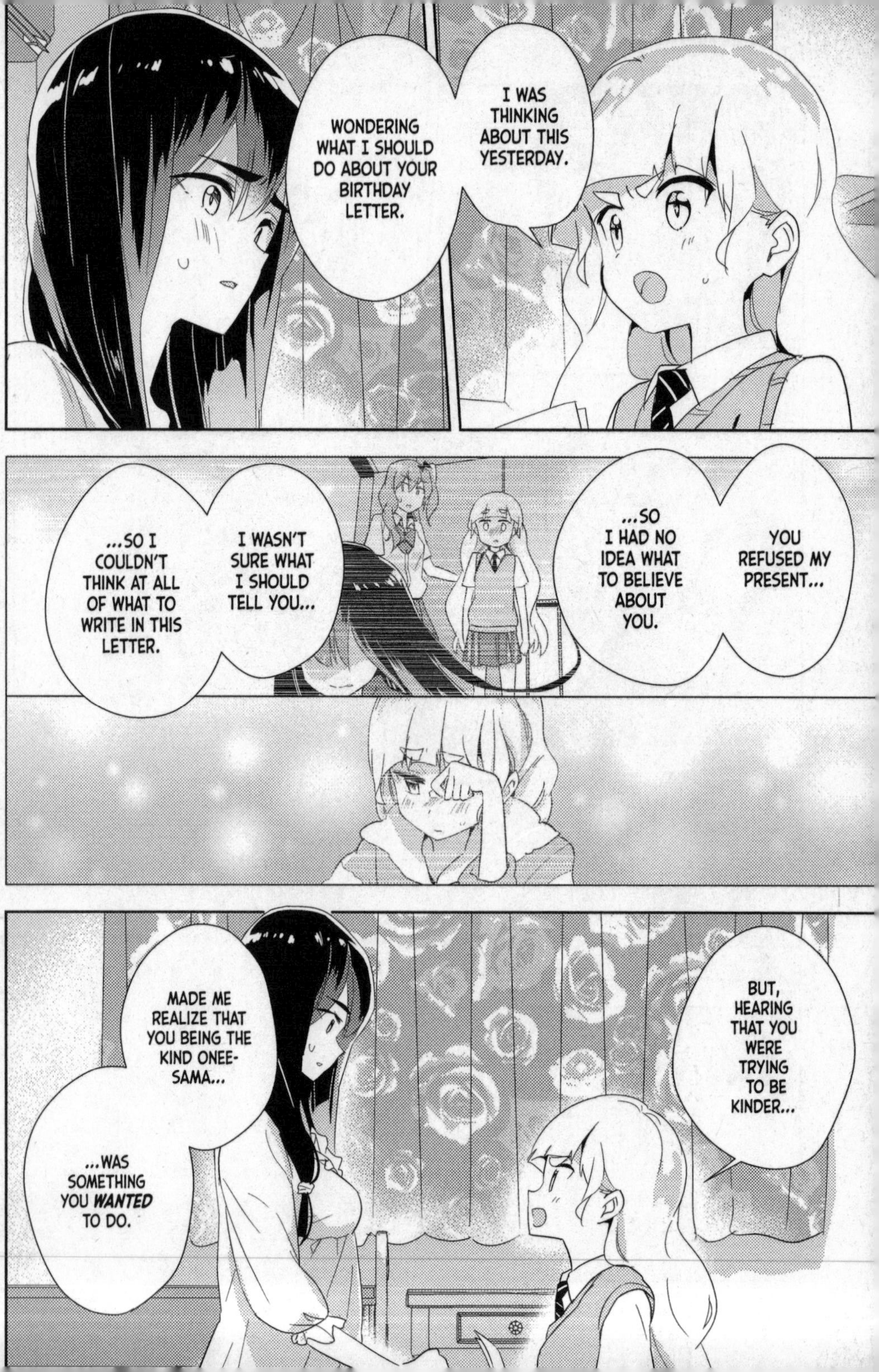
I WAS THINKING ABOUT THIS YESTERDAY.
WONDERING WHAT I SHOULD DO ABOUT YOUR BIRTHDAY LETTER.
YOU REFUSED MY PRESENT...
...SO I HAD NO IDEA WHAT TO BELIEVE ABOUT YOU.
I WASN'T SURE WHAT I SHOULD TELL YOU...
...SO I COULDN'T THINK AT ALL OF WHAT TO WRITE IN THIS LETTER.
BUT, HEARING THAT YOU WERE TRYING TO BE KINDER...
MADE ME REALIZE THAT YOU BEING THE KIND ONEE-SAMA...
...WAS SOMETHING YOU *WANTED* TO DO.

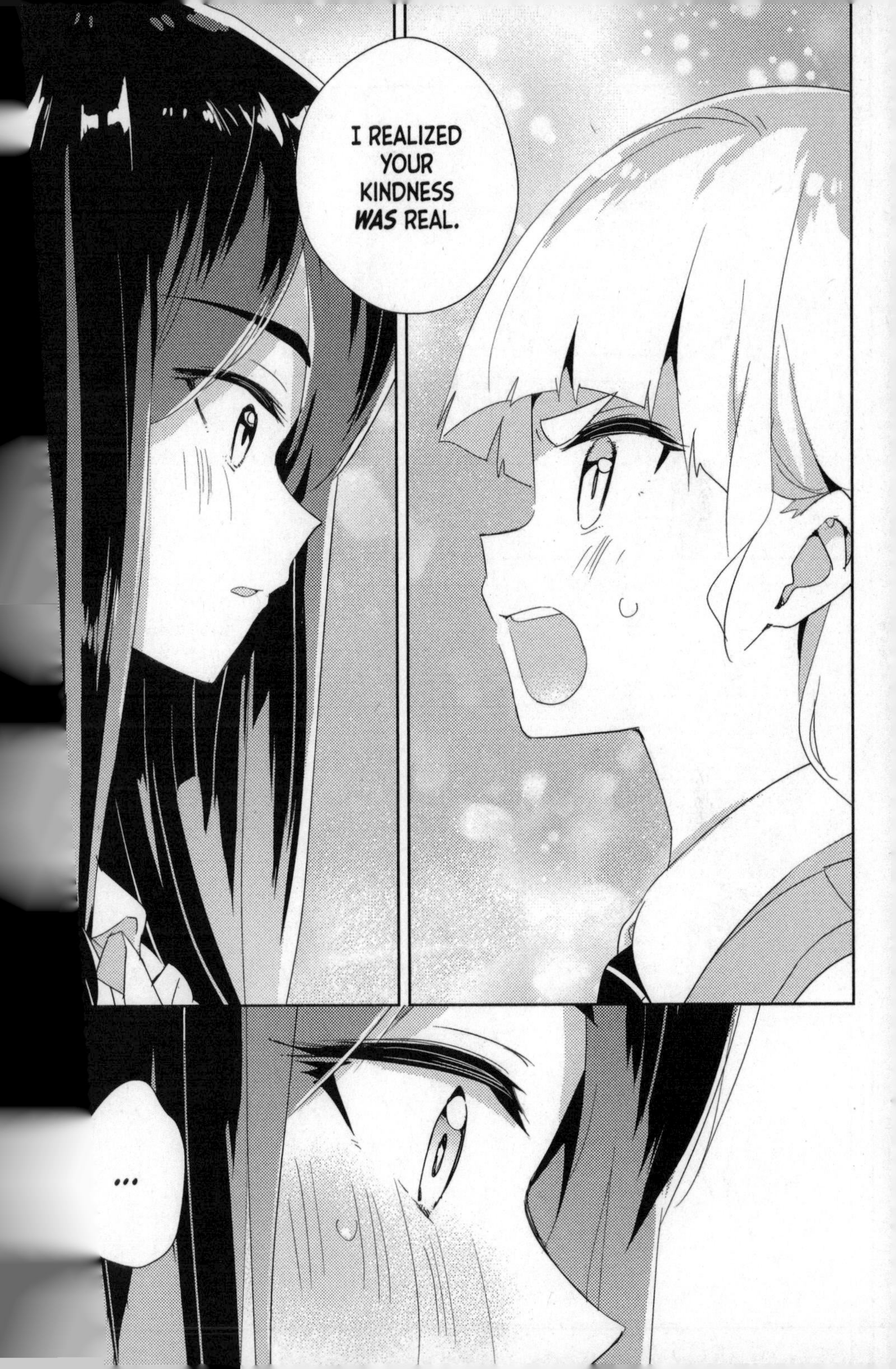
I REALIZED YOUR KINDNESS WAS REAL.
...

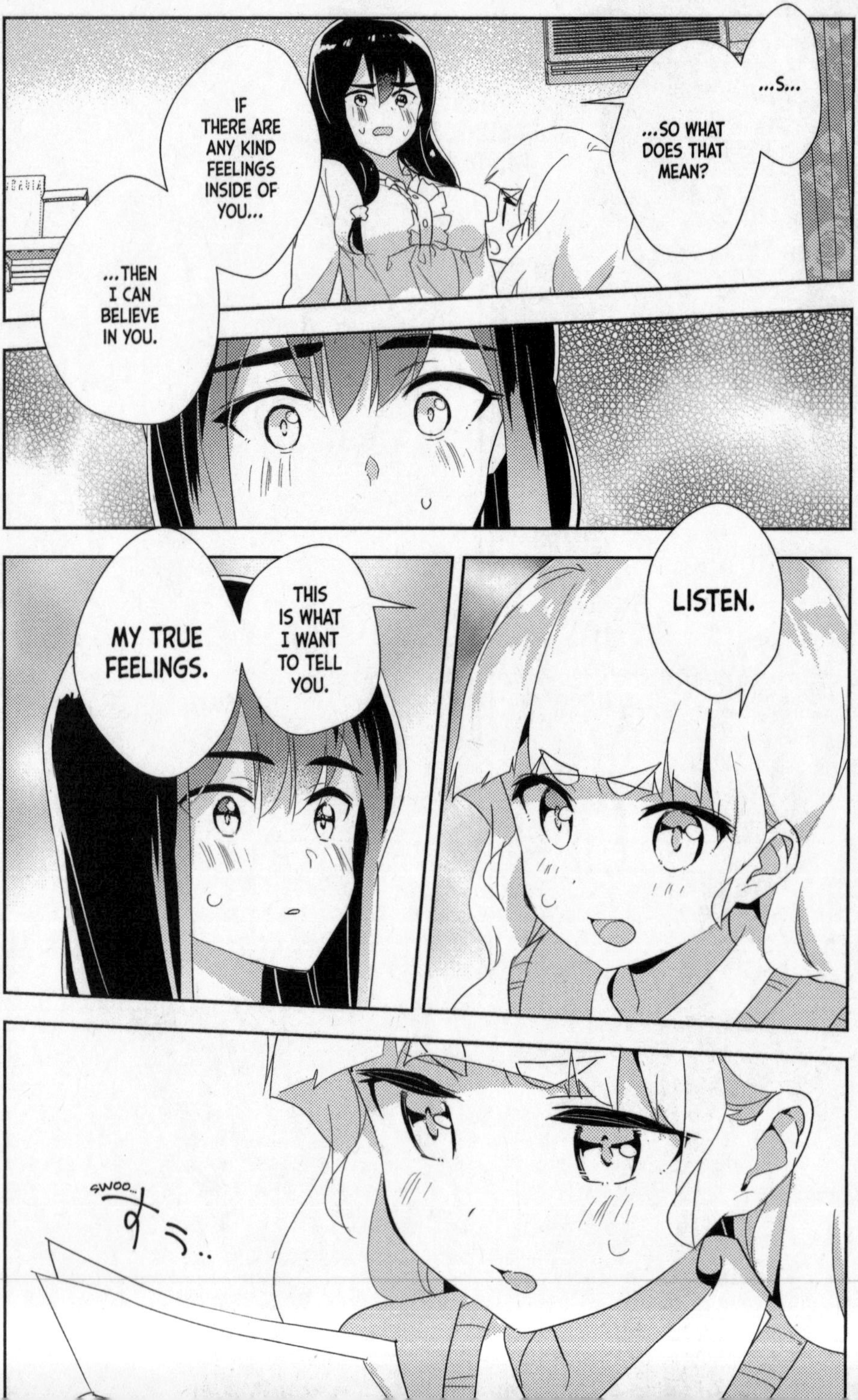
...S...
...SO WHAT DOES THAT MEAN?
IF THERE ARE ANY KIND FEELINGS INSIDE OF YOU...
...THEN I CAN BELIEVE IN YOU.
LISTEN.
THIS IS WHAT I WANT TO TELL YOU.
MY TRUE FEELINGS.
SWOO...
すぅ..

DEAR AYANOKOUJI ONEE-SAMA...

THANK YOU FOR ALWAYS BEING SO KIND TO ME IN THE SALON.

I'M WRITING YOU THIS LETTER TODAY...

...TO EXPRESS THAT GRATITUDE TO YOU.

Dear Ayanokouji Onee-sama,
Thank you for always being so kind to me in the salon.
I'm writing you this letter today to express that gratitude to you. There are still many tasks I can't perform. I blunder
to you. There are still many tasks I can't perform. I blu
cause trouble for everyone around. But whenever
you're always there to help me.

THERE ARE STILL MANY TASKS I CAN'T PERFORM.

I BLUNDER, AND I CAUSE TROUBLE FOR EVERYONE AROUND.

BUT WHENEVER I DO, YOU'RE ALWAYS THERE TO HELP ME.

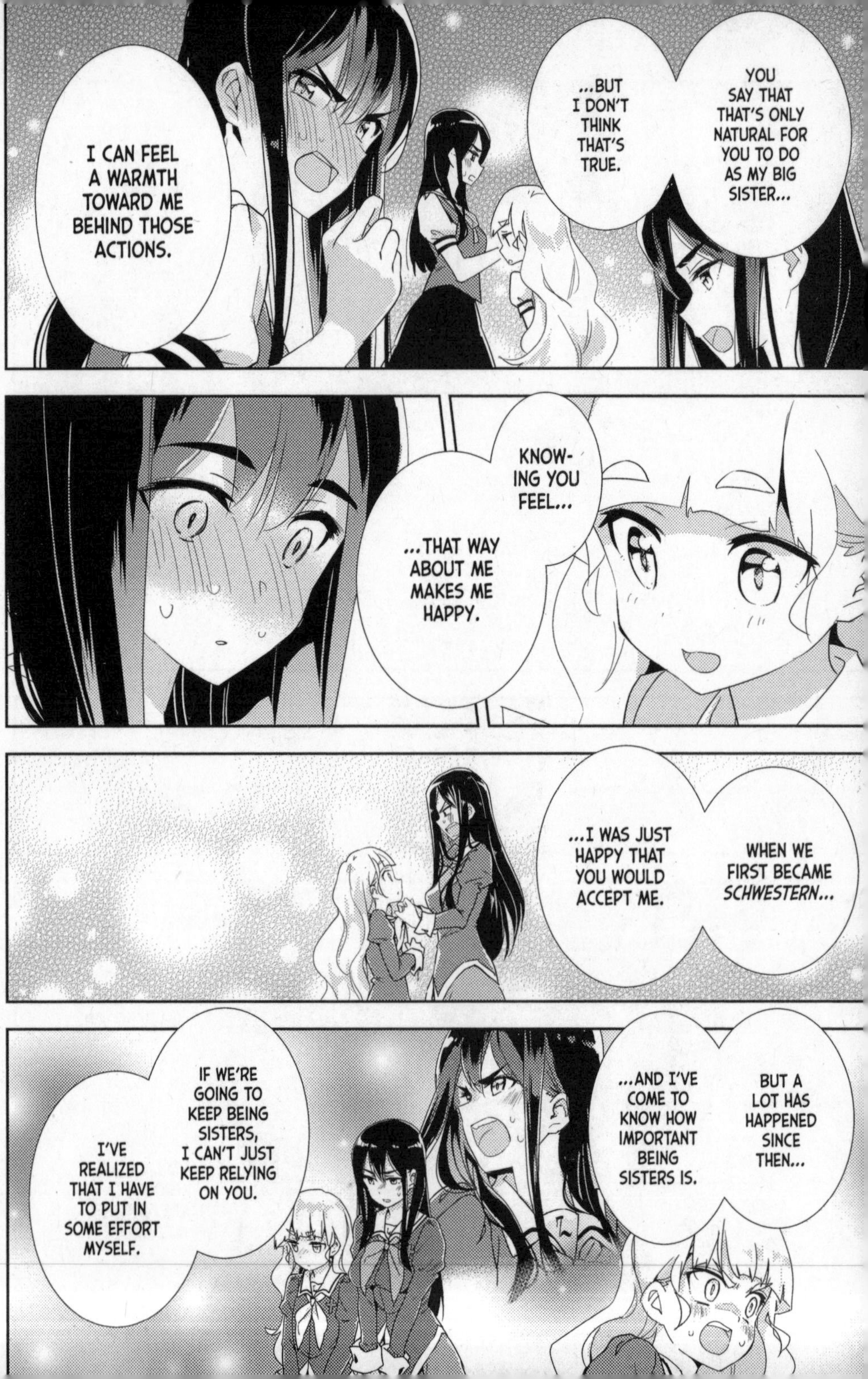
YOU SAY THAT THAT'S ONLY NATURAL FOR YOU TO DO AS MY BIG SISTER...
...BUT I DON'T THINK THAT'S TRUE.
I CAN FEEL A WARMTH TOWARD ME BEHIND THOSE ACTIONS.
KNOWING YOU FEEL...
...THAT WAY ABOUT ME MAKES ME HAPPY.
WHEN WE FIRST BECAME *SCHWESTERN*...
...I WAS JUST HAPPY THAT YOU WOULD ACCEPT ME.
BUT A LOT HAS HAPPENED SINCE THEN...
...AND I'VE COME TO KNOW HOW IMPORTANT BEING SISTERS IS.
IF WE'RE GOING TO KEEP BEING SISTERS, I CAN'T JUST KEEP RELYING ON YOU.
I'VE REALIZED THAT I HAVE TO PUT IN SOME EFFORT MYSELF.

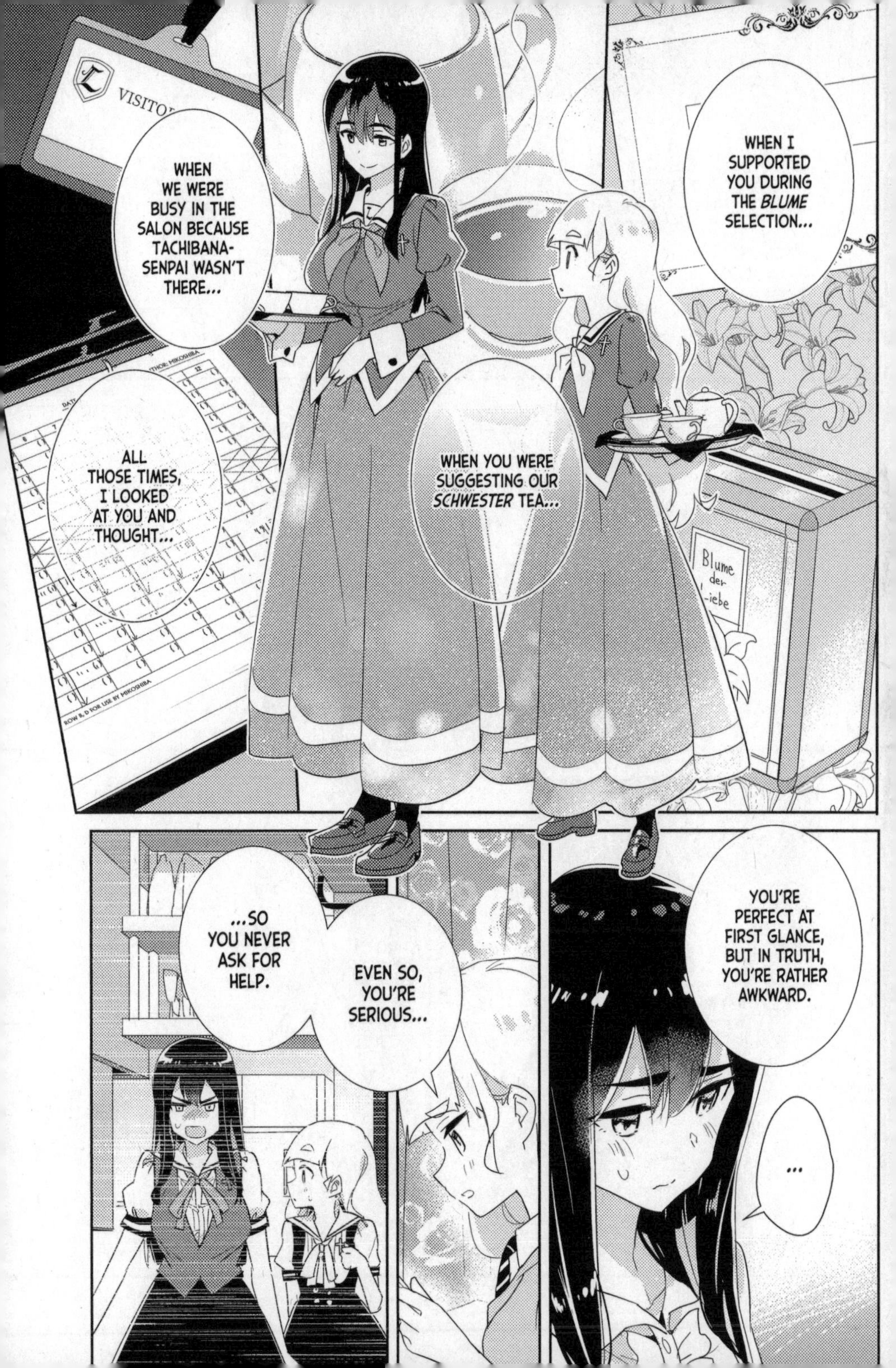
WHEN I SUPPORTED YOU DURING THE *BLUME* SELECTION...
WHEN YOU WERE SUGGESTING OUR *SCHWESTER* TEA...
Blume der Liebe
WHEN WE WERE BUSY IN THE SALON BECAUSE TACHIBANA-SENPAI WASN'T THERE...
ALL THOSE TIMES, I LOOKED AT YOU AND THOUGHT...
YOU'RE PERFECT AT FIRST GLANCE, BUT IN TRUTH, YOU'RE RATHER AWKWARD.
...
EVEN SO, YOU'RE SERIOUS...
...SO YOU NEVER ASK FOR HELP.

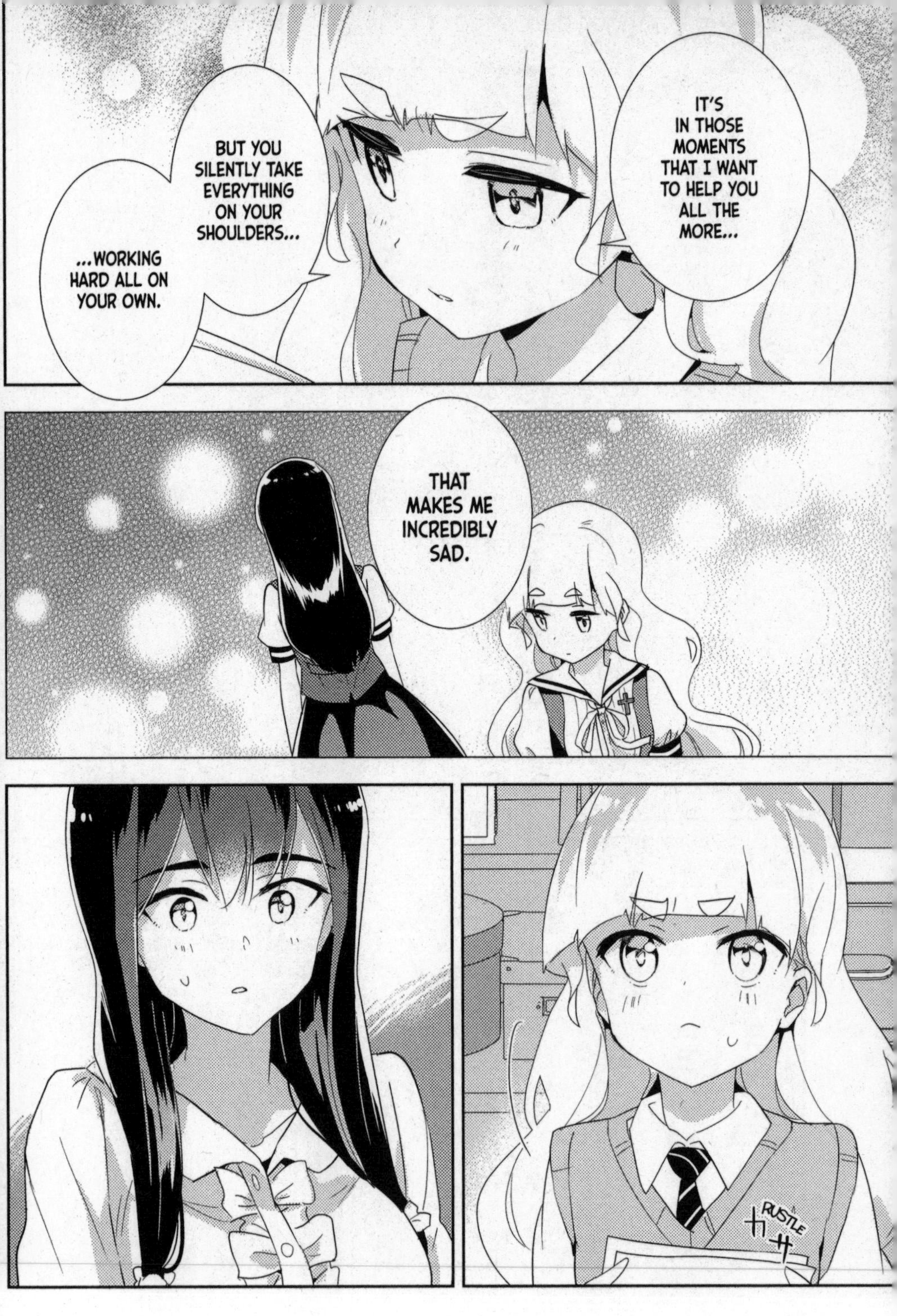
IT'S IN THOSE MOMENTS THAT I WANT TO HELP YOU ALL THE MORE...
BUT YOU SILENTLY TAKE EVERYTHING ON YOUR SHOULDERS...
...WORKING HARD ALL ON YOUR OWN.
THAT MAKES ME INCREDIBLY SAD.
RUSTLE

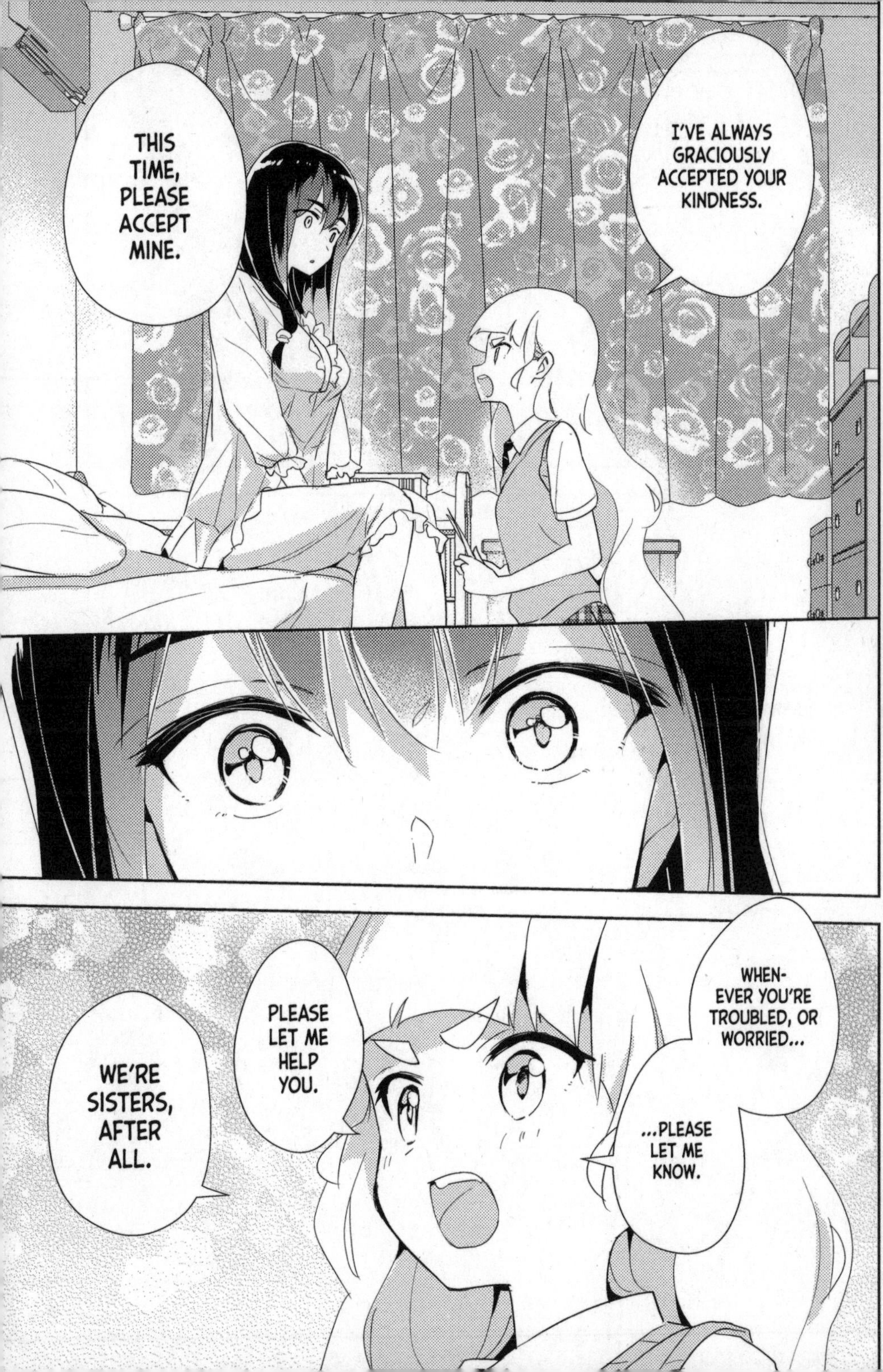
I'VE ALWAYS GRACIOUSLY ACCEPTED YOUR KINDNESS.
THIS TIME, PLEASE ACCEPT MINE.
WHEN-EVER YOU'RE TROUBLED, OR WORRIED...
...PLEASE LET ME KNOW.
PLEASE LET ME HELP YOU.
WE'RE SISTERS, AFTER ALL.

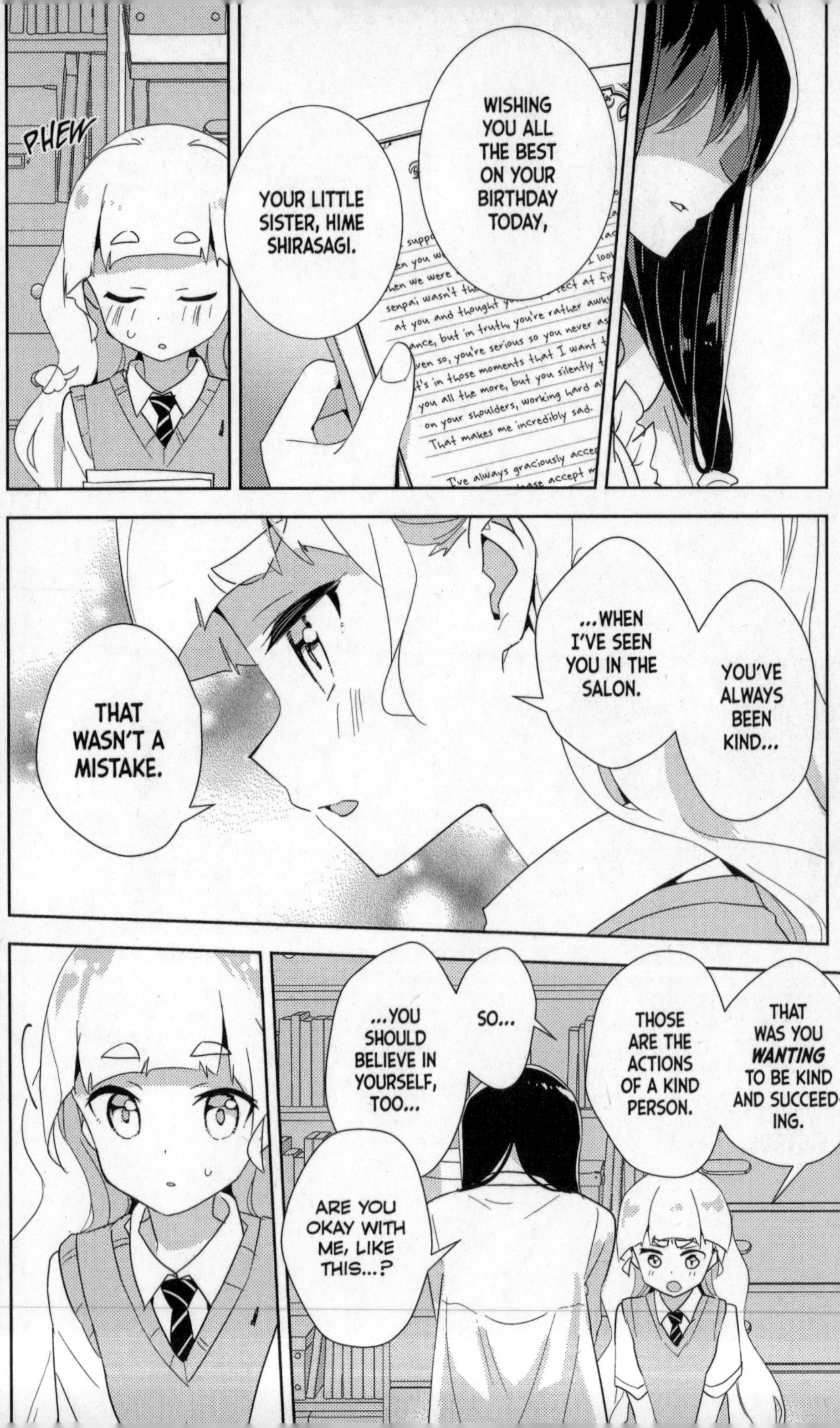
WISHING YOU ALL THE BEST ON YOUR BIRTHDAY TODAY,
YOUR LITTLE SISTER, HIME SHIRASAGI.
That makes me incredibly sad.
PHEW
YOU'VE ALWAYS BEEN KIND...
...WHEN I'VE SEEN YOU IN THE SALON.
THAT WASN'T A MISTAKE.
THAT WAS YOU *WANTING* TO BE KIND AND SUCCEEDING.
THOSE ARE THE ACTIONS OF A KIND PERSON.
SO...
...YOU SHOULD BELIEVE IN YOURSELF, TOO...
ARE YOU OKAY WITH ME, LIKE THIS...?

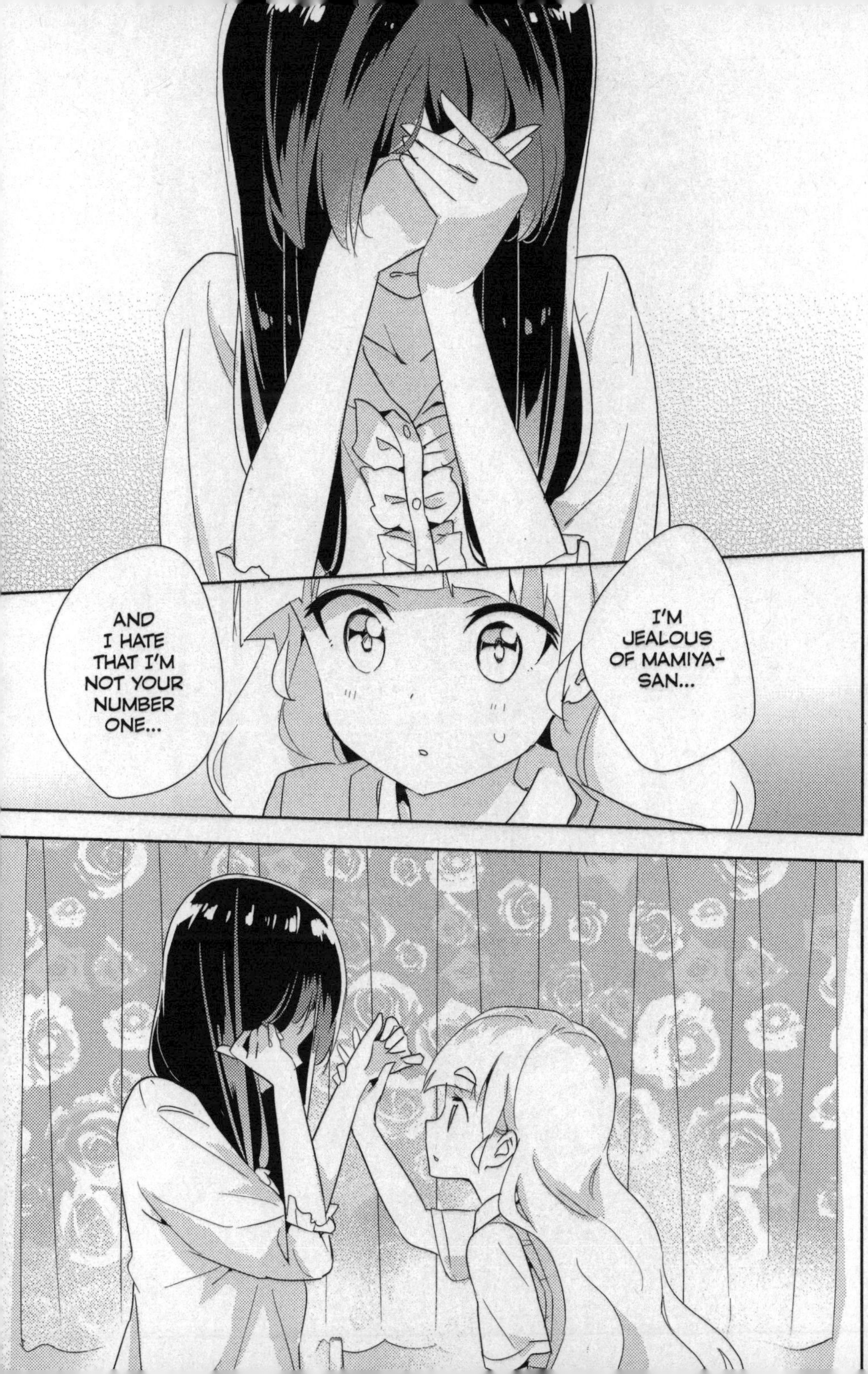
I'M JEALOUS OF MAMIYA-SAN...
AND I HATE THAT I'M NOT YOUR NUMBER ONE...

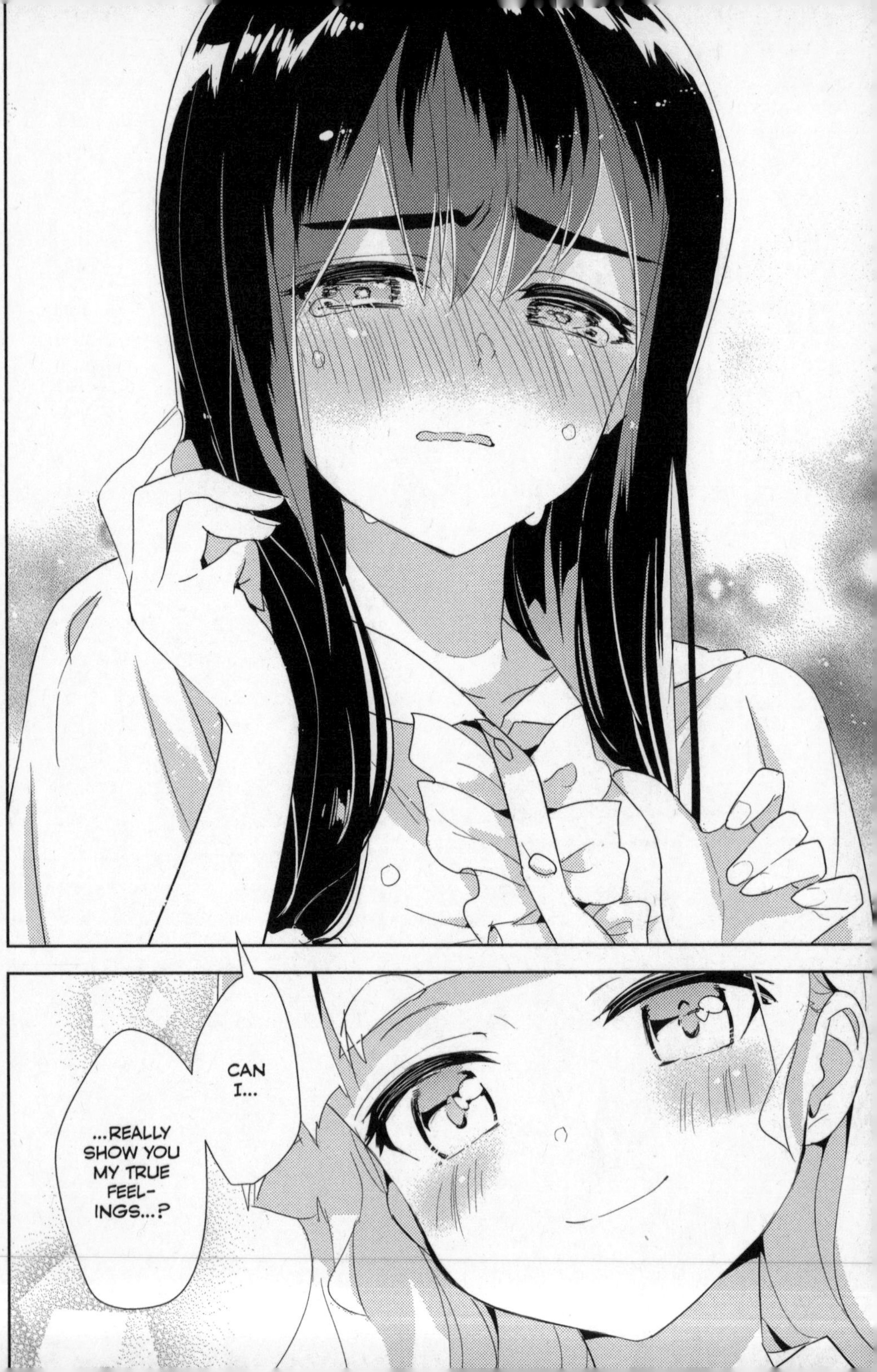
CAN I... ...REALLY SHOW YOU MY TRUE FEEL-INGS...?

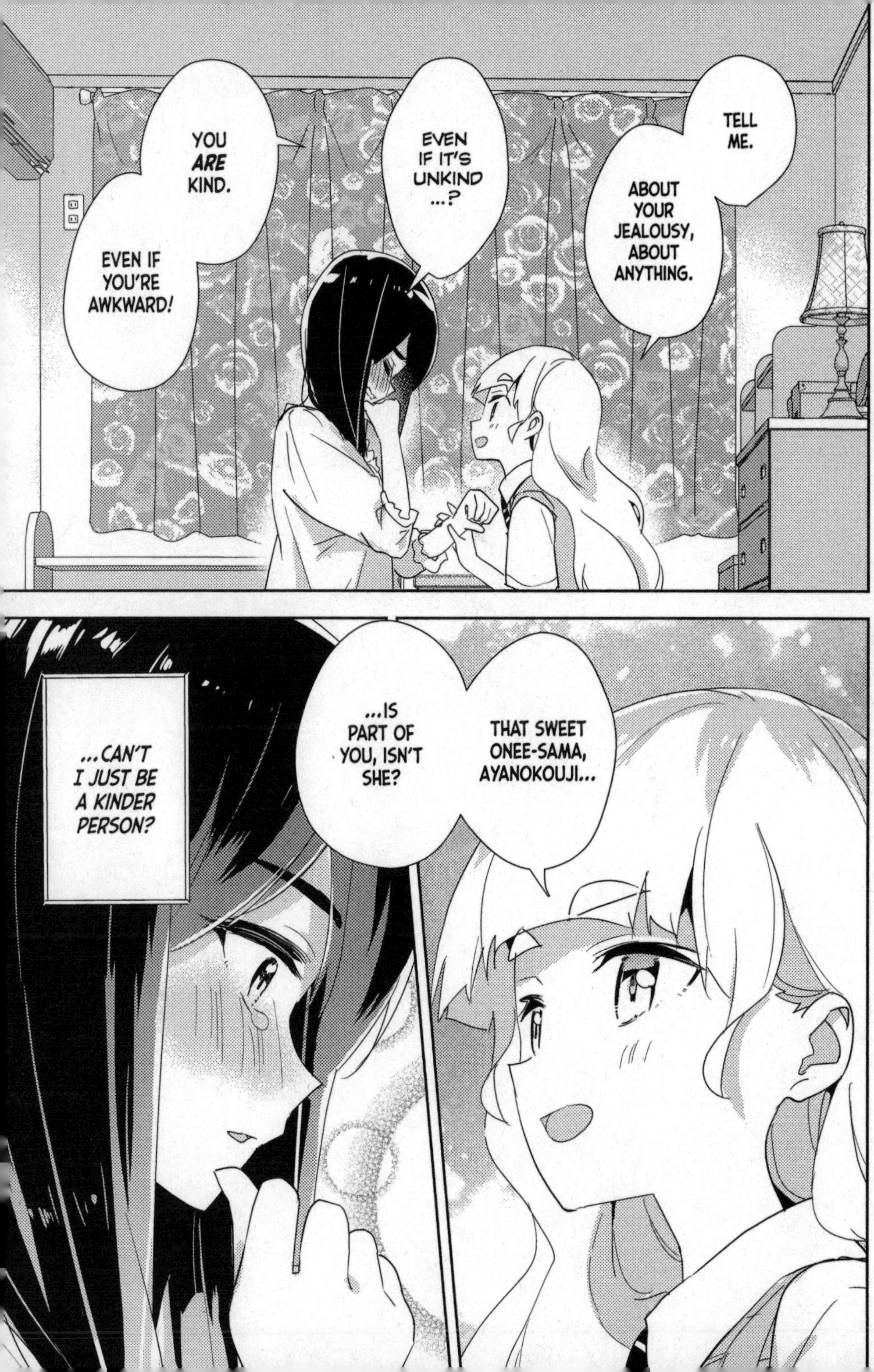
TELL ME.
ABOUT YOUR JEALOUSY, ABOUT ANYTHING.
EVEN IF IT'S UNKIND ...?
YOU **ARE** KIND.
EVEN IF YOU'RE AWKWARD!
THAT SWEET ONEE-SAMA, AYANOKOUJI...
...IS PART OF YOU, ISN'T SHE?
...CAN'T I JUST BE A KINDER PERSON?

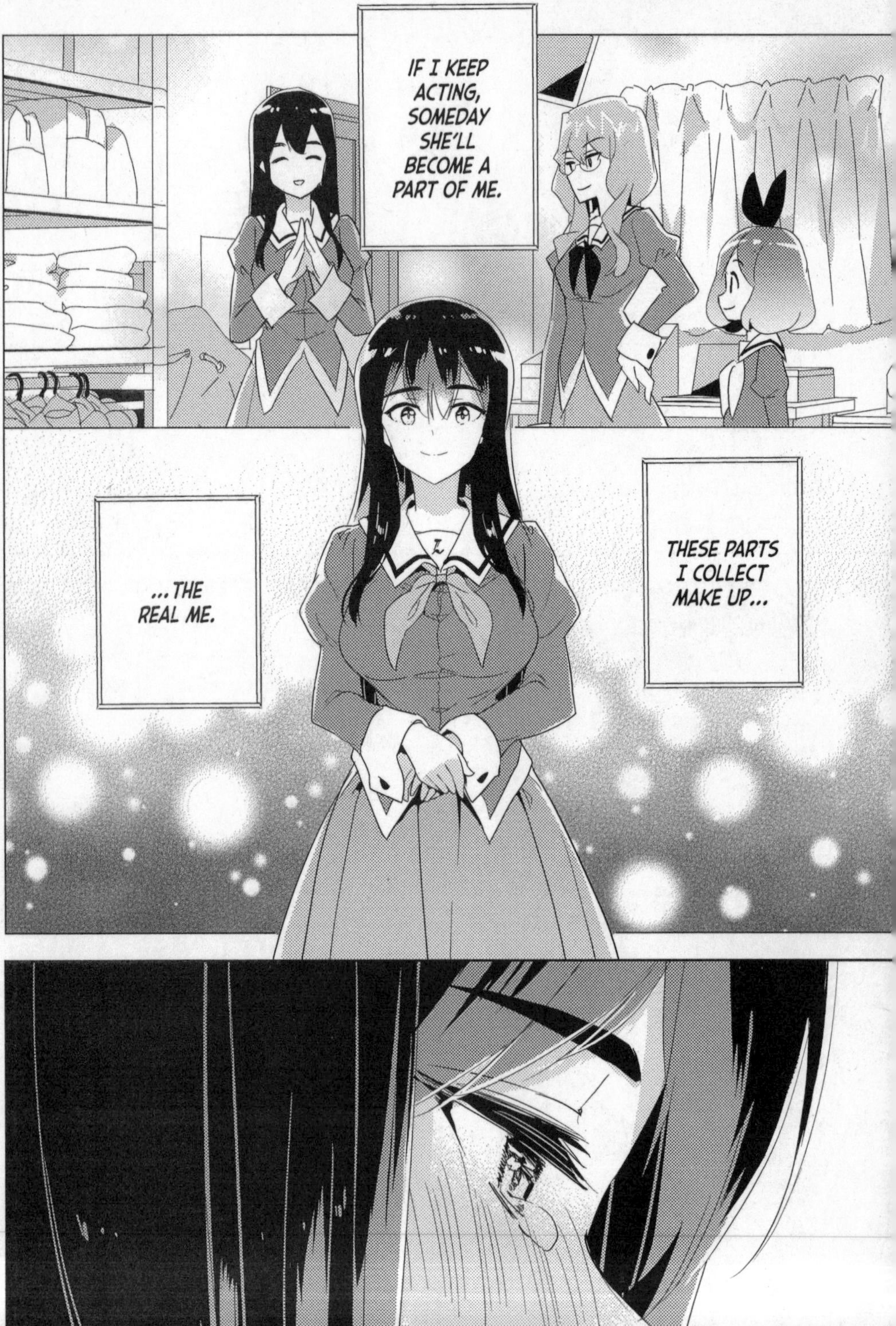
IF I KEEP ACTING, SOMEDAY SHE'LL BECOME A PART OF ME.
THESE PARTS I COLLECT MAKE UP...
...THE REAL ME.

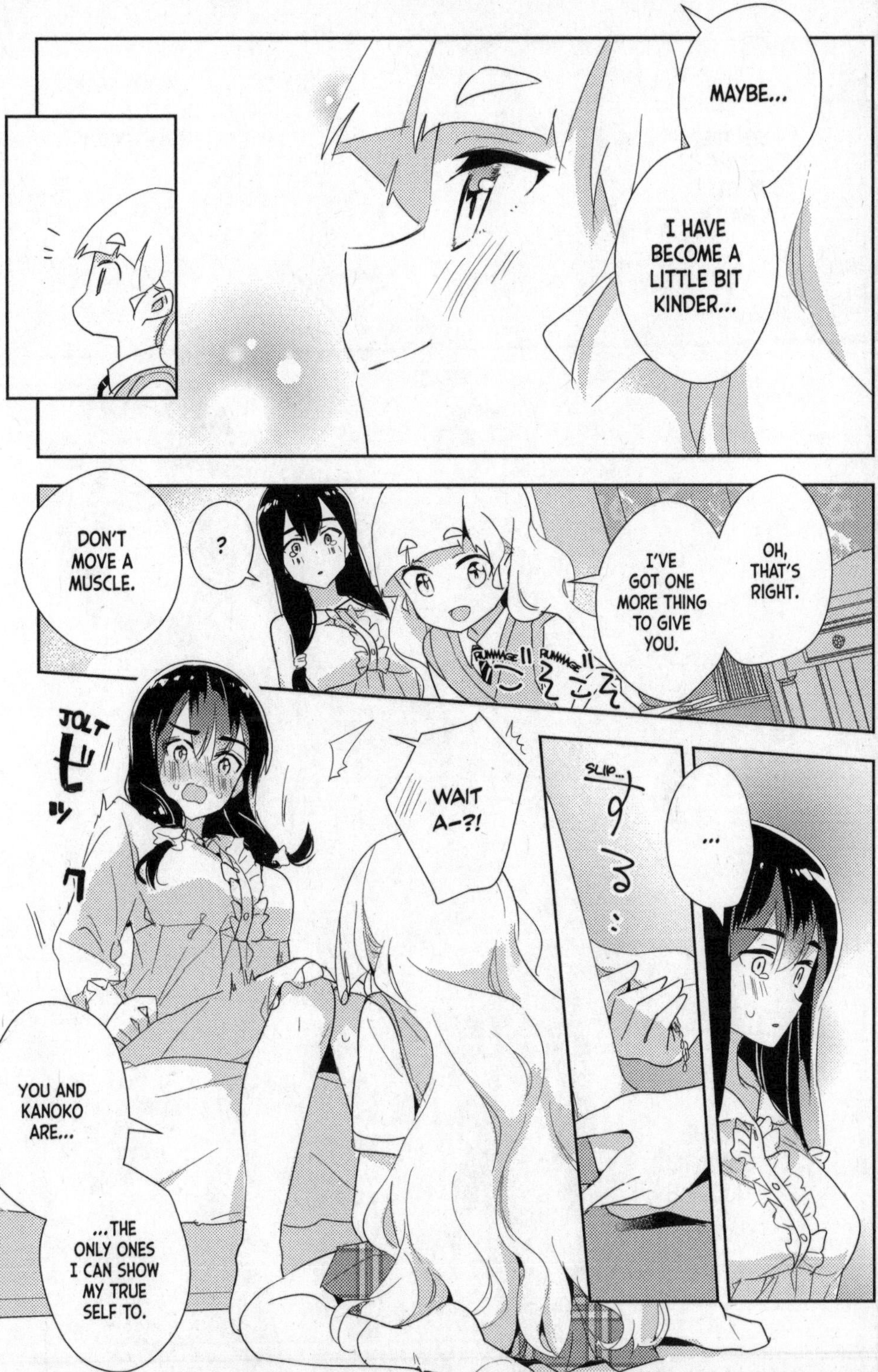
MAYBE...
I HAVE BECOME A LITTLE BIT KINDER...
OH, THAT'S RIGHT.
I'VE GOT ONE MORE THING TO GIVE YOU.
RUMMAGE RUMMAGE
?
DON'T MOVE A MUSCLE.
...
SLIP...
WAIT A-?!
JOLT
YOU AND KANOKO ARE...
...THE ONLY ONES I CAN SHOW MY TRUE SELF TO.

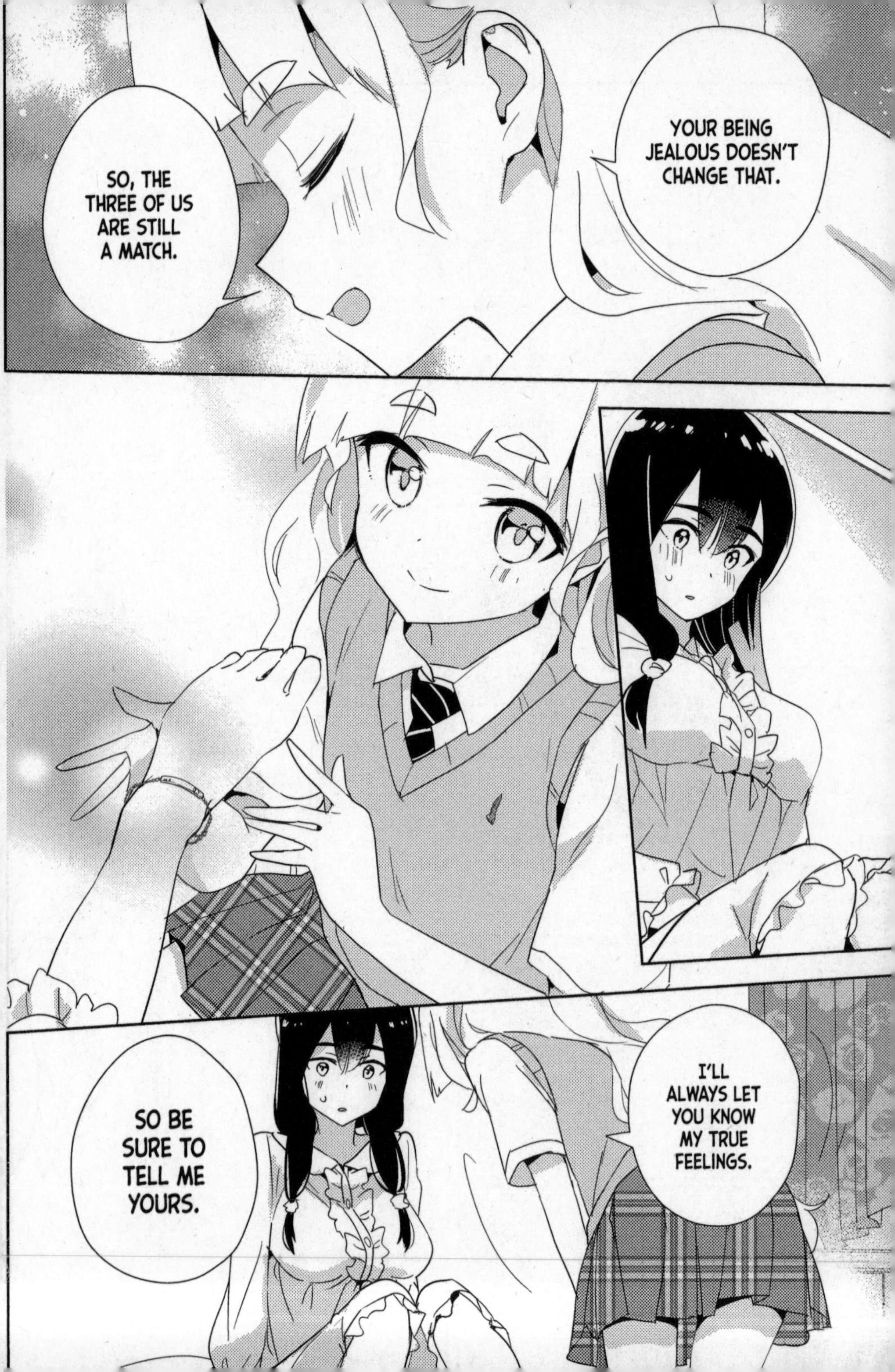
YOUR BEING JEALOUS DOESN'T CHANGE THAT.
SO, THE THREE OF US ARE STILL A MATCH.
I'LL ALWAYS LET YOU KNOW MY TRUE FEELINGS.
SO BE SURE TO TELL ME YOURS.

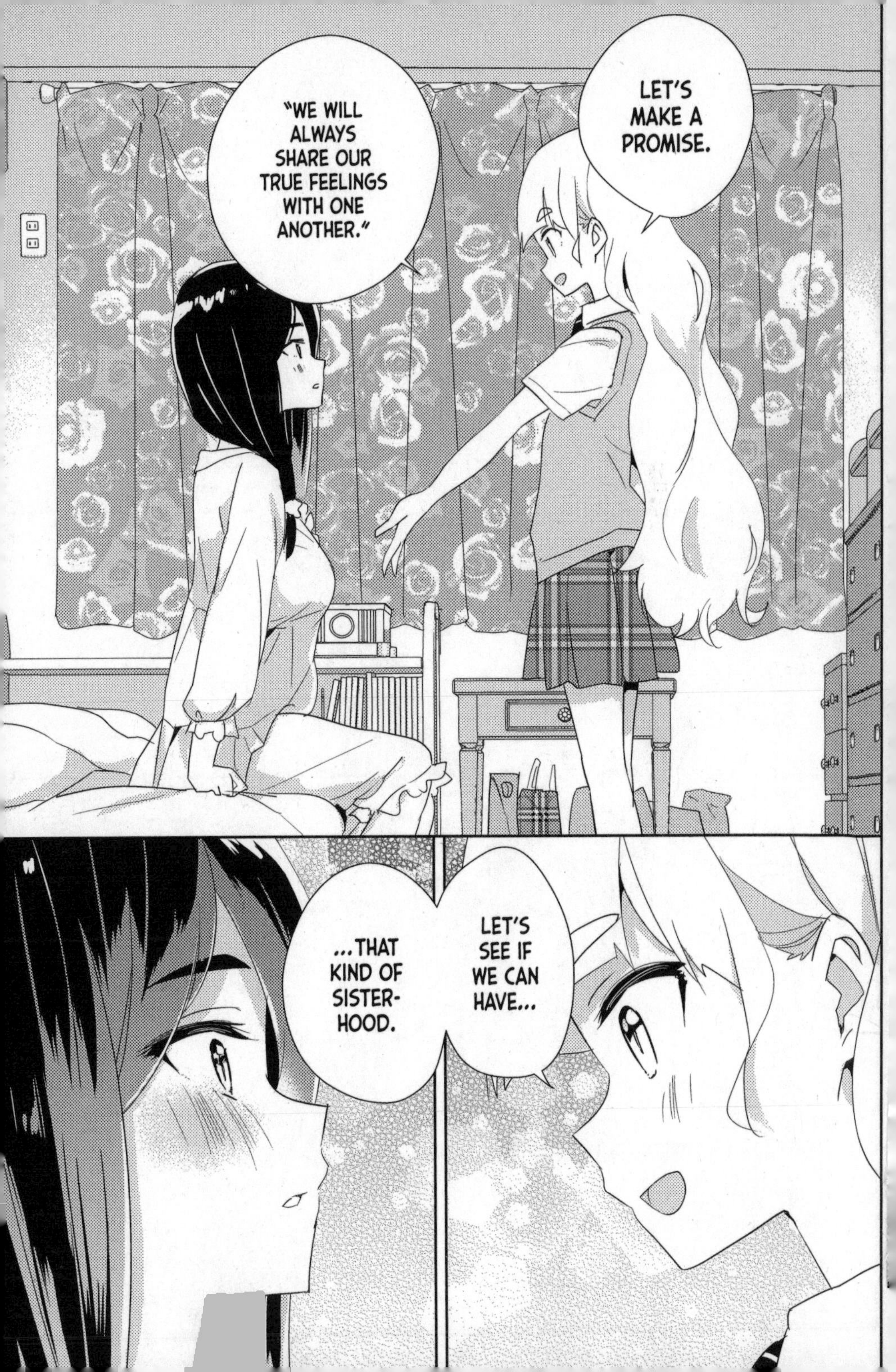
LET'S MAKE A PROMISE.
"WE WILL ALWAYS SHARE OUR TRUE FEELINGS WITH ONE ANOTHER."
LET'S SEE IF WE CAN HAVE...
...THAT KIND OF SISTER-HOOD.

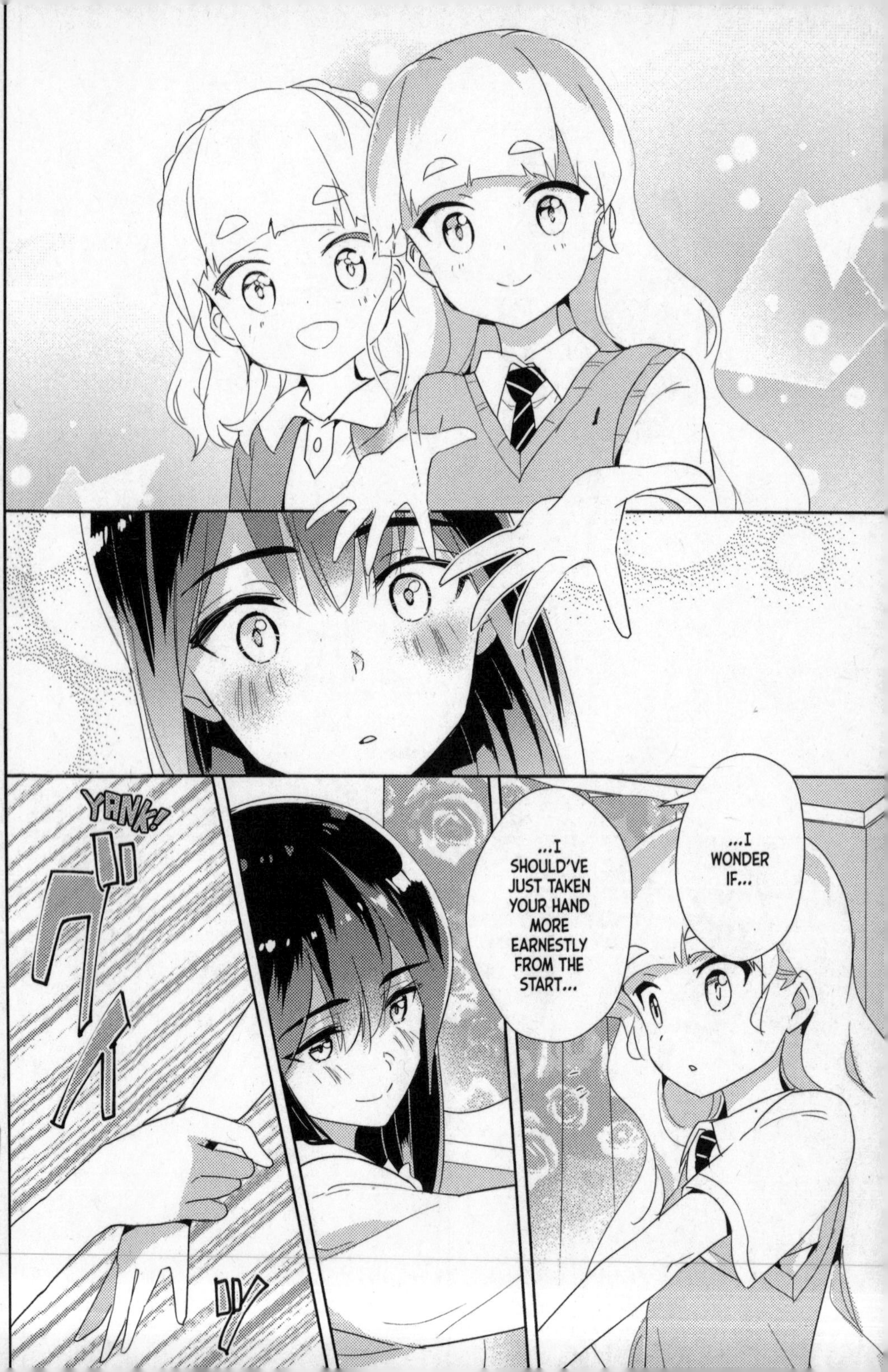
...I WONDER IF...
...I SHOULD'VE JUST TAKEN YOUR HAND MORE EARNESTLY FROM THE START...
YANK!

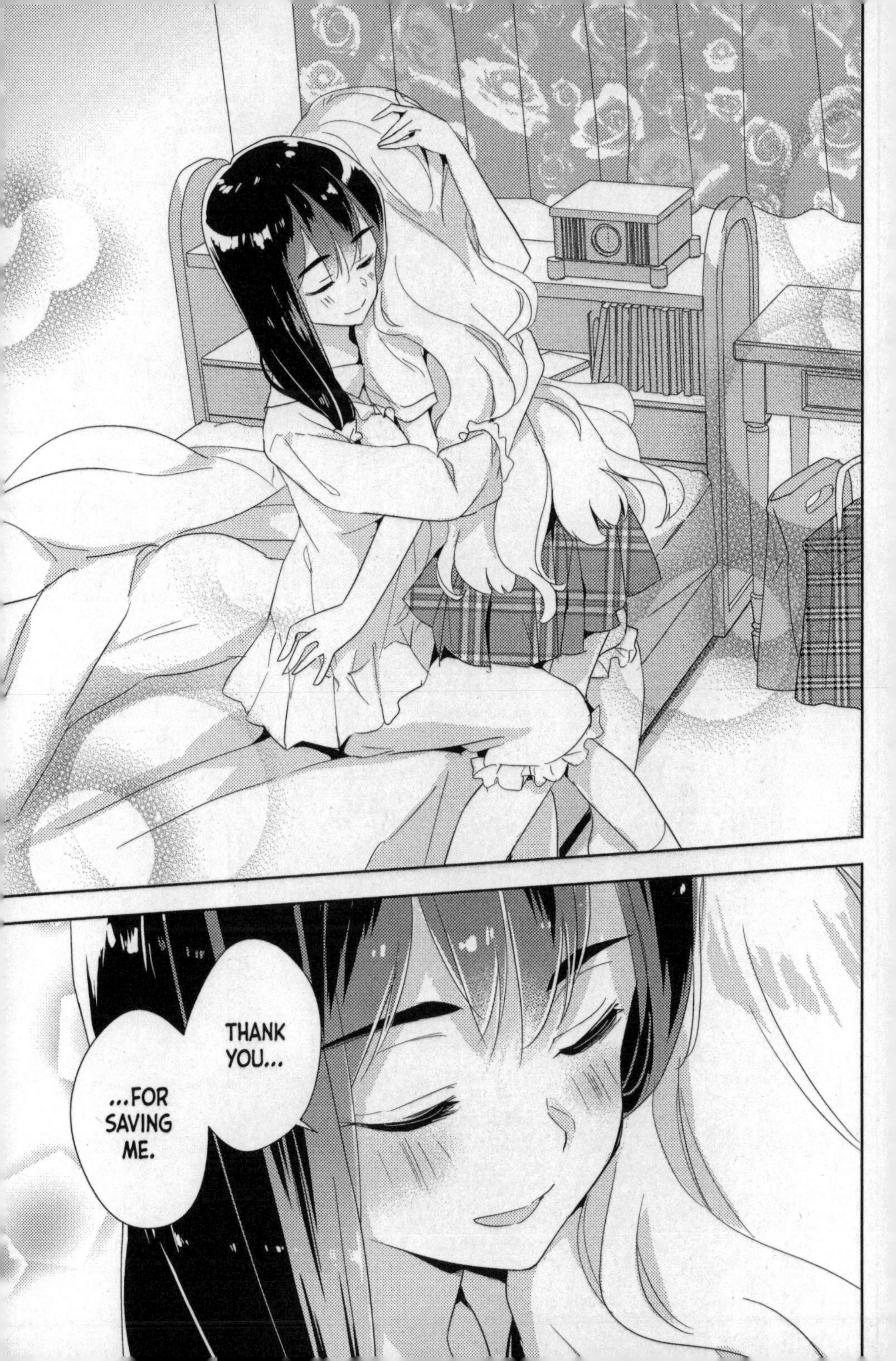
THANK YOU...
...FOR SAVING ME.

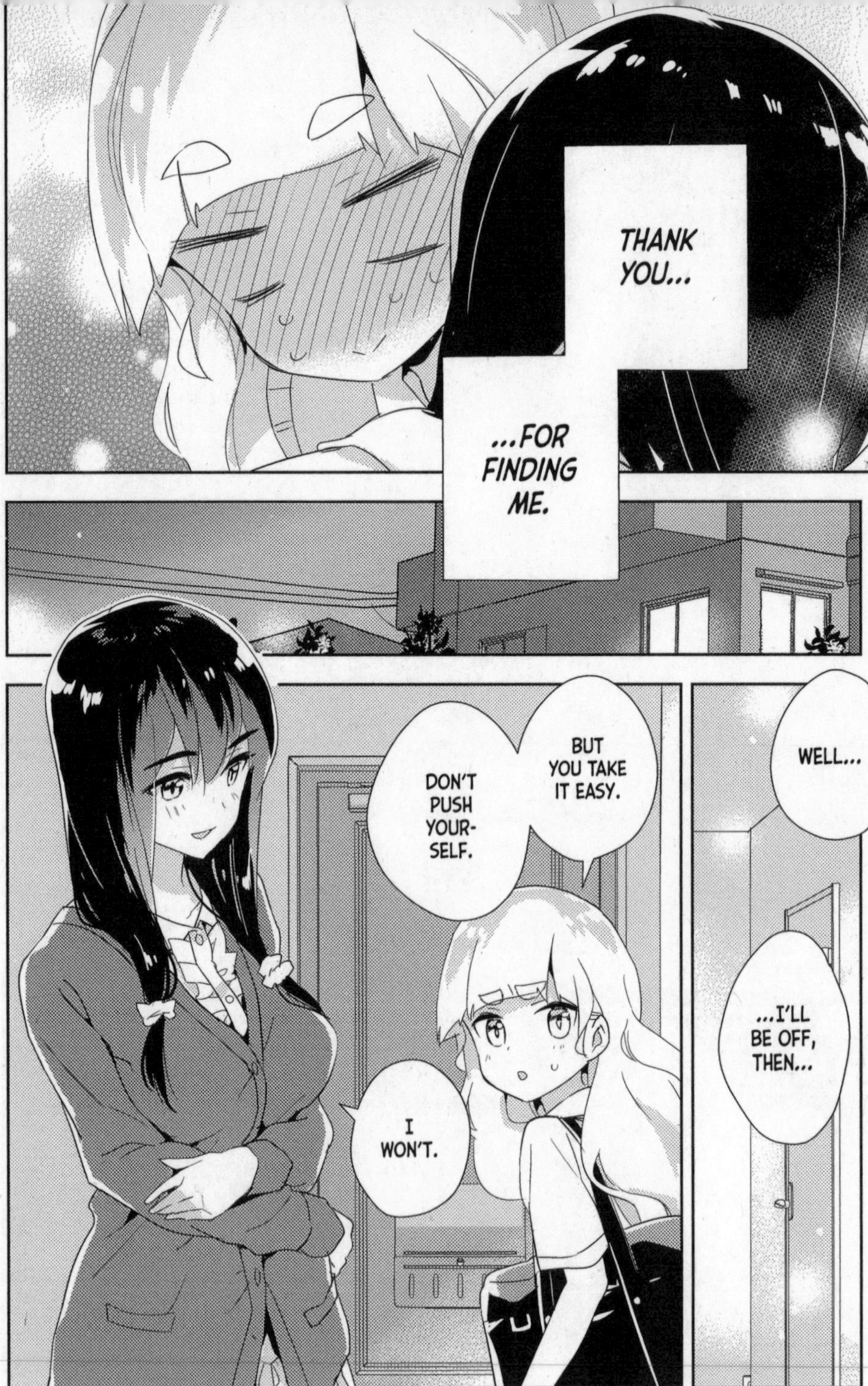
THANK YOU...
...FOR FINDING ME.
WELL...
...I'LL BE OFF, THEN...
BUT YOU TAKE IT EASY.
DON'T PUSH YOUR-SELF.
I WON'T.

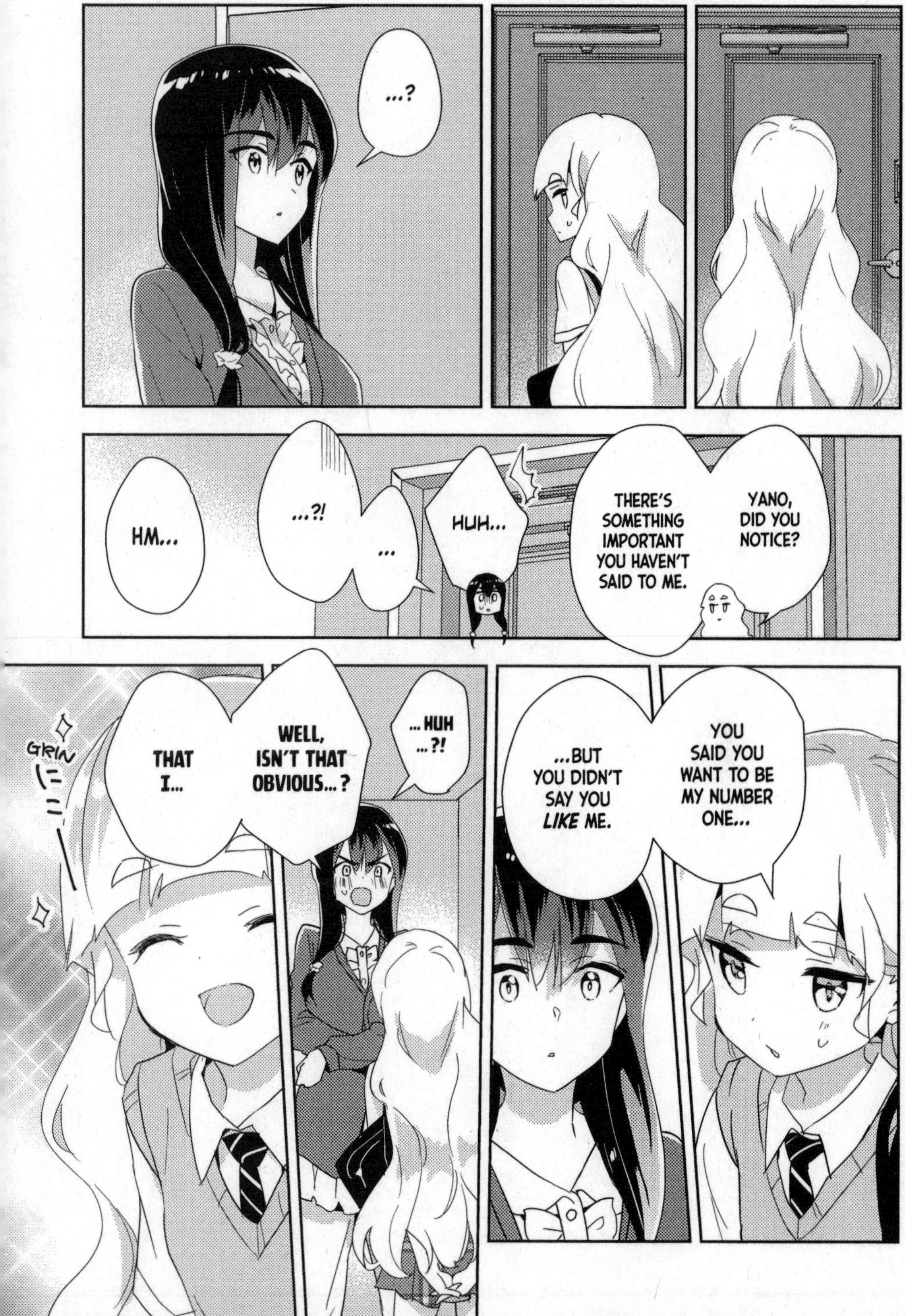
...?
YANO, DID YOU NOTICE?
THERE'S SOMETHING IMPORTANT YOU HAVEN'T SAID TO ME.
HUH...
...
...?!
HM...
YOU SAID YOU WANT TO BE MY NUMBER ONE...
...BUT YOU DIDN'T SAY YOU *LIKE* ME.
...HUH ...?!
WELL, ISN'T THAT OBVIOUS...?
THAT I...
GRIN

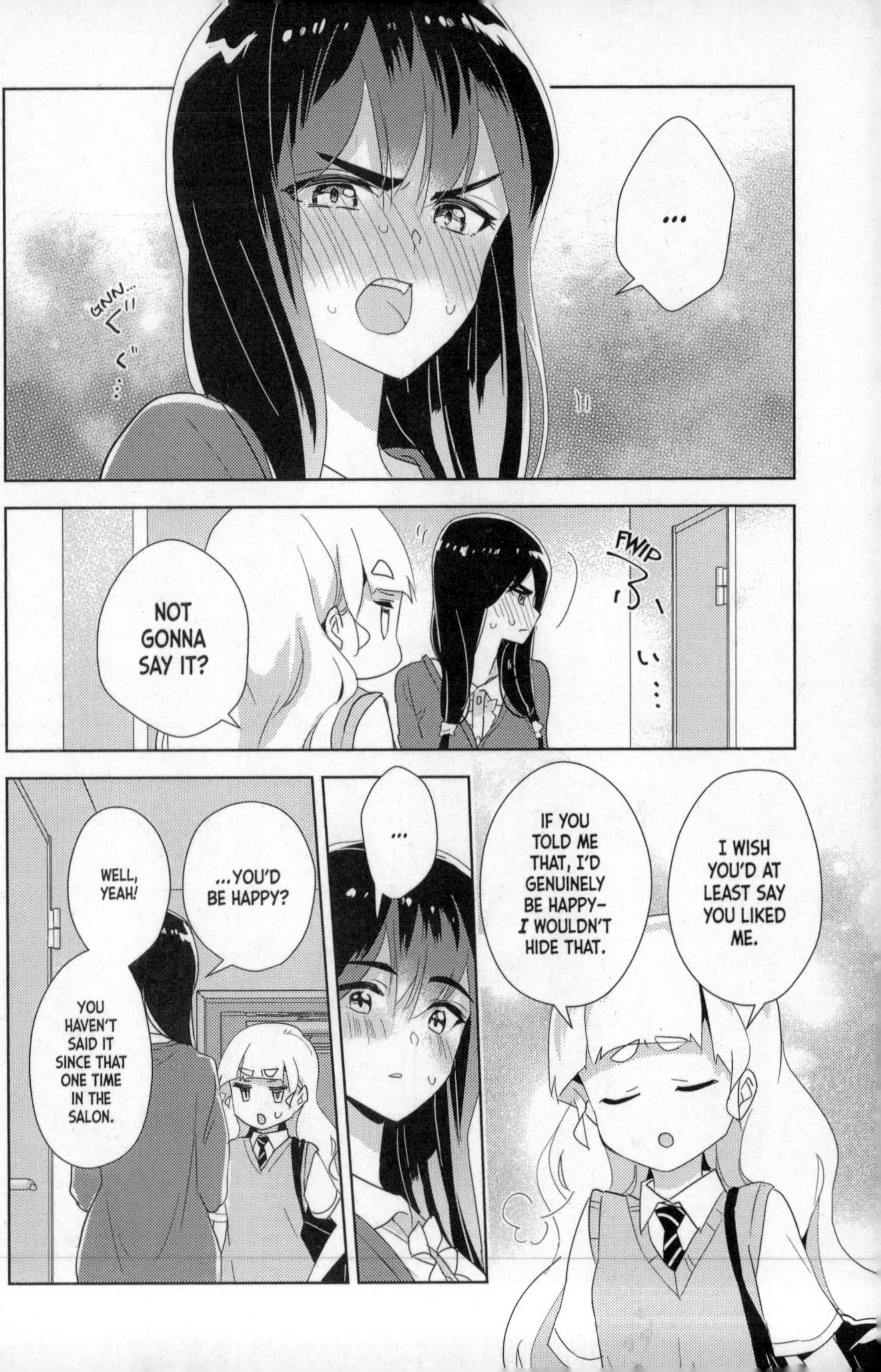
...
GNN...
FWIP
NOT GONNA SAY IT?
I WISH YOU'D AT LEAST SAY YOU LIKED ME.
IF YOU TOLD ME THAT, I'D GENUINELY BE HAPPY– *I* WOULDN'T HIDE THAT.
...
...YOU'D BE HAPPY?
WELL, YEAH!
YOU HAVEN'T SAID IT SINCE THAT ONE TIME IN THE SALON.

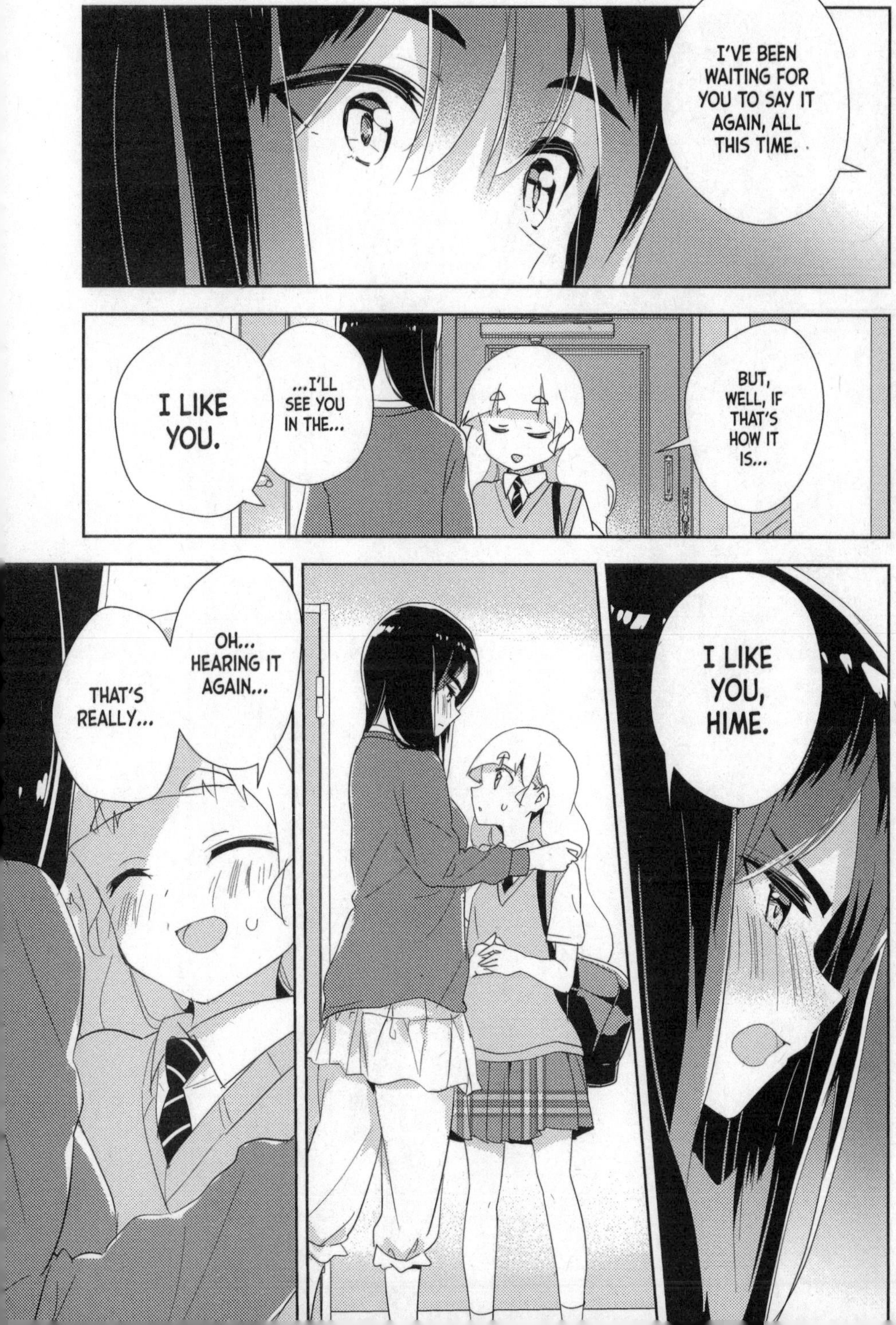
I'VE BEEN WAITING FOR YOU TO SAY IT AGAIN, ALL THIS TIME.
BUT, WELL, IF THAT'S HOW IT IS...
...I'LL SEE YOU IN THE...
I LIKE YOU.
I LIKE YOU, HIME.
OH... HEARING IT AGAIN...
THAT'S REALLY...

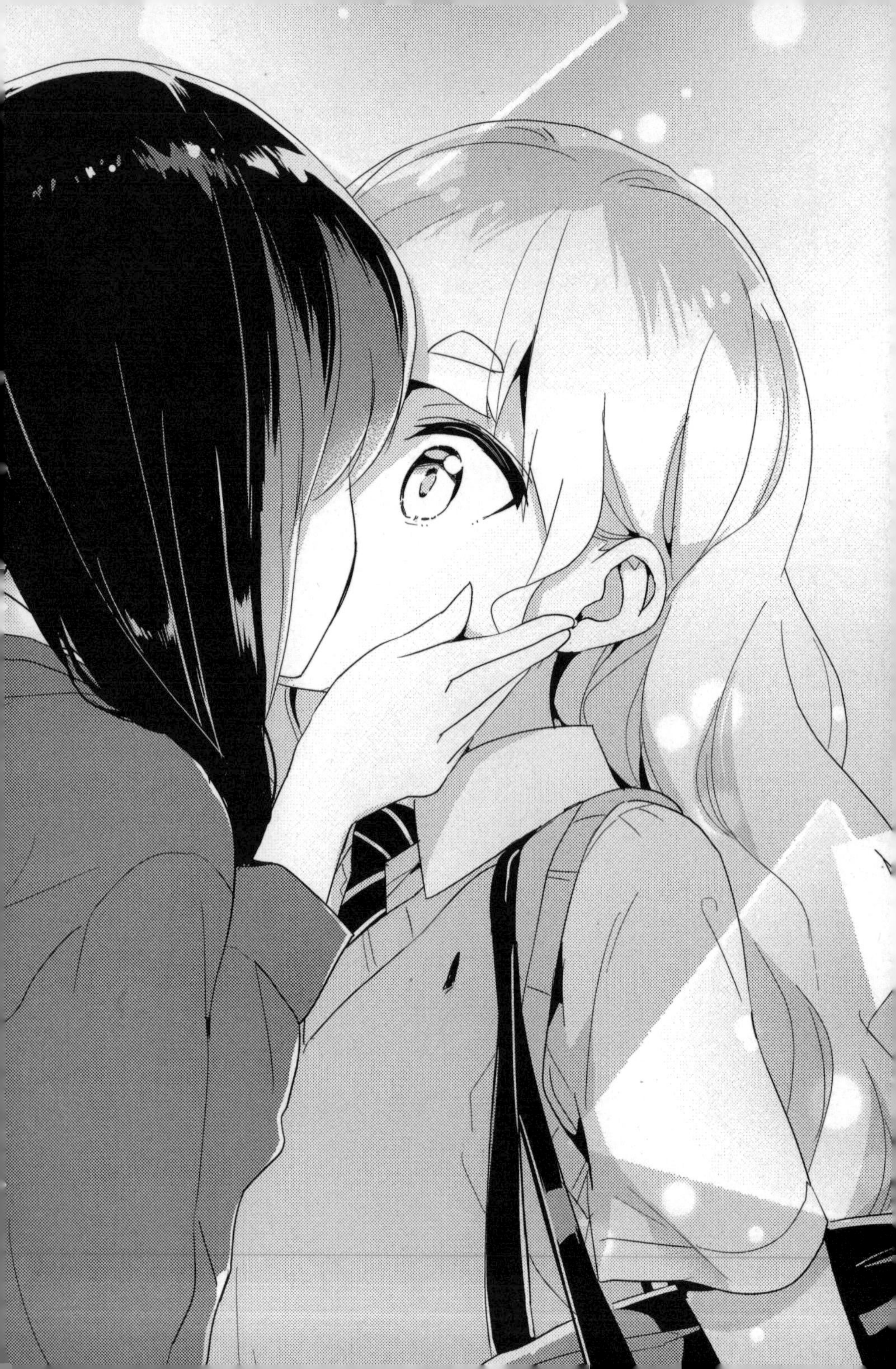

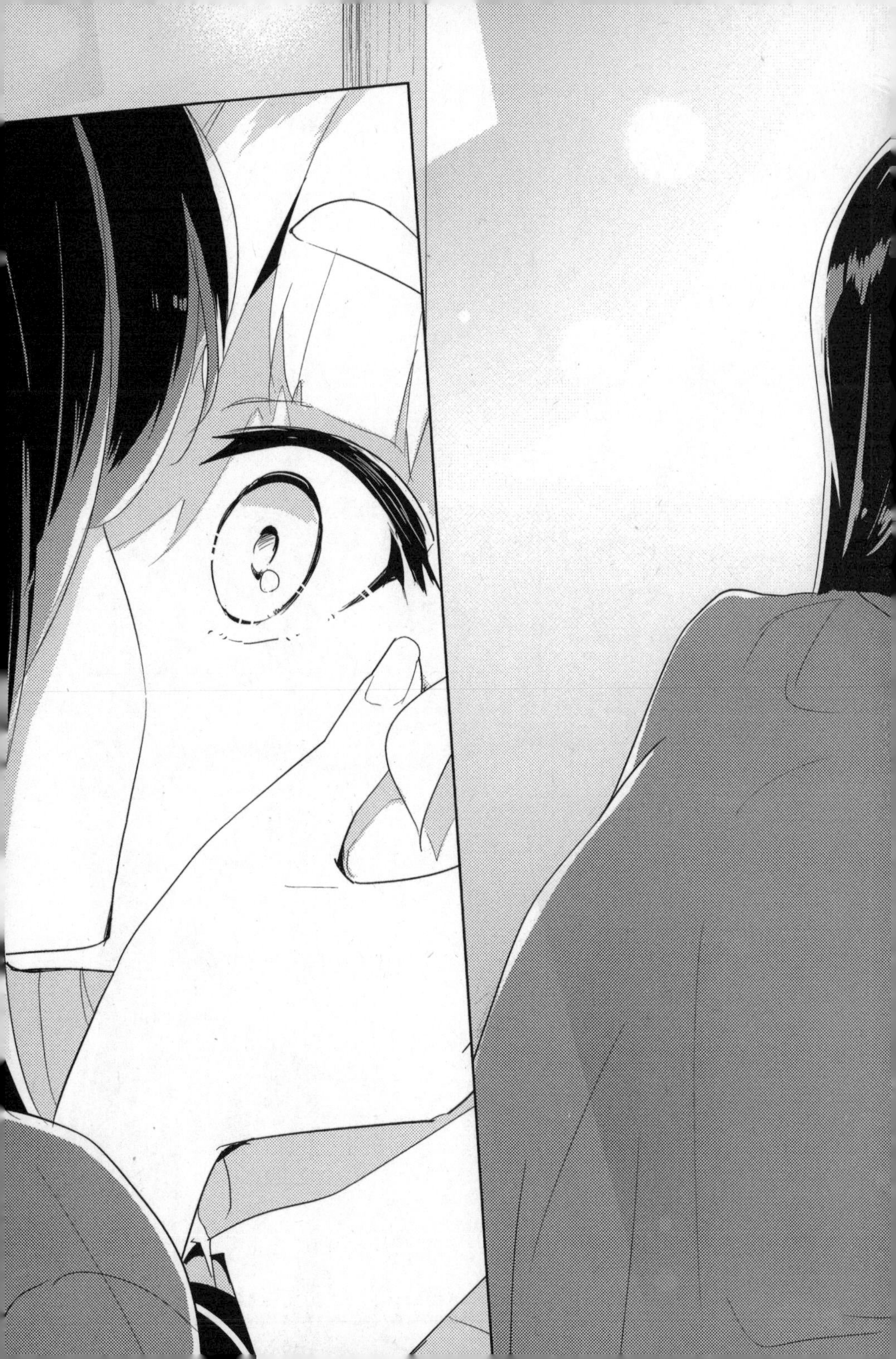

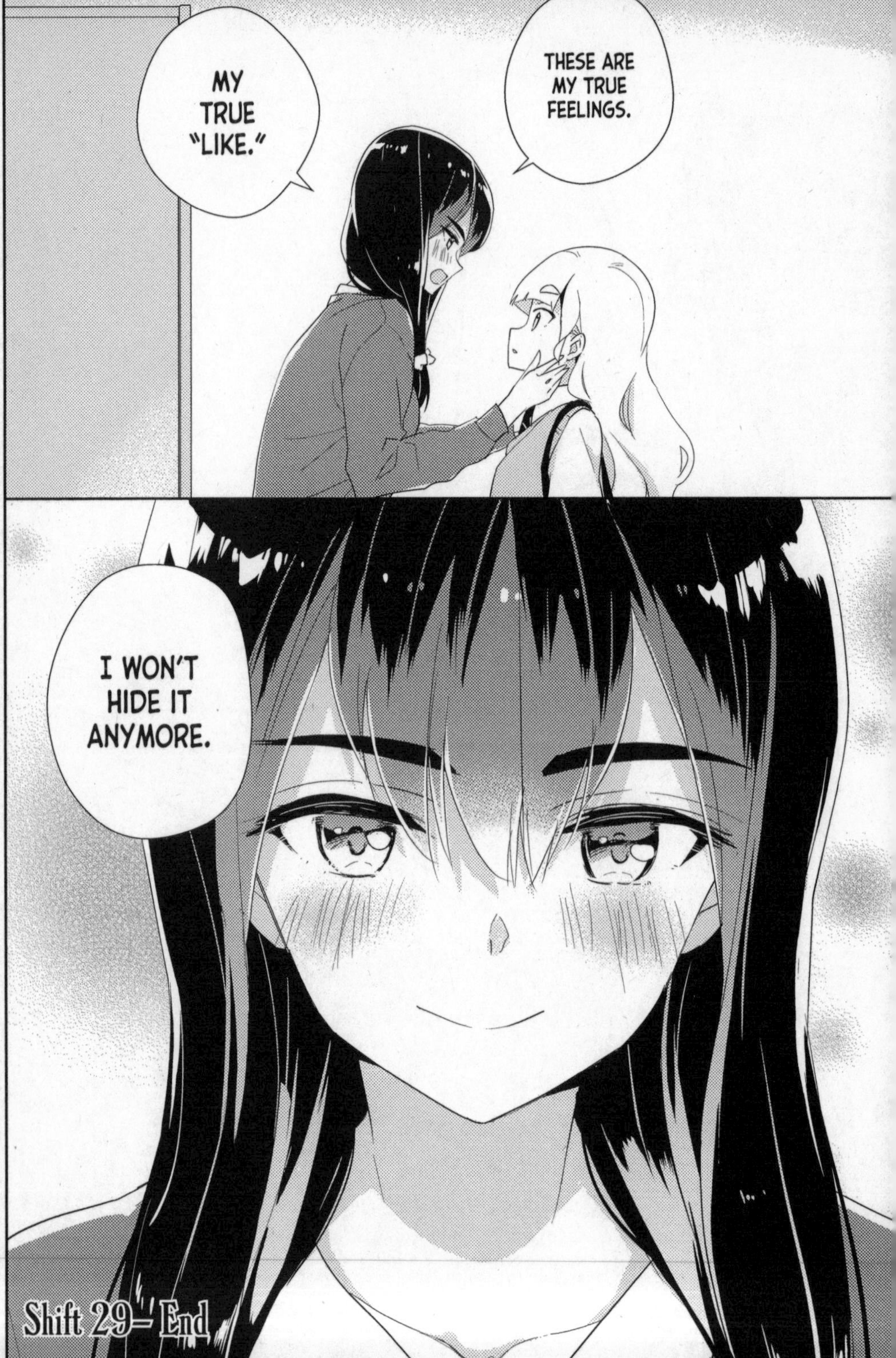
THESE ARE MY TRUE FEELINGS.
MY TRUE "LIKE."
I WON'T HIDE IT ANYMORE.
Shift 29 - End

Yuri Is My Job!

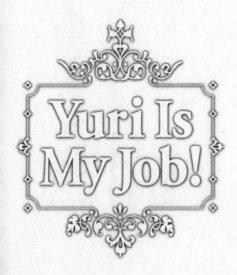

Yuri Is My Job!

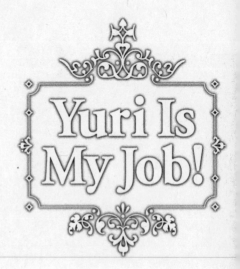

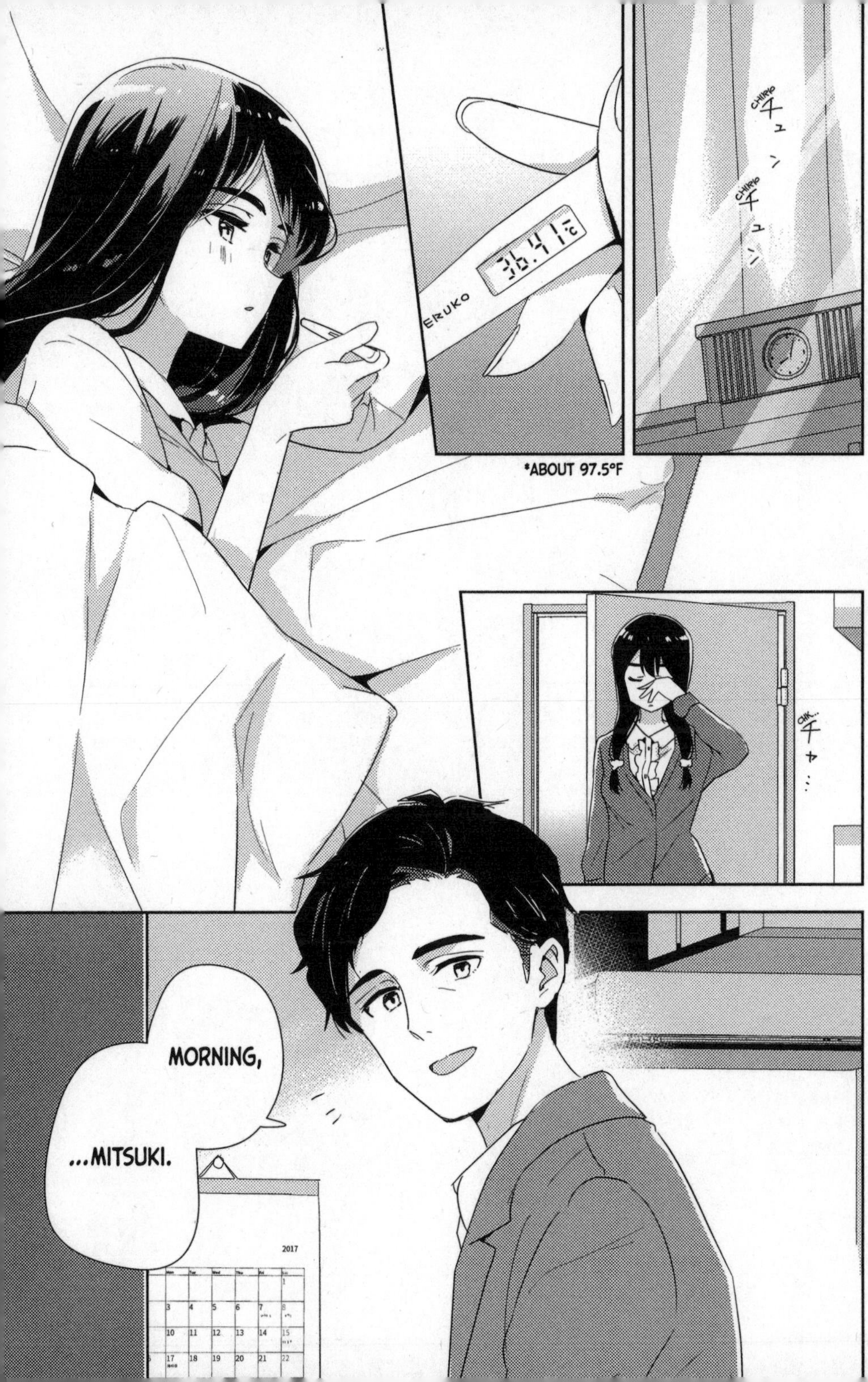
CHIRP チュン
CHIRP チュン
ERUKO
36.41°C
*ABOUT 97.5°F
CHK... チャ...
MORNING,
...MITSUKI.
2017

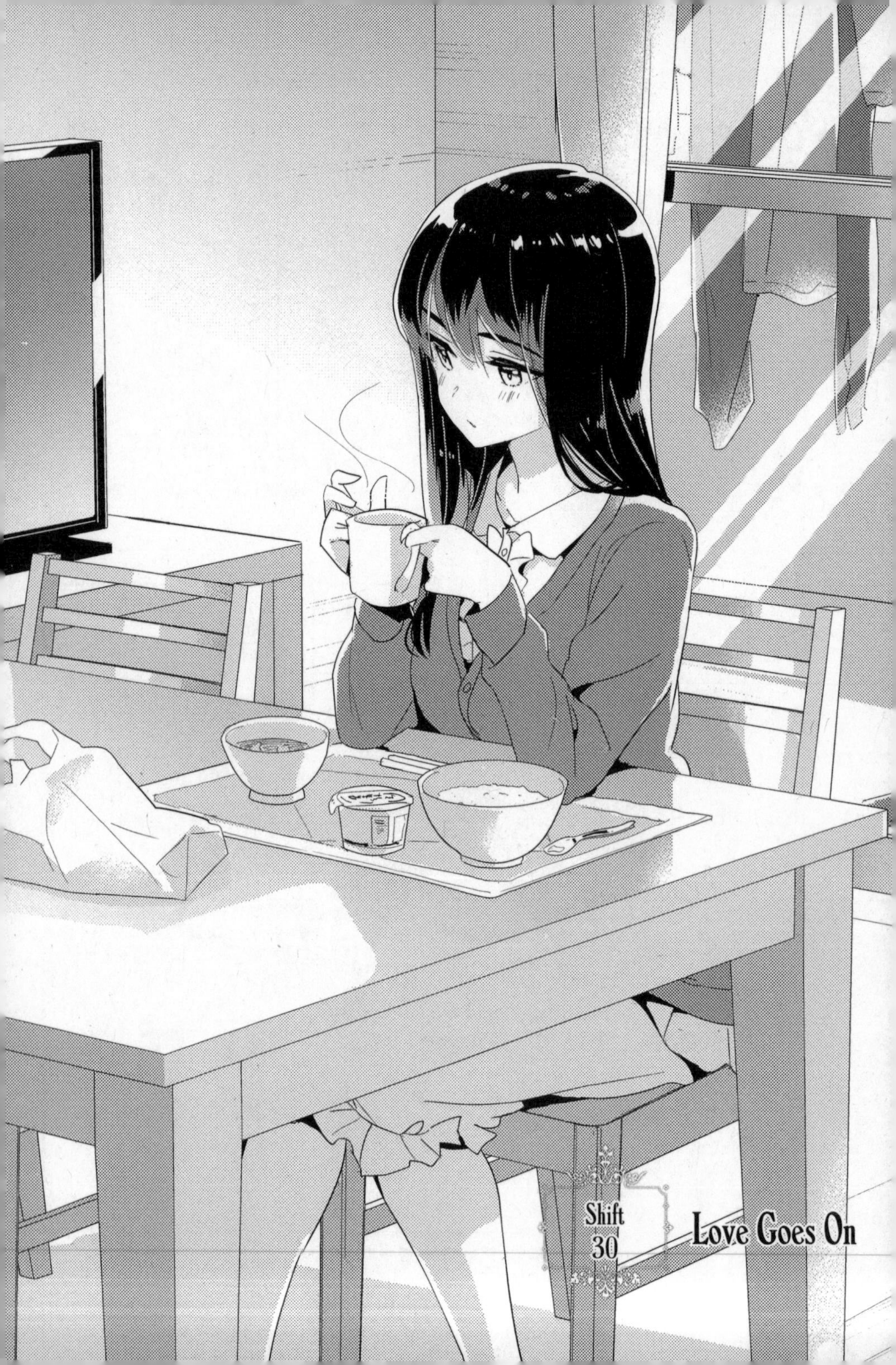
Shift 30
Love Goes On

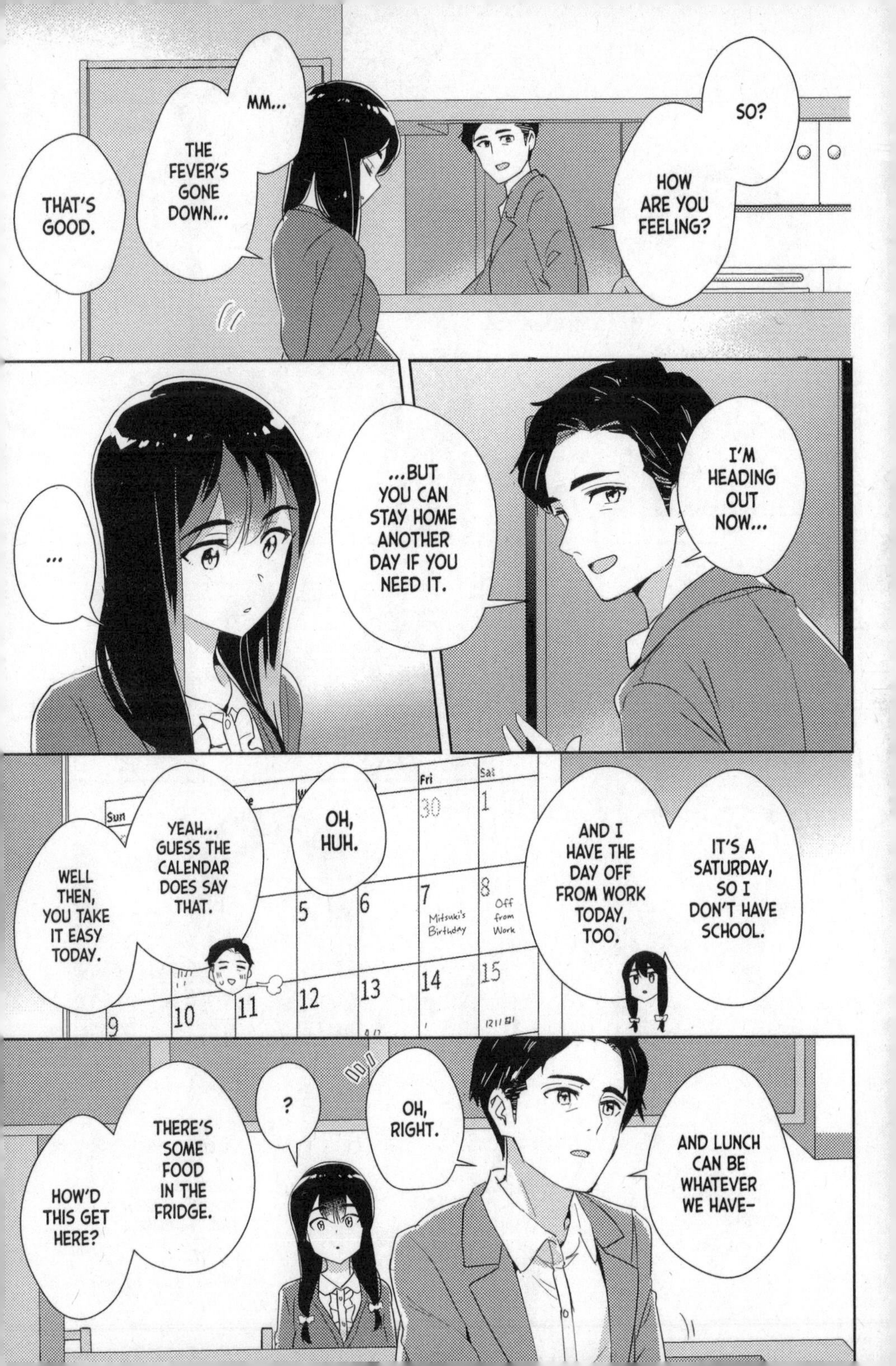
SO?
HOW ARE YOU FEELING?
MM...
THE FEVER'S GONE DOWN...
THAT'S GOOD.
I'M HEADING OUT NOW...
...BUT YOU CAN STAY HOME ANOTHER DAY IF YOU NEED IT.
...
IT'S A SATURDAY, SO I DON'T HAVE SCHOOL.
AND I HAVE THE DAY OFF FROM WORK TODAY, TOO.
Fri
Sat
Sun
Mitsuki's Birthday
Off from Work
OH, HUH.
YEAH... GUESS THE CALENDAR DOES SAY THAT.
WELL THEN, YOU TAKE IT EASY TODAY.
AND LUNCH CAN BE WHATEVER WE HAVE–
OH, RIGHT.
?
THERE'S SOME FOOD IN THE FRIDGE.
HOW'D THIS GET HERE?

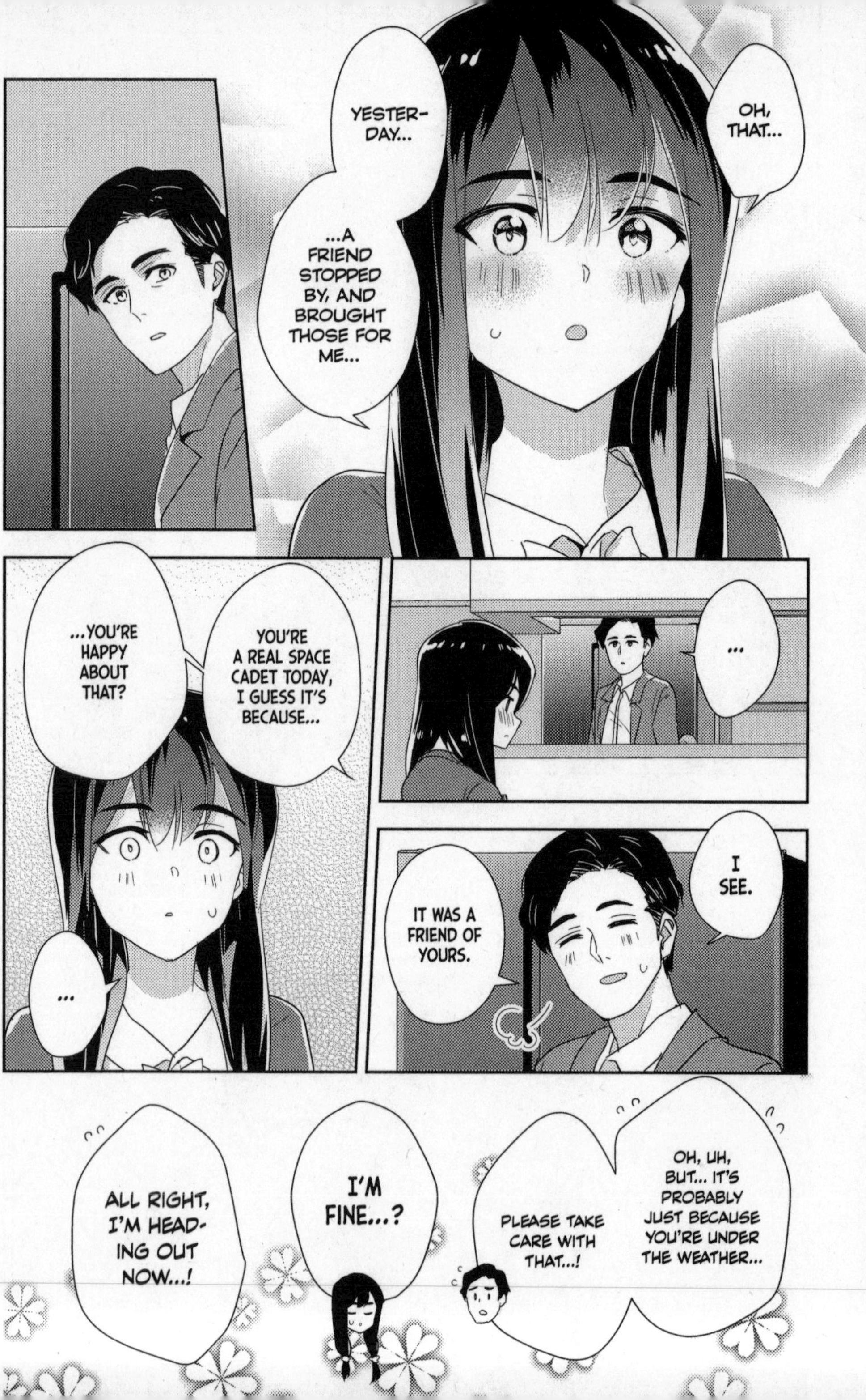

OH, THAT...
YESTER-DAY...
...A FRIEND STOPPED BY, AND BROUGHT THOSE FOR ME...
...
I SEE.
IT WAS A FRIEND OF YOURS.
YOU'RE A REAL SPACE CADET TODAY, I GUESS IT'S BECAUSE...
...YOU'RE HAPPY ABOUT THAT?
...
OH, UH, BUT... IT'S PROBABLY JUST BECAUSE YOU'RE UNDER THE WEATHER...
PLEASE TAKE CARE WITH THAT...!
I'M FINE...?
ALL RIGHT, I'M HEADING OUT NOW...!

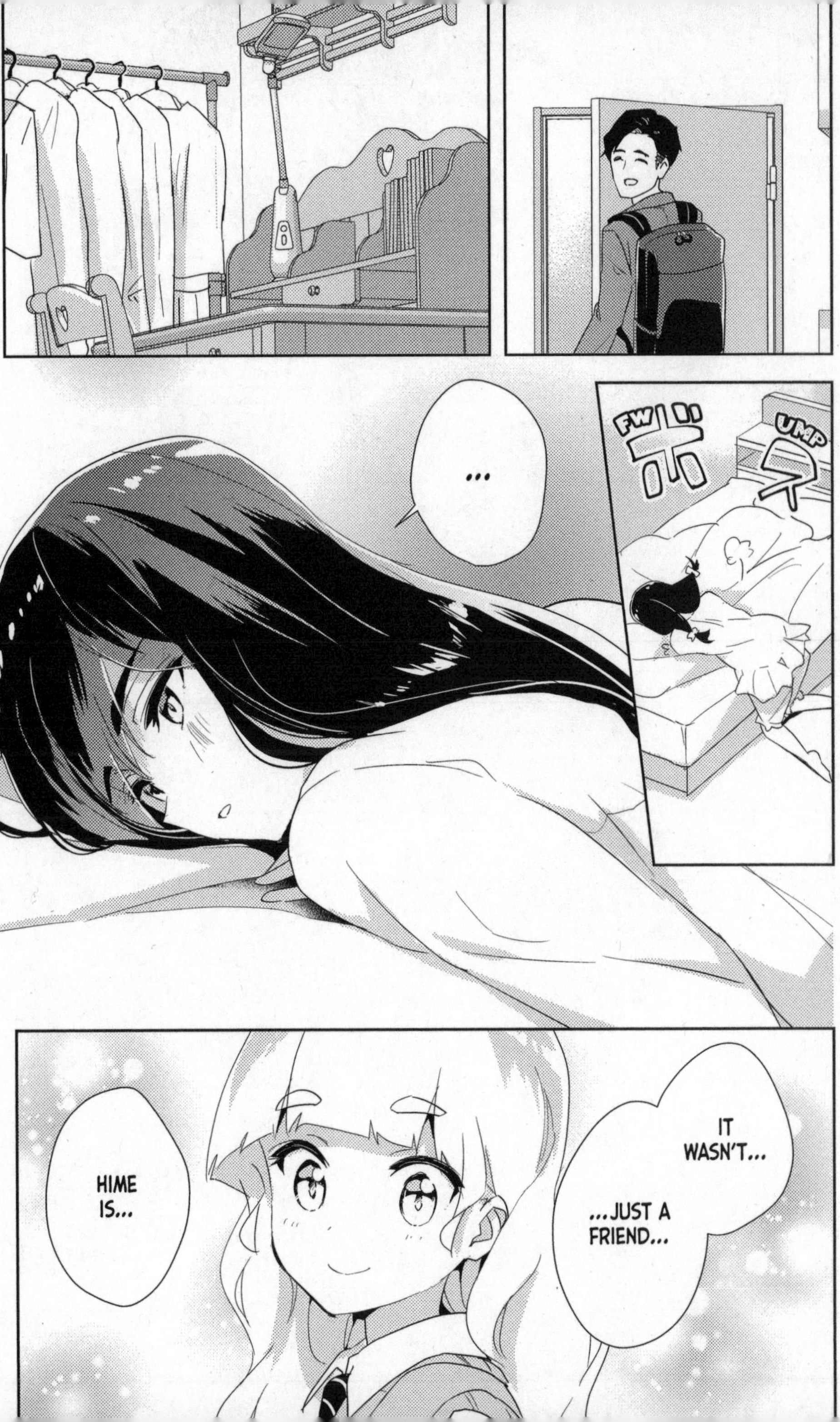
FW
UMP
...
IT WASN'T...
...JUST A FRIEND...
HIME IS...

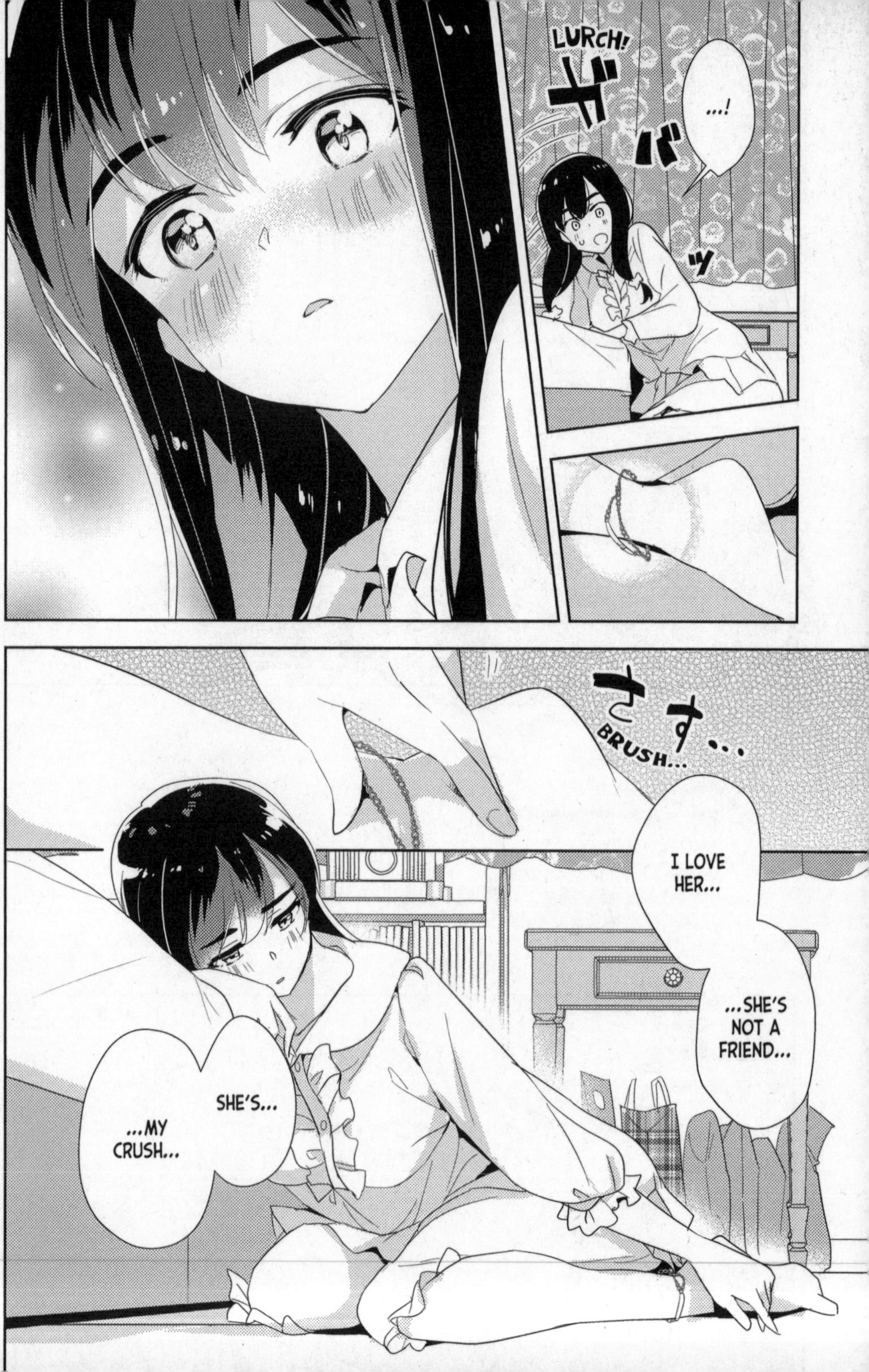
LURCH!
ガバ
...!
さす...
BRUSH...
I LOVE HER...
...SHE'S NOT A FRIEND...
SHE'S...
...MY CRUSH...

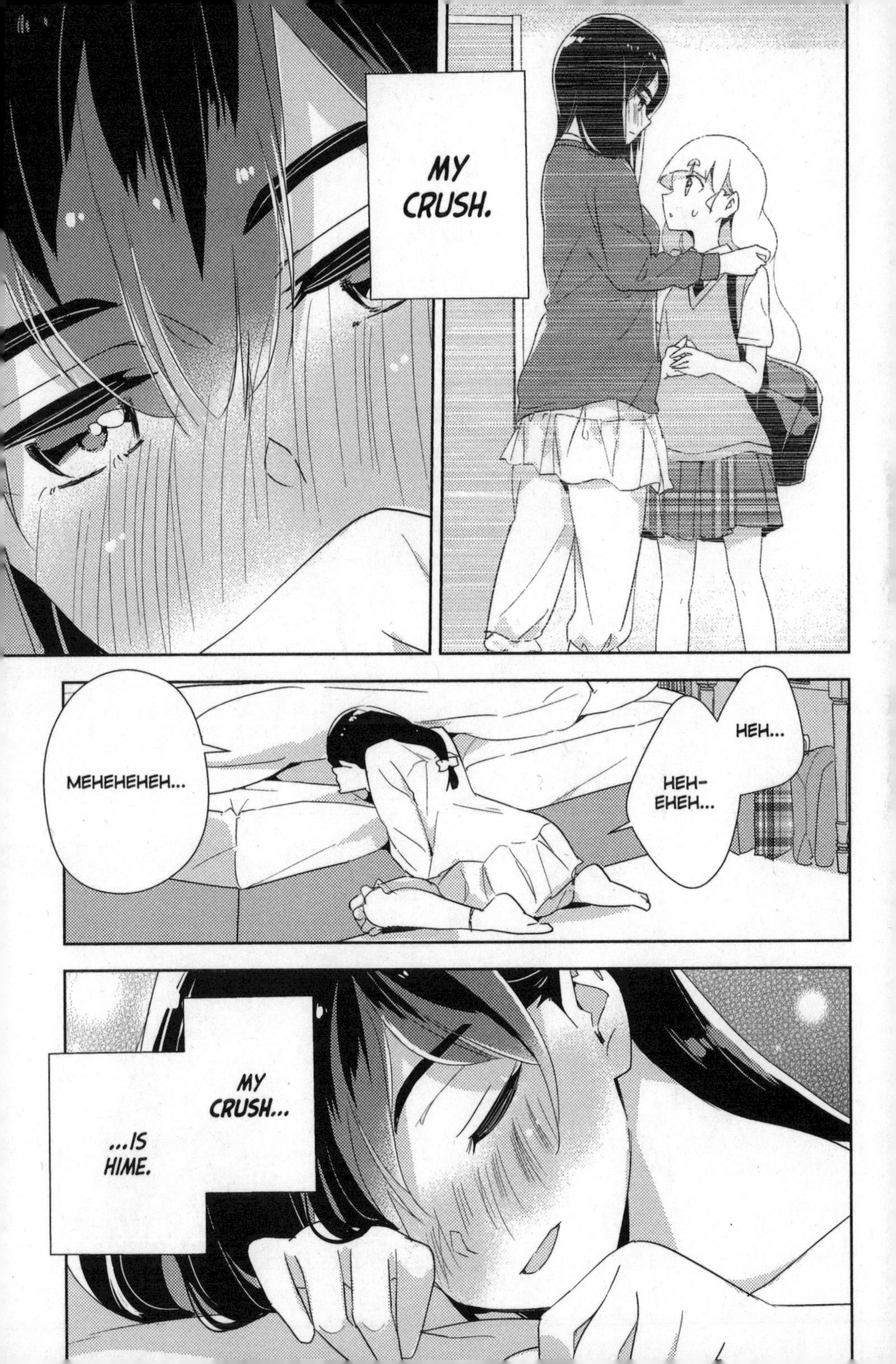
MY CRUSH.
HEH...
HEH-EHEH...
MEHEHEHEH...
MY CRUSH...
...IS HIME.

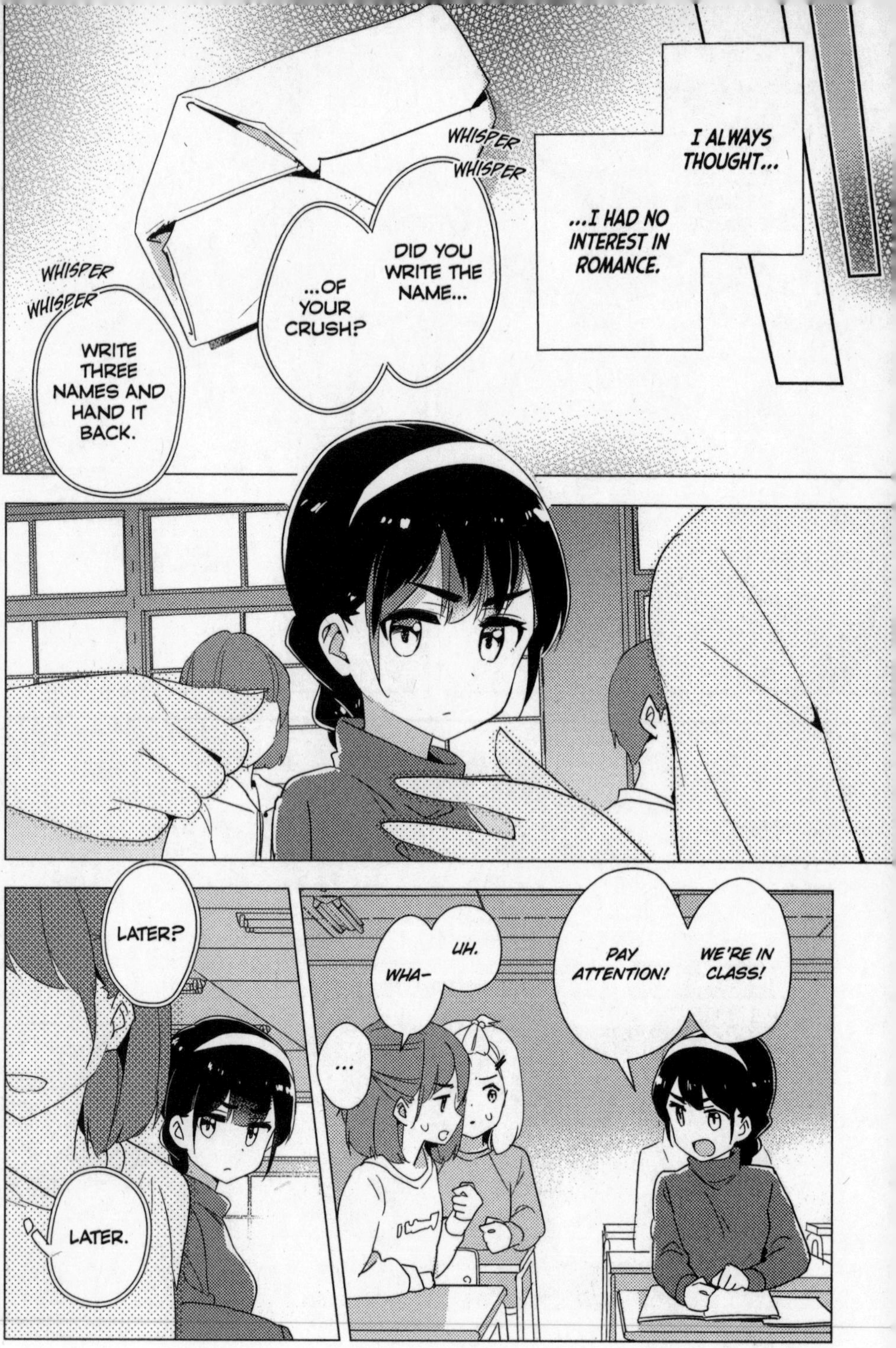
I ALWAYS THOUGHT...
...I HAD NO INTEREST IN ROMANCE.
WHISPER
WHISPER
DID YOU WRITE THE NAME... ...OF YOUR CRUSH?
WHISPER
WHISPER
WRITE THREE NAMES AND HAND IT BACK.
WE'RE IN CLASS! PAY ATTENTION!
UH. WHA-
...
LATER?
LATER.

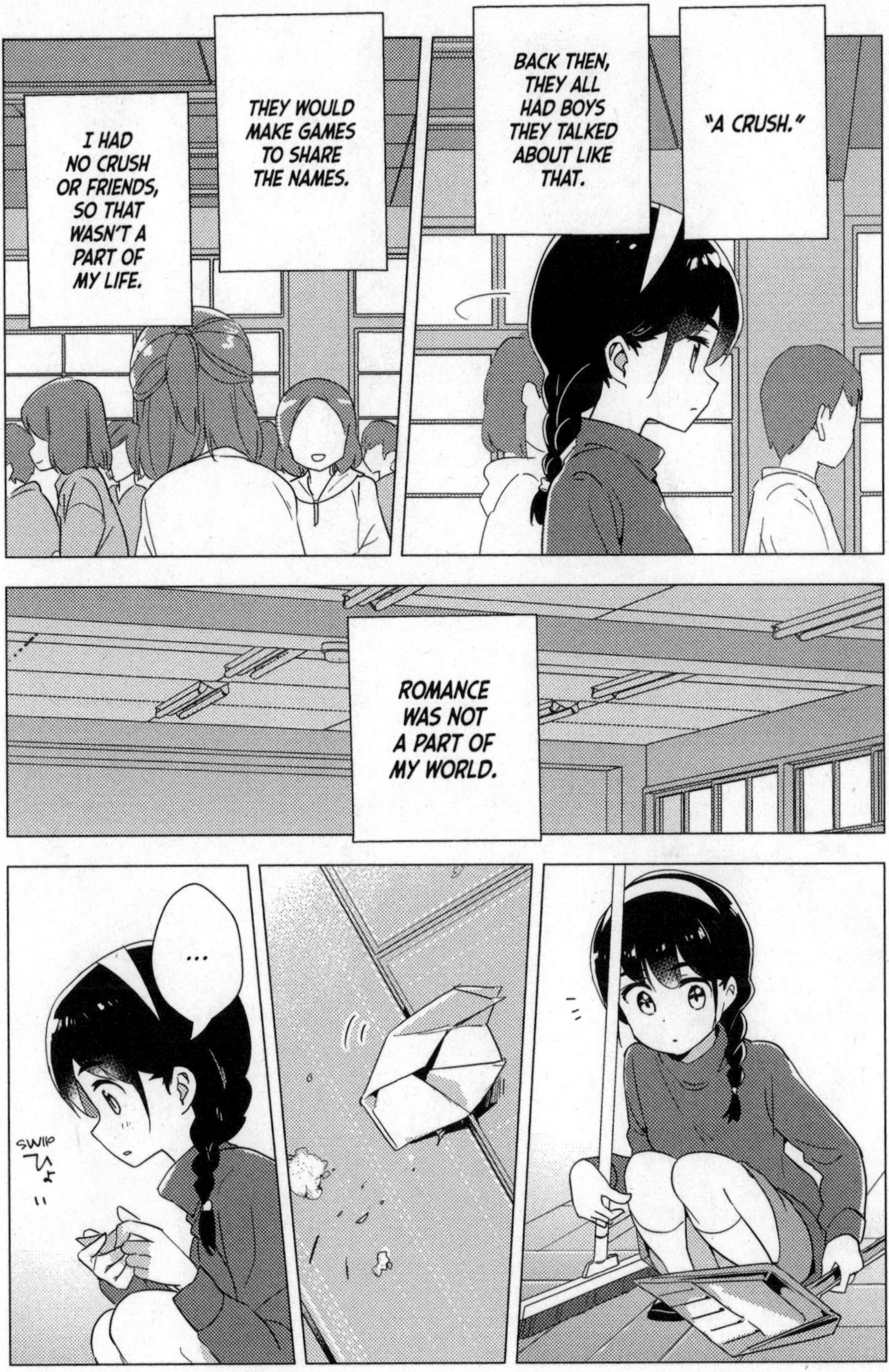
"A CRUSH."
BACK THEN, THEY ALL HAD BOYS THEY TALKED ABOUT LIKE THAT.
THEY WOULD MAKE GAMES TO SHARE THE NAMES.
I HAD NO CRUSH OR FRIENDS, SO THAT WASN'T A PART OF MY LIFE.
ROMANCE WAS NOT A PART OF MY WORLD.
...
SWIP
ぴょ

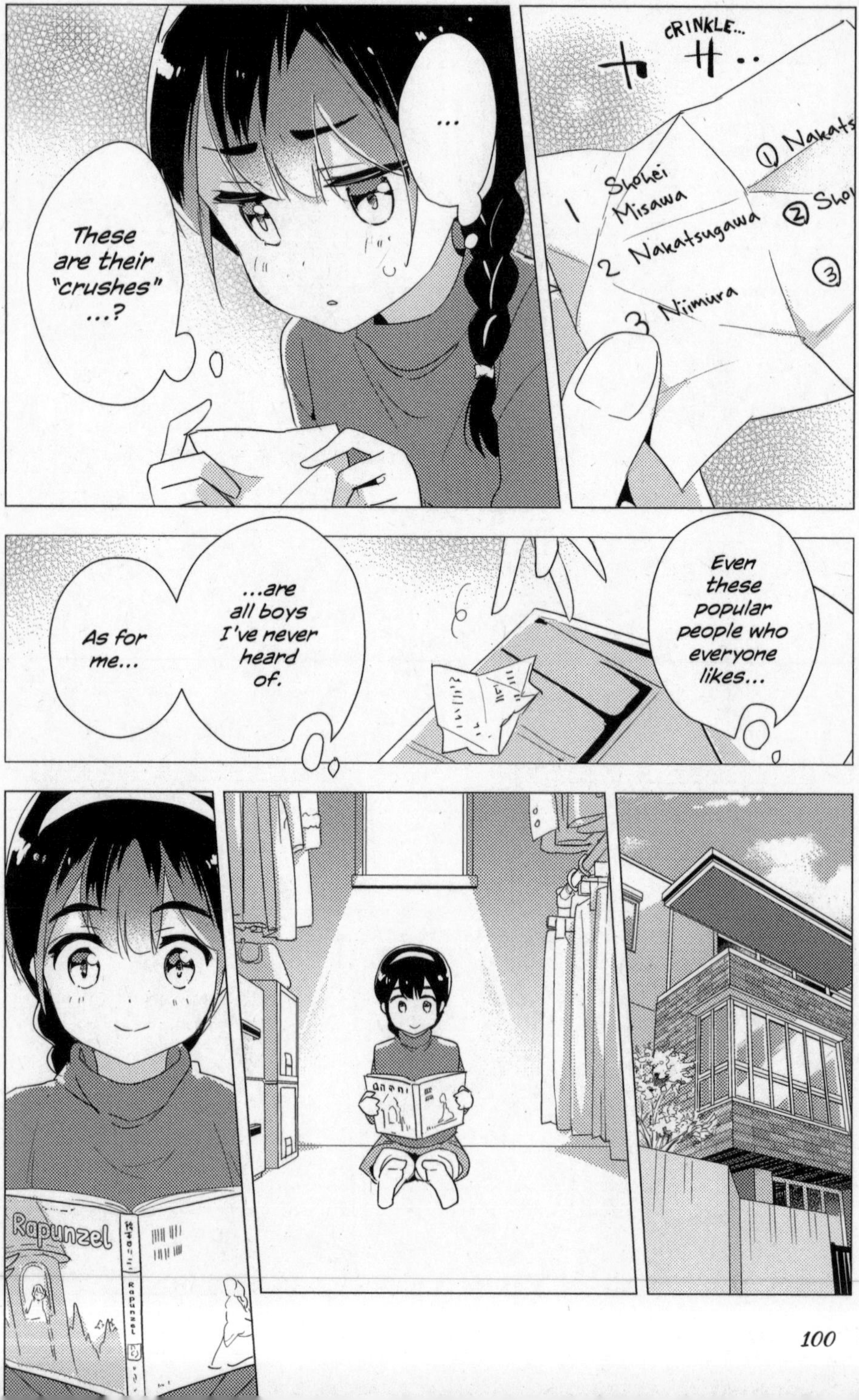

CRINKLE...
1 Shohei Misawa
2 Nakatsugawa
3 Niimura
① Nakats
② Sho
③
...
These are their "crushes" ...?
Even these popular people who everyone likes...
...are all boys I've never heard of.
As for me...
Rapunzel
Rapunzel

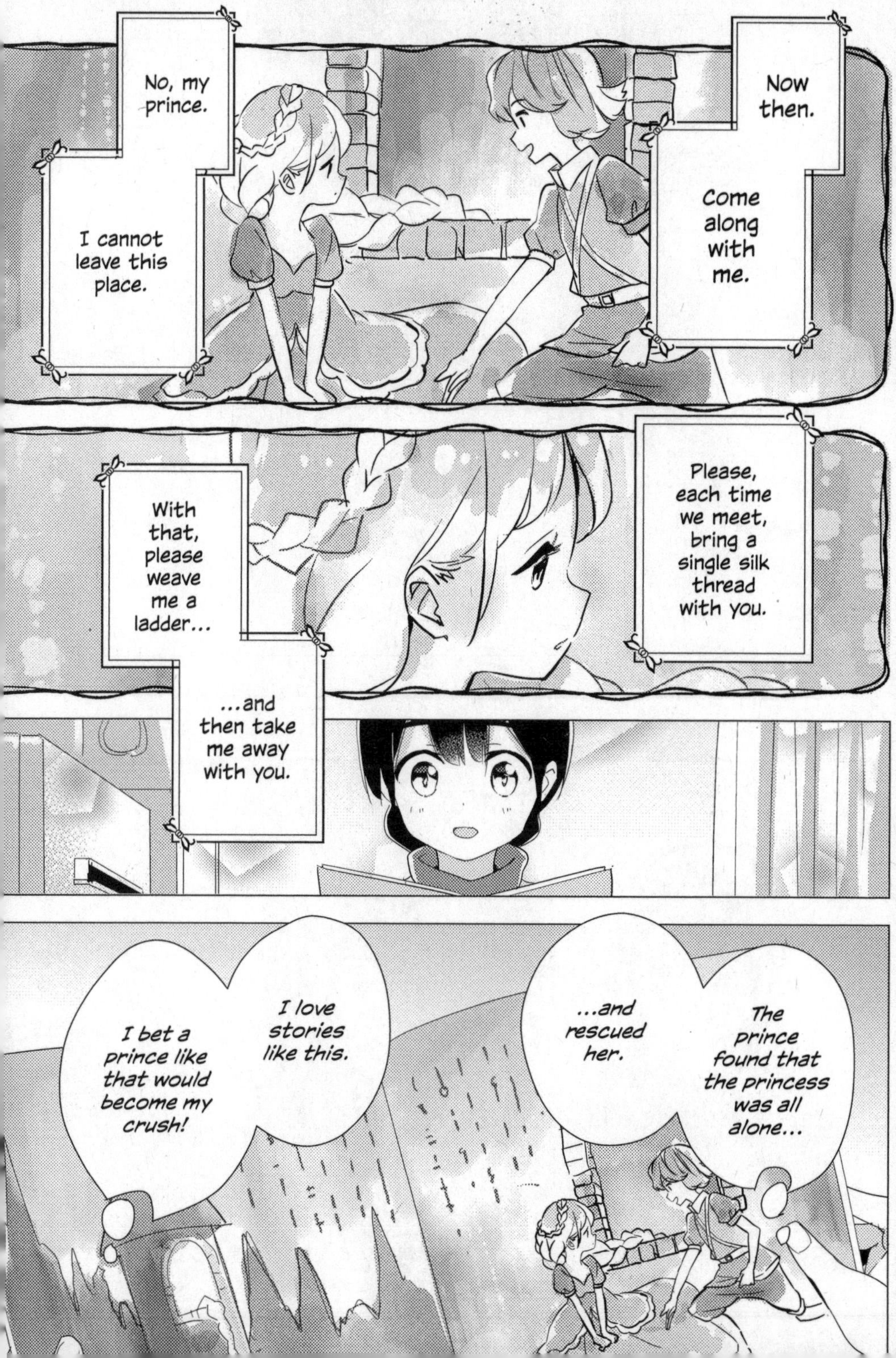
Now then.
Come along with me.
No, my prince.
I cannot leave this place.
Please, each time we meet, bring a single silk thread with you.
With that, please weave me a ladder...
...and then take me away with you.
The prince found that the princess was all alone...
...and rescued her.
I love stories like this.
I bet a prince like that would become my crush!

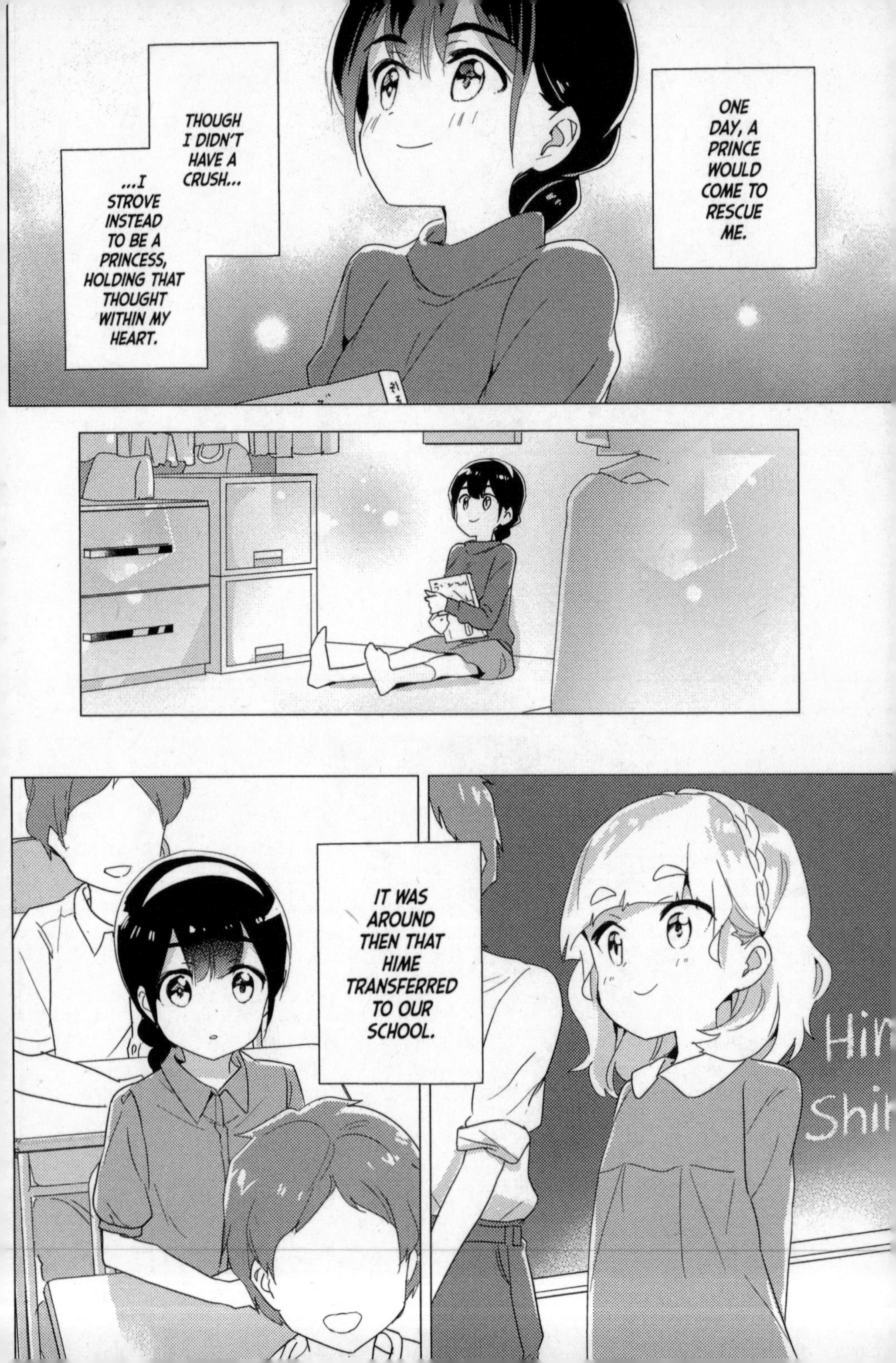
ONE DAY, A PRINCE WOULD COME TO RESCUE ME.
THOUGH I DIDN'T HAVE A CRUSH...
...I STROVE INSTEAD TO BE A PRINCESS, HOLDING THAT THOUGHT WITHIN MY HEART.
IT WAS AROUND THEN THAT HIME TRANSFERRED TO OUR SCHOOL.

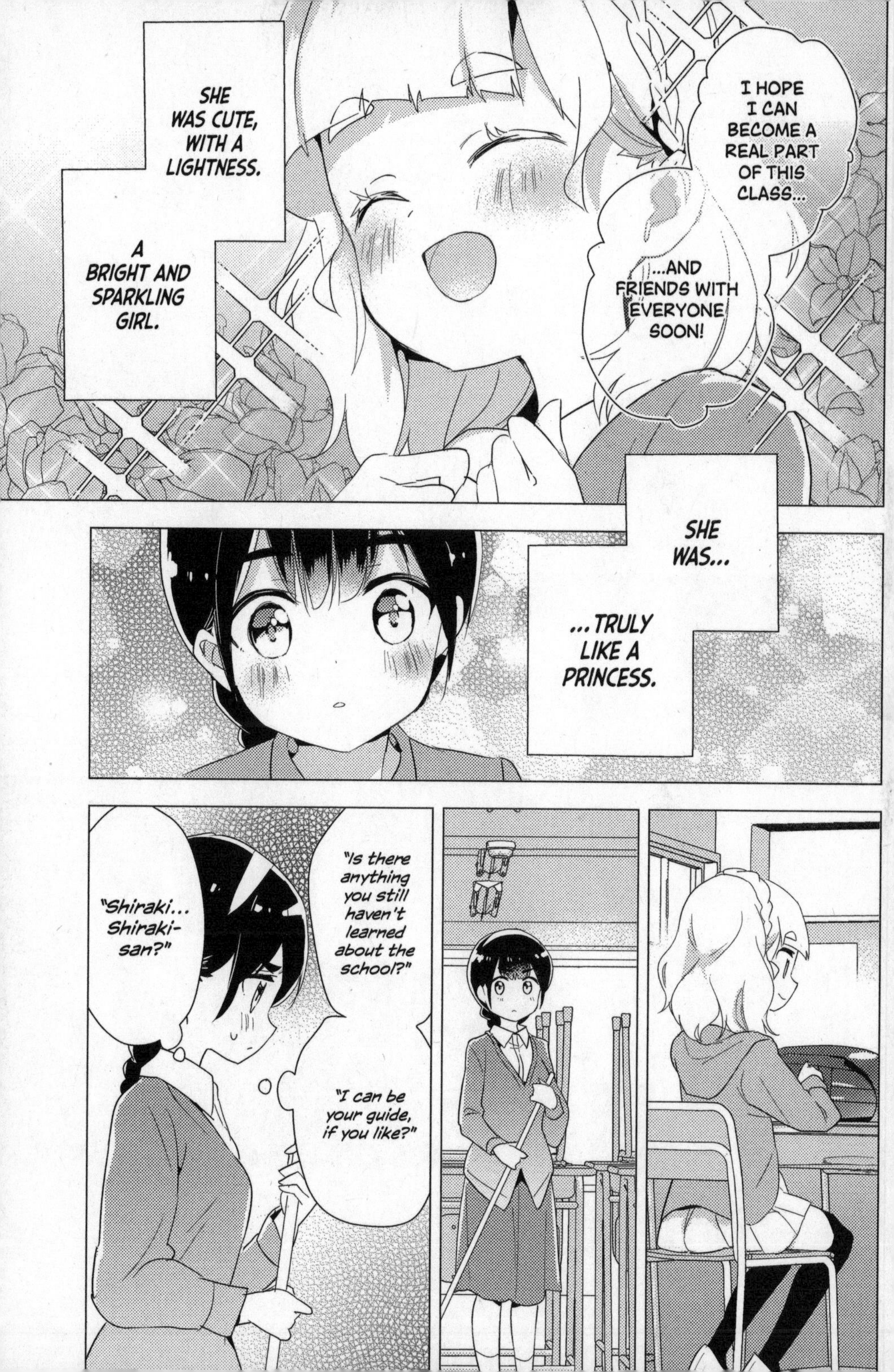
I HOPE I CAN BECOME A REAL PART OF THIS CLASS...
...AND FRIENDS WITH EVERYONE SOON!
SHE WAS CUTE, WITH A LIGHTNESS.
A BRIGHT AND SPARKLING GIRL.
SHE WAS...
...TRULY LIKE A PRINCESS.
"Is there anything you still haven't learned about the school?"
"I can be your guide, if you like?"
"Shiraki... Shiraki-san?"

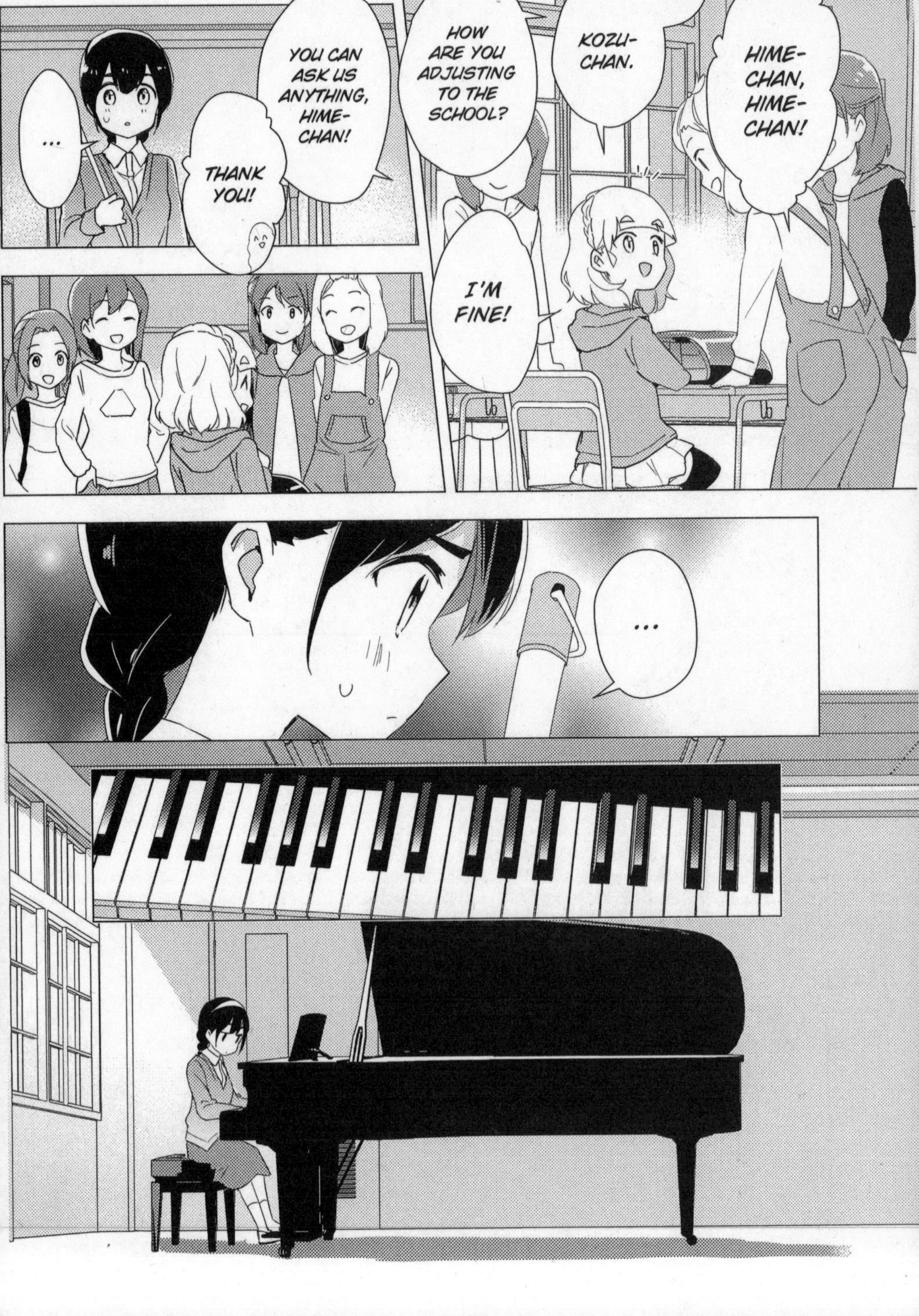
HIME-CHAN, HIME-CHAN!
OH!
KOZU-CHAN.
HOW ARE YOU ADJUSTING TO THE SCHOOL?
I'M FINE!
YOU CAN ASK US ANYTHING, HIME-CHAN!
THANK YOU!
...
...

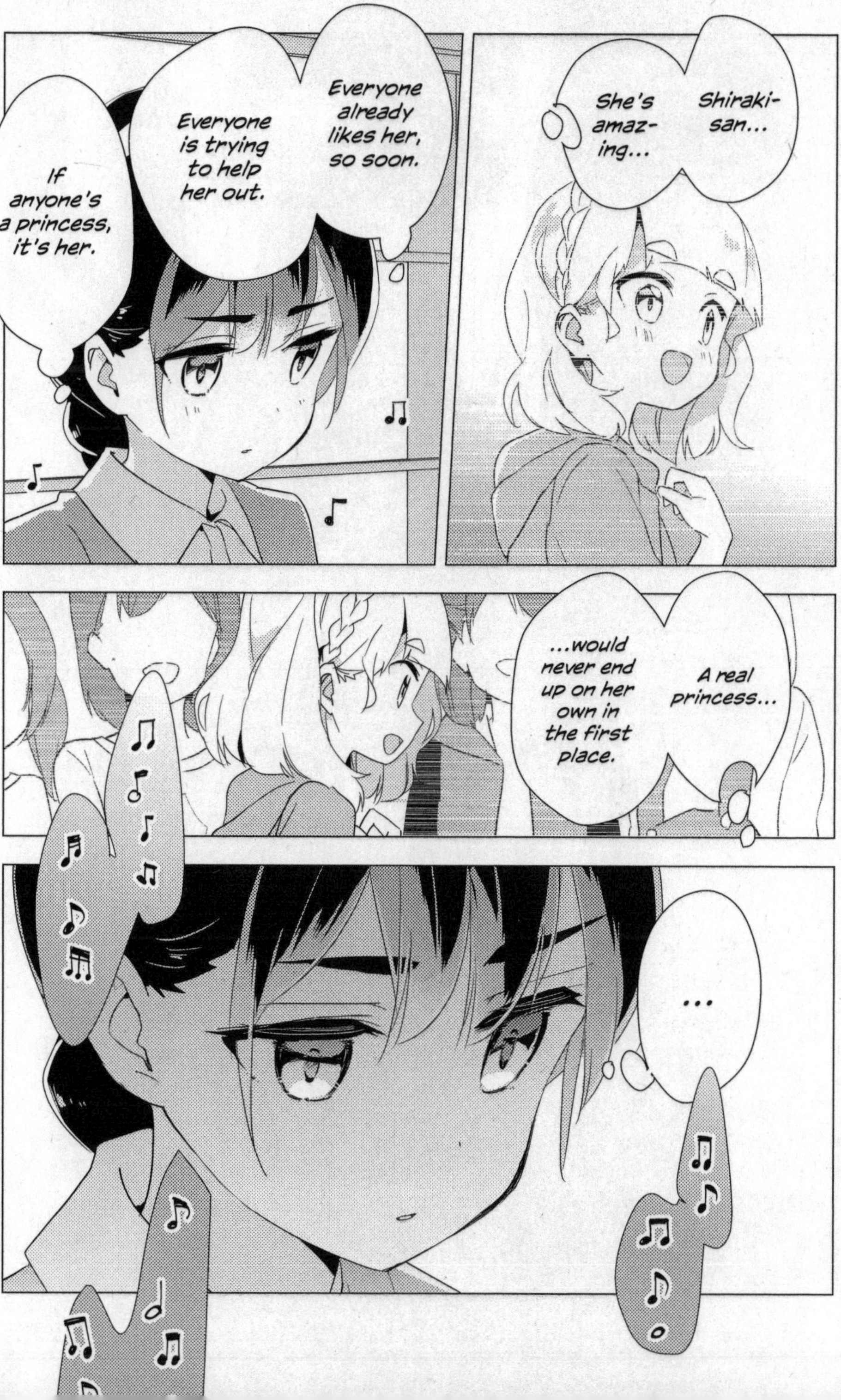
Shiraki-san...
She's amaz-ing...
Everyone already likes her, so soon.
Everyone is trying to help her out.
If anyone's a princess, it's her.
A real princess...
...would never end up on her own in the first place.
...

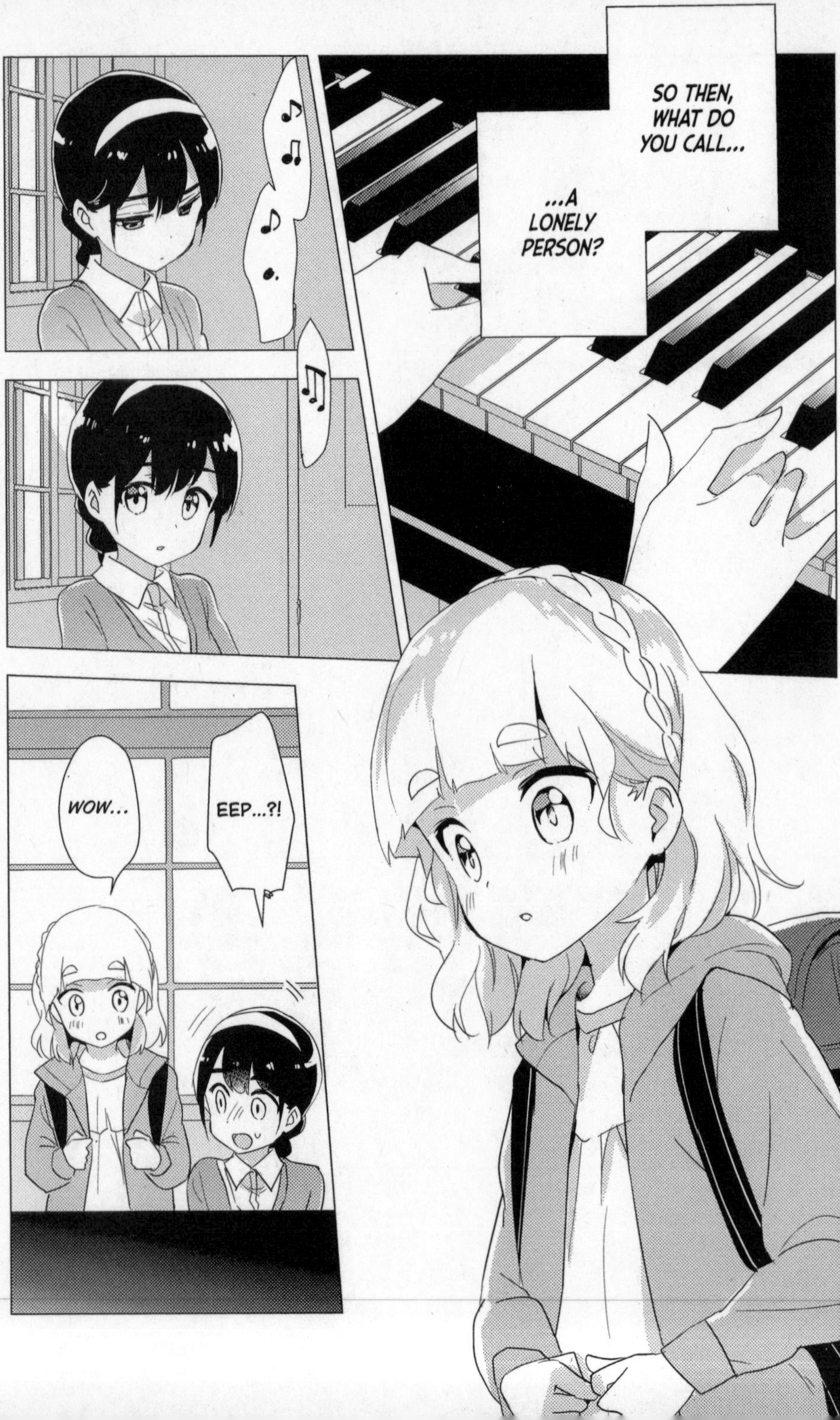
SO THEN, WHAT DO YOU CALL...
...A LONELY PERSON?
EEP...?!
WOW...

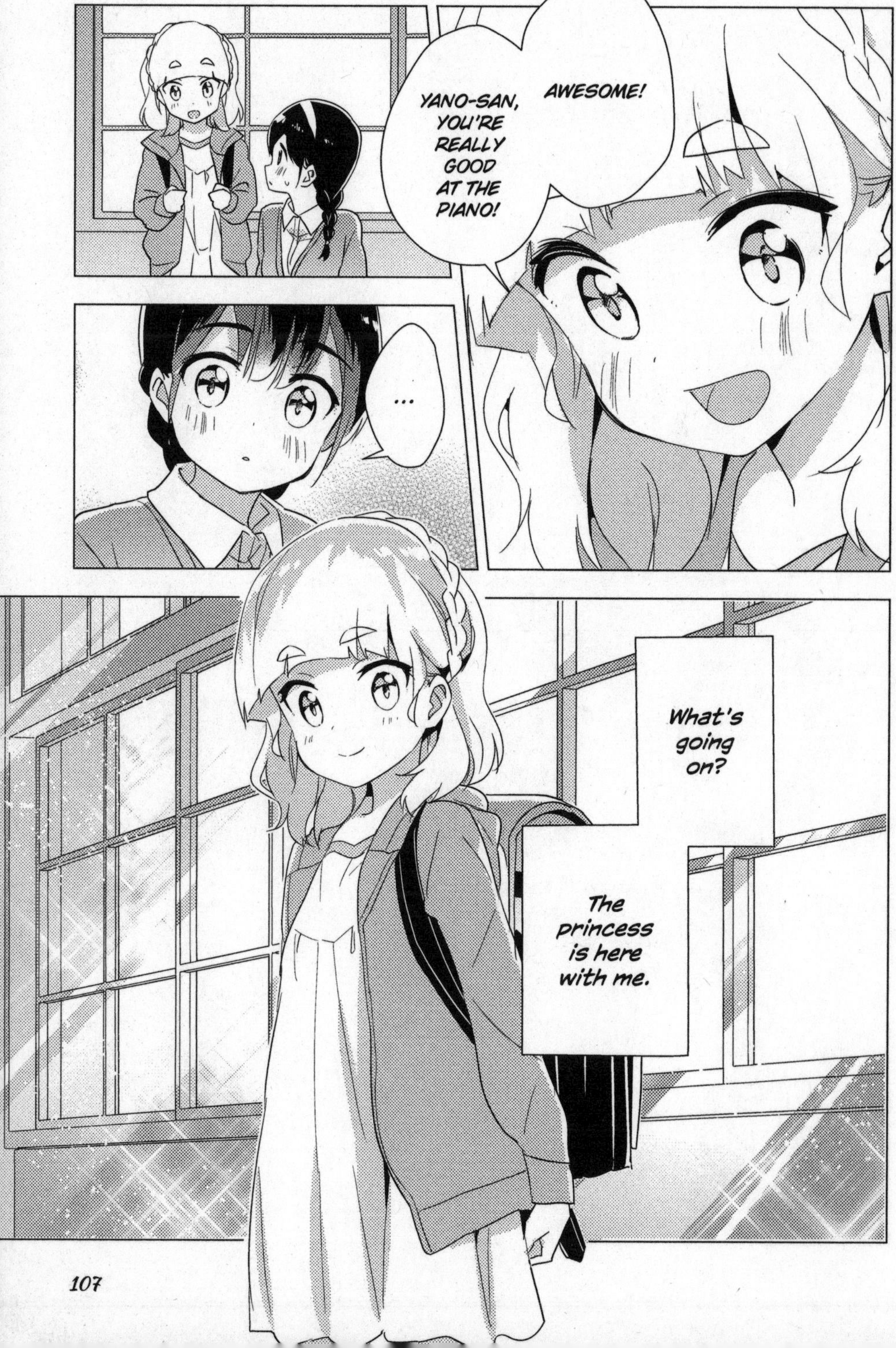
AWESOME!
YANO-SAN, YOU'RE REALLY GOOD AT THE PIANO!
...
What's going on?
The princess is here with me.

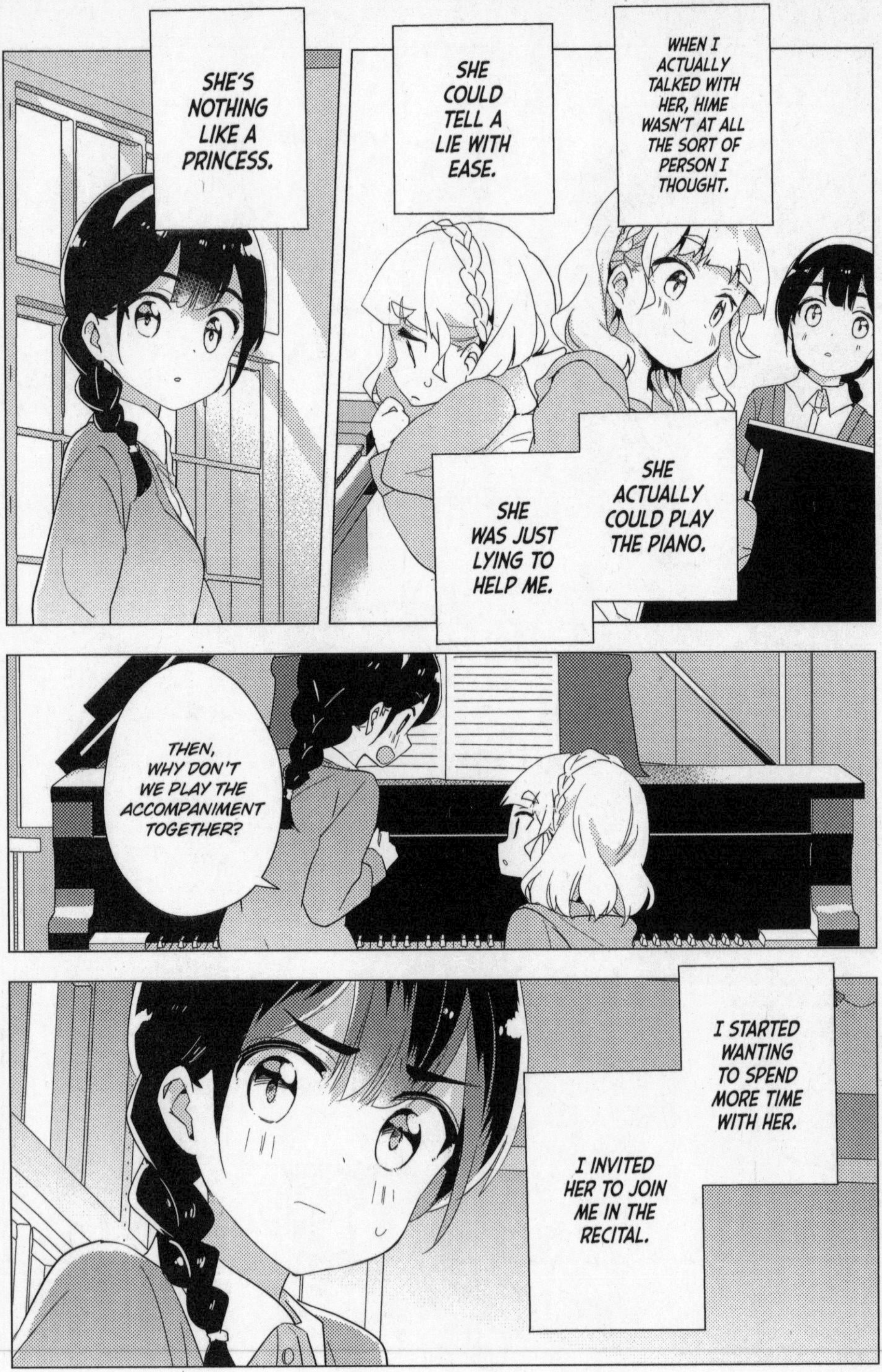
WHEN I ACTUALLY TALKED WITH HER, HIME WASN'T AT ALL THE SORT OF PERSON I THOUGHT.
SHE COULD TELL A LIE WITH EASE.
SHE ACTUALLY COULD PLAY THE PIANO.
SHE WAS JUST LYING TO HELP ME.
SHE'S NOTHING LIKE A PRINCESS.
THEN, WHY DON'T WE PLAY THE ACCOMPANIMENT TOGETHER?
I STARTED WANTING TO SPEND MORE TIME WITH HER.
I INVITED HER TO JOIN ME IN THE RECITAL.

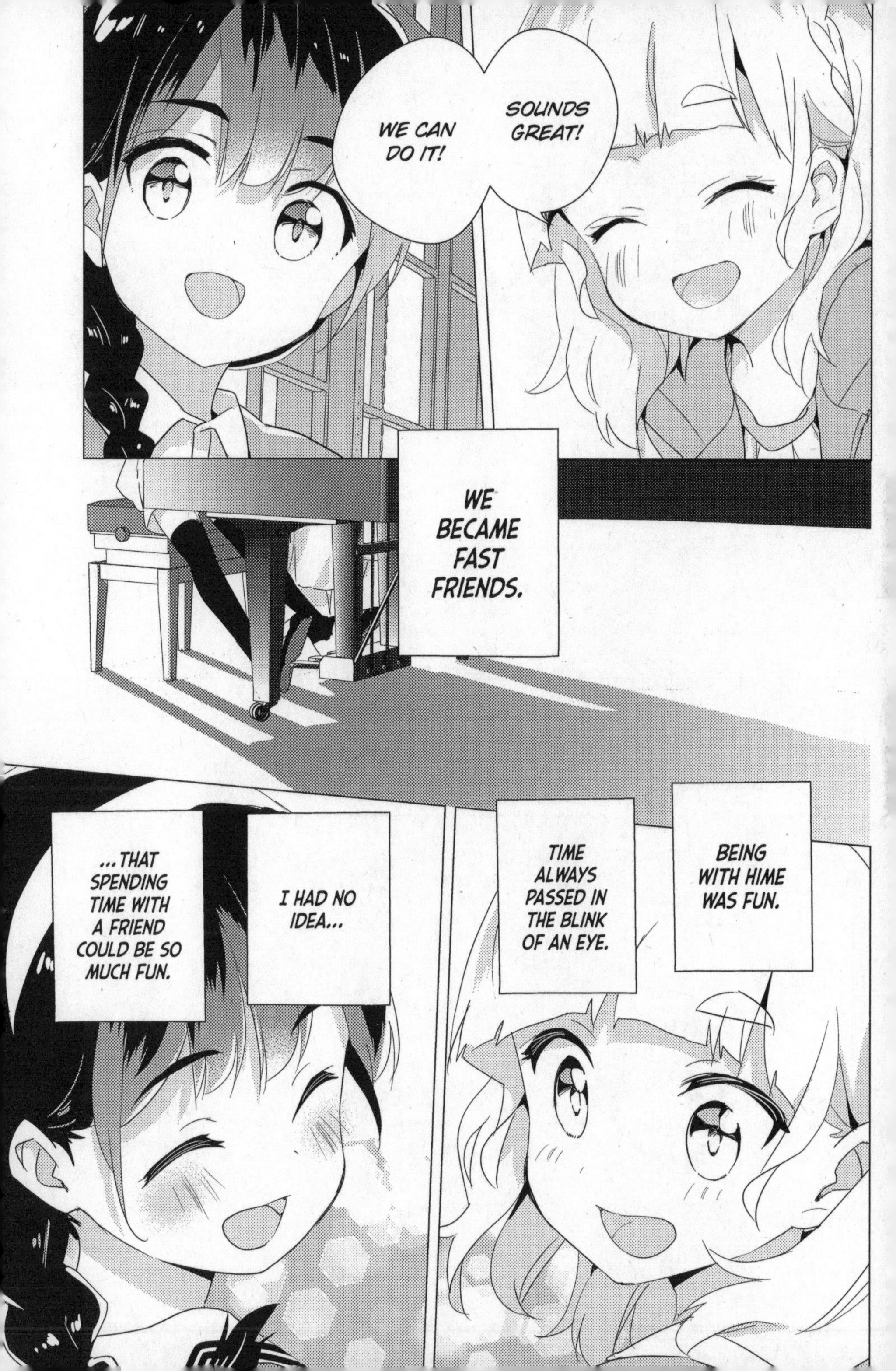
SOUNDS GREAT!
WE CAN DO IT!
WE BECAME FAST FRIENDS.
BEING WITH HIME WAS FUN.
TIME ALWAYS PASSED IN THE BLINK OF AN EYE.
I HAD NO IDEA...
...THAT SPENDING TIME WITH A FRIEND COULD BE SO MUCH FUN.

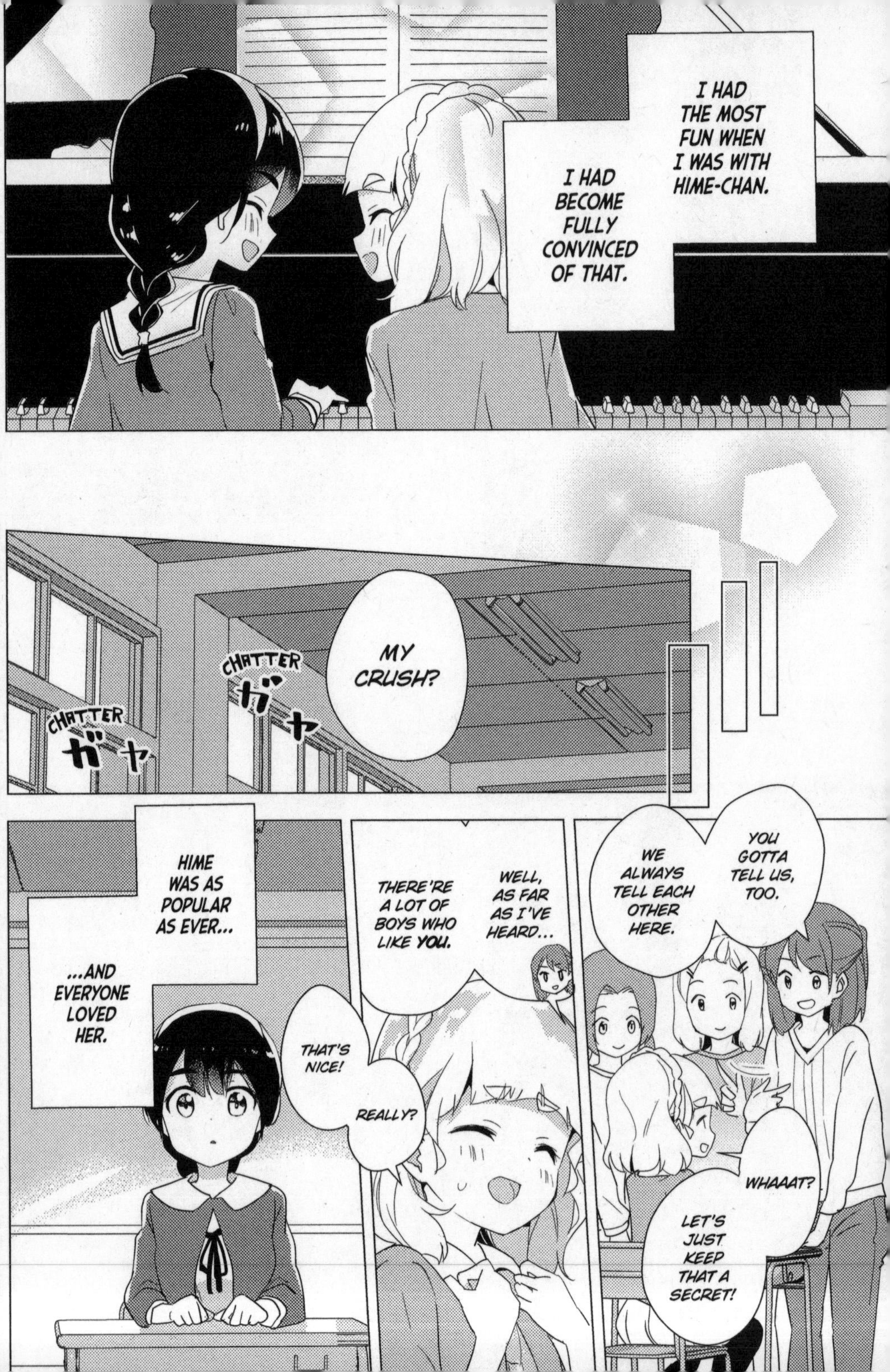
I HAD THE MOST FUN WHEN I WAS WITH HIME-CHAN.
I HAD BECOME FULLY CONVINCED OF THAT.
MY CRUSH?
CHATTER ガヤ
CHATTER ガヤ
YOU GOTTA TELL US, TOO.
WE ALWAYS TELL EACH OTHER HERE.
WHAAAT?
LET'S JUST KEEP THAT A SECRET!
WELL, AS FAR AS I'VE HEARD...
THERE'RE A LOT OF BOYS WHO LIKE YOU.
THAT'S NICE!
REALLY?
HIME WAS AS POPULAR AS EVER...
...AND EVERYONE LOVED HER.

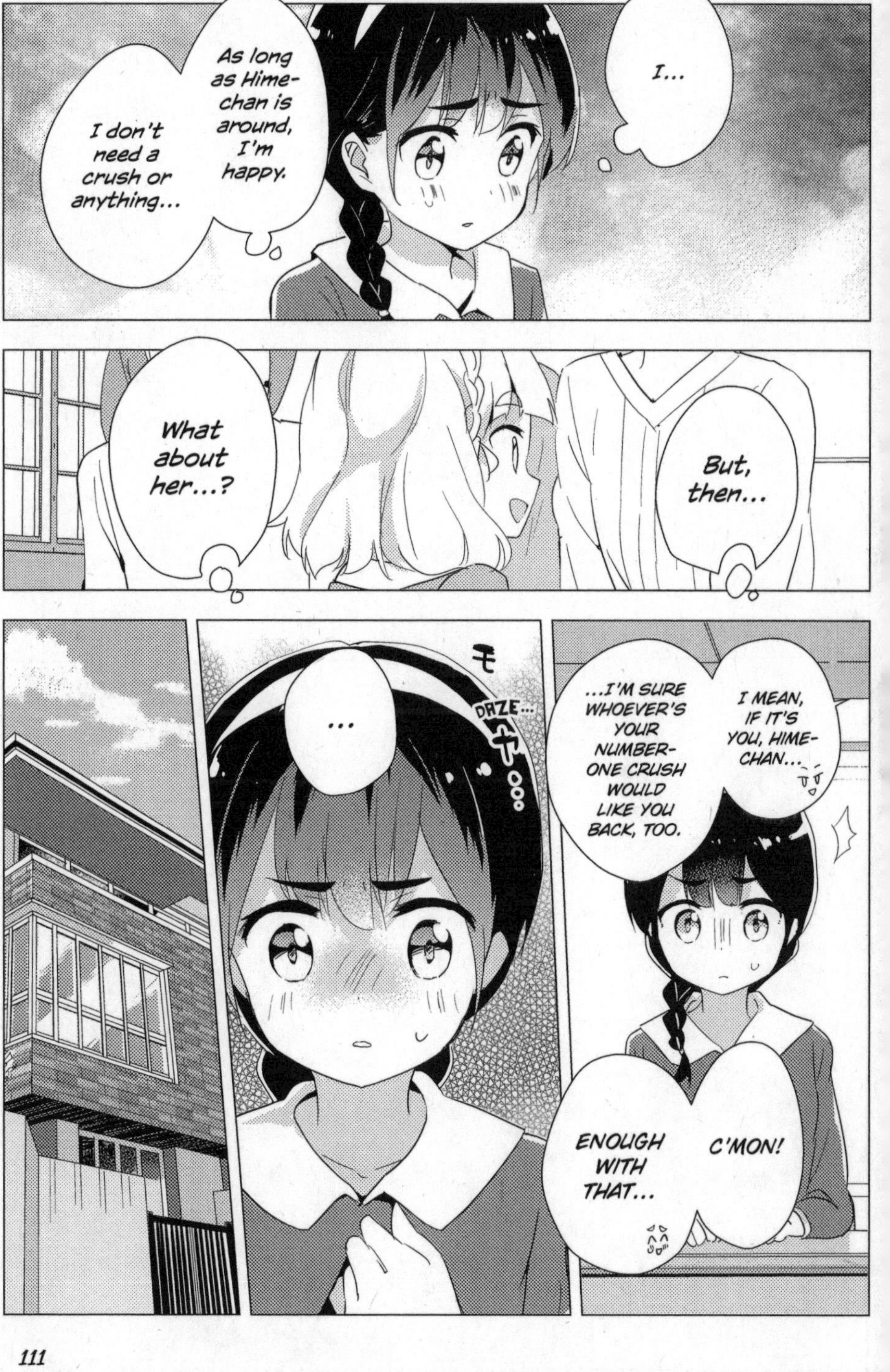
I...
As long as Hime-chan is around, I'm happy.
I don't need a crush or anything...
But, then...
What about her...?
I MEAN, IF IT'S YOU, HIME-CHAN...
...I'M SURE WHOEVER'S YOUR NUMBER-ONE CRUSH WOULD LIKE YOU BACK, TOO.
C'MON!
ENOUGH WITH THAT...
DAZE...
...

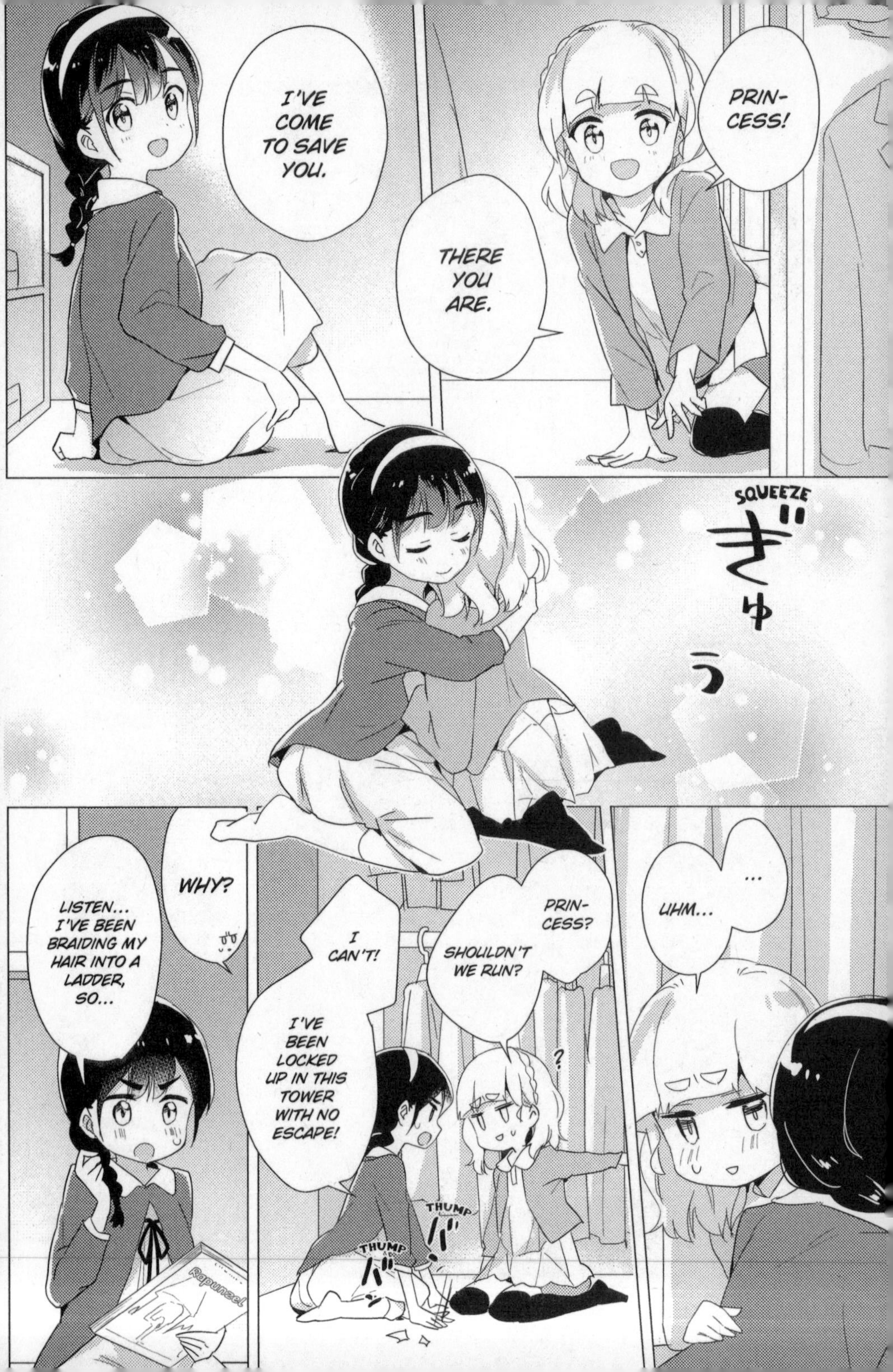
PRIN-CESS!
THERE YOU ARE.
I'VE COME TO SAVE YOU.
SQUEEZE
ぎゅう
...
UHM...
PRIN-CESS? SHOULDN'T WE RUN?
?
I CAN'T!
I'VE BEEN LOCKED UP IN THIS TOWER WITH NO ESCAPE!
THUMP
バ
THUMP
バ
WHY?
LISTEN... I'VE BEEN BRAIDING MY HAIR INTO A LADDER, SO...
Rapunzel

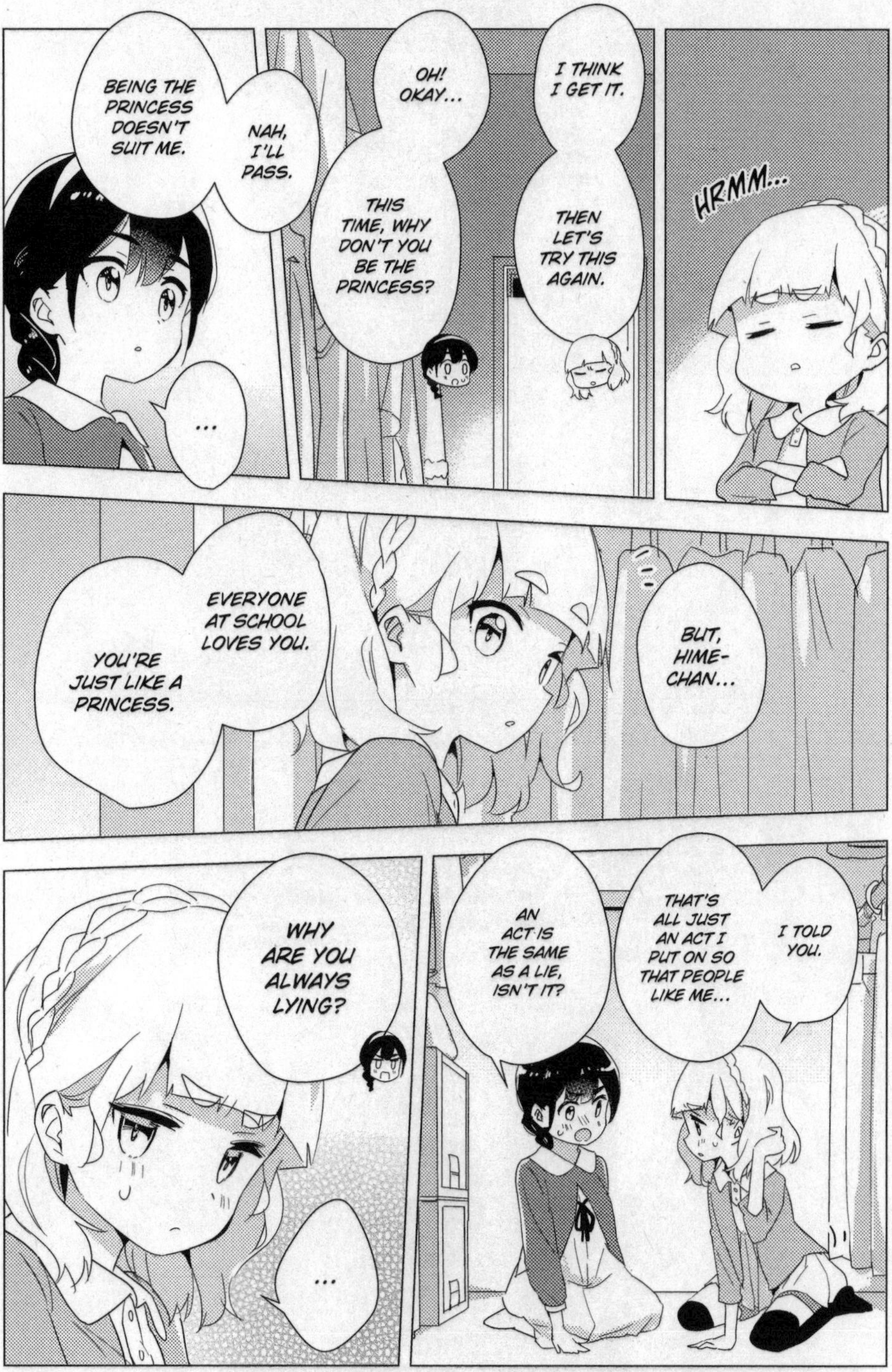
HRMM...
I THINK I GET IT.
THEN LET'S TRY THIS AGAIN.
OH! OKAY...
THIS TIME, WHY DON'T YOU BE THE PRINCESS?
NAH, I'LL PASS.
BEING THE PRINCESS DOESN'T SUIT ME.
...
BUT, HIME-CHAN...
EVERYONE AT SCHOOL LOVES YOU.
YOU'RE JUST LIKE A PRINCESS.
I TOLD YOU.
THAT'S ALL JUST AN ACT I PUT ON SO THAT PEOPLE LIKE ME...
AN ACT IS THE SAME AS A LIE, ISN'T IT?
WHY ARE YOU ALWAYS LYING?
...

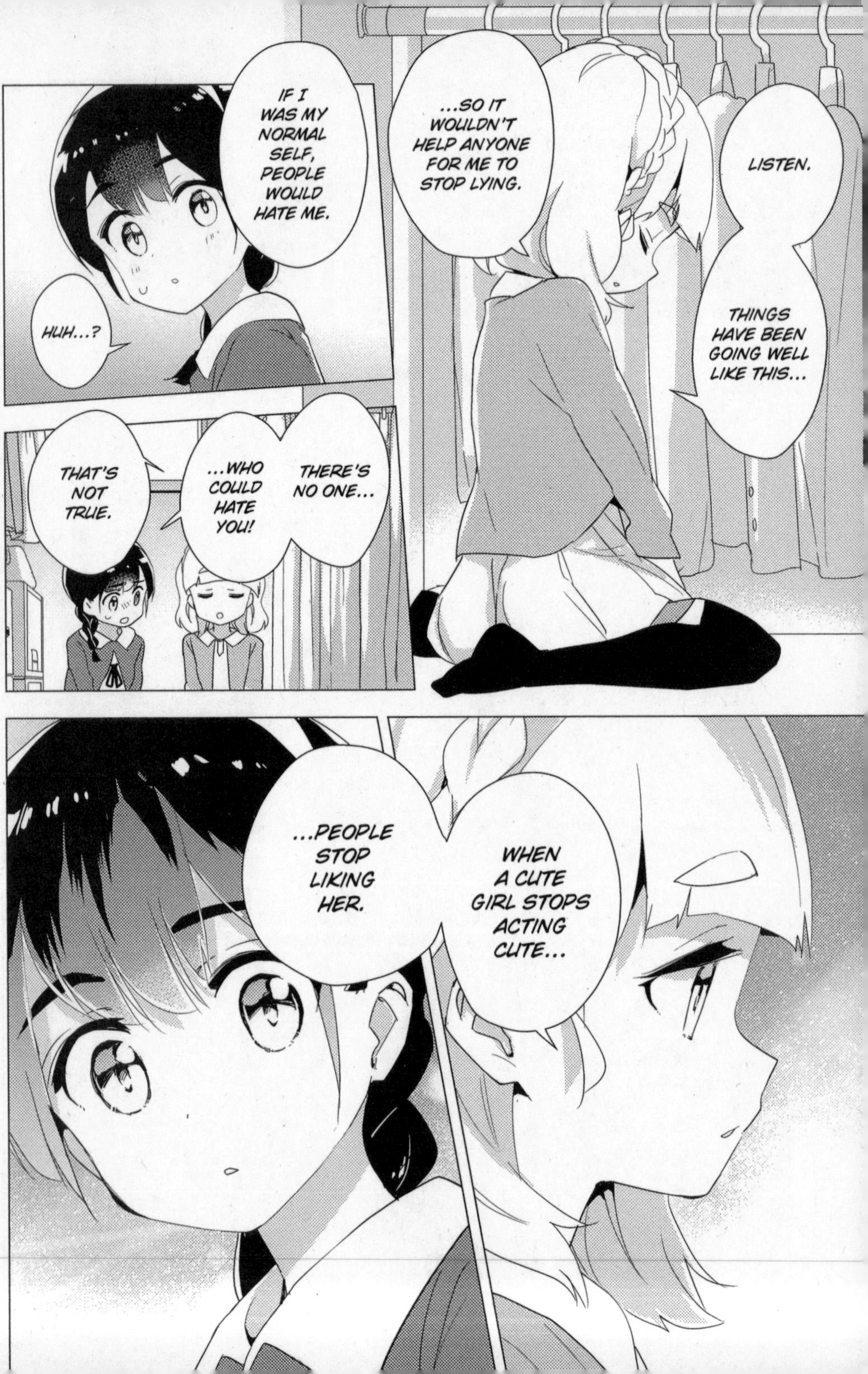
LISTEN.
THINGS HAVE BEEN GOING WELL LIKE THIS...
...SO IT WOULDN'T HELP ANYONE FOR ME TO STOP LYING.
IF I WAS MY NORMAL SELF, PEOPLE WOULD HATE ME.
HUH...?
THERE'S NO ONE...
...WHO COULD HATE YOU!
THAT'S NOT TRUE.
WHEN A CUTE GIRL STOPS ACTING CUTE...
...PEOPLE STOP LIKING HER.

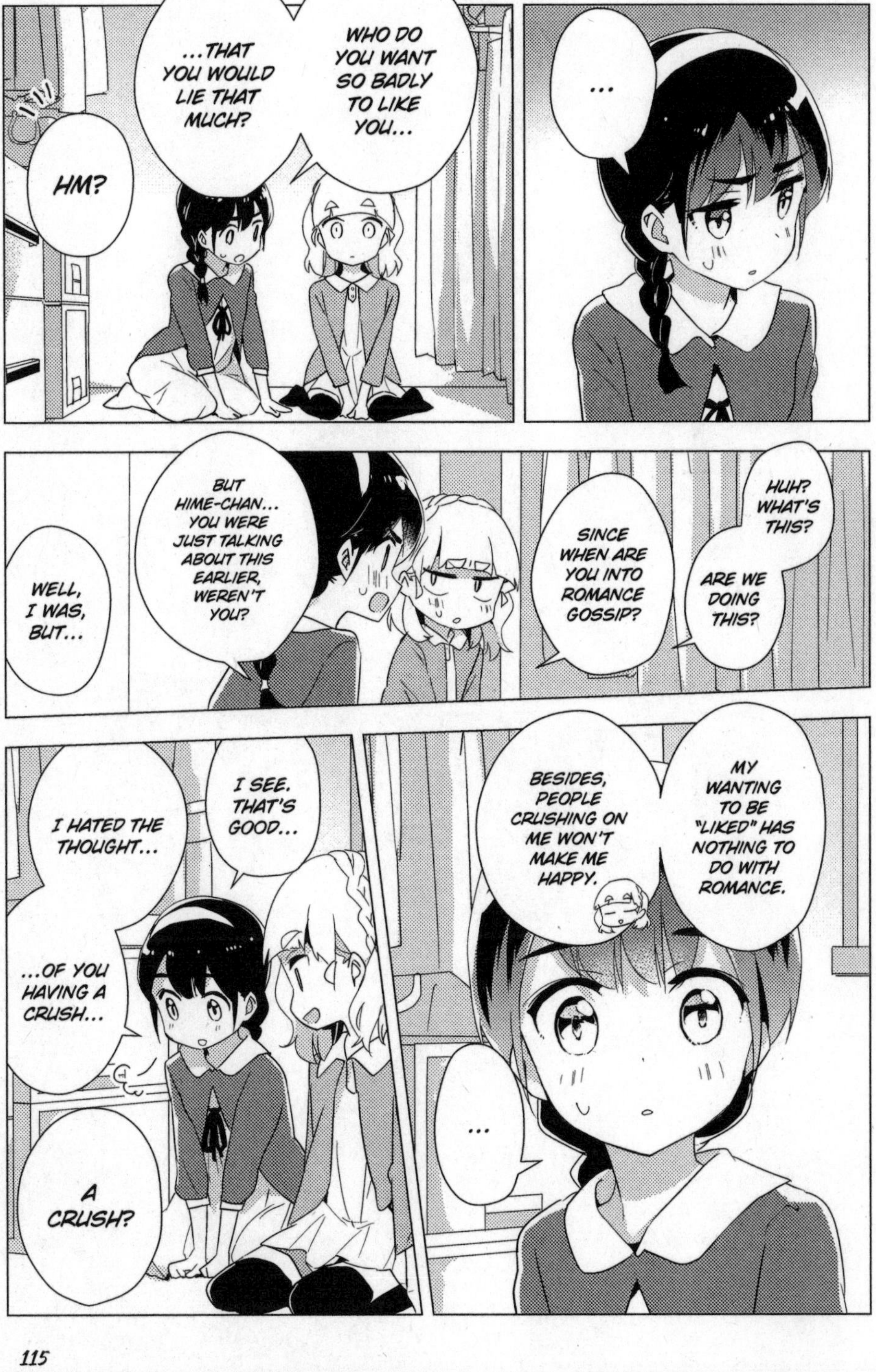
...
WHO DO YOU WANT SO BADLY TO LIKE YOU...
...THAT YOU WOULD LIE THAT MUCH?
HM?
HUH? WHAT'S THIS?
SINCE WHEN ARE YOU INTO ROMANCE GOSSIP?
ARE WE DOING THIS?
BUT HIME-CHAN... YOU WERE JUST TALKING ABOUT THIS EARLIER, WEREN'T YOU?
WELL, I WAS, BUT...
MY WANTING TO BE "LIKED" HAS NOTHING TO DO WITH ROMANCE.
BESIDES, PEOPLE CRUSHING ON ME WON'T MAKE ME HAPPY.
...
I SEE. THAT'S GOOD...
I HATED THE THOUGHT...
...OF YOU HAVING A CRUSH...
A CRUSH?

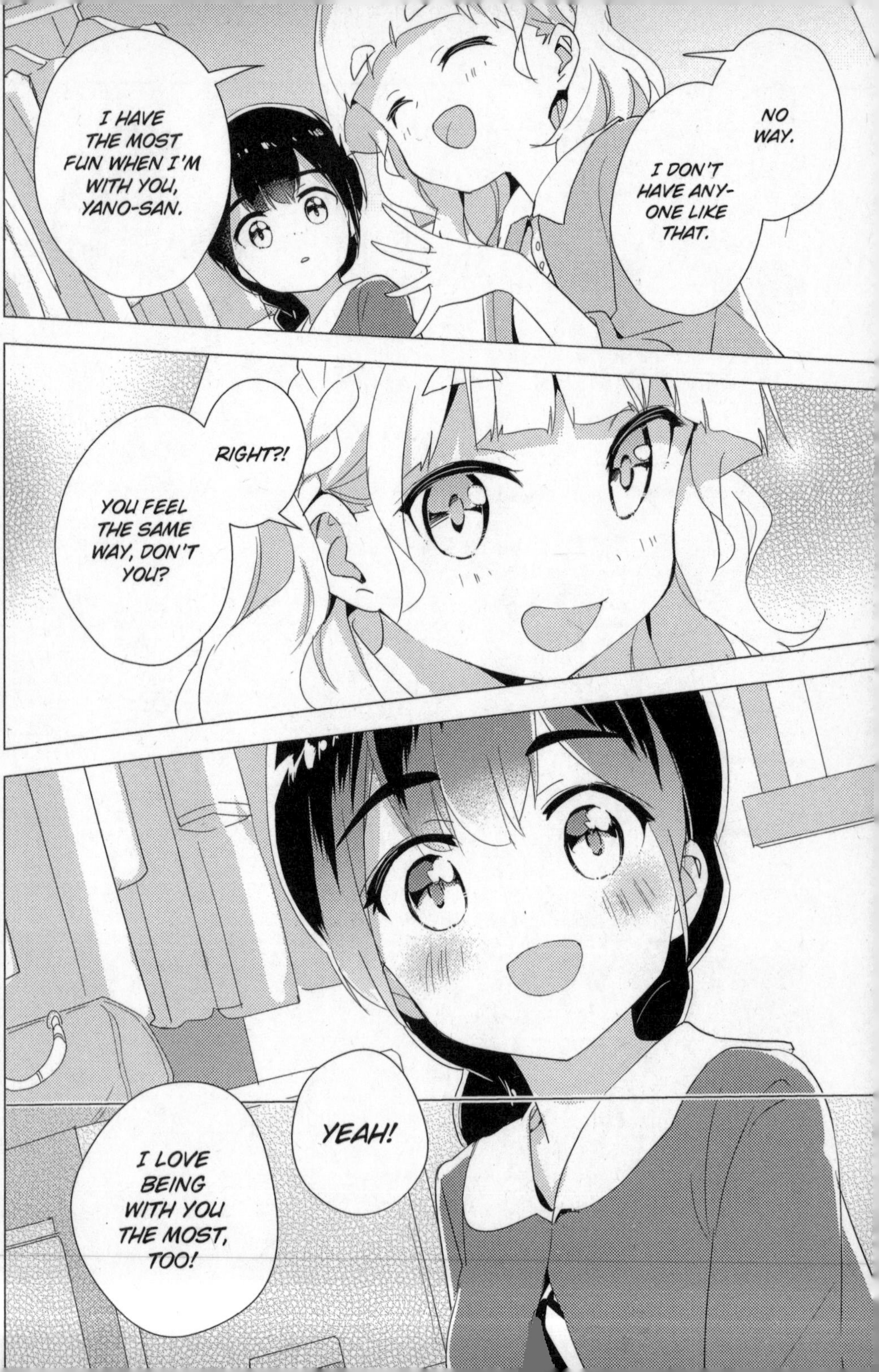
NO WAY.
I DON'T HAVE ANY-ONE LIKE THAT.
I HAVE THE MOST FUN WHEN I'M WITH YOU, YANO-SAN.
RIGHT?!
YOU FEEL THE SAME WAY, DON'T YOU?
YEAH!
I LOVE BEING WITH YOU THE MOST, TOO!

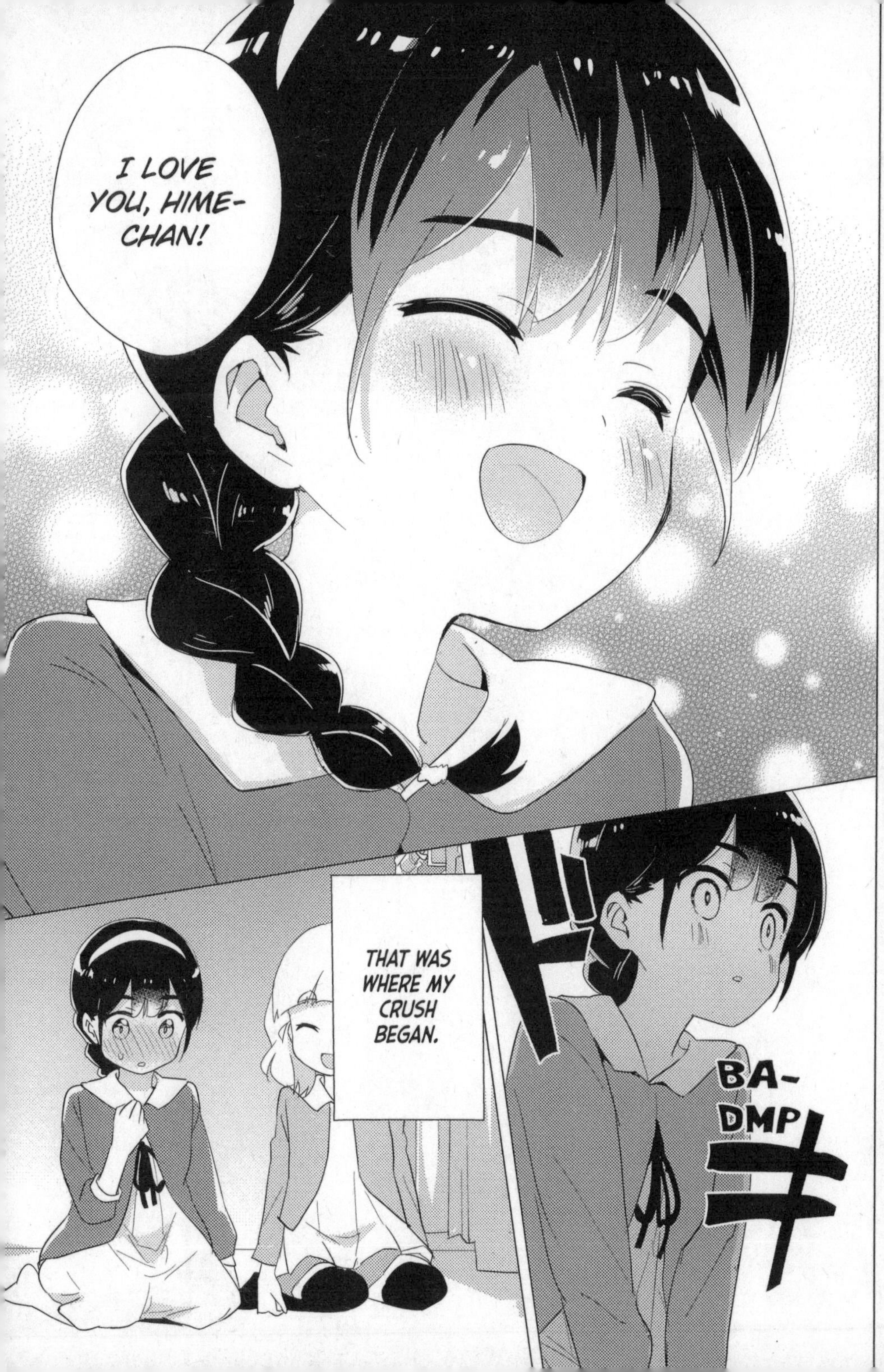
I LOVE YOU, HIME-CHAN!
BA-DMP
THAT WAS WHERE MY CRUSH BEGAN.

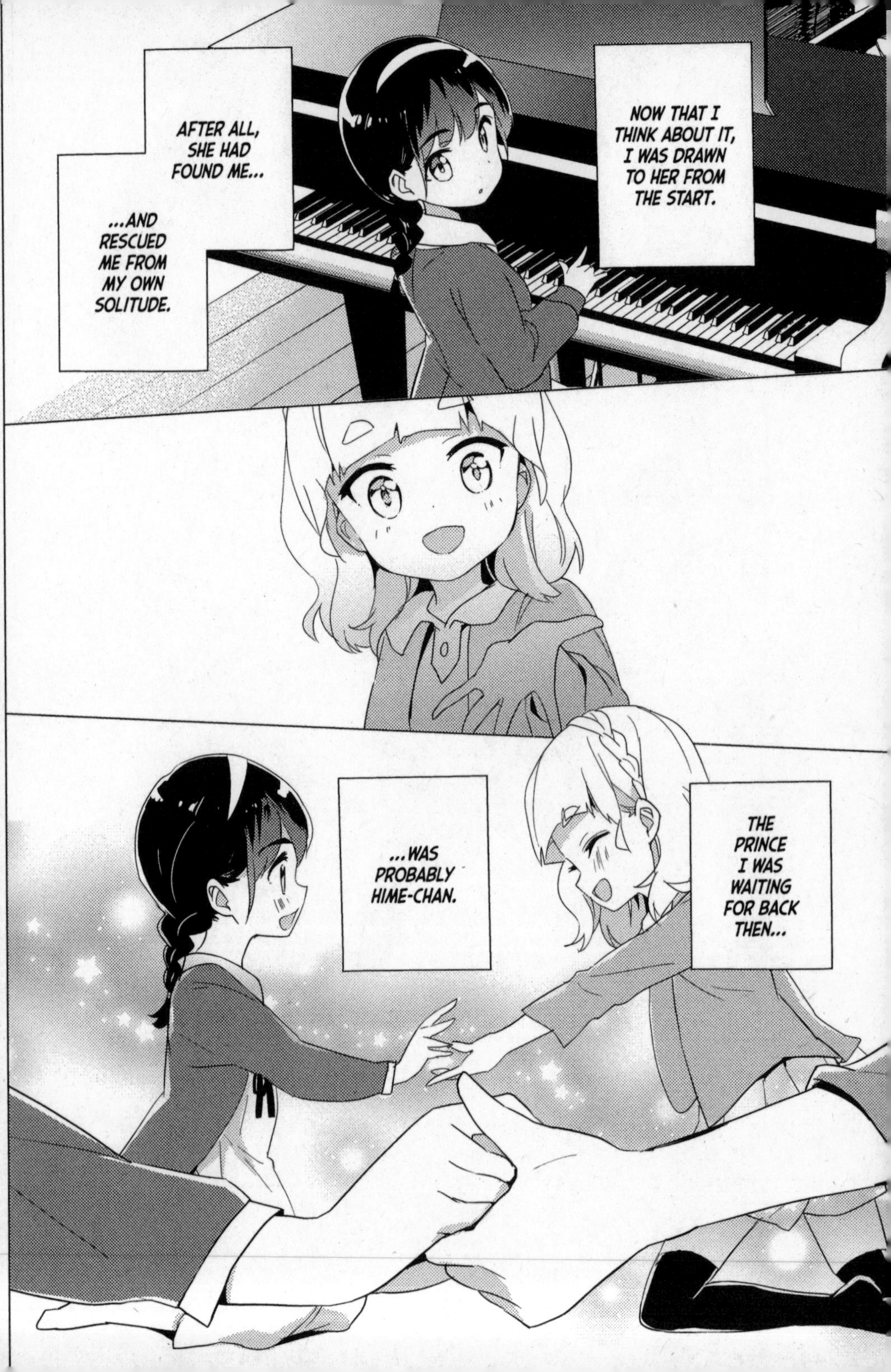
NOW THAT I THINK ABOUT IT, I WAS DRAWN TO HER FROM THE START.
AFTER ALL, SHE HAD FOUND ME...
...AND RESCUED ME FROM MY OWN SOLITUDE.
THE PRINCE I WAS WAITING FOR BACK THEN...
...WAS PROBABLY HIME-CHAN.

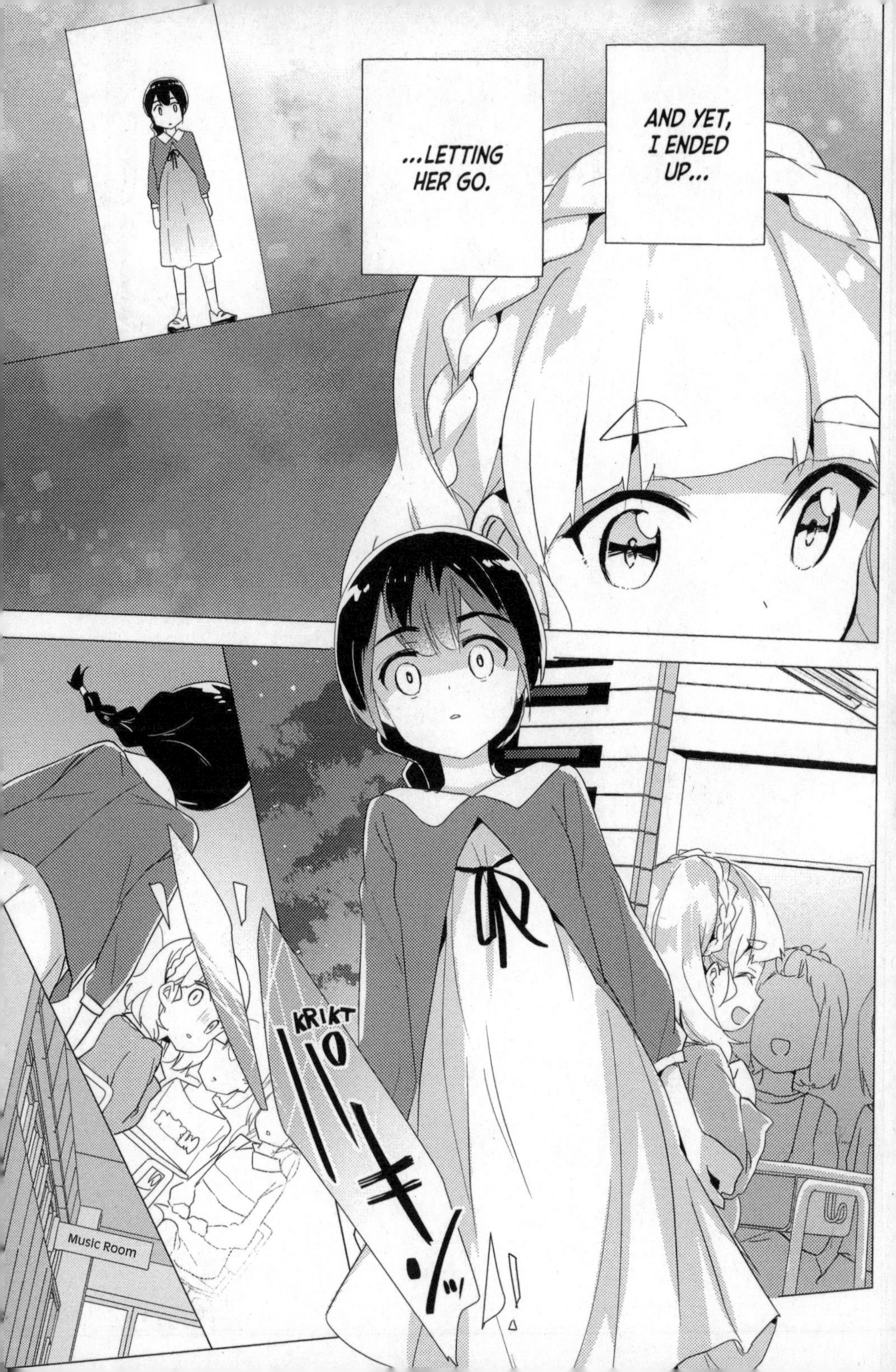
AND YET, I ENDED UP...
...LETTING HER GO.
KRIKT
Music Room

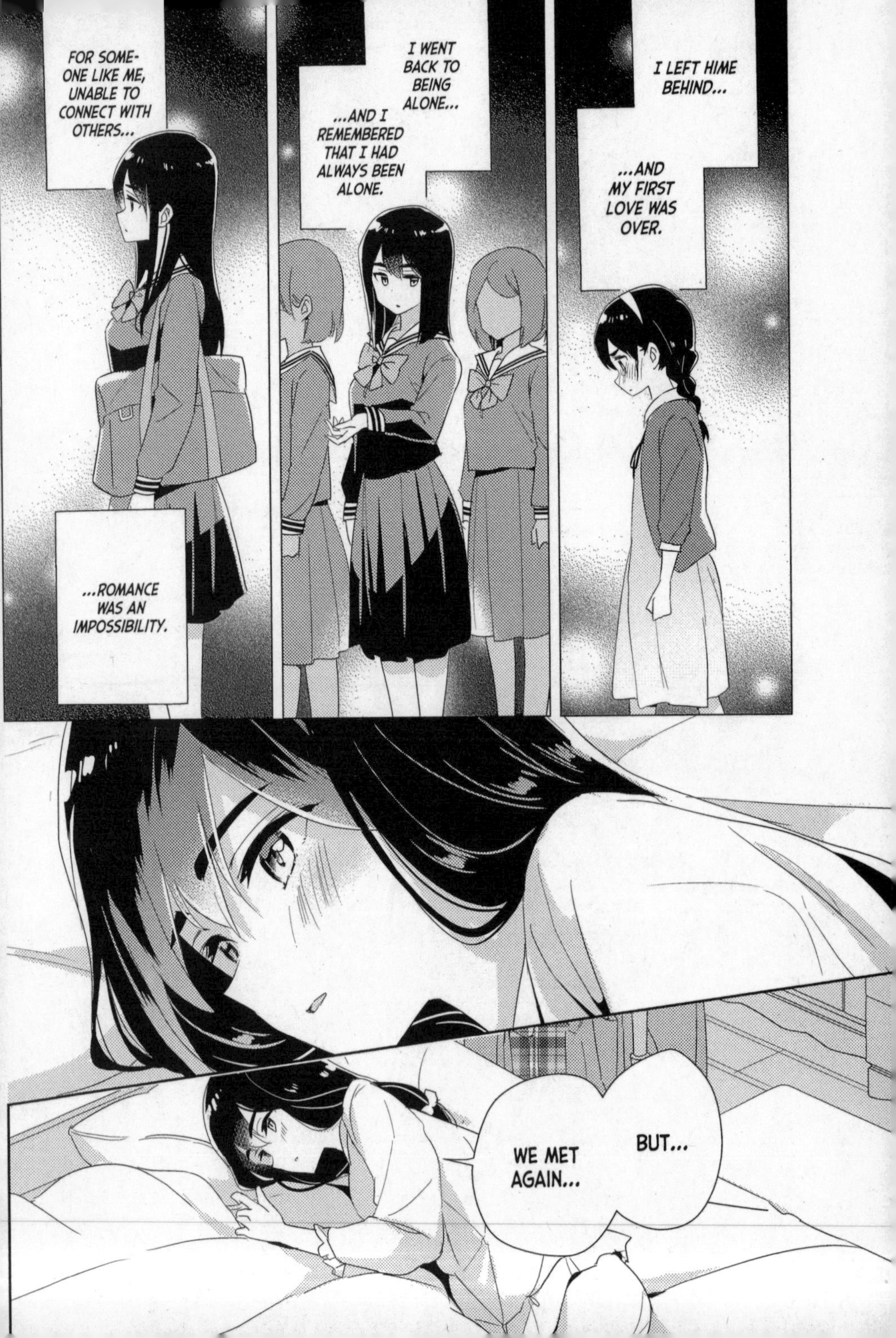
I LEFT HIME BEHIND...
...AND MY FIRST LOVE WAS OVER.
I WENT BACK TO BEING ALONE...
...AND I REMEMBERED THAT I HAD ALWAYS BEEN ALONE.
FOR SOME-ONE LIKE ME, UNABLE TO CONNECT WITH OTHERS...
...ROMANCE WAS AN IMPOSSIBILITY.
BUT...
WE MET AGAIN...

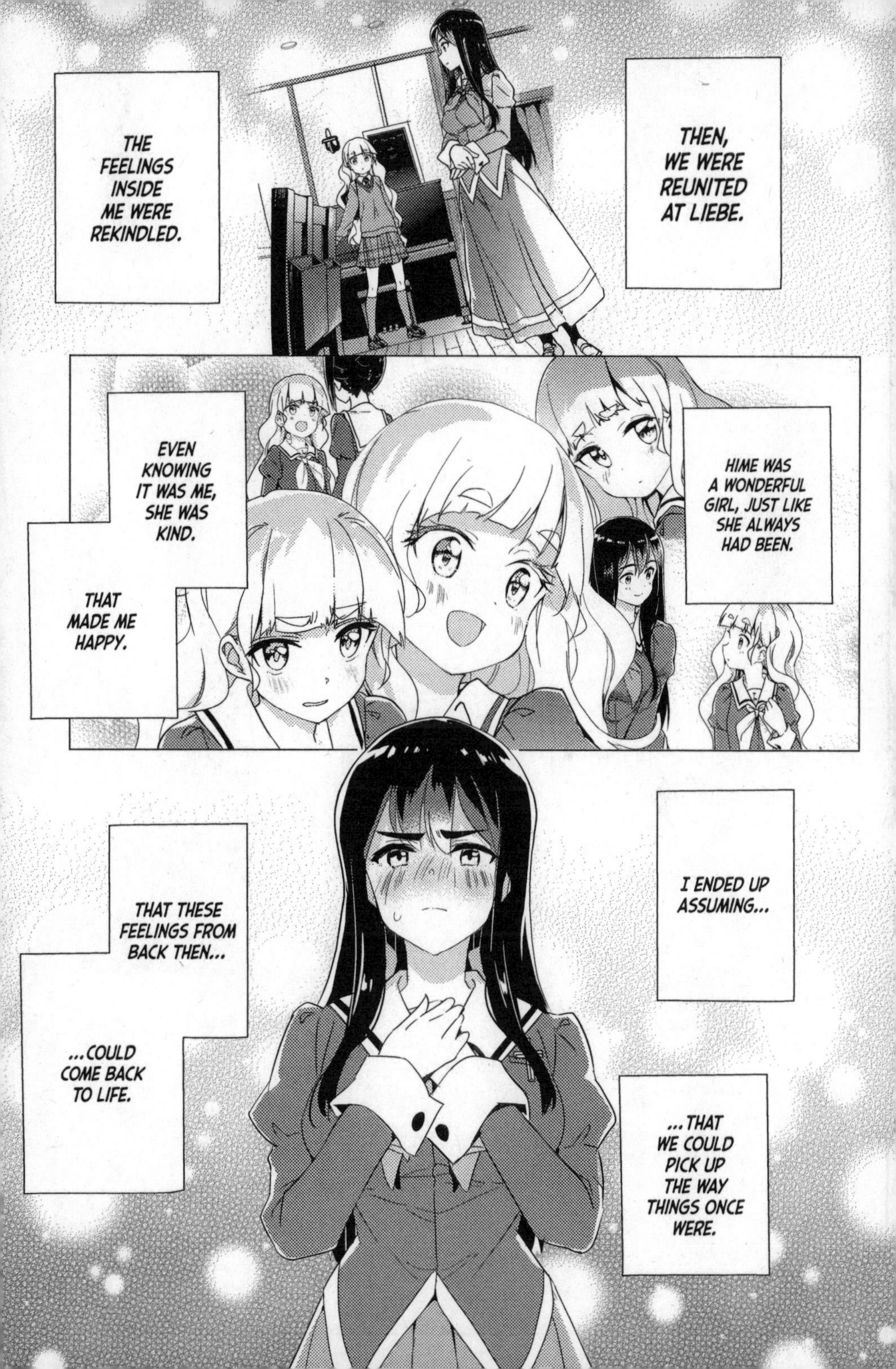
THEN, WE WERE REUNITED AT LIEBE.
THE FEELINGS INSIDE ME WERE REKINDLED.
HIME WAS A WONDERFUL GIRL, JUST LIKE SHE ALWAYS HAD BEEN.
EVEN KNOWING IT WAS ME, SHE WAS KIND.
THAT MADE ME HAPPY.
I ENDED UP ASSUMING...
THAT THESE FEELINGS FROM BACK THEN...
...COULD COME BACK TO LIFE.
...THAT WE COULD PICK UP THE WAY THINGS ONCE WERE.

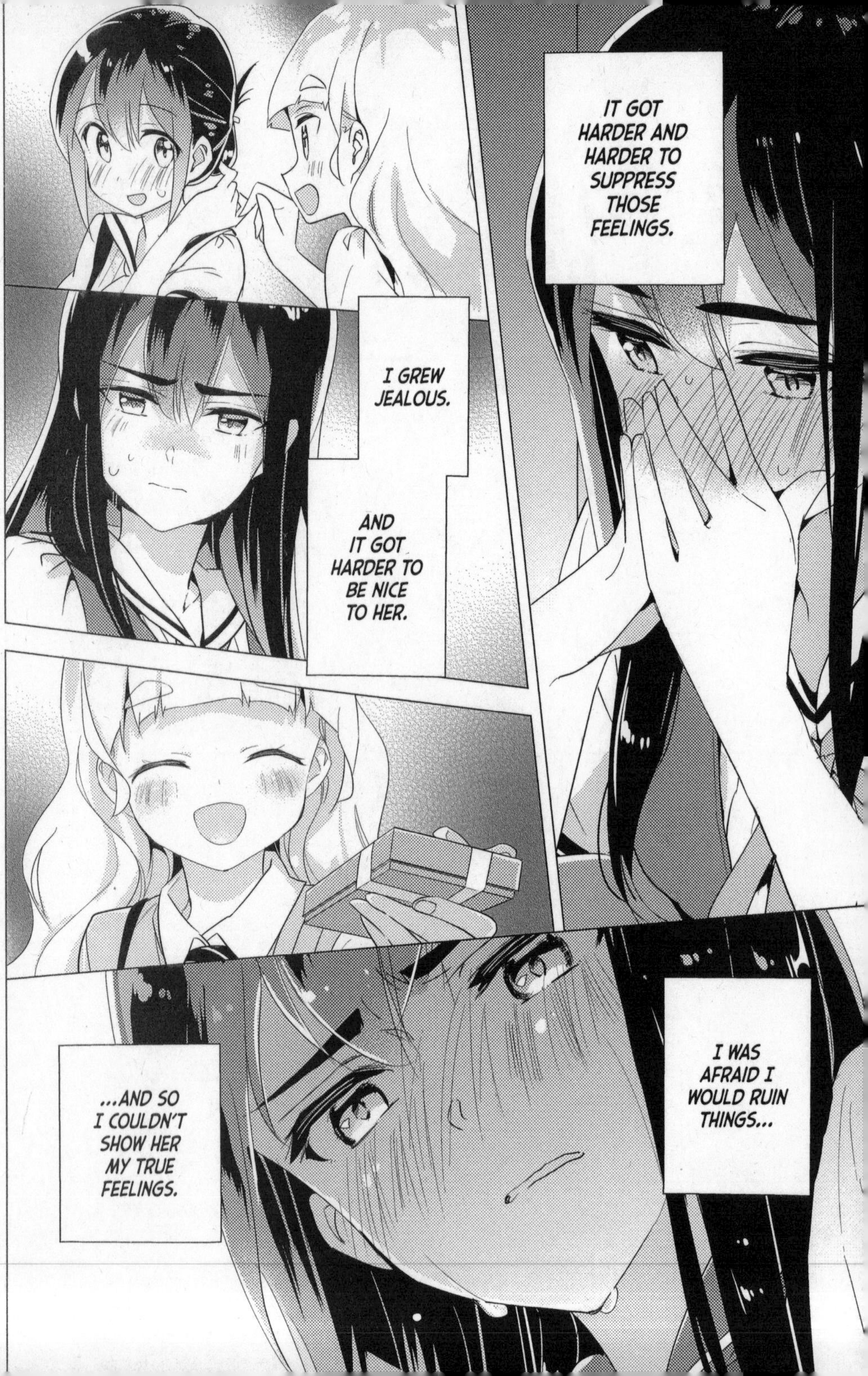
IT GOT HARDER AND HARDER TO SUPPRESS THOSE FEELINGS.
I GREW JEALOUS.
AND IT GOT HARDER TO BE NICE TO HER.
I WAS AFRAID I WOULD RUIN THINGS...
...AND SO I COULDN'T SHOW HER MY TRUE FEELINGS.

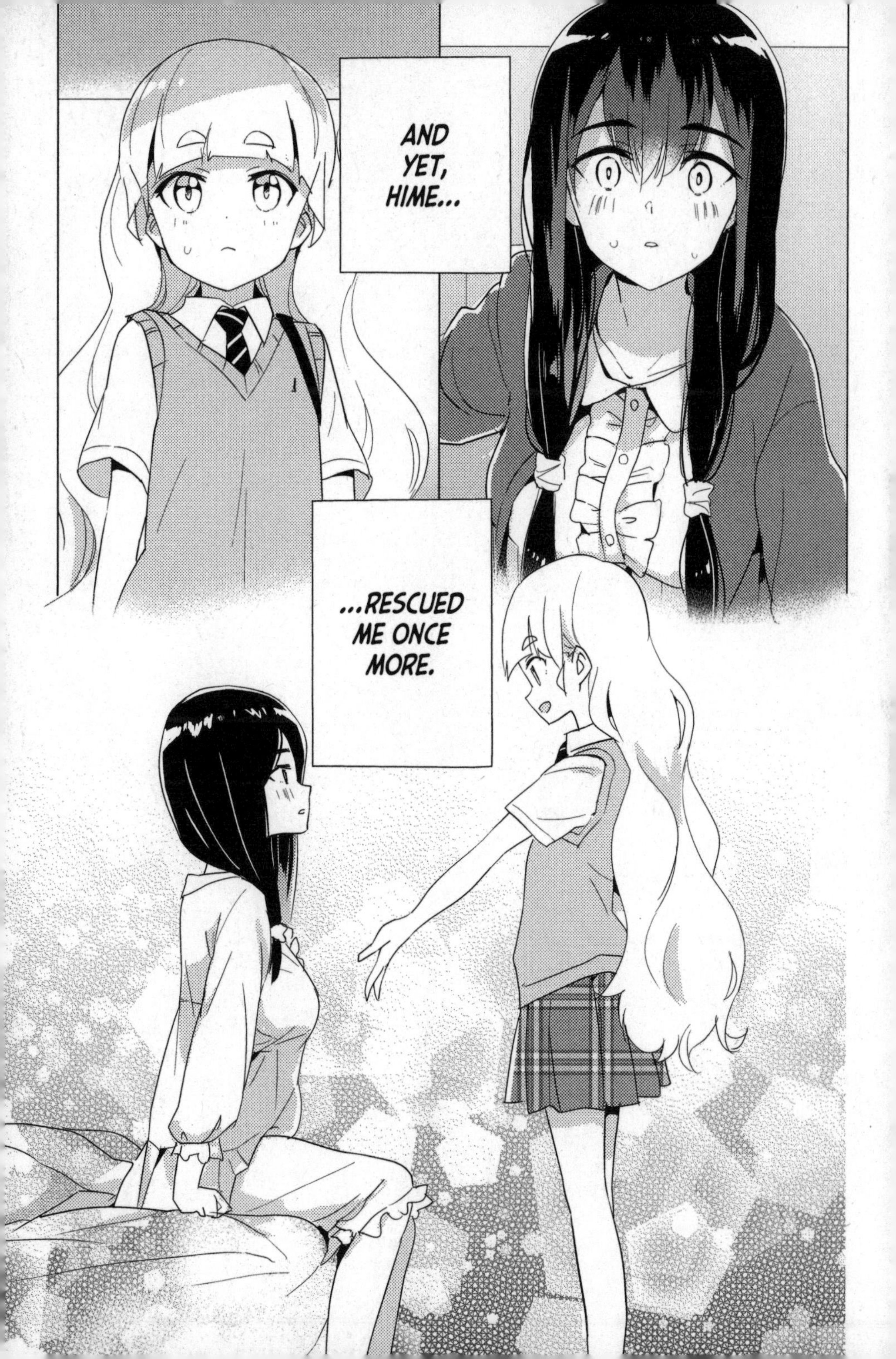
AND YET, HIME...
...RESCUED ME ONCE MORE.

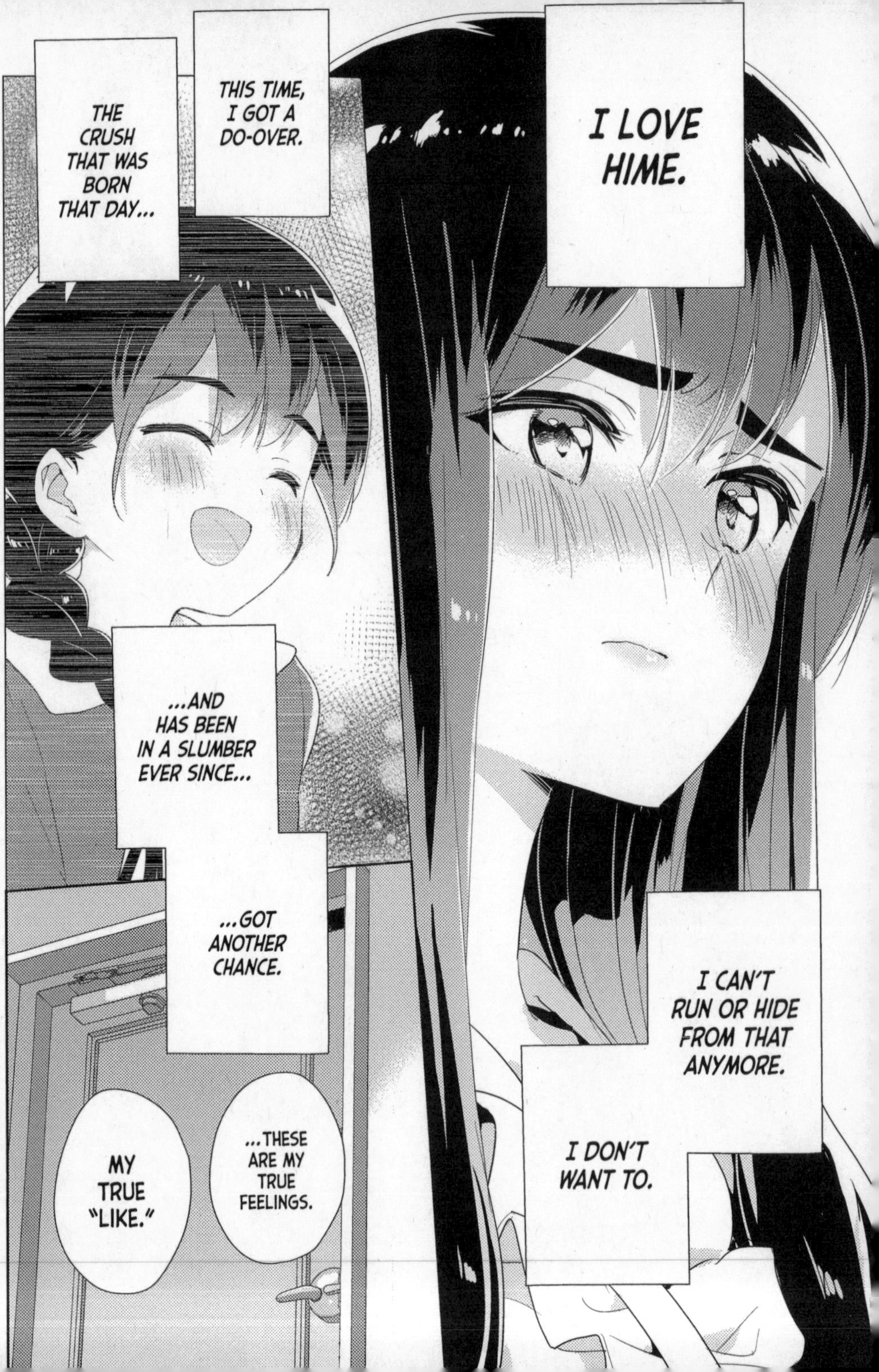
I LOVE HIME.
I CAN'T RUN OR HIDE FROM THAT ANYMORE.
I DON'T WANT TO.
THIS TIME, I GOT A DO-OVER.
THE CRUSH THAT WAS BORN THAT DAY...
...AND HAS BEEN IN A SLUMBER EVER SINCE...
...GOT ANOTHER CHANCE.
...THESE ARE MY TRUE FEELINGS.
MY TRUE "LIKE."

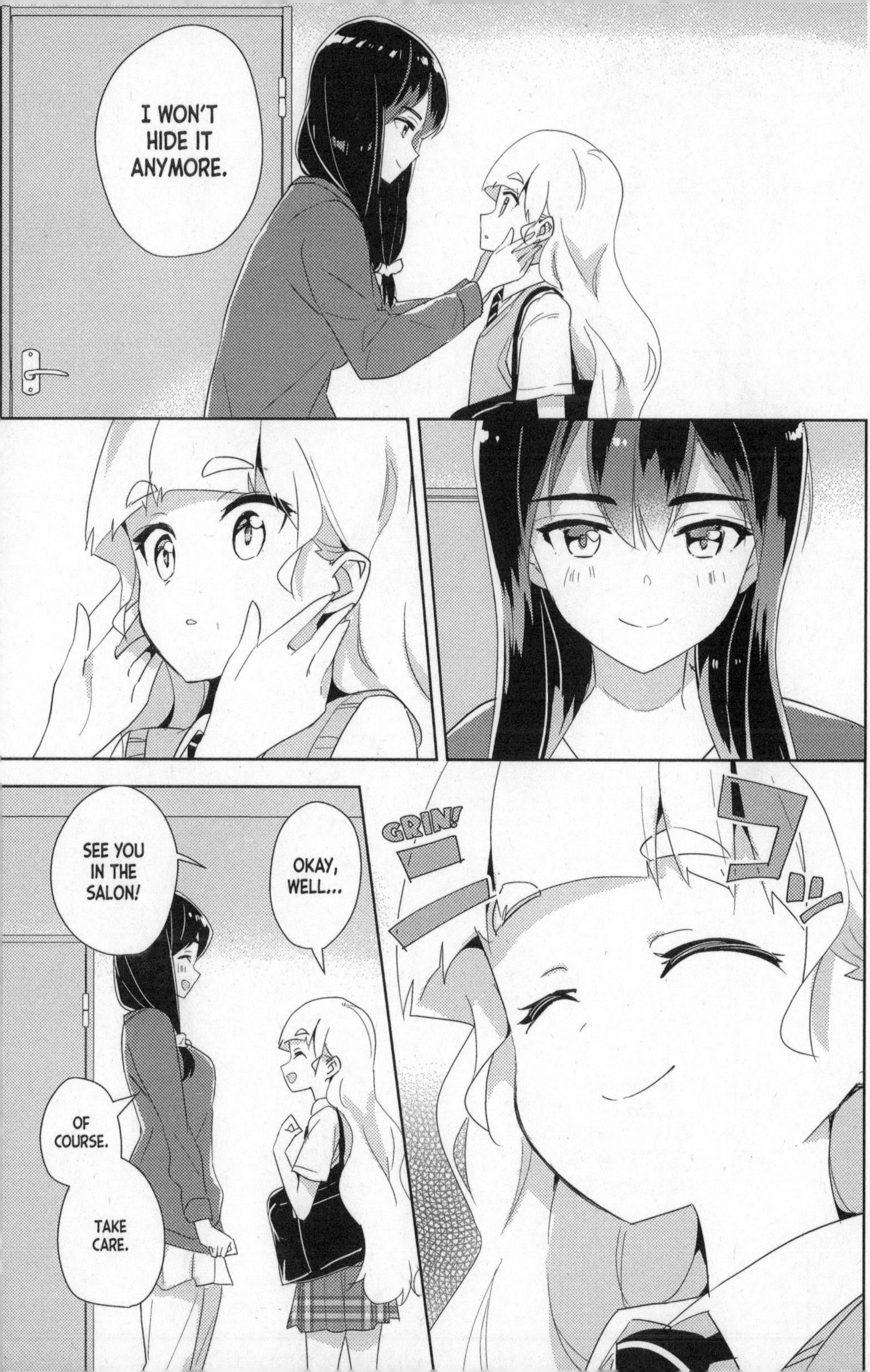
I WON'T HIDE IT ANYMORE.
GRIN!
OKAY, WELL...
SEE YOU IN THE SALON!
OF COURSE.
TAKE CARE.

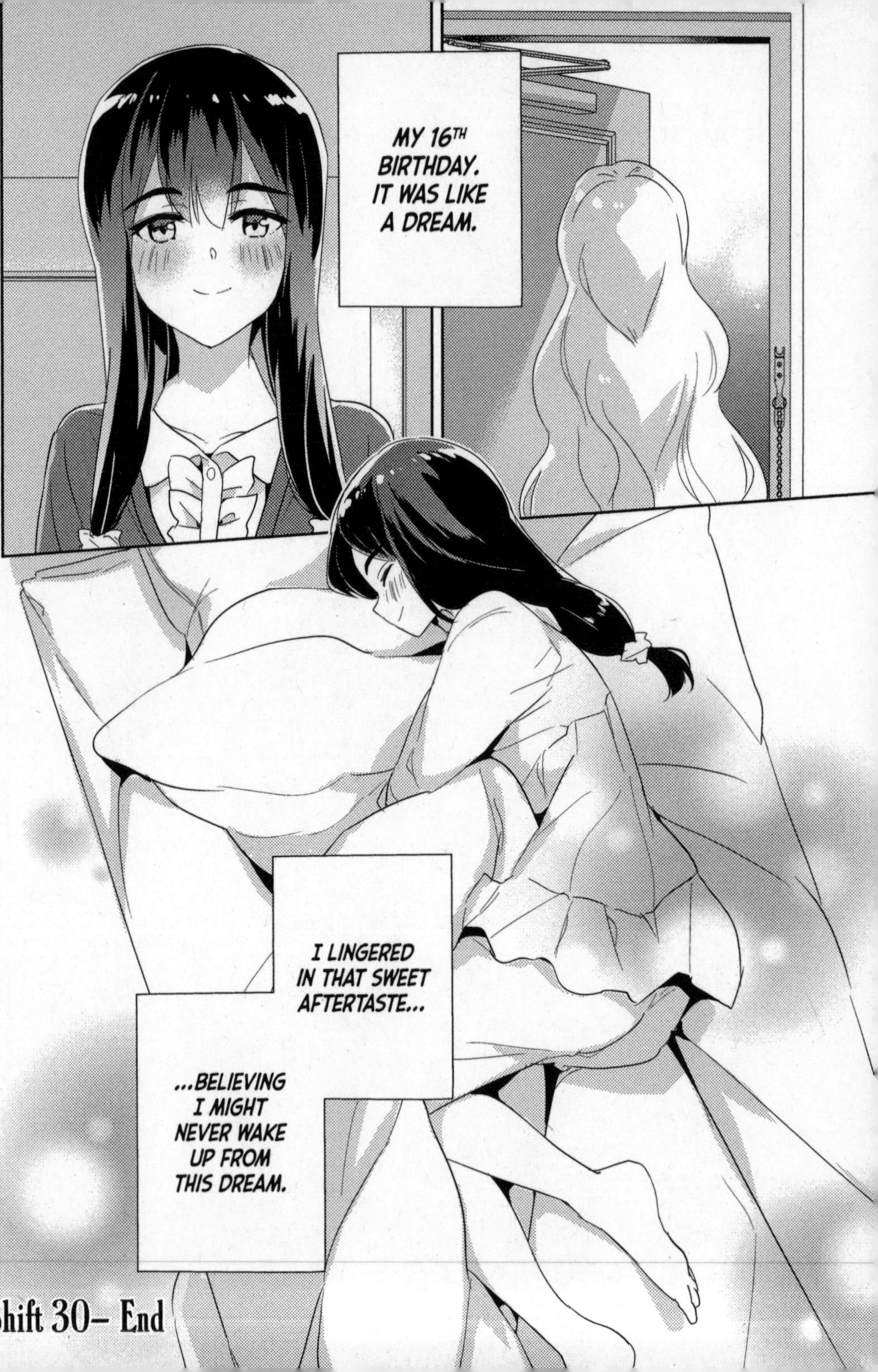
MY 16TH BIRTHDAY. IT WAS LIKE A DREAM.
I LINGERED IN THAT SWEET AFTERTASTE...
...BELIEVING I MIGHT NEVER WAKE UP FROM THIS DREAM.

Shift 30– End

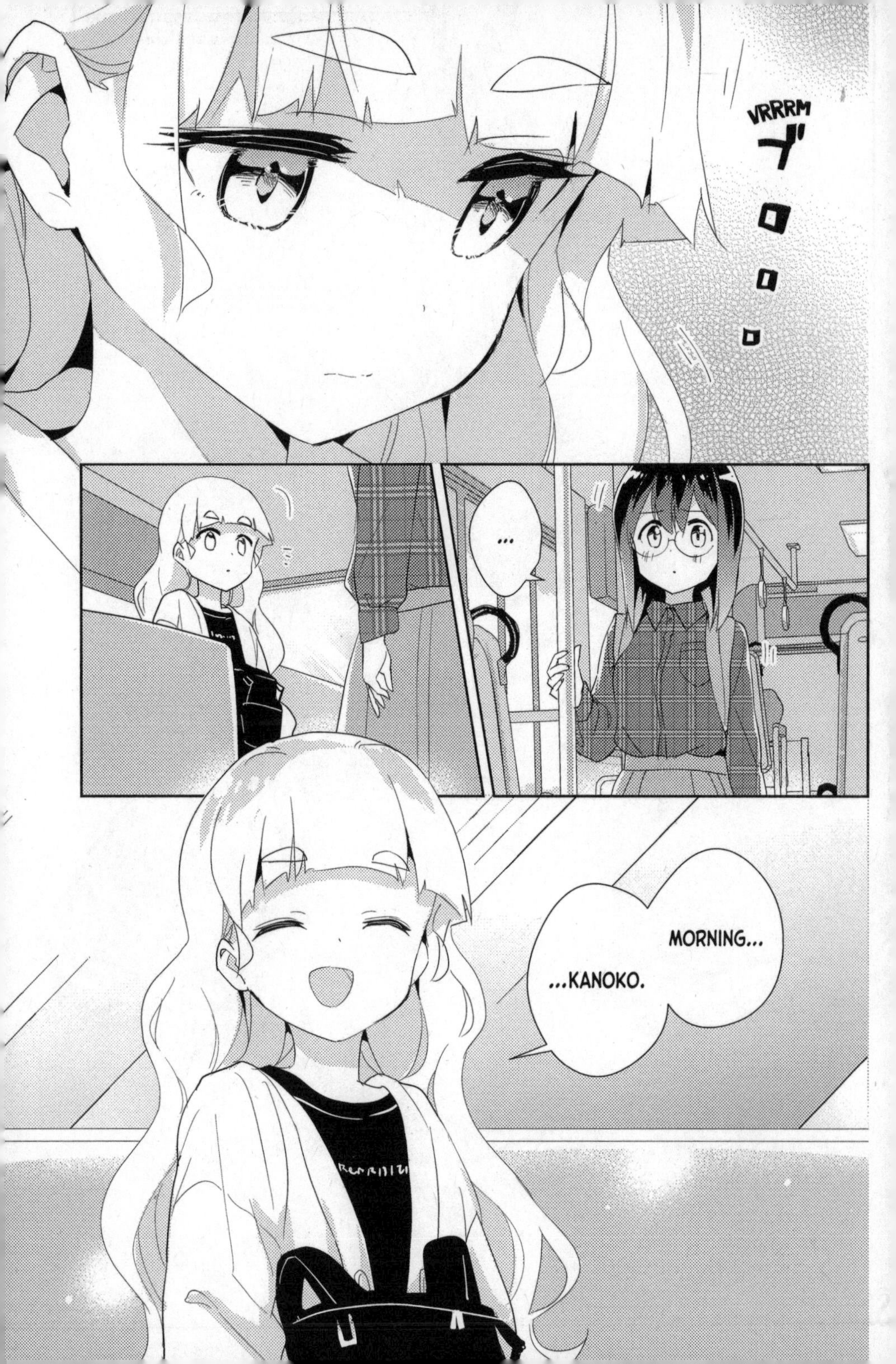
VRRRM
ブロロロ
...
MORNING...
...KANOKO.

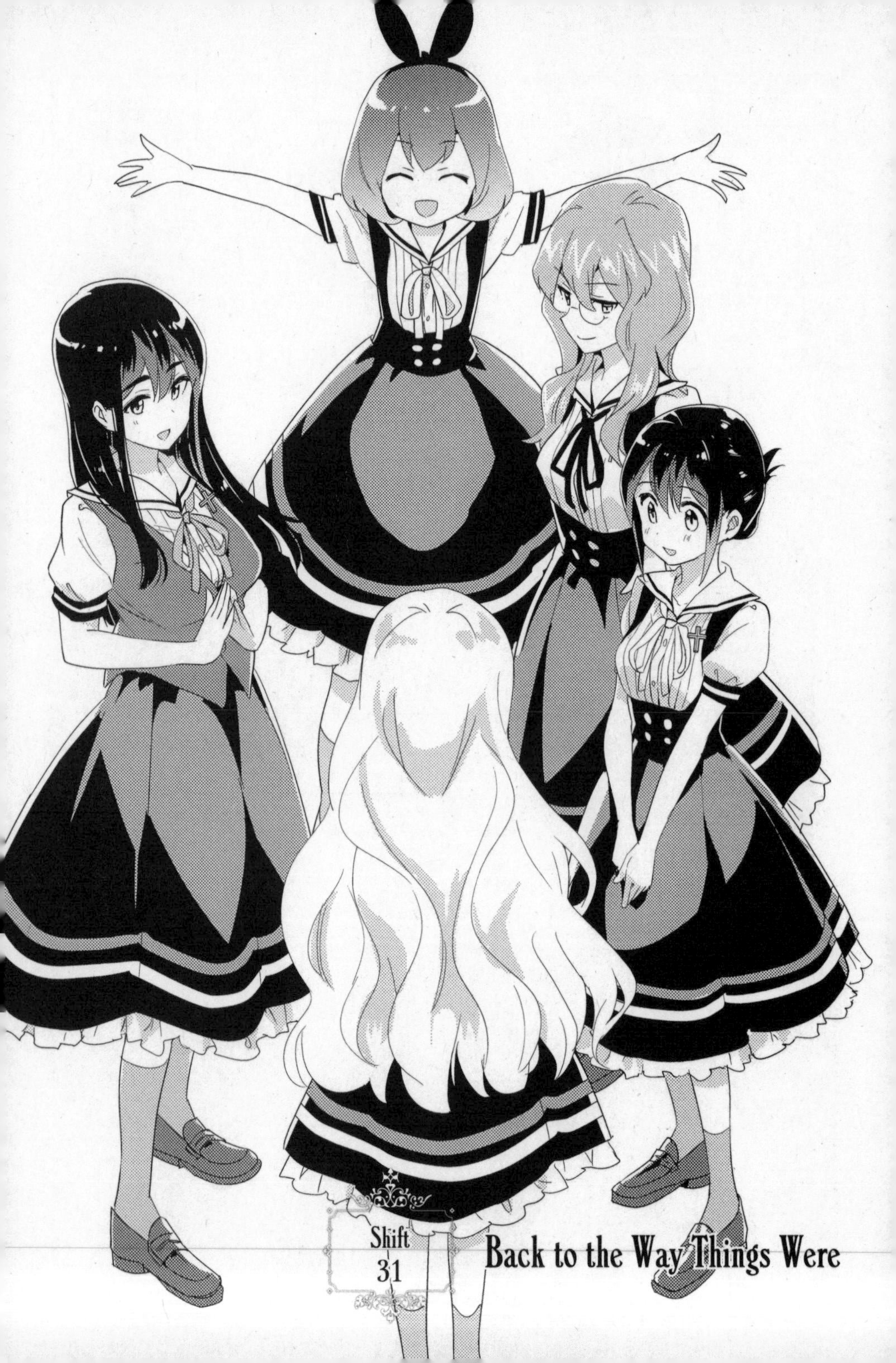

Shift 31 Back to the Way Things Were

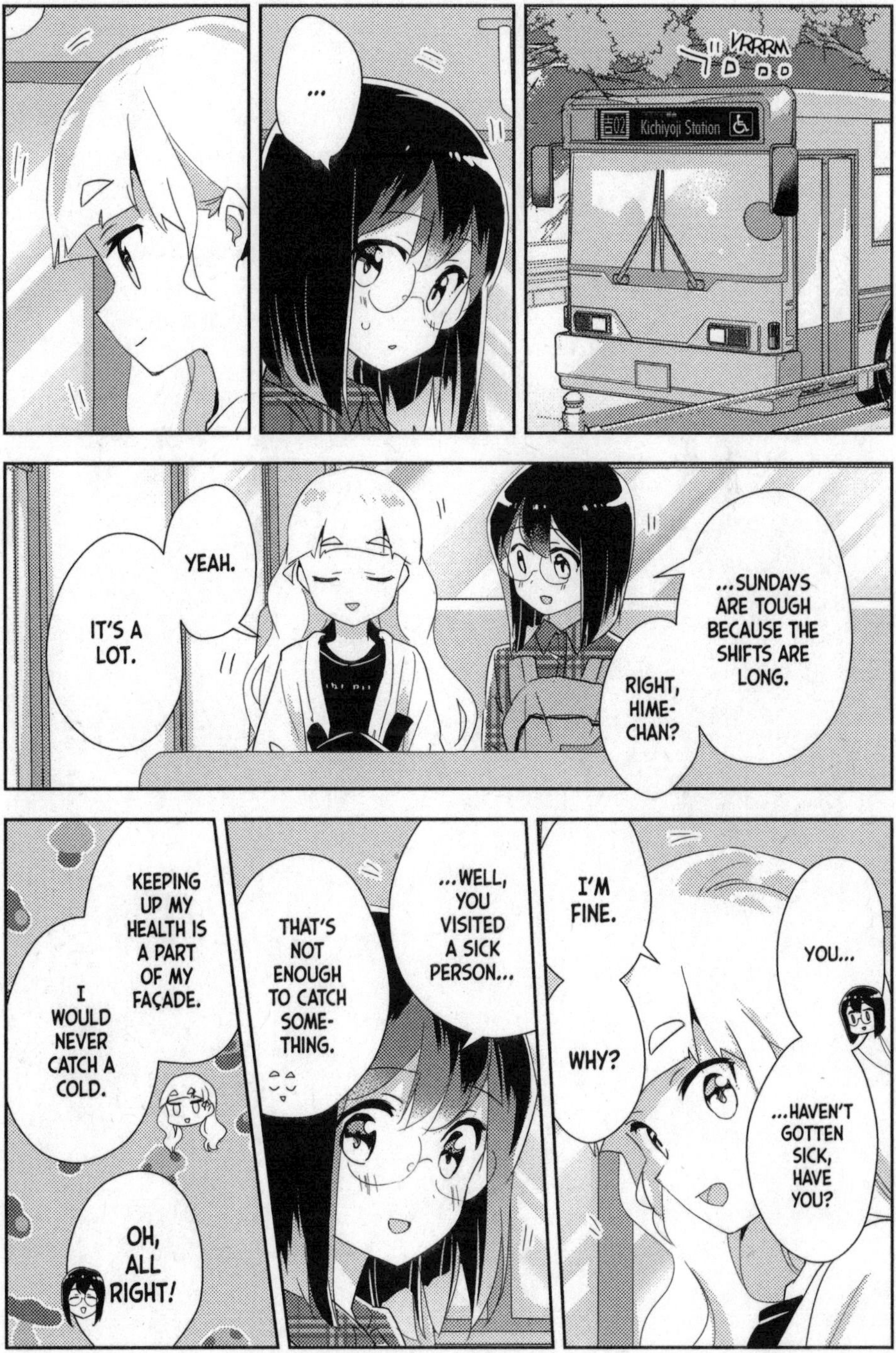
VRRRM
Kichiyoji Station
...
...SUNDAYS ARE TOUGH BECAUSE THE SHIFTS ARE LONG.
RIGHT, HIME-CHAN?
YEAH.
IT'S A LOT.
YOU...
...HAVEN'T GOTTEN SICK, HAVE YOU?
I'M FINE.
WHY?
...WELL, YOU VISITED A SICK PERSON...
THAT'S NOT ENOUGH TO CATCH SOMETHING.
KEEPING UP MY HEALTH IS A PART OF MY FAÇADE.
I WOULD NEVER CATCH A COLD.
OH, ALL RIGHT!

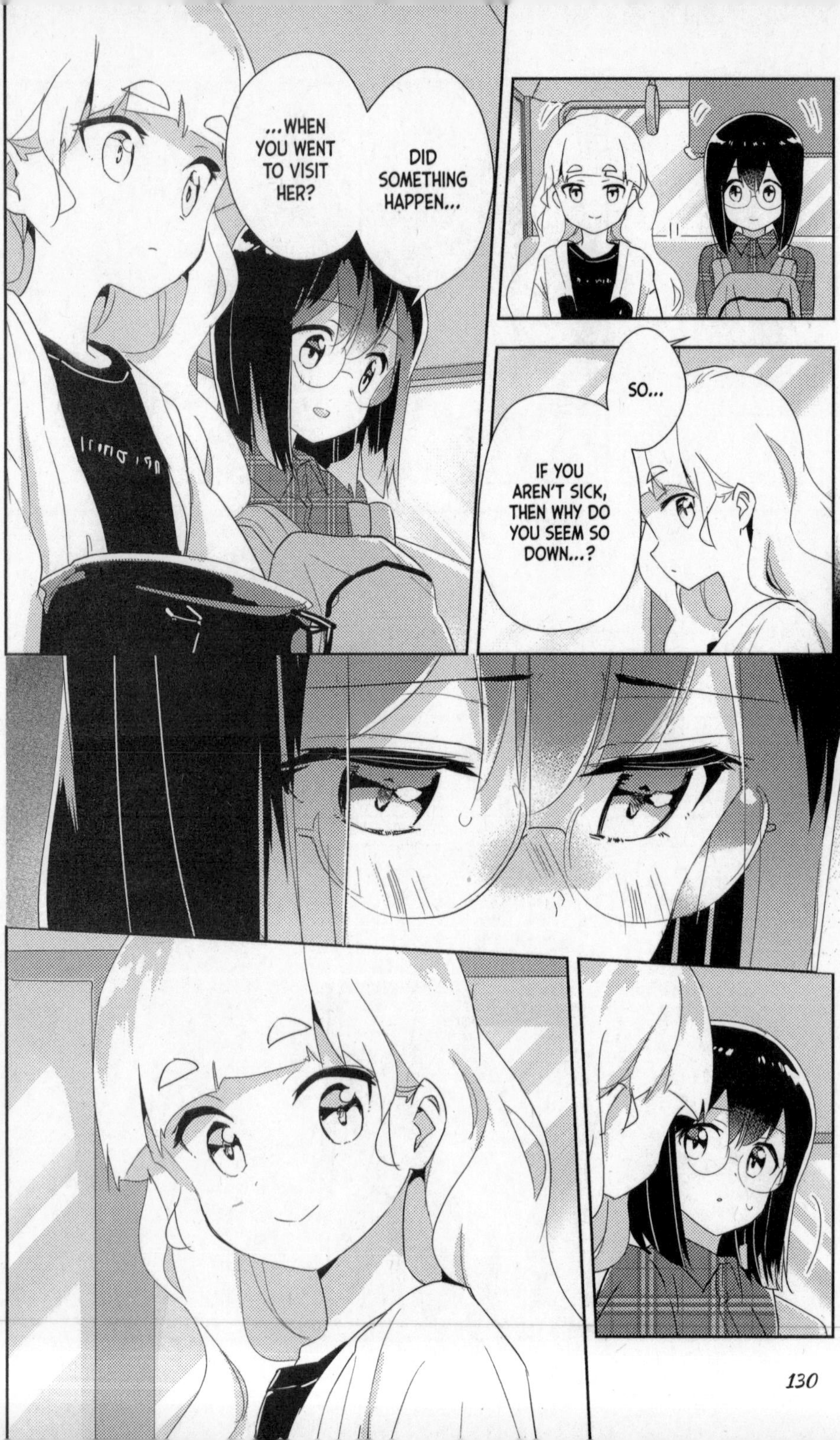
SO...
IF YOU AREN'T SICK, THEN WHY DO YOU SEEM SO DOWN...?
DID SOMETHING HAPPEN...
...WHEN YOU WENT TO VISIT HER?

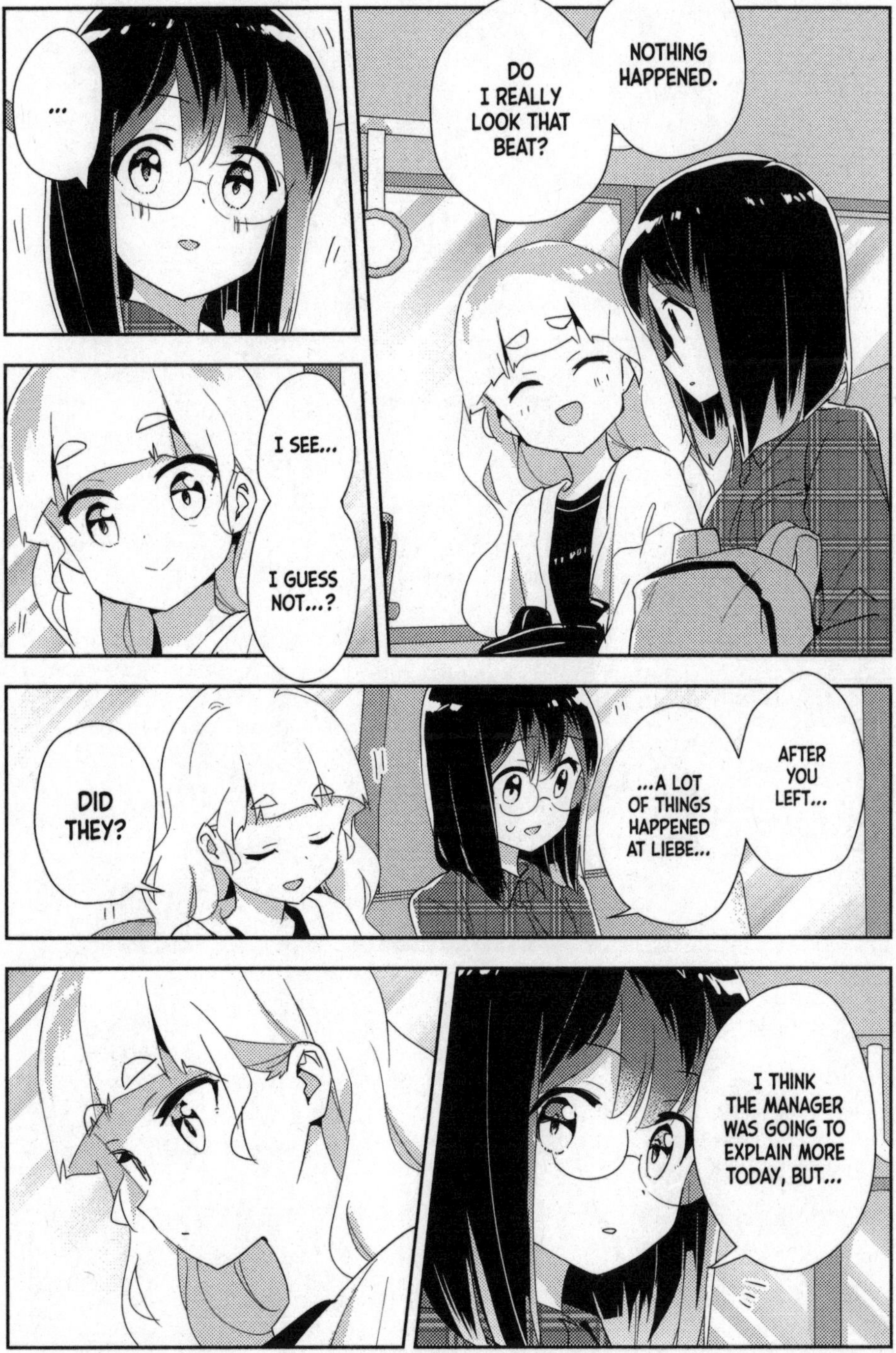
NOTHING HAPPENED.
DO I REALLY LOOK THAT BEAT?
...
I SEE...
I GUESS NOT...?
AFTER YOU LEFT...
...A LOT OF THINGS HAPPENED AT LIEBE...
DID THEY?
I THINK THE MANAGER WAS GOING TO EXPLAIN MORE TODAY, BUT...

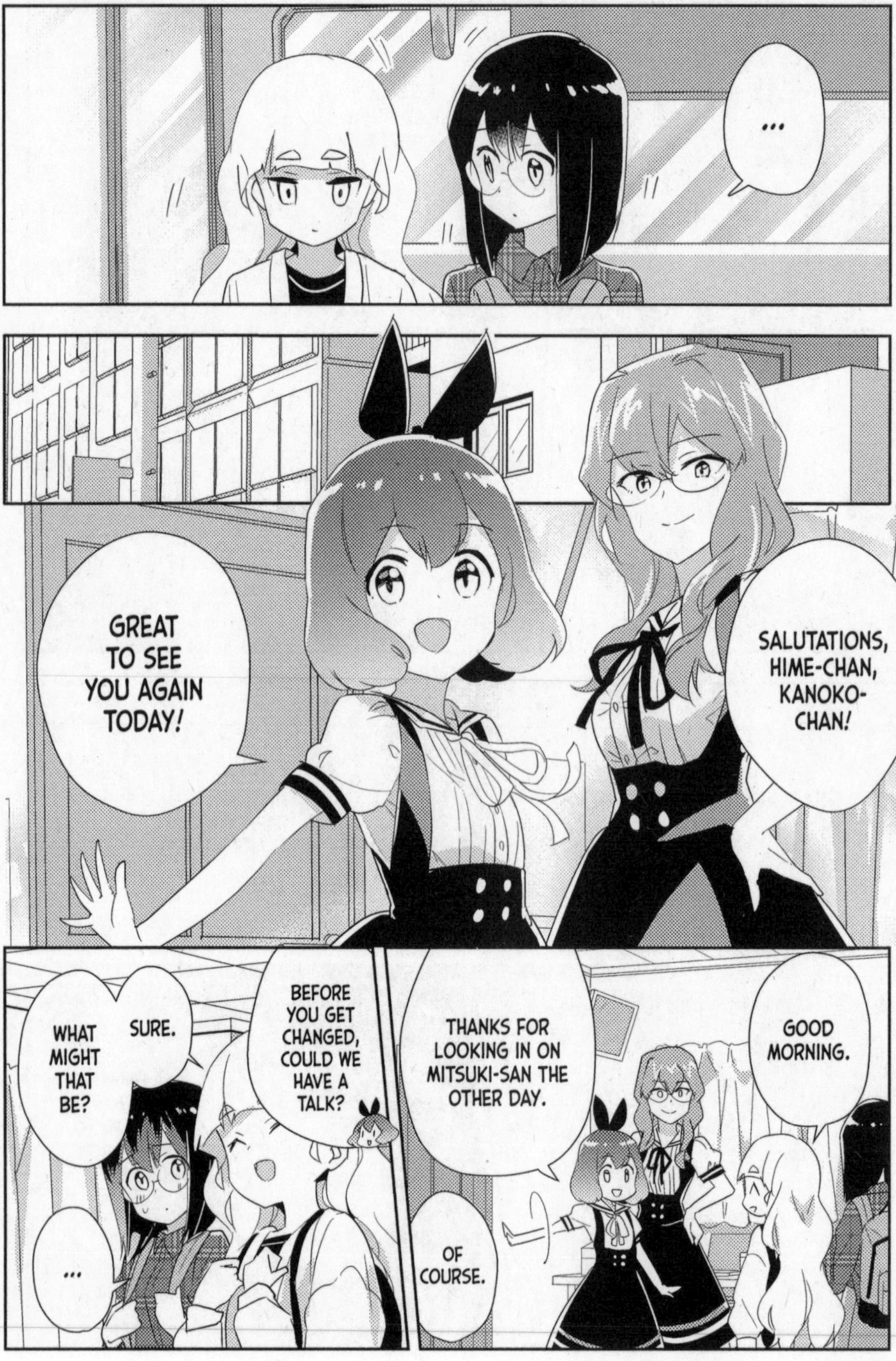
...
SALUTATIONS, HIME-CHAN, KANOKO-CHAN!
GREAT TO SEE YOU AGAIN TODAY!
GOOD MORNING.
THANKS FOR LOOKING IN ON MITSUKI-SAN THE OTHER DAY.
OF COURSE.
BEFORE YOU GET CHANGED, COULD WE HAVE A TALK?
SURE.
WHAT MIGHT THAT BE?
...

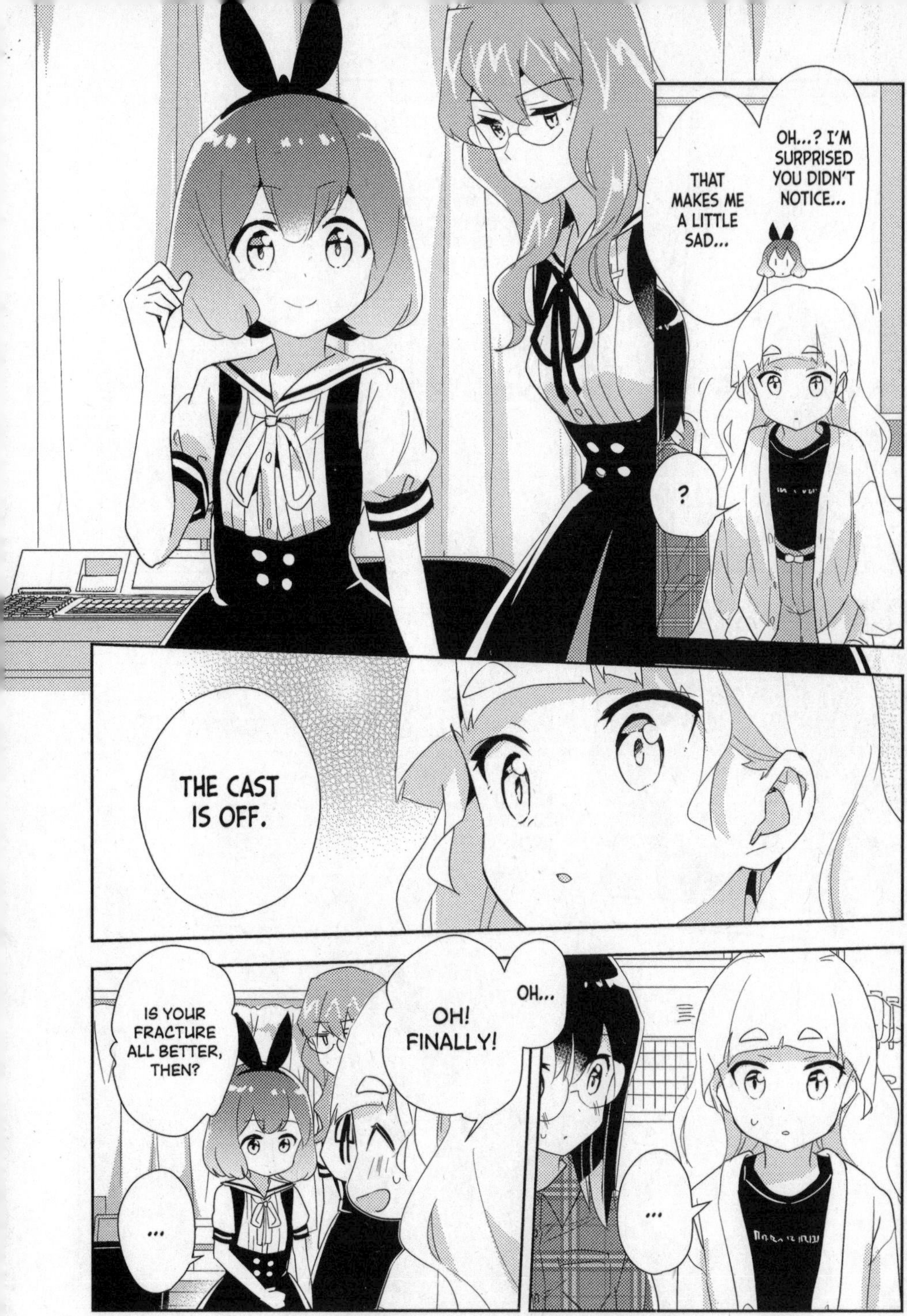
OH...? I'M SURPRISED YOU DIDN'T NOTICE...
THAT MAKES ME A LITTLE SAD...
?
THE CAST IS OFF.
...
OH...
OH! FINALLY!
IS YOUR FRACTURE ALL BETTER, THEN?
...

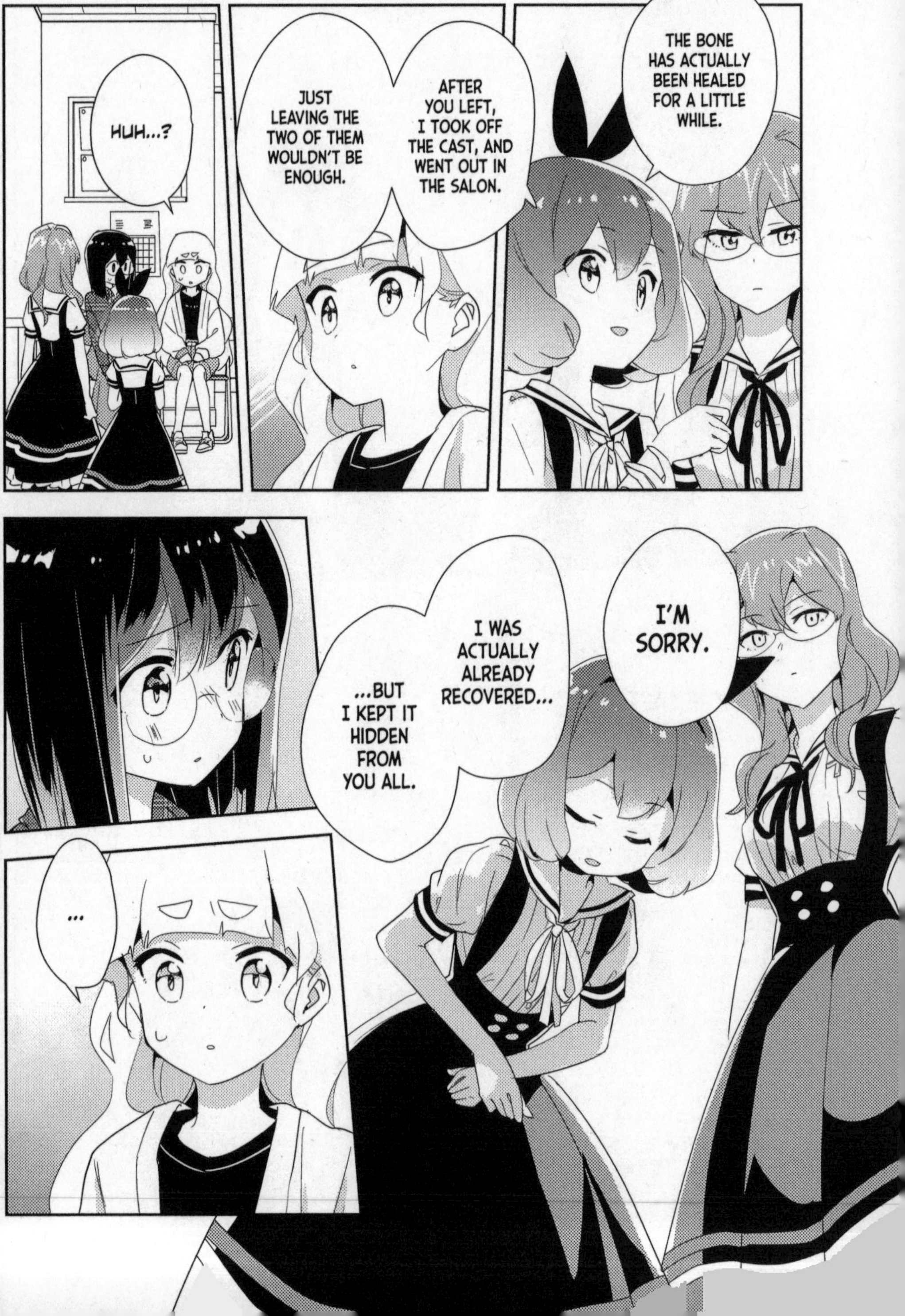
THE BONE HAS ACTUALLY BEEN HEALED FOR A LITTLE WHILE.
AFTER YOU LEFT, I TOOK OFF THE CAST, AND WENT OUT IN THE SALON.
JUST LEAVING THE TWO OF THEM WOULDN'T BE ENOUGH.
HUH...?
I'M SORRY.
I WAS ACTUALLY ALREADY RECOVERED...
...BUT I KEPT IT HIDDEN FROM YOU ALL.
...

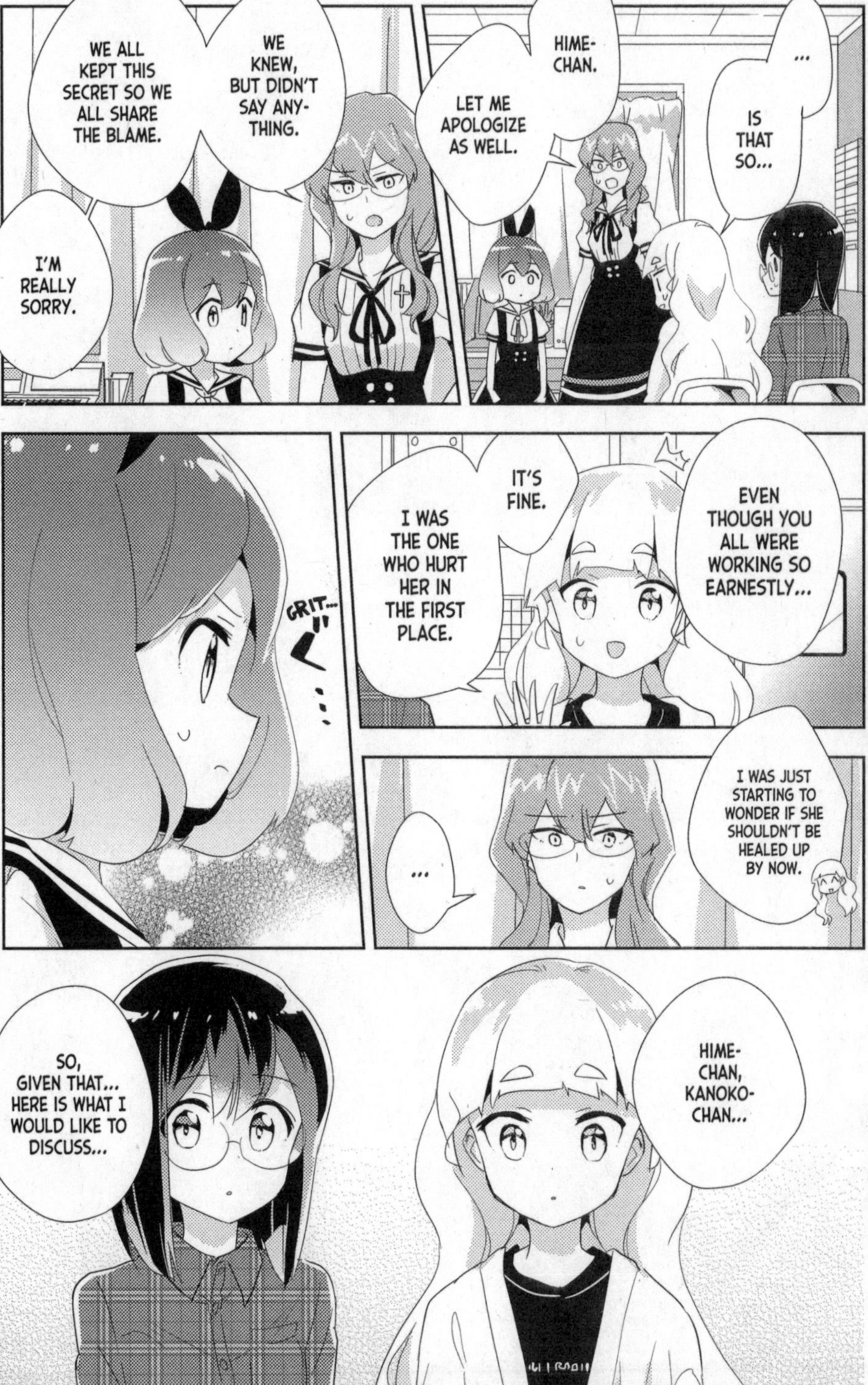
...
IS THAT SO...
HIME-CHAN.
LET ME APOLOGIZE AS WELL.
WE KNEW, BUT DIDN'T SAY ANY-THING.
WE ALL KEPT THIS SECRET SO WE ALL SHARE THE BLAME.
I'M REALLY SORRY.
EVEN THOUGH YOU ALL WERE WORKING SO EARNESTLY...
IT'S FINE.
I WAS THE ONE WHO HURT HER IN THE FIRST PLACE.
I WAS JUST STARTING TO WONDER IF SHE SHOULDN'T BE HEALED UP BY NOW.
...
GRIT...
HIME-CHAN, KANOKO-CHAN...
SO, GIVEN THAT... HERE IS WHAT I WOULD LIKE TO DISCUSS...

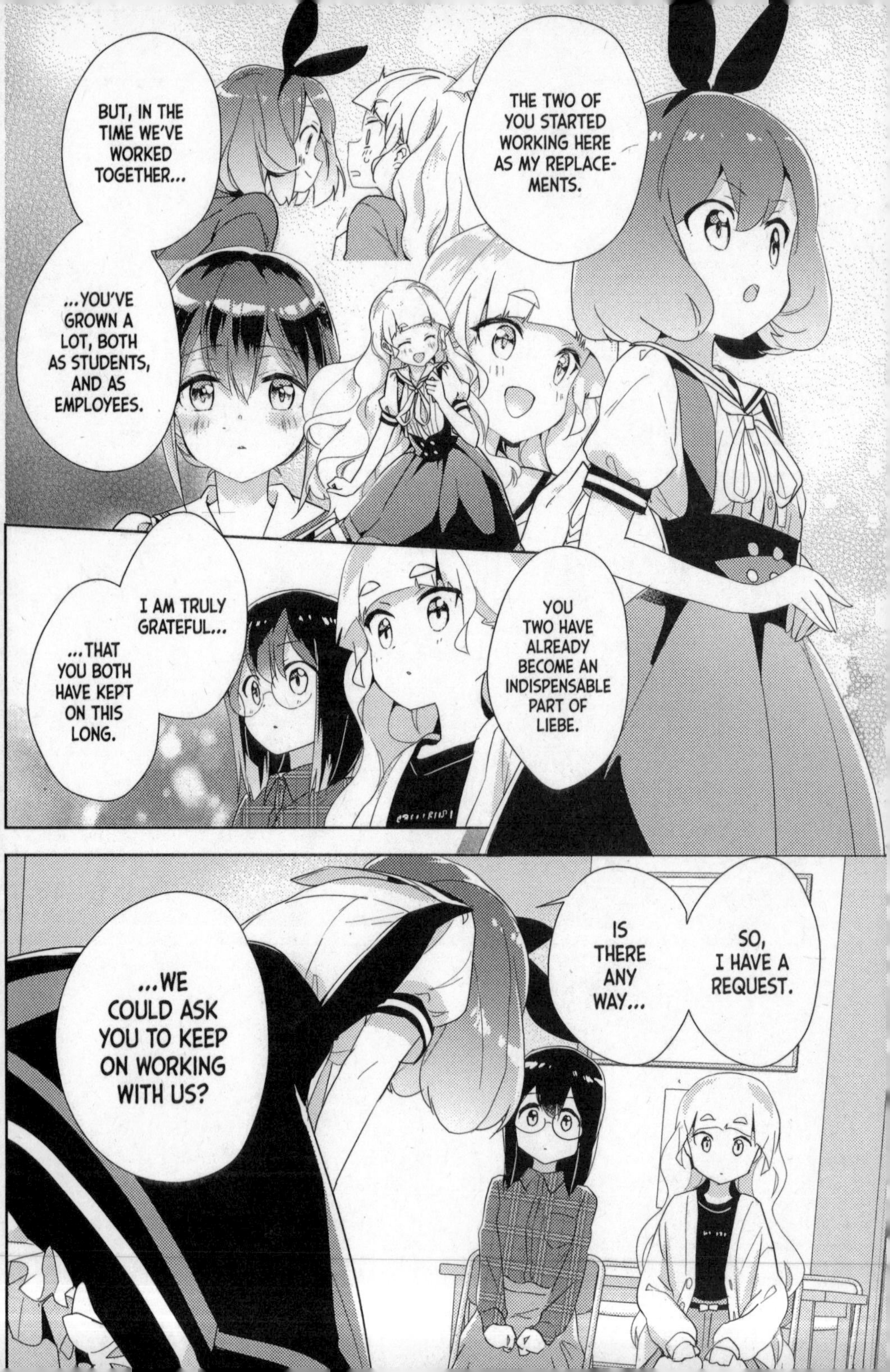
THE TWO OF YOU STARTED WORKING HERE AS MY REPLACE-MENTS.
BUT, IN THE TIME WE'VE WORKED TOGETHER...
...YOU'VE GROWN A LOT, BOTH AS STUDENTS, AND AS EMPLOYEES.
YOU TWO HAVE ALREADY BECOME AN INDISPENSABLE PART OF LIEBE.
I AM TRULY GRATEFUL...
...THAT YOU BOTH HAVE KEPT ON THIS LONG.
SO, I HAVE A REQUEST.
IS THERE ANY WAY...
...WE COULD ASK YOU TO KEEP ON WORKING WITH US?

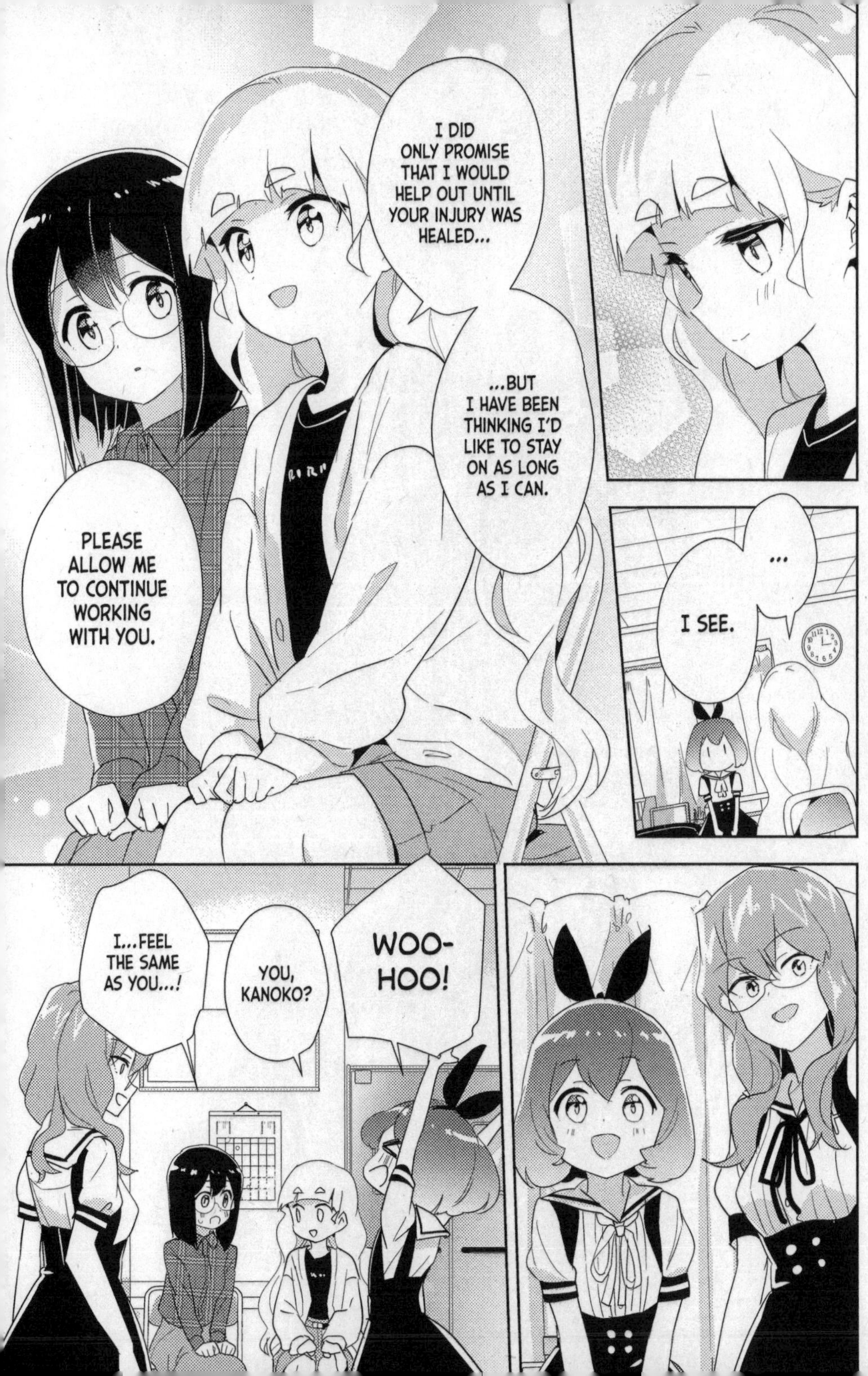
...
I SEE.
I DID ONLY PROMISE THAT I WOULD HELP OUT UNTIL YOUR INJURY WAS HEALED...
...BUT I HAVE BEEN THINKING I'D LIKE TO STAY ON AS LONG AS I CAN.
PLEASE ALLOW ME TO CONTINUE WORKING WITH YOU.
WOO-HOO!
YOU, KANOKO?
I...FEEL THE SAME AS YOU...!

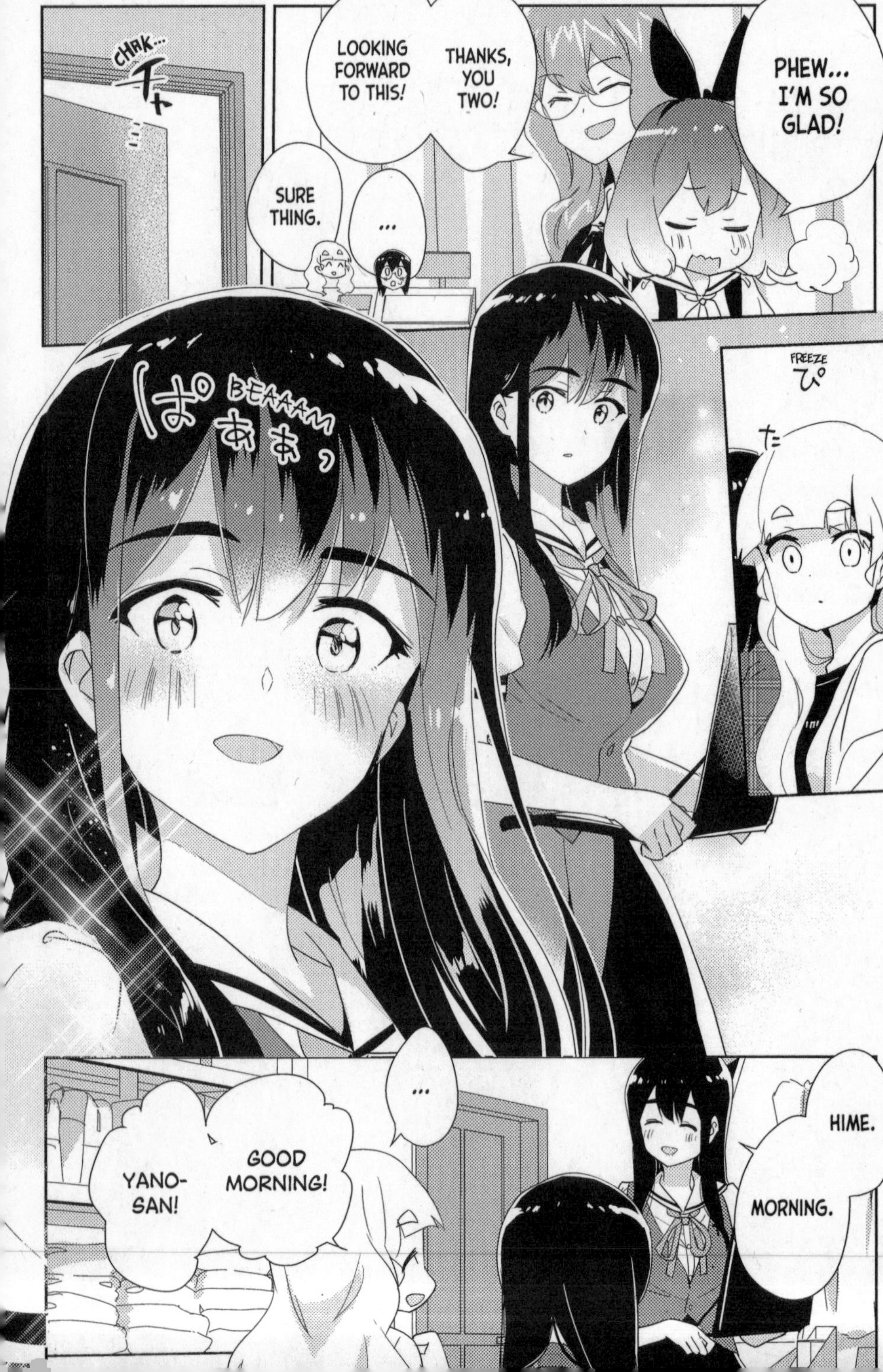
PHEW... I'M SO GLAD!
THANKS, YOU TWO!
LOOKING FORWARD TO THIS!
...
SURE THING.
CHAK...
FREEZE
BEAAAM
HIME.
MORNING.
...
GOOD MORNING!
YANO-SAN!

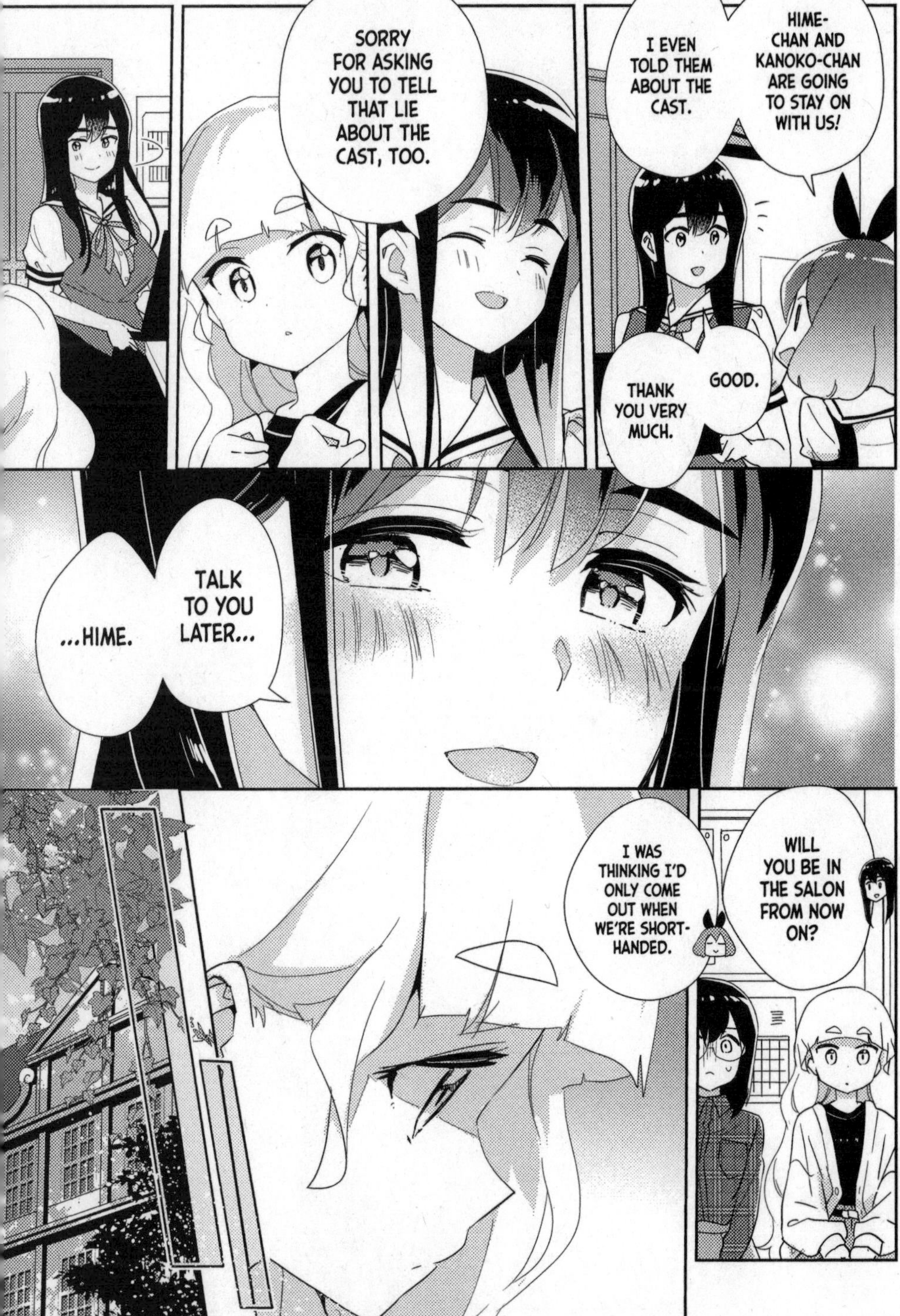
HIME-CHAN AND KANOKO-CHAN ARE GOING TO STAY ON WITH US!
I EVEN TOLD THEM ABOUT THE CAST.
GOOD.
THANK YOU VERY MUCH.
SORRY FOR ASKING YOU TO TELL THAT LIE ABOUT THE CAST, TOO.
TALK TO YOU LATER...
...HIME.
WILL YOU BE IN THE SALON FROM NOW ON?
I WAS THINKING I'D ONLY COME OUT WHEN WE'RE SHORT-HANDED.

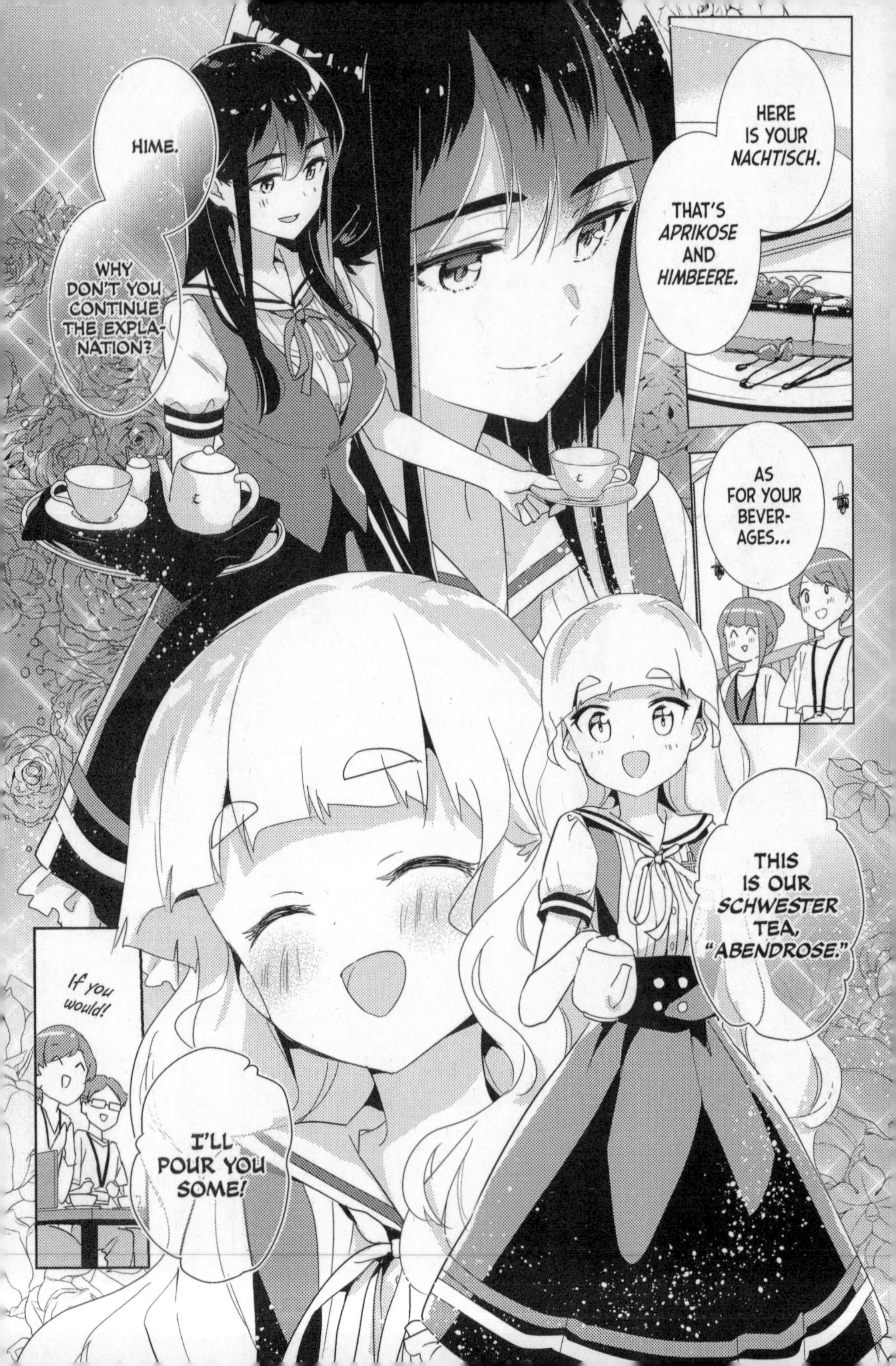

HERE IS YOUR NACHTISCH.
THAT'S APRIKOSE AND HIMBEERE.
HIME.
WHY DON'T YOU CONTINUE THE EXPLA-NATION?
AS FOR YOUR BEVER-AGES...
THIS IS OUR SCHWESTER TEA, "ABENDROSE."
I'LL POUR YOU SOME!
If you would!

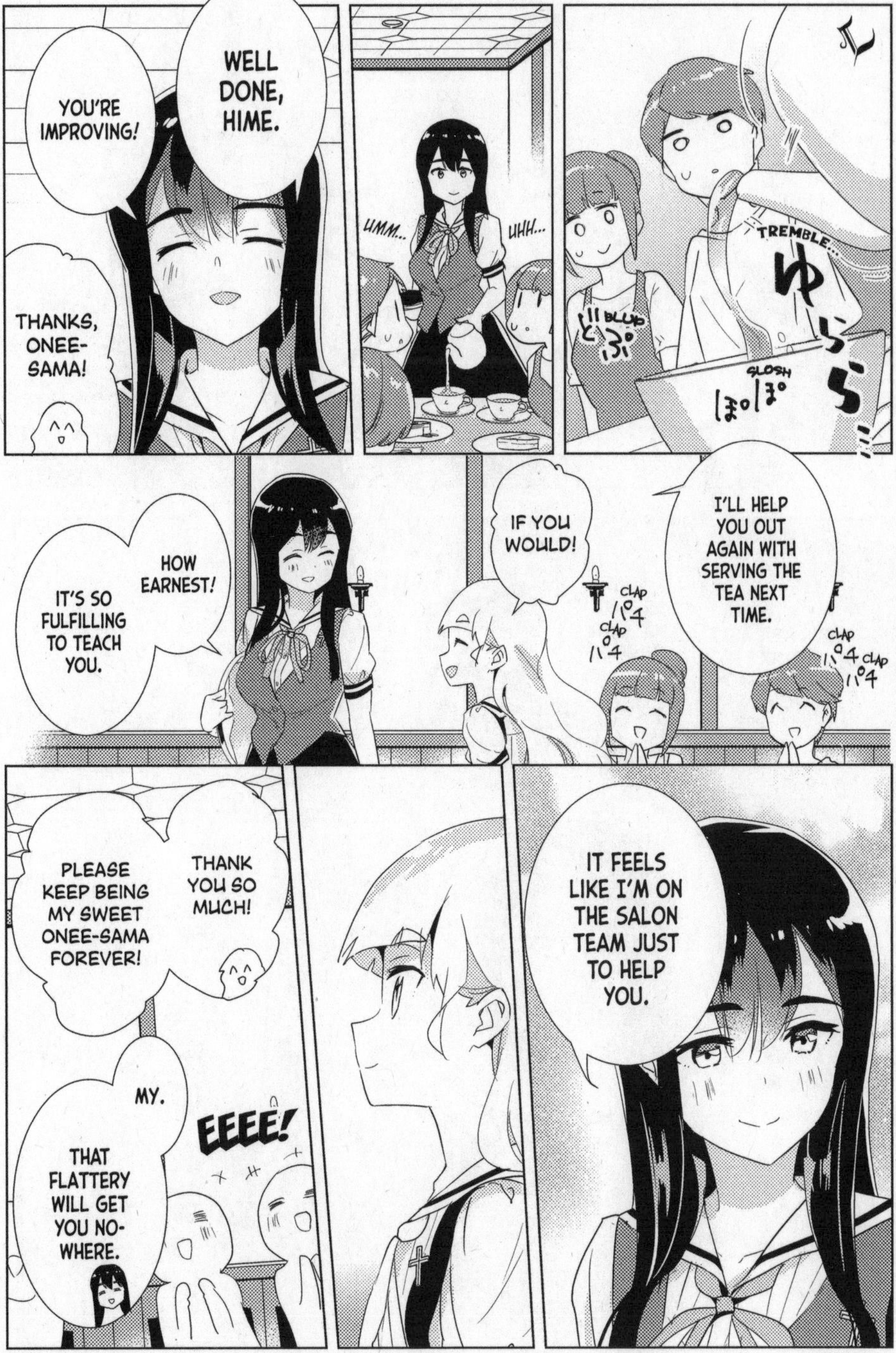
TREMBLE...
ゆらら
BLUP
とぷ
SLOSH
ぽぽ
UHH...
UMM...
WELL DONE, HIME.
YOU'RE IMPROVING!
THANKS, ONEE-SAMA!
I'LL HELP YOU OUT AGAIN WITH SERVING THE TEA NEXT TIME.
CLAP パチ CLAP パチ
IF YOU WOULD!
CLAP パチ CLAP パチ
HOW EARNEST!
IT'S SO FULFILLING TO TEACH YOU.
IT FEELS LIKE I'M ON THE SALON TEAM JUST TO HELP YOU.
THANK YOU SO MUCH!
PLEASE KEEP BEING MY SWEET ONEE-SAMA FOREVER!
EEEE!
MY.
THAT FLATTERY WILL GET YOU NO-WHERE.

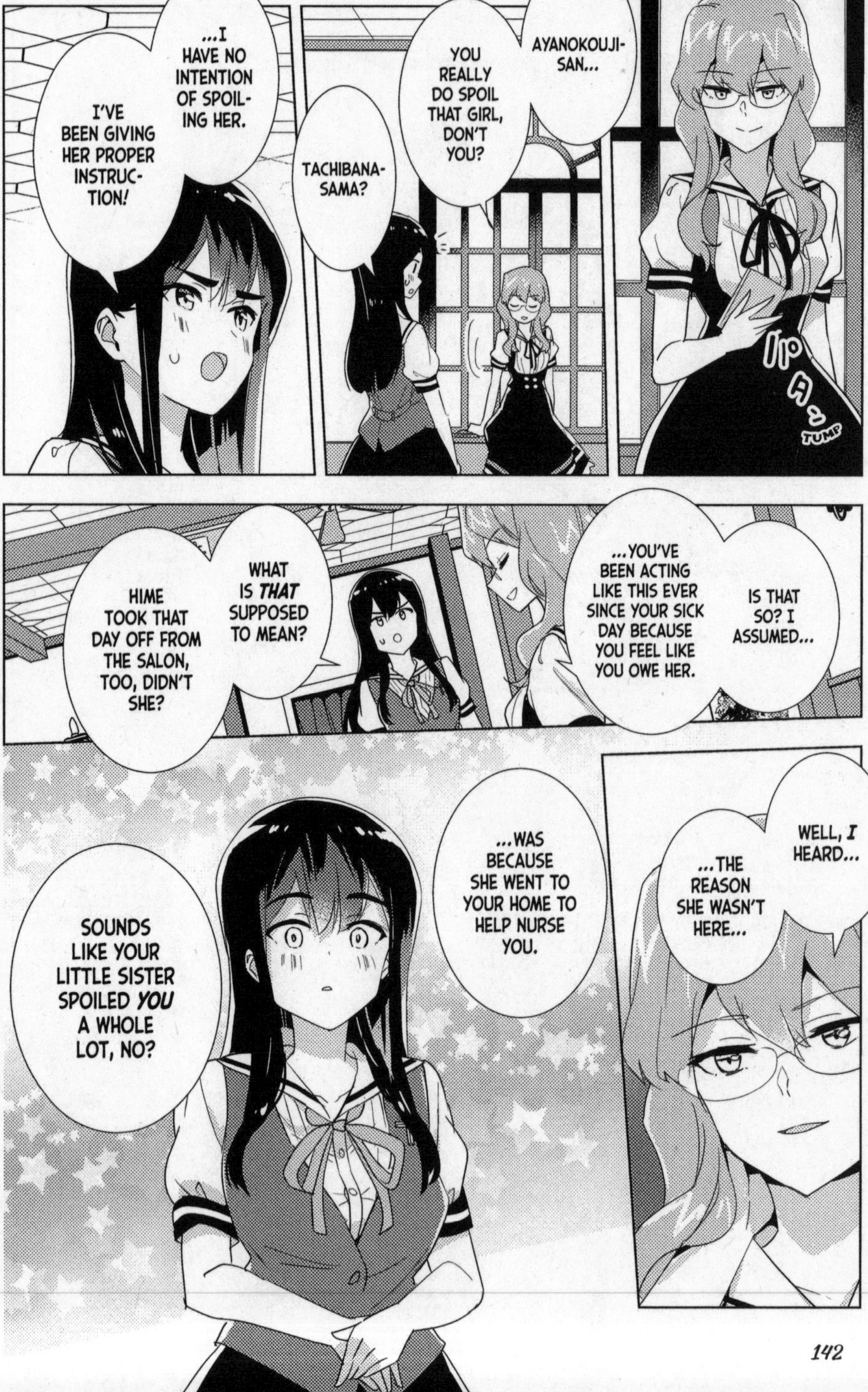
AYANOKOUJI-SAN...
YOU REALLY DO SPOIL THAT GIRL, DON'T YOU?
TUMP
TACHIBANA-SAMA?
...I HAVE NO INTENTION OF SPOIL-ING HER.
I'VE BEEN GIVING HER PROPER INSTRUC-TION!
IS THAT SO? I ASSUMED...
...YOU'VE BEEN ACTING LIKE THIS EVER SINCE YOUR SICK DAY BECAUSE YOU FEEL LIKE YOU OWE HER.
WHAT IS *THAT* SUPPOSED TO MEAN?
HIME TOOK THAT DAY OFF FROM THE SALON, TOO, DIDN'T SHE?
WELL, *I* HEARD...
...THE REASON SHE WASN'T HERE...
...WAS BECAUSE SHE WENT TO YOUR HOME TO HELP NURSE YOU.
SOUNDS LIKE YOUR LITTLE SISTER SPOILED *YOU* A WHOLE LOT, NO?

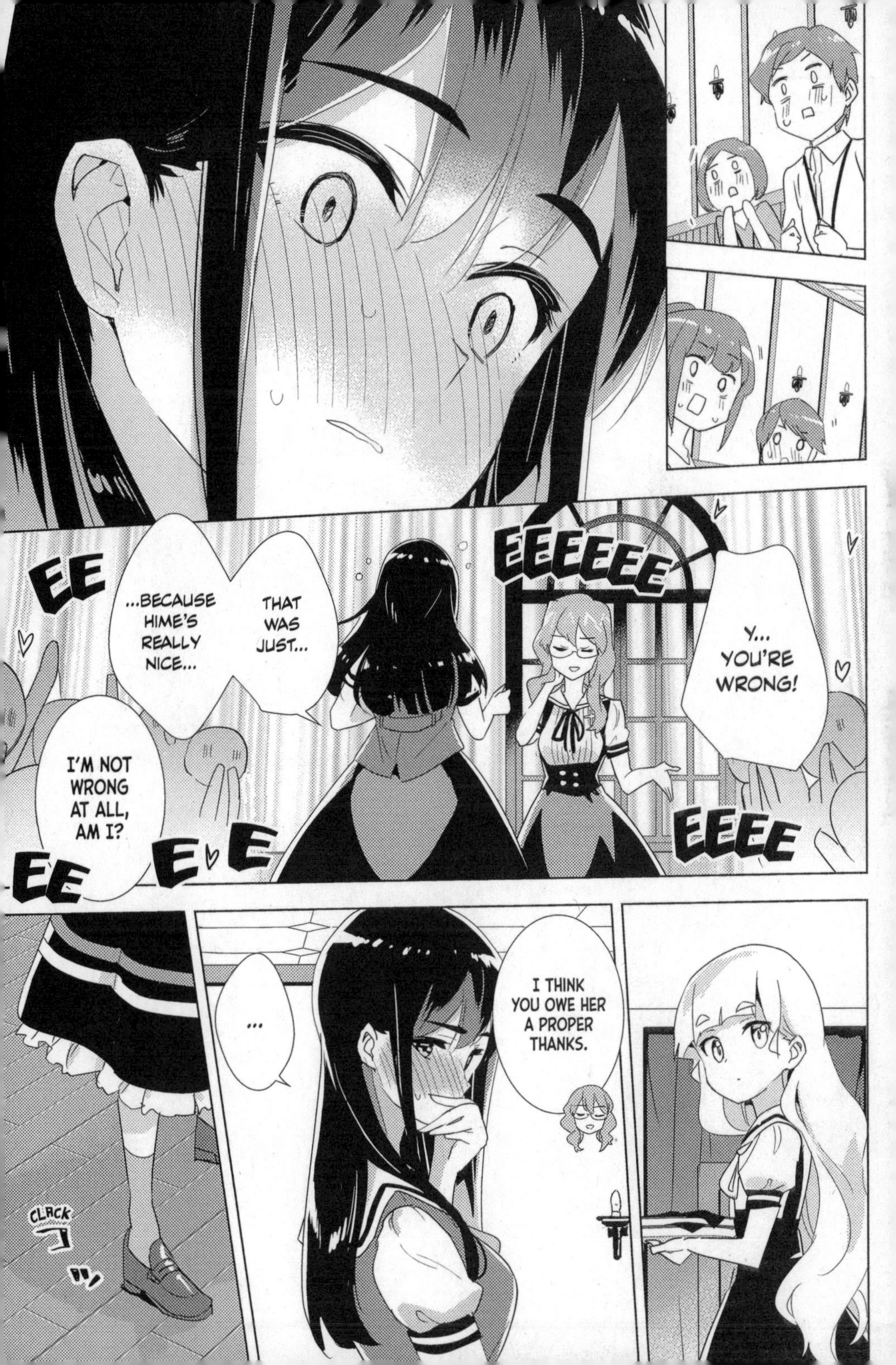

EEEEEE
Y... YOU'RE WRONG!
THAT WAS JUST...
...BECAUSE HIME'S REALLY NICE...
EE
EEEE
I'M NOT WRONG AT ALL, AM I?
E
E
EE
I THINK YOU OWE HER A PROPER THANKS.
...
CLACK

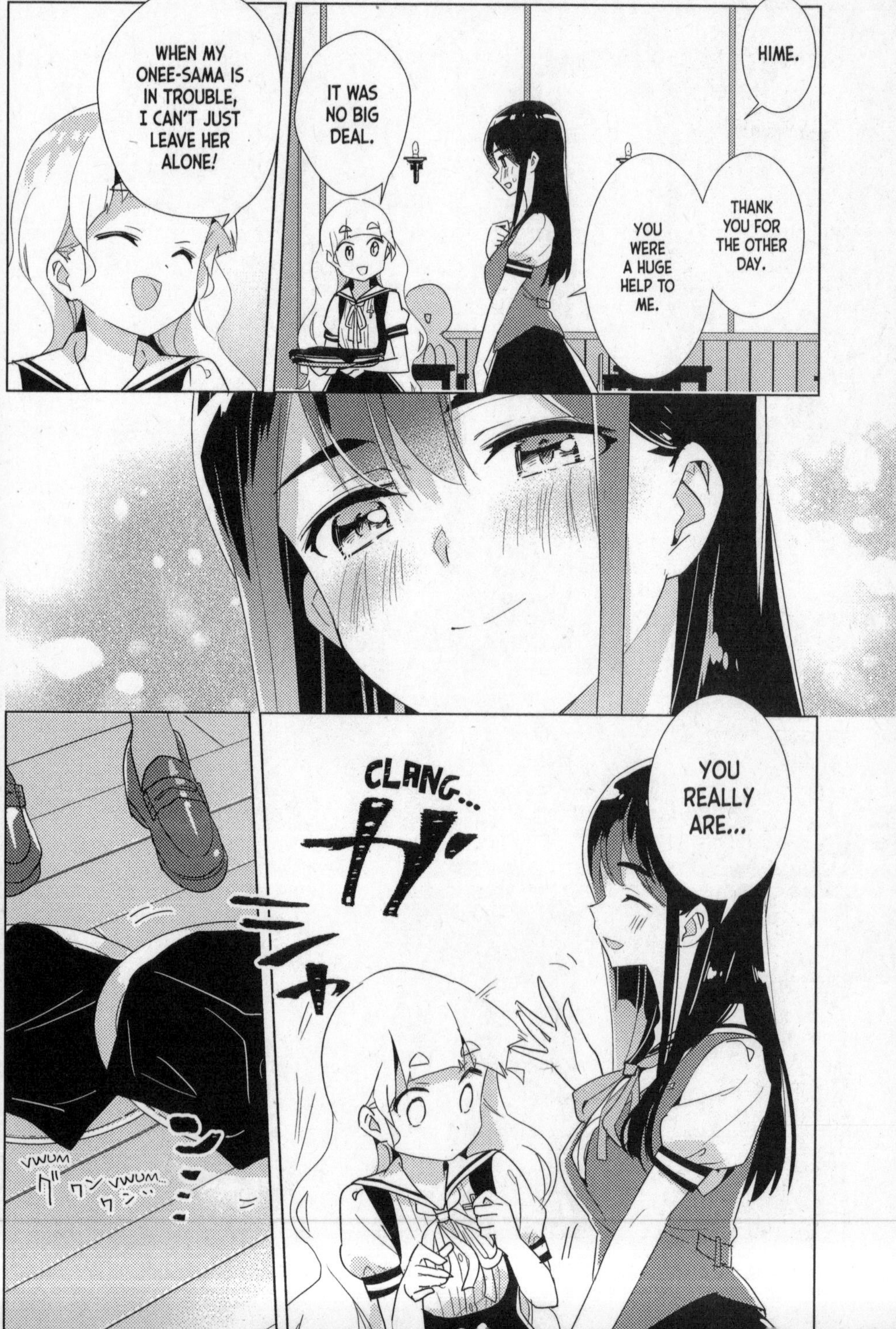
HIME.
THANK YOU FOR THE OTHER DAY.
YOU WERE A HUGE HELP TO ME.
IT WAS NO BIG DEAL.
WHEN MY ONEE-SAMA IS IN TROUBLE, I CAN'T JUST LEAVE HER ALONE!
YOU REALLY ARE...
CLANG...
VWUM
VWUM...

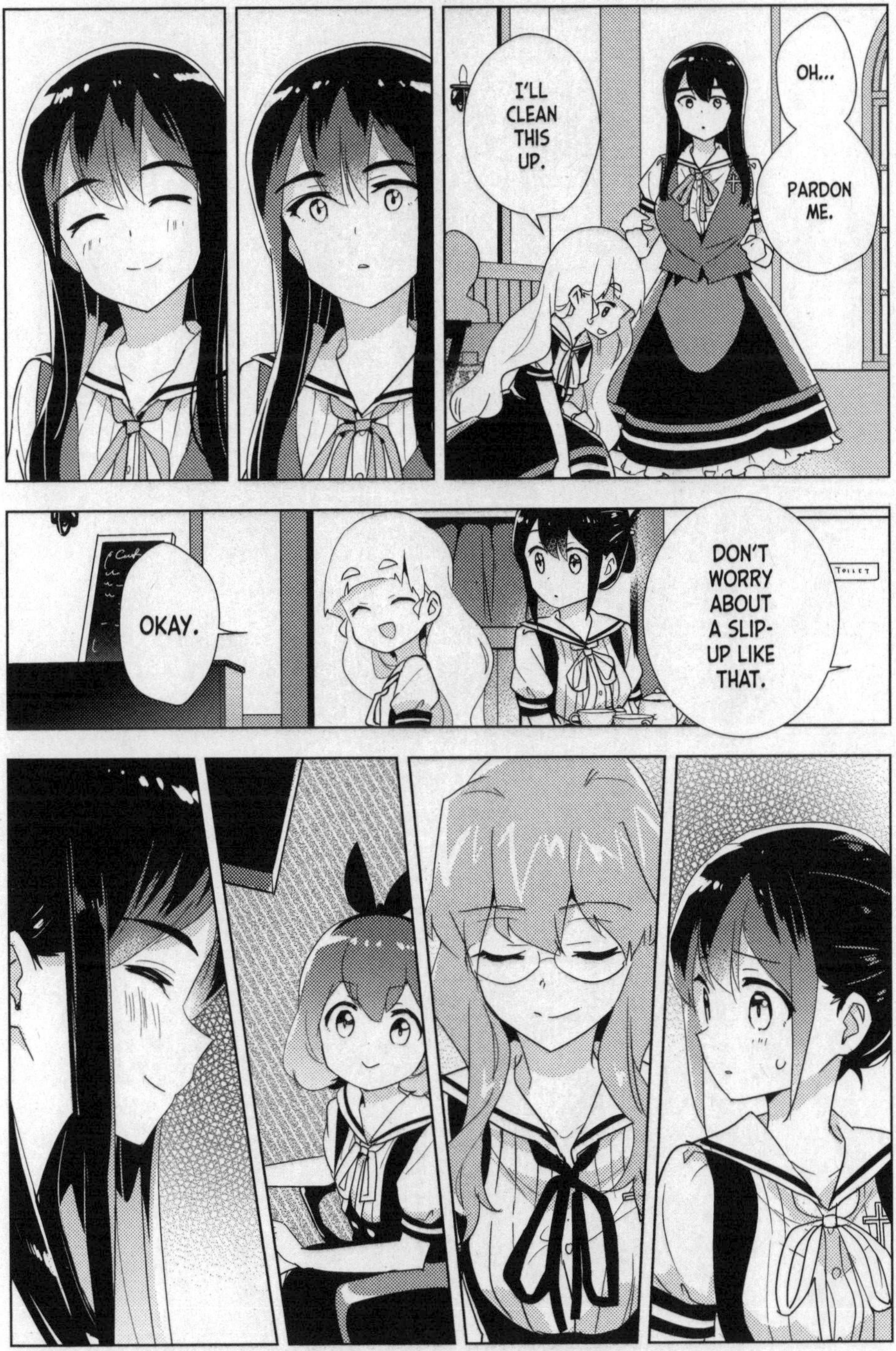
OH... PARDON ME.
I'LL CLEAN THIS UP.
DON'T WORRY ABOUT A SLIP-UP LIKE THAT.
OKAY.

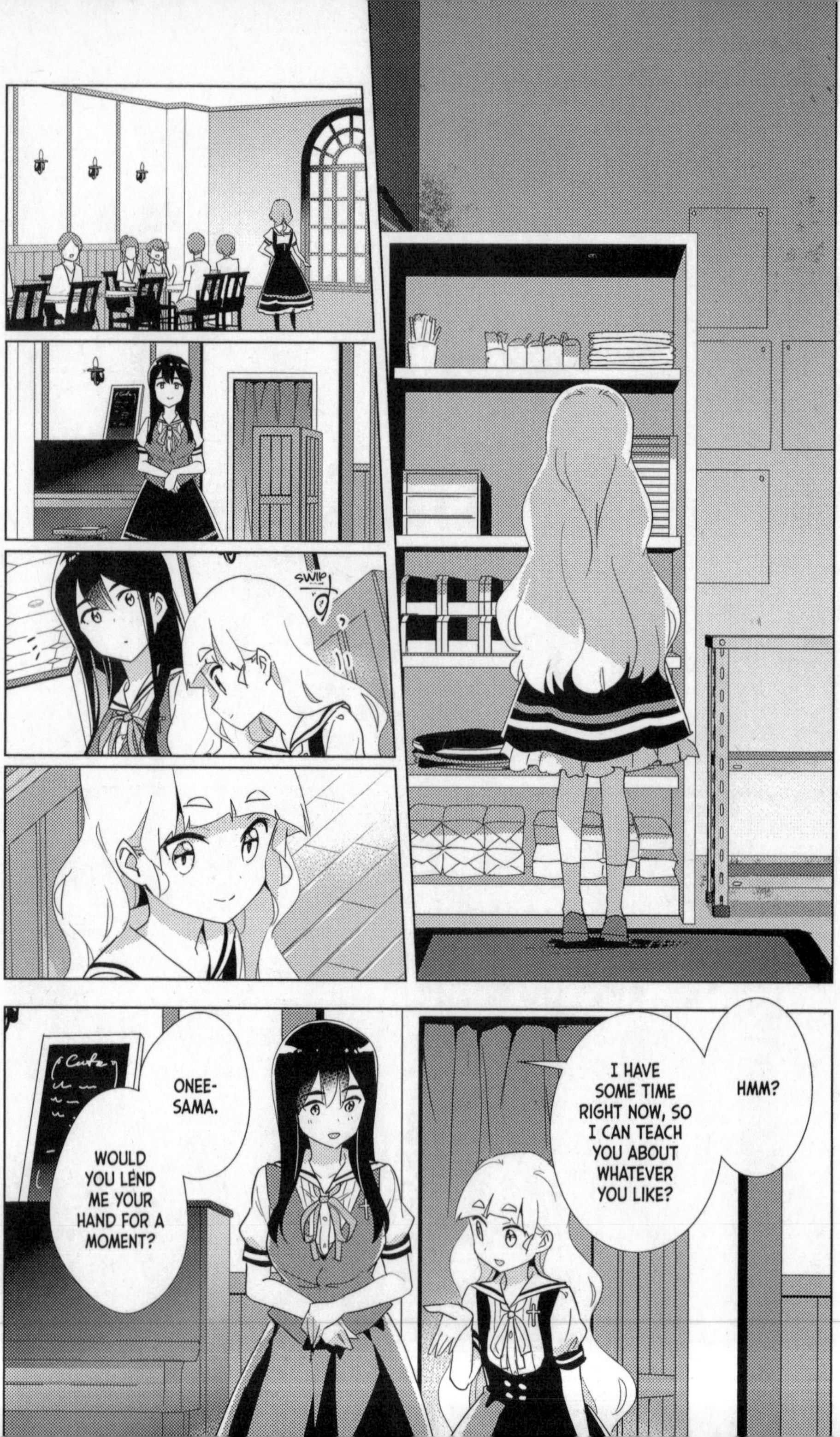
SWIP
HMM?
I HAVE SOME TIME RIGHT NOW, SO I CAN TEACH YOU ABOUT WHATEVER YOU LIKE?
ONEE-SAMA.
WOULD YOU LEND ME YOUR HAND FOR A MOMENT?

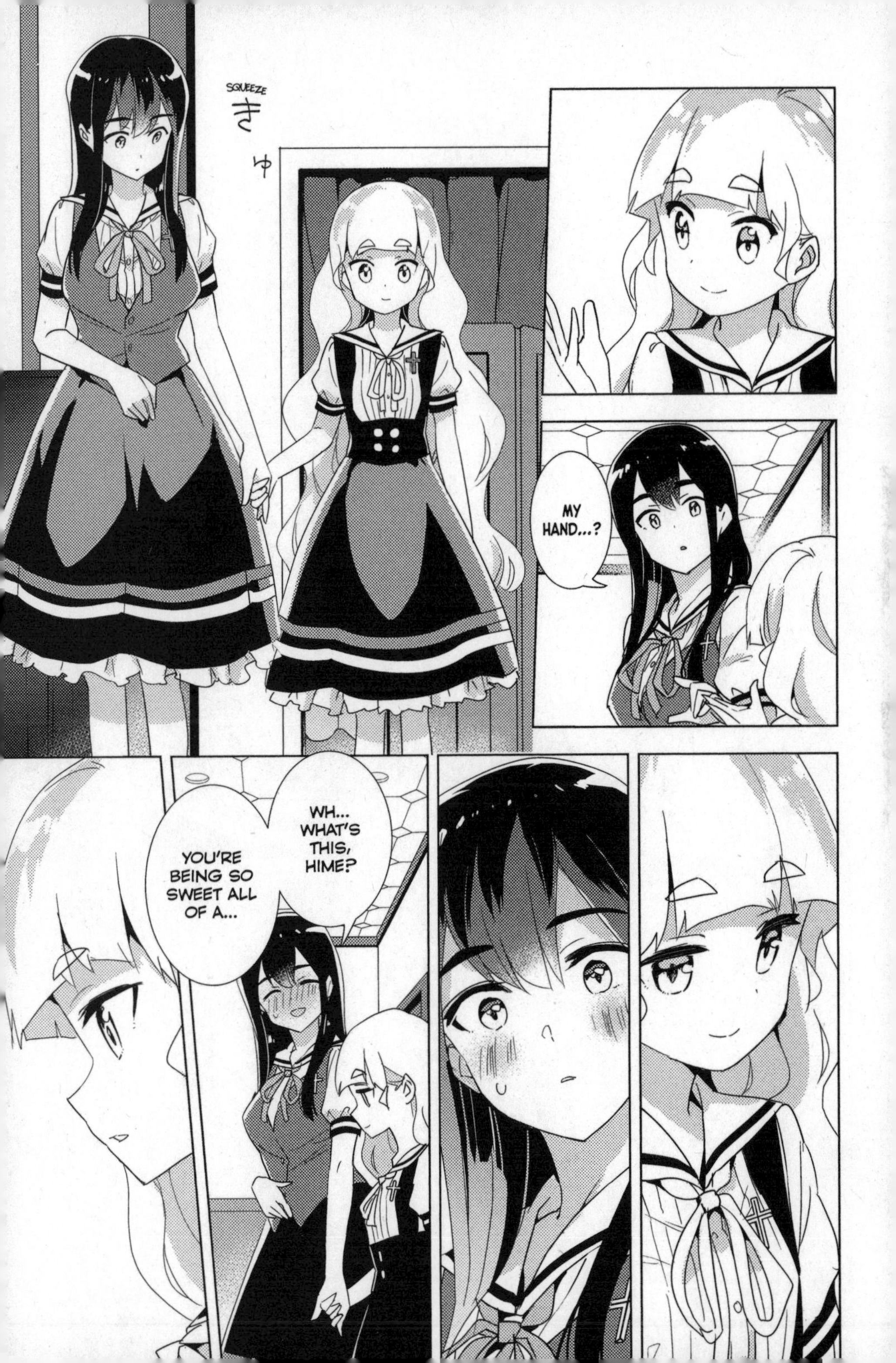
MY HAND...?
SQUEEZE
きゅ
WH... WHAT'S THIS, HIME?
YOU'RE BEING SO SWEET ALL OF A...

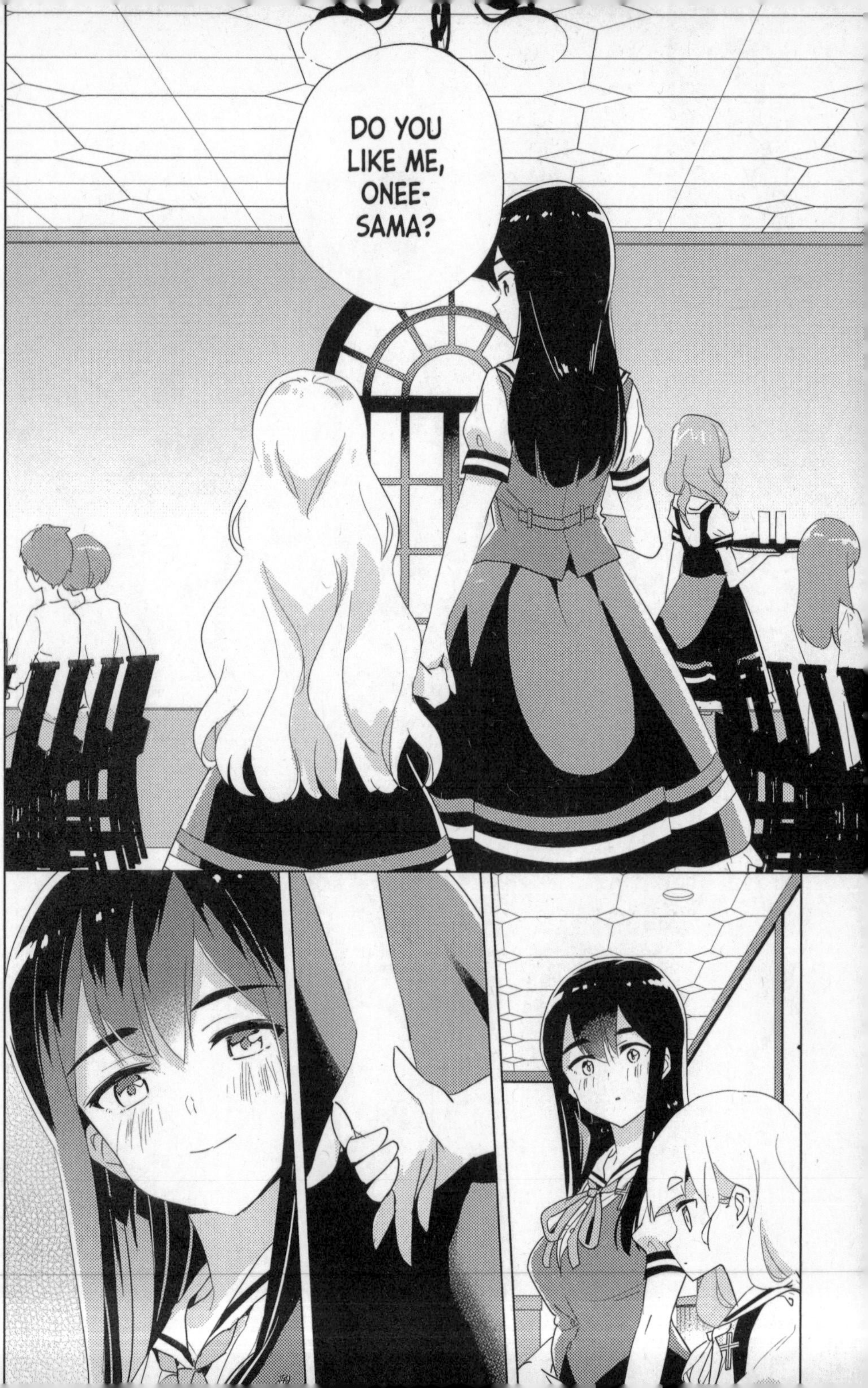
DO YOU LIKE ME, ONEE-SAMA?

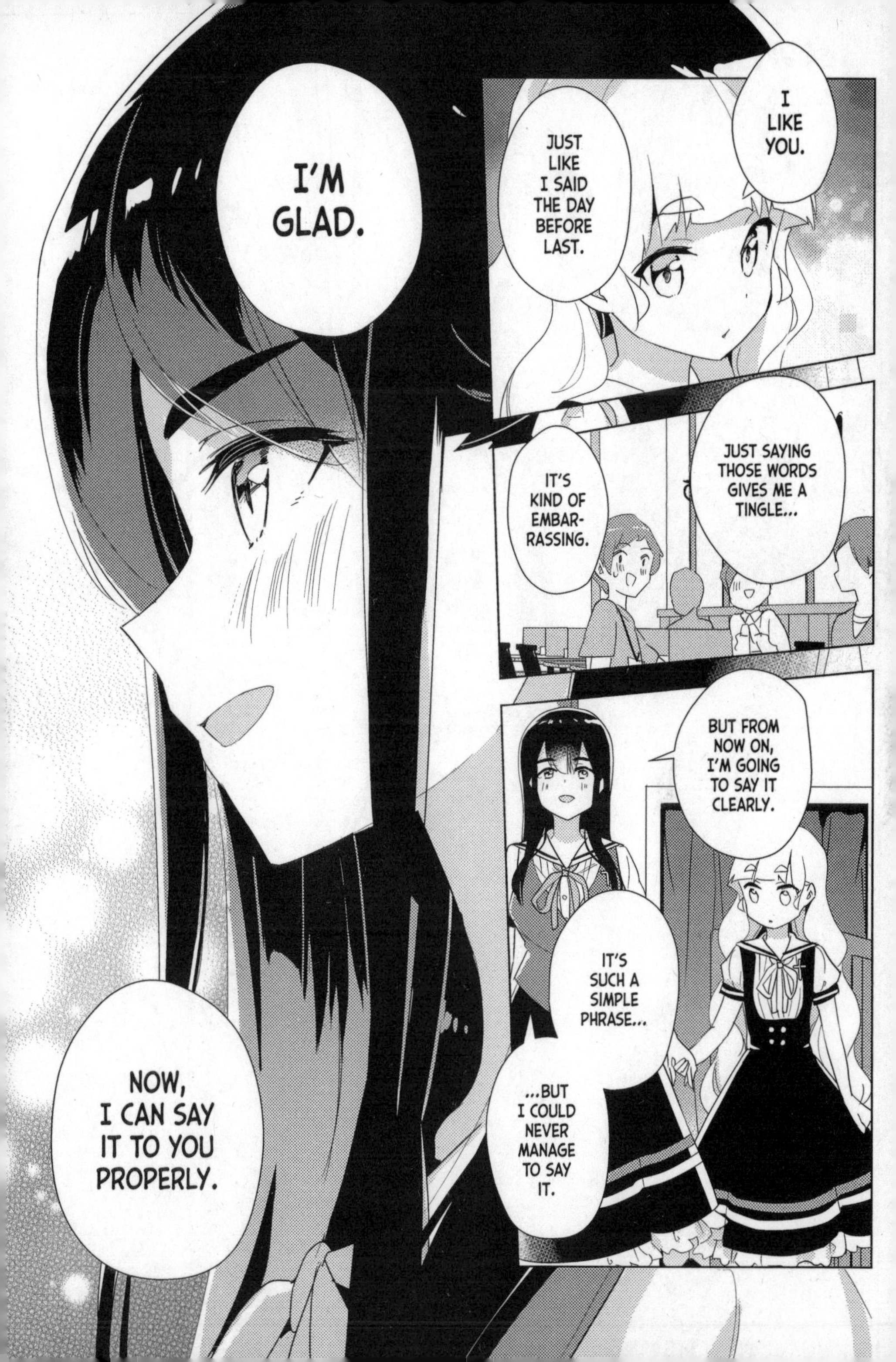
I LIKE YOU.
JUST LIKE I SAID THE DAY BEFORE LAST.
JUST SAYING THOSE WORDS GIVES ME A TINGLE...
IT'S KIND OF EMBARRASSING.
BUT FROM NOW ON, I'M GOING TO SAY IT CLEARLY.
IT'S SUCH A SIMPLE PHRASE...
...BUT I COULD NEVER MANAGE TO SAY IT.
I'M GLAD.
NOW, I CAN SAY IT TO YOU PROPERLY.

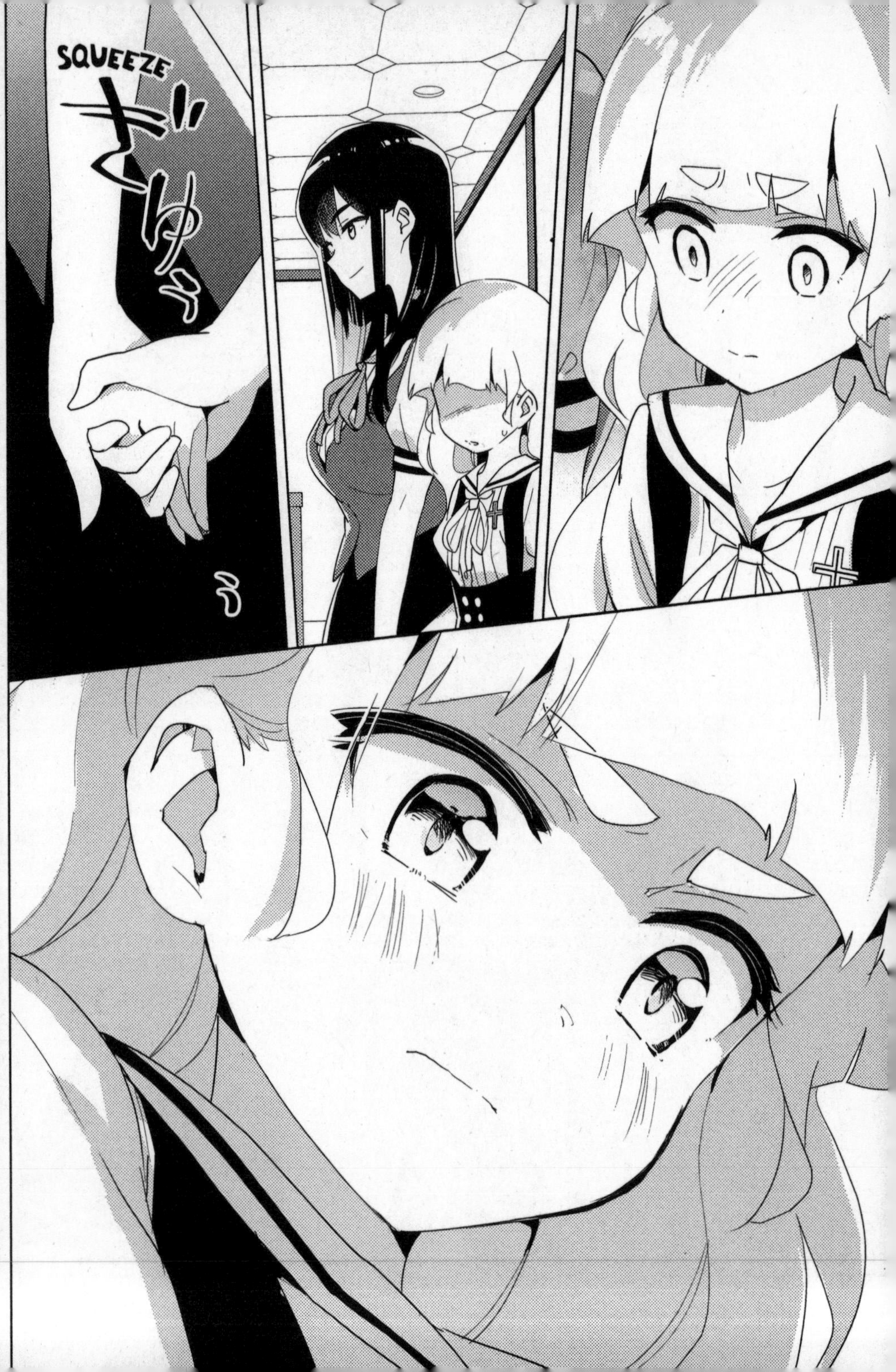
SQUEEZE

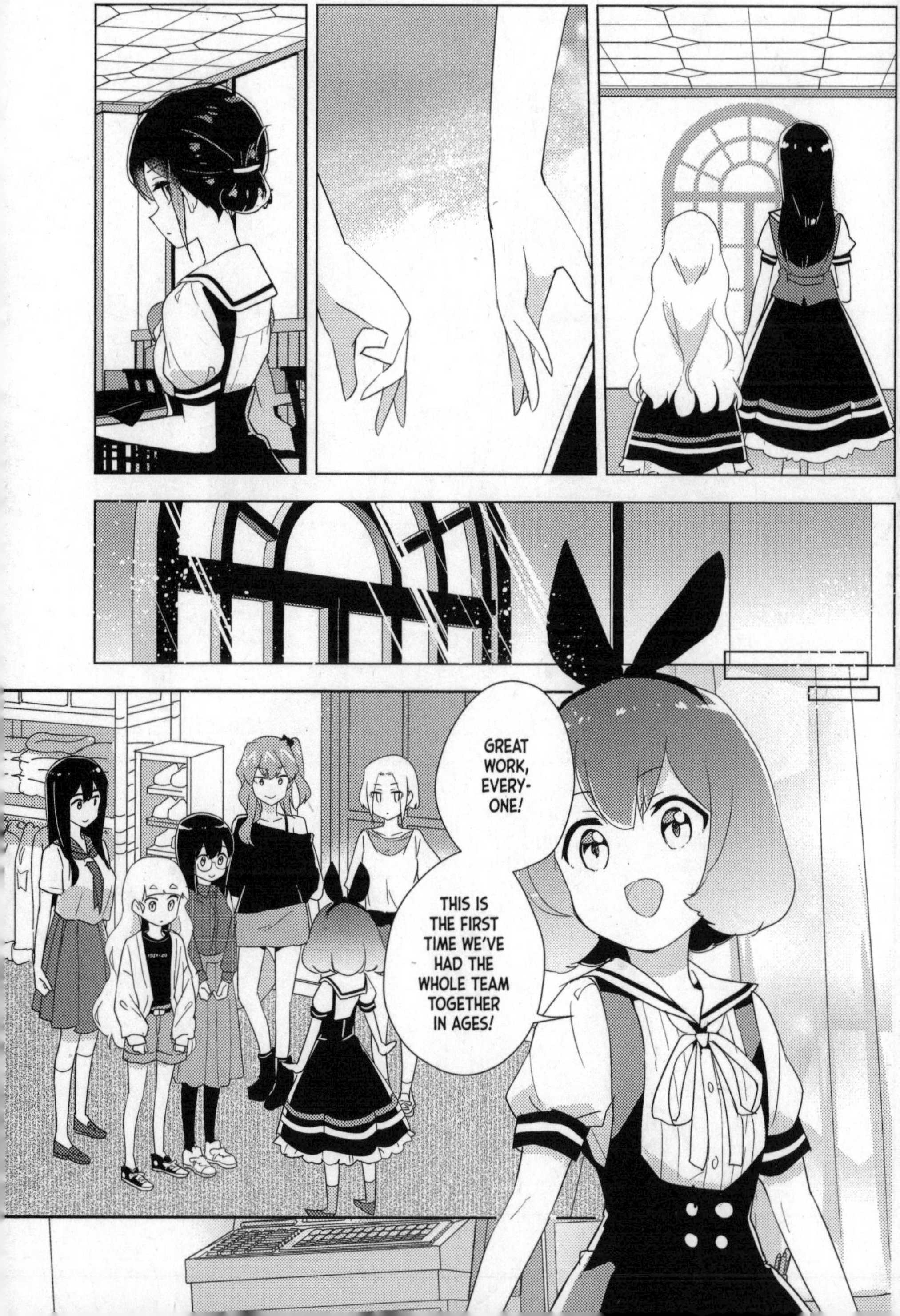
GREAT WORK, EVERY-ONE!
THIS IS THE FIRST TIME WE'VE HAD THE WHOLE TEAM TOGETHER IN AGES!

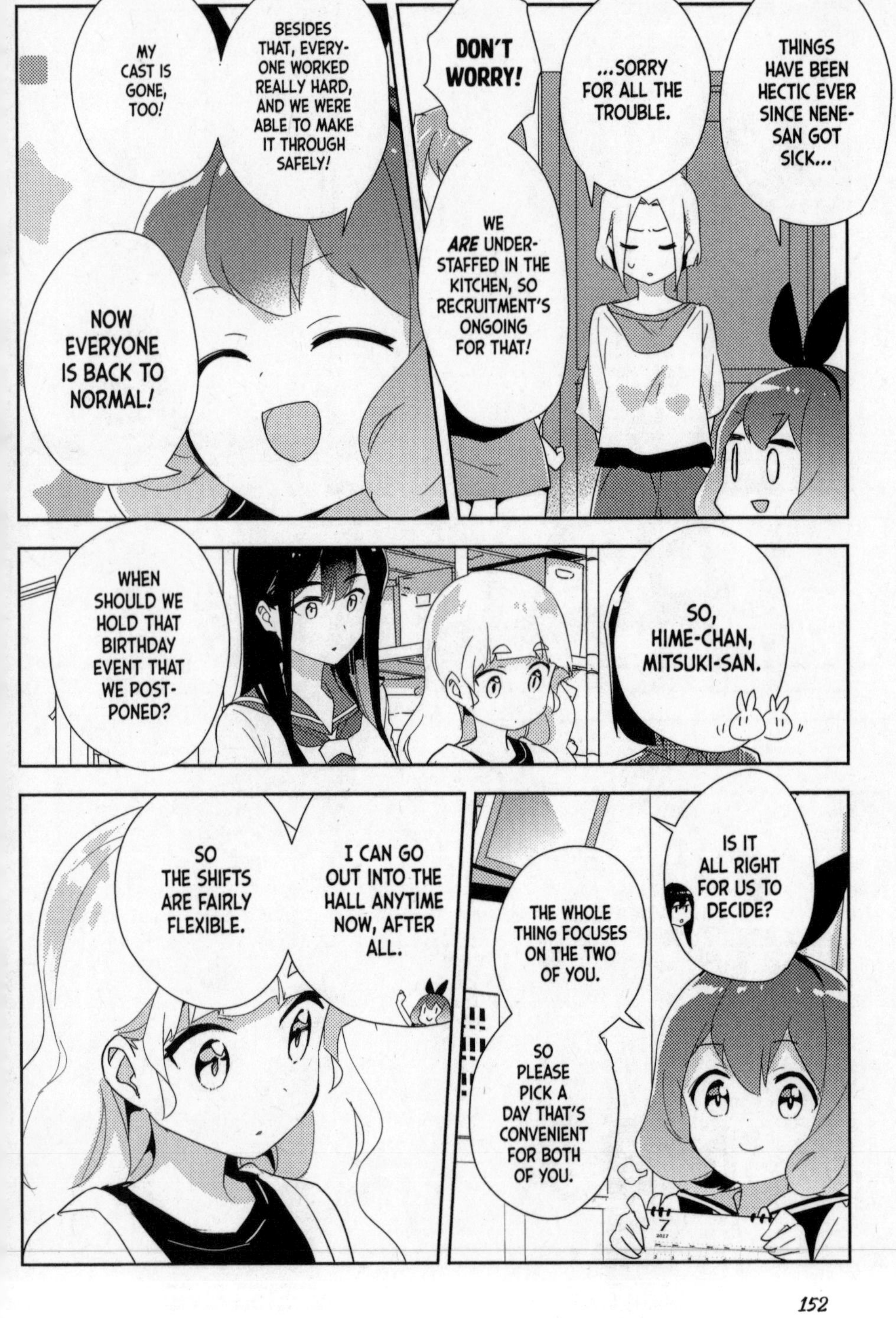
THINGS HAVE BEEN HECTIC EVER SINCE NENE-SAN GOT SICK...
...SORRY FOR ALL THE TROUBLE.
DON'T WORRY!
WE *ARE* UNDER-STAFFED IN THE KITCHEN, SO RECRUITMENT'S ONGOING FOR THAT!
BESIDES THAT, EVERY-ONE WORKED REALLY HARD, AND WE WERE ABLE TO MAKE IT THROUGH SAFELY!
MY CAST IS GONE, TOO!
NOW EVERYONE IS BACK TO NORMAL!
SO, HIME-CHAN, MITSUKI-SAN.
WHEN SHOULD WE HOLD THAT BIRTHDAY EVENT THAT WE POST-PONED?
IS IT ALL RIGHT FOR US TO DECIDE?
THE WHOLE THING FOCUSES ON THE TWO OF YOU.
SO PLEASE PICK A DAY THAT'S CONVENIENT FOR BOTH OF YOU.
I CAN GO OUT INTO THE HALL ANYTIME NOW, AFTER ALL.
SO THE SHIFTS ARE FAIRLY FLEXIBLE.

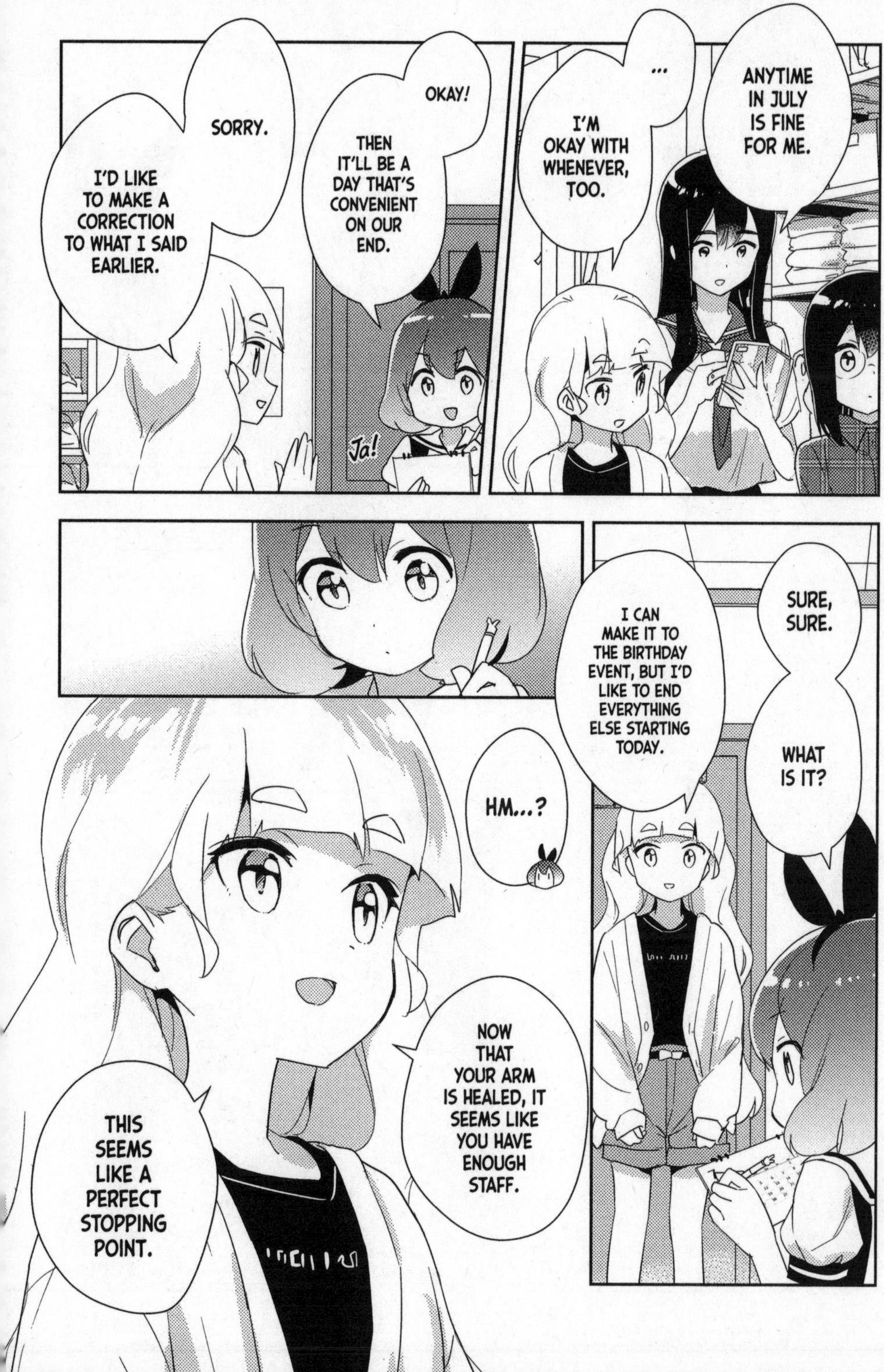
ANYTIME IN JULY IS FINE FOR ME.
...
I'M OKAY WITH WHENEVER, TOO.
OKAY!
THEN IT'LL BE A DAY THAT'S CONVENIENT ON OUR END.
Ja!
SORRY.
I'D LIKE TO MAKE A CORRECTION TO WHAT I SAID EARLIER.
SURE, SURE.
WHAT IS IT?
I CAN MAKE IT TO THE BIRTHDAY EVENT, BUT I'D LIKE TO END EVERYTHING ELSE STARTING TODAY.
HM...?
NOW THAT YOUR ARM IS HEALED, IT SEEMS LIKE YOU HAVE ENOUGH STAFF.
THIS SEEMS LIKE A PERFECT STOPPING POINT.

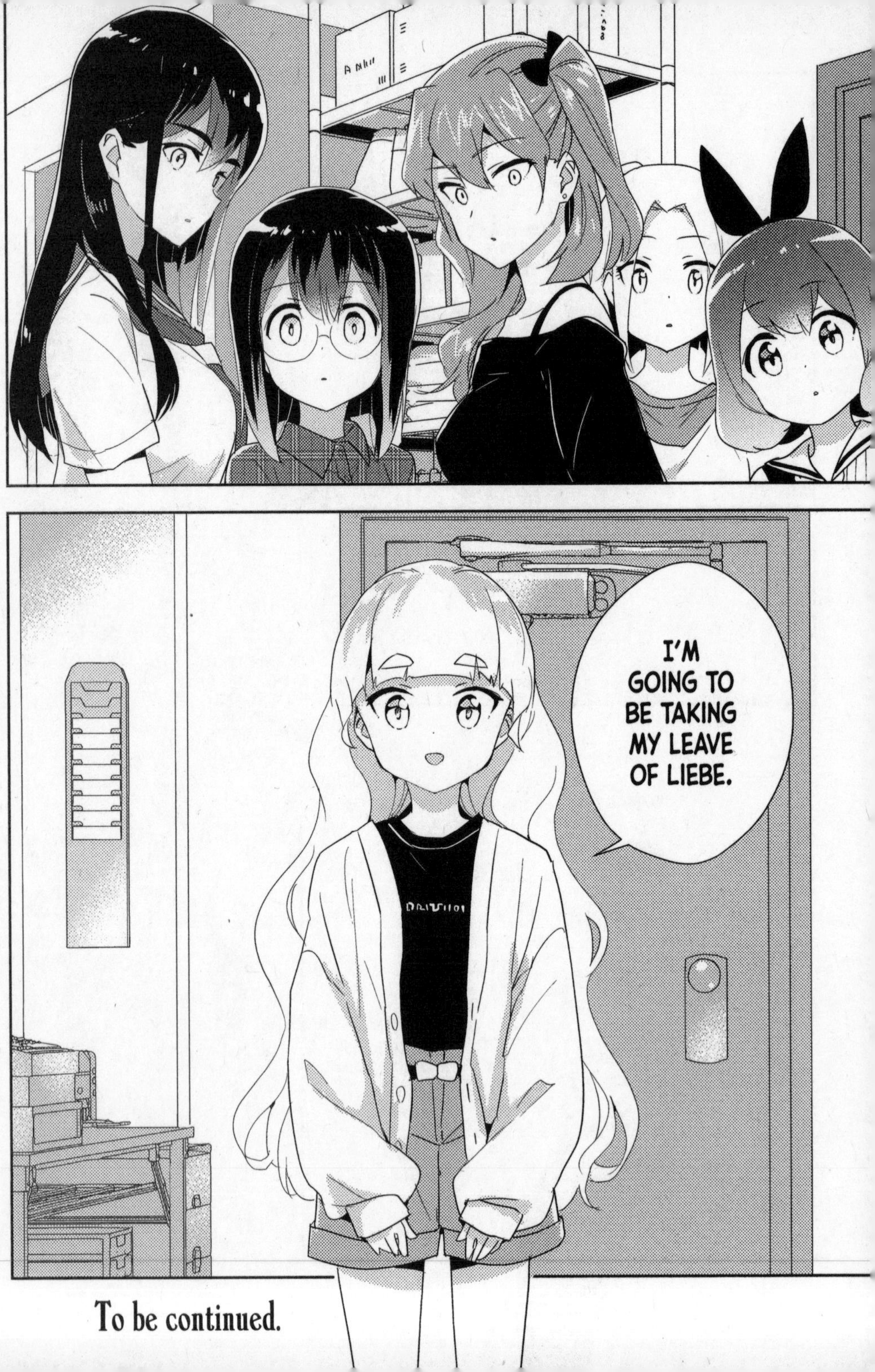
I'M GOING TO BE TAKING MY LEAVE OF LIEBE.

To be continued.

Yuri Is My Job!

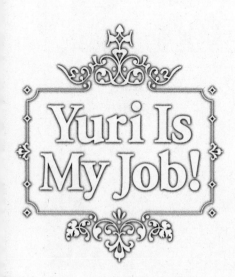

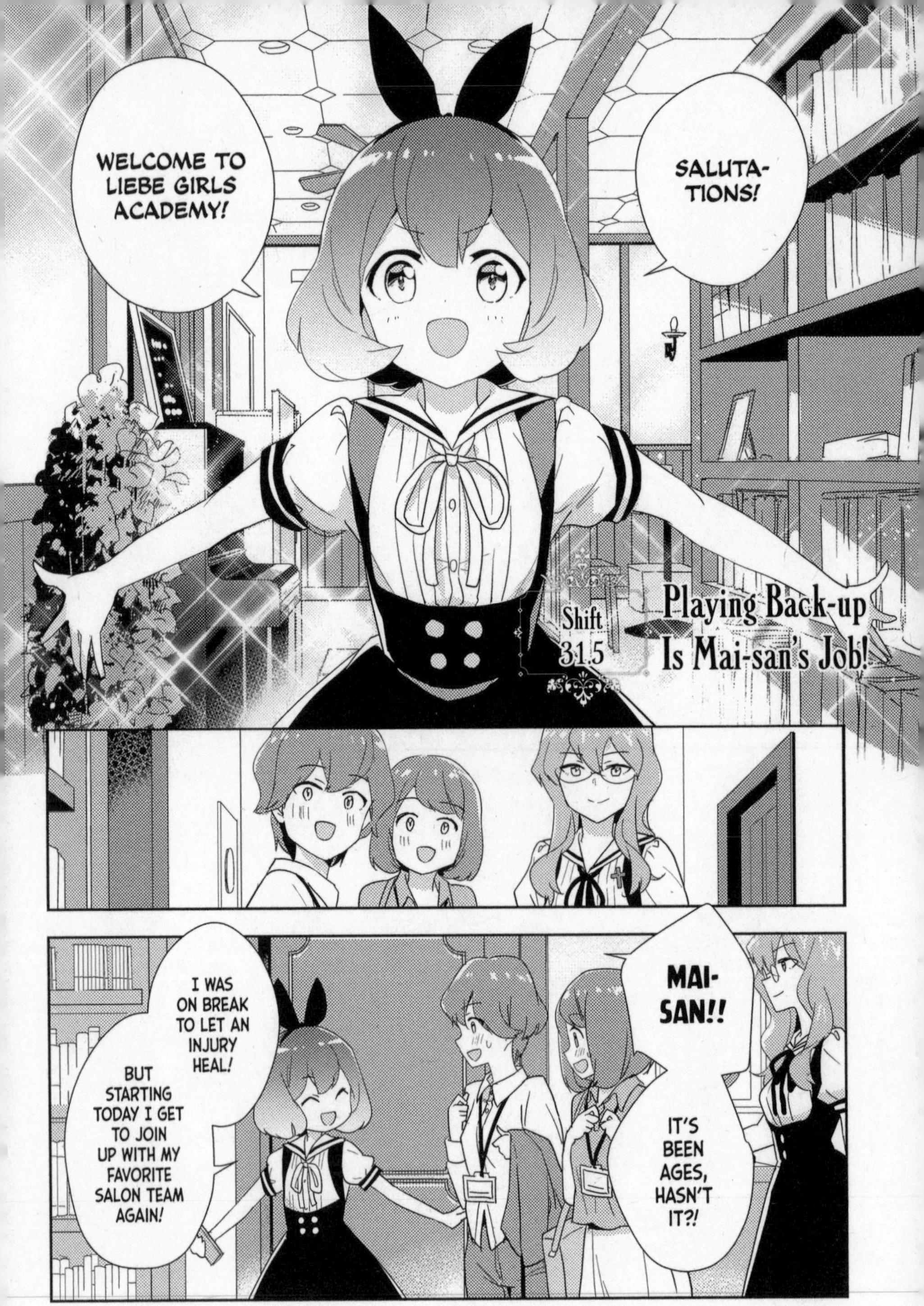
SALUTATIONS!
WELCOME TO LIEBE GIRLS ACADEMY!
Shift 31.5 Playing Back-up Is Mai-san's Job!
MAI-SAN!!
IT'S BEEN AGES, HASN'T IT?!
I WAS ON BREAK TO LET AN INJURY HEAL!
BUT STARTING TODAY I GET TO JOIN UP WITH MY FAVORITE SALON TEAM AGAIN!

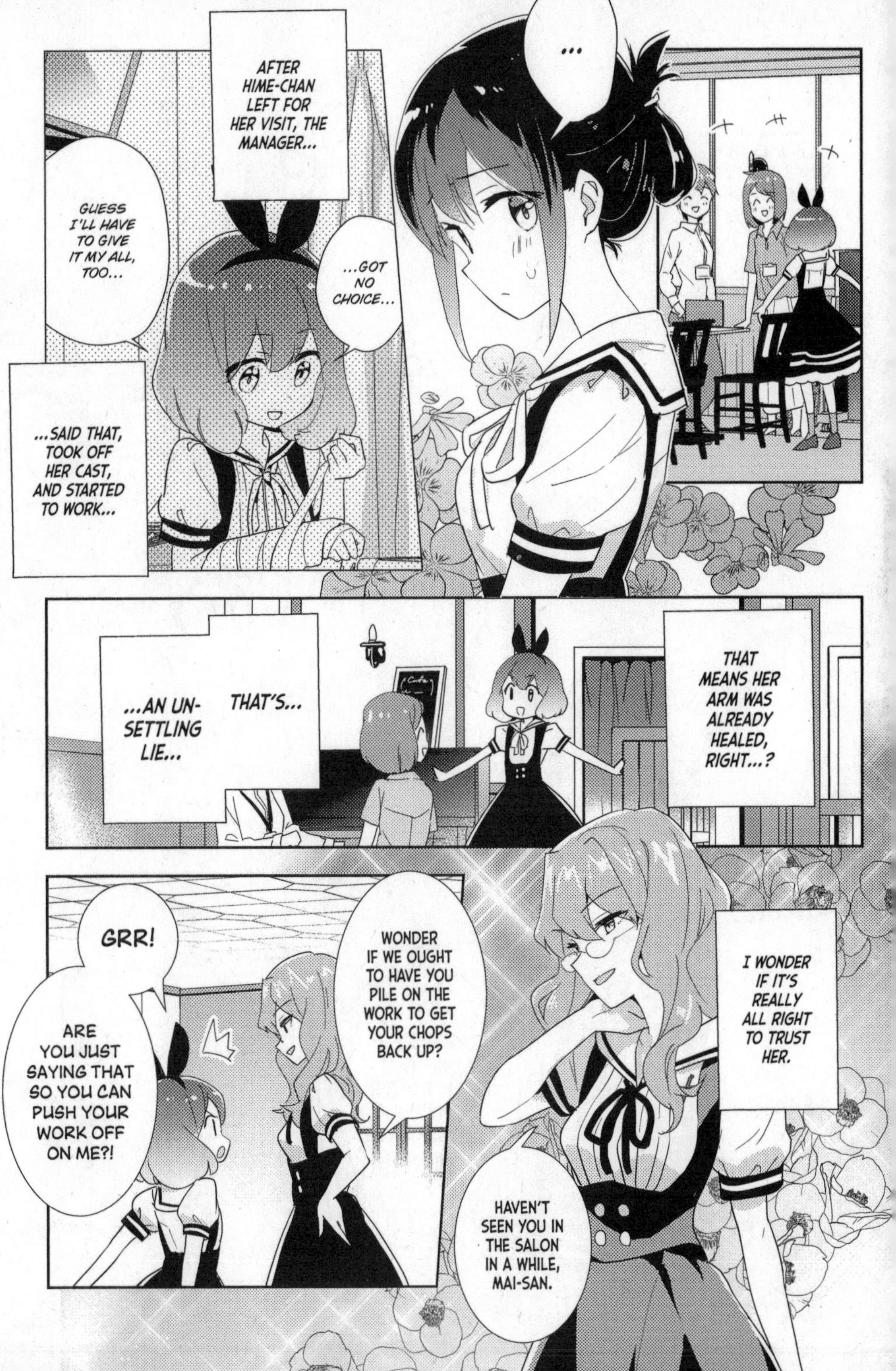
...
AFTER HIME-CHAN LEFT FOR HER VISIT, THE MANAGER...
...GOT NO CHOICE...
GUESS I'LL HAVE TO GIVE IT MY ALL, TOO...
...SAID THAT, TOOK OFF HER CAST, AND STARTED TO WORK...
THAT MEANS HER ARM WAS ALREADY HEALED, RIGHT...?
THAT'S...
...AN UN-SETTLING LIE...
I WONDER IF IT'S REALLY ALL RIGHT TO TRUST HER.
HAVEN'T SEEN YOU IN THE SALON IN A WHILE, MAI-SAN.
WONDER IF WE OUGHT TO HAVE YOU PILE ON THE WORK TO GET YOUR CHOPS BACK UP?
GRR!
ARE YOU JUST SAYING THAT SO YOU CAN PUSH YOUR WORK OFF ON ME?!

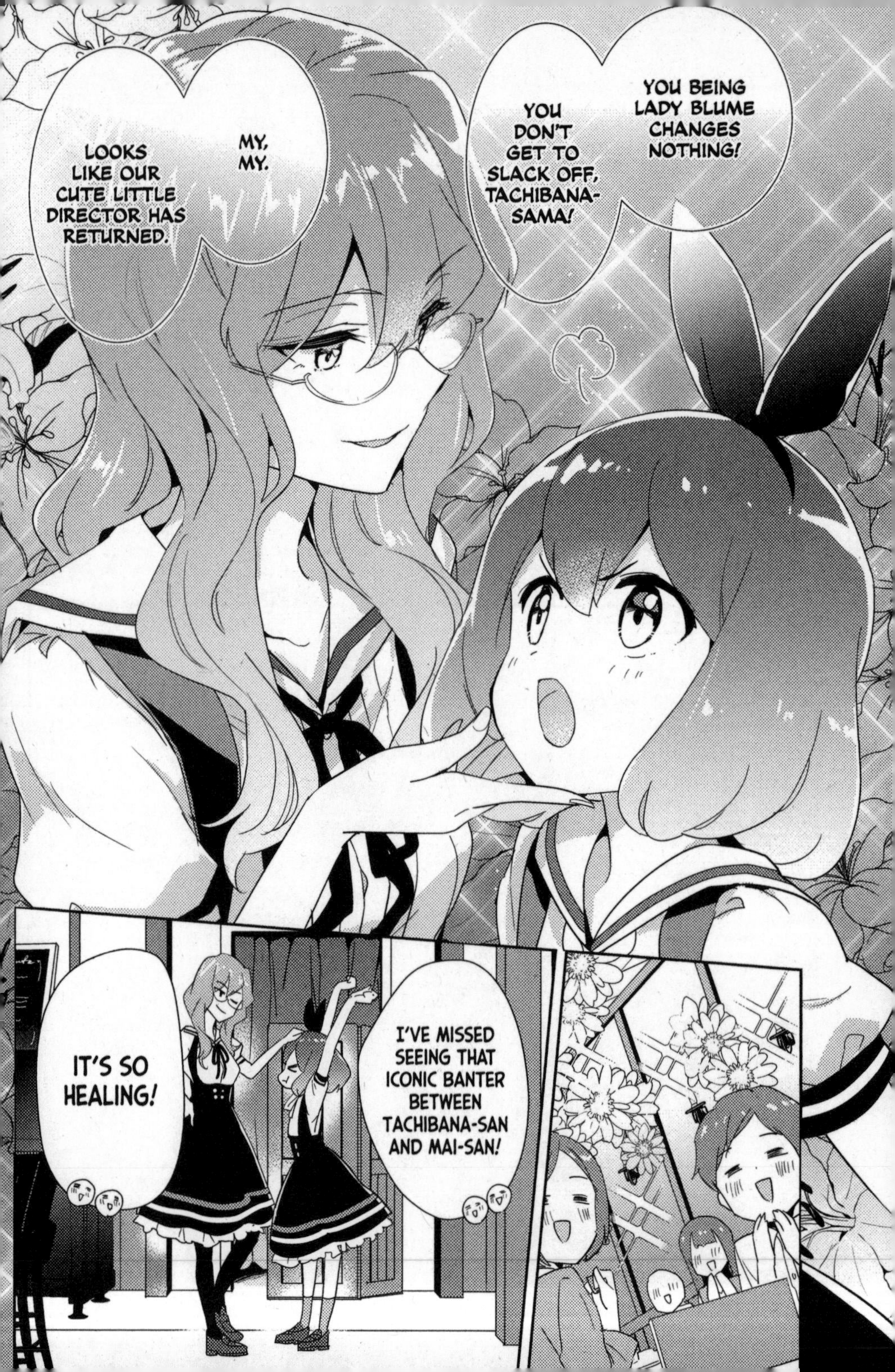
YOU BEING LADY BLUME CHANGES NOTHING!
YOU DON'T GET TO SLACK OFF, TACHIBANA-SAMA!
MY, MY.
LOOKS LIKE OUR CUTE LITTLE DIRECTOR HAS RETURNED.
I'VE MISSED SEEING THAT ICONIC BANTER BETWEEN TACHIBANA-SAN AND MAI-SAN!
IT'S SO HEALING!

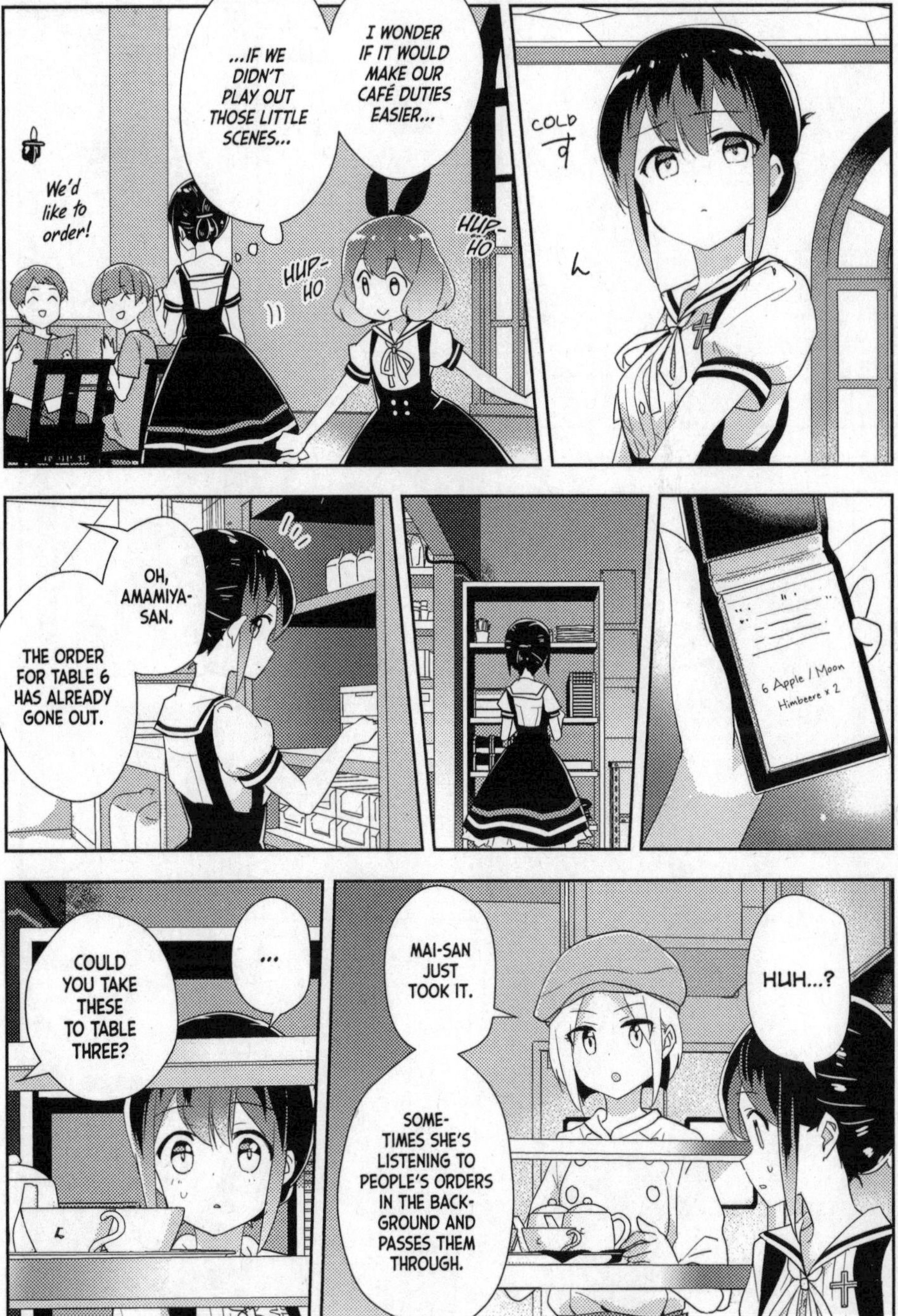
COLD す
ん
I WONDER IF IT WOULD MAKE OUR CAFÉ DUTIES EASIER...
...IF WE DIDN'T PLAY OUT THOSE LITTLE SCENES...
HUP-HO
HUP-HO
We'd like to order!
6 Apple / Moon
Himbeere x 2
OH, AMAMIYA-SAN.
THE ORDER FOR TABLE 6 HAS ALREADY GONE OUT.
HUH...?
MAI-SAN JUST TOOK IT.
SOME-TIMES SHE'S LISTENING TO PEOPLE'S ORDERS IN THE BACK-GROUND AND PASSES THEM THROUGH.
...
COULD YOU TAKE THESE TO TABLE THREE?

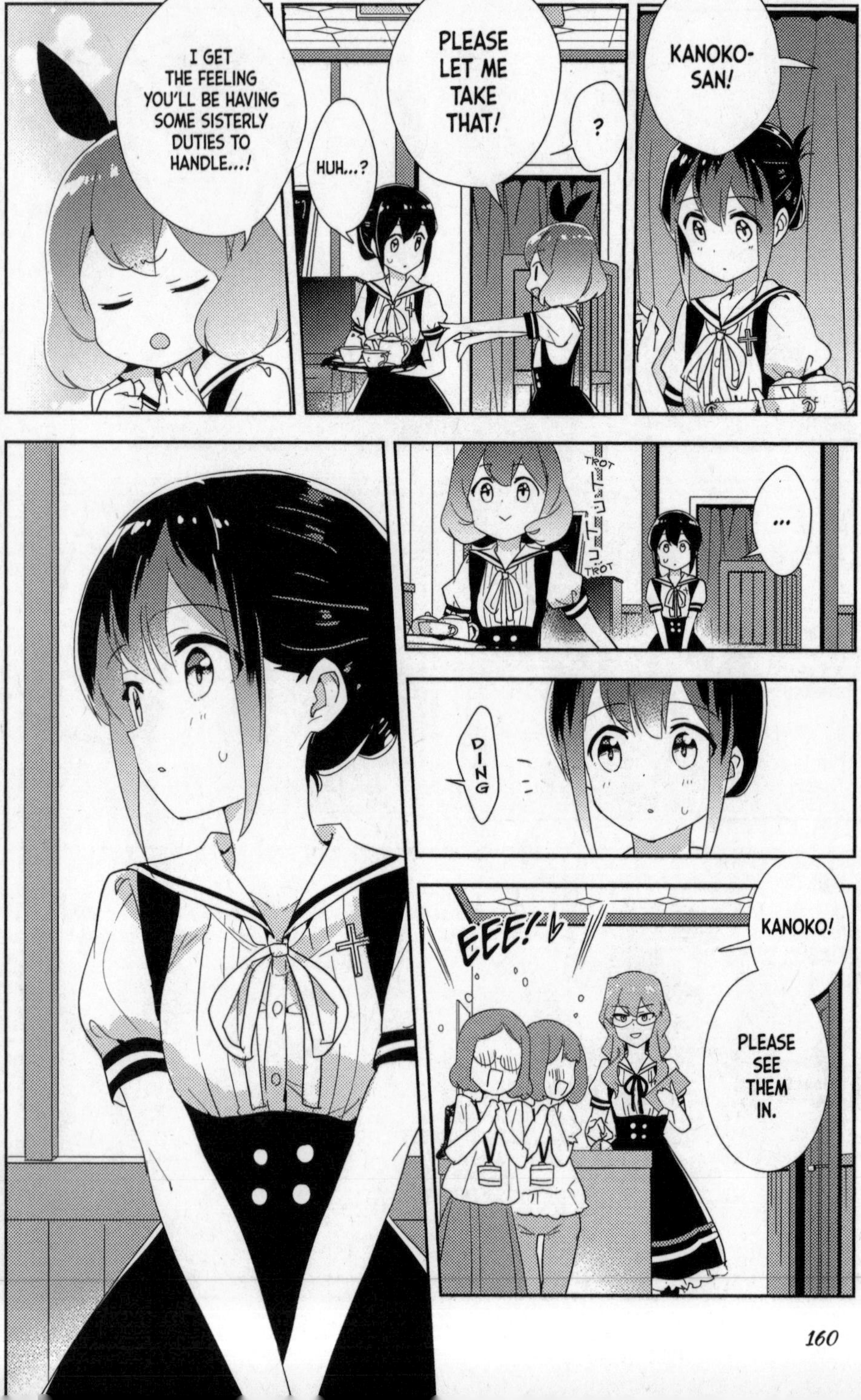
KANOKO-SAN!
?
PLEASE LET ME TAKE THAT!
HUH...?
I GET THE FEELING YOU'LL BE HAVING SOME SISTERLY DUTIES TO HANDLE...!
...
TROT TROT
DING
KANOKO!
PLEASE SEE THEM IN.
EEE!

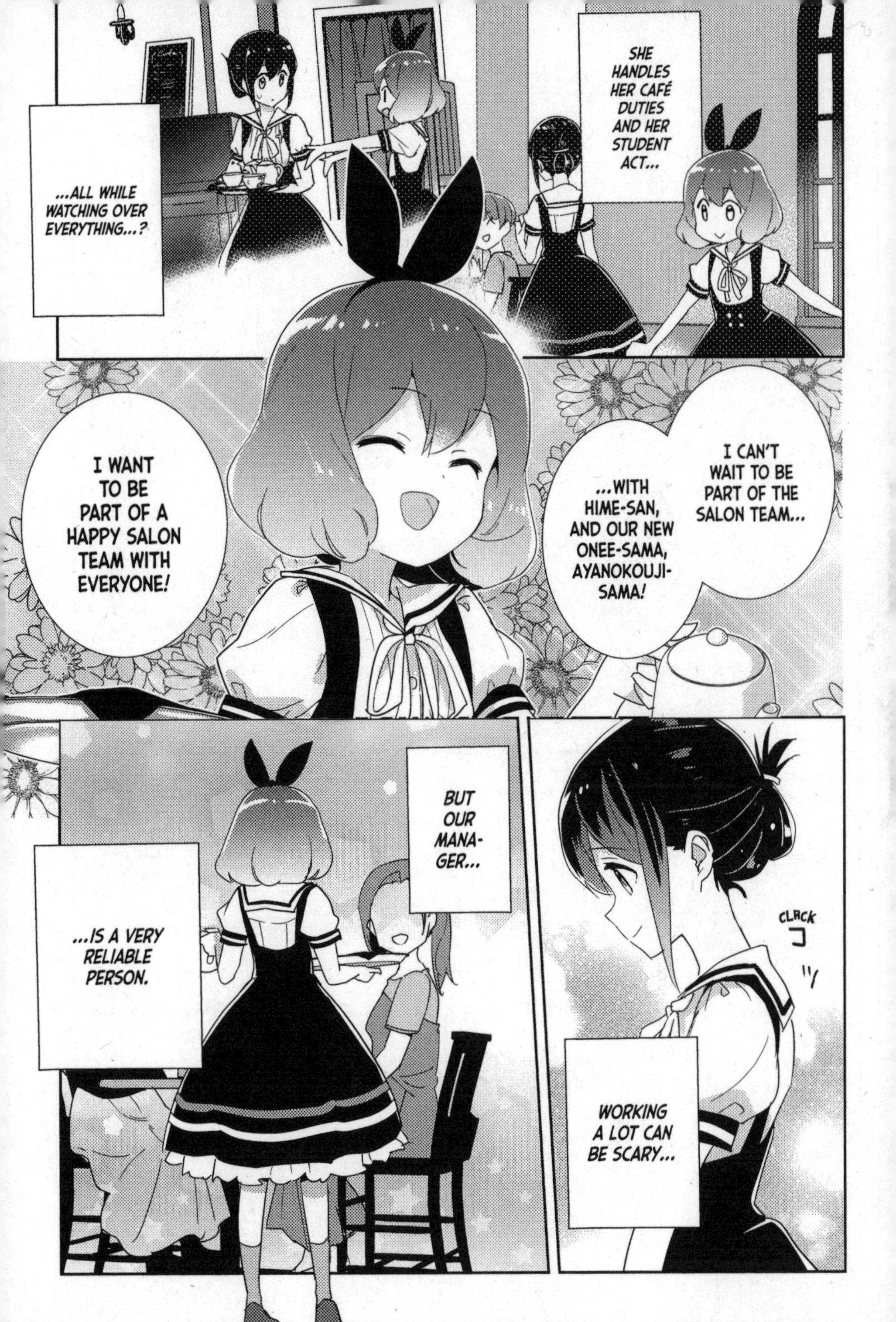
SHE HANDLES HER CAFÉ DUTIES AND HER STUDENT ACT...
...ALL WHILE WATCHING OVER EVERYTHING...?
I CAN'T WAIT TO BE PART OF THE SALON TEAM...
...WITH HIME-SAN, AND OUR NEW ONEE-SAMA, AYANOKOUJI-SAMA!
I WANT TO BE PART OF A HAPPY SALON TEAM WITH EVERYONE!
CLACK
WORKING A LOT CAN BE SCARY...
BUT OUR MANA-GER...
...IS A VERY RELIABLE PERSON.

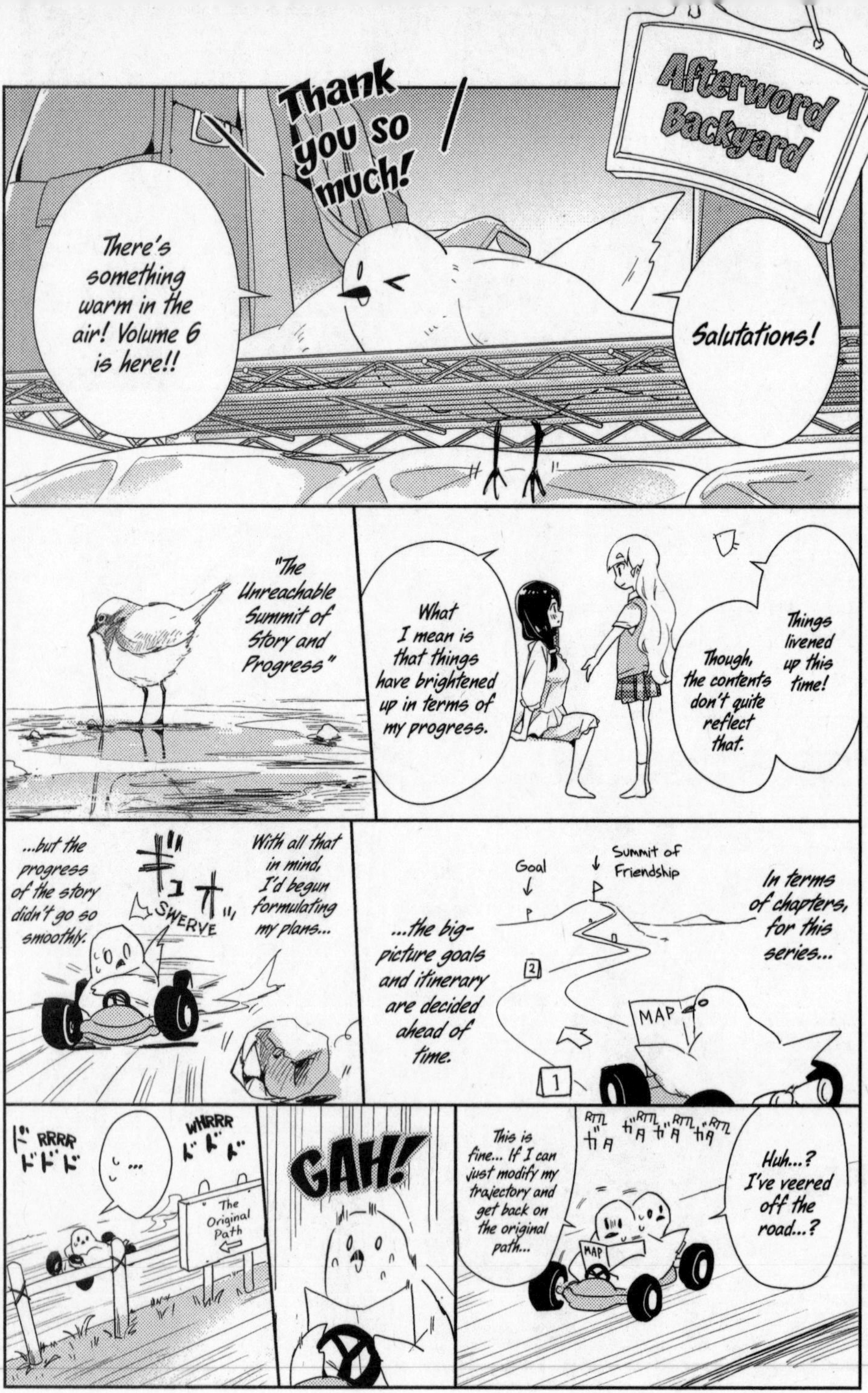
Afterword Backyard
Salutations!
Thank you so much!
There's something warm in the air! Volume 6 is here!!
Things livened up this time!
Though, the contents don't quite reflect that.
What I mean is that things have brightened up in terms of my progress.
"The Unreachable Summit of Story and Progress"
In terms of chapters, for this series...
Summit of Friendship
Goal
2
MAP
1
...the big-picture goals and itinerary are decided ahead of time.
With all that in mind, I'd begun formulating my plans...
SWERVE
...but the progress of the story didn't go so smoothly.
Huh...? I've veered off the road...?
RTTL
MAP
This is fine... If I can just modify my trajectory and get back on the original path...
GAH!
WHRRR
...
RRRR
The Original Path

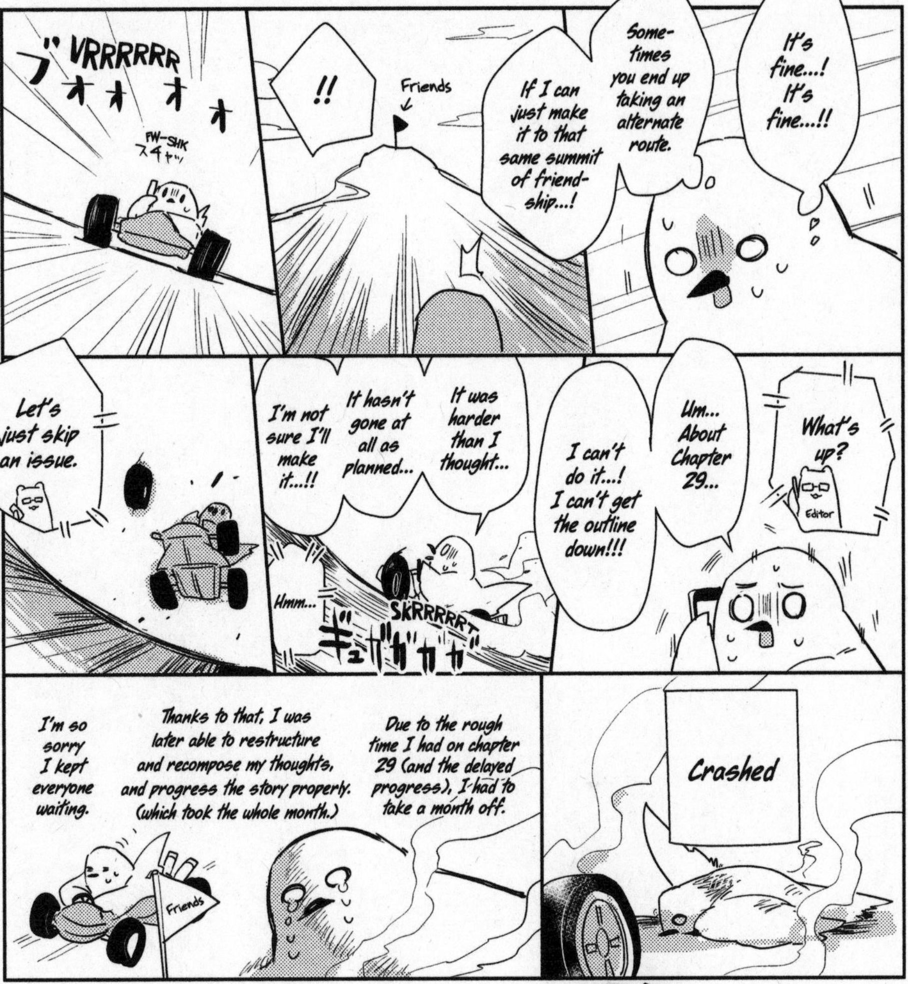
It's fine...! It's fine...!!
Sometimes you end up taking an alternate route.
If I can just make it to that same summit of friendship...!
!!
Friends
VRRRRRR
ブオオオオ
FW-SHK
スチャッ
What's up?
Editor
Um... About Chapter 29...
I can't do it...! I can't get the outline down!!!
It was harder than I thought...
It hasn't gone at all as planned...
I'm not sure I'll make it...!!
Hmm...
SKRRRRRT
ギュガガガガ
Let's just skip an issue.
Crashed
Due to the rough time I had on chapter 29 (and the delayed progress), I had to take a month off.
Thanks to that, I was later able to restructure and recompose my thoughts, and progress the story properly. (which took the whole month.)
I'm so sorry I kept everyone waiting.
Friends

...And this is how I crashed and burned once, then took my time and was able to climb that hill and finish Volume 6.

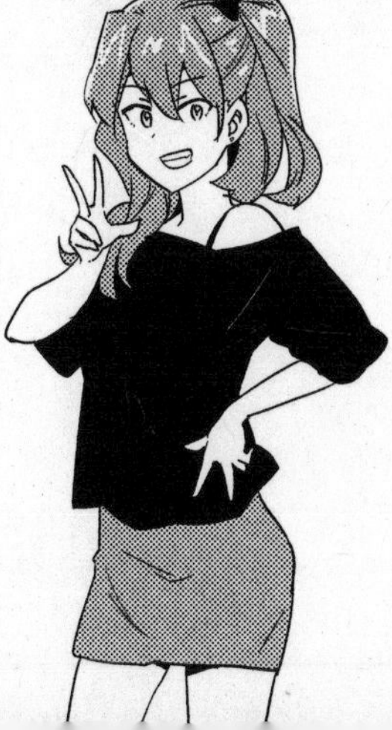

It was an important summit for Hime and Mitsuki, though, so I'm glad I was able to reach it.

I get the feeling that the path to the goal is a steep one yet, but...I'll do my best! I wish I had more strength!!

Until the day that we might meet again!

WHOOSH

2020

special thanx

Yuuri

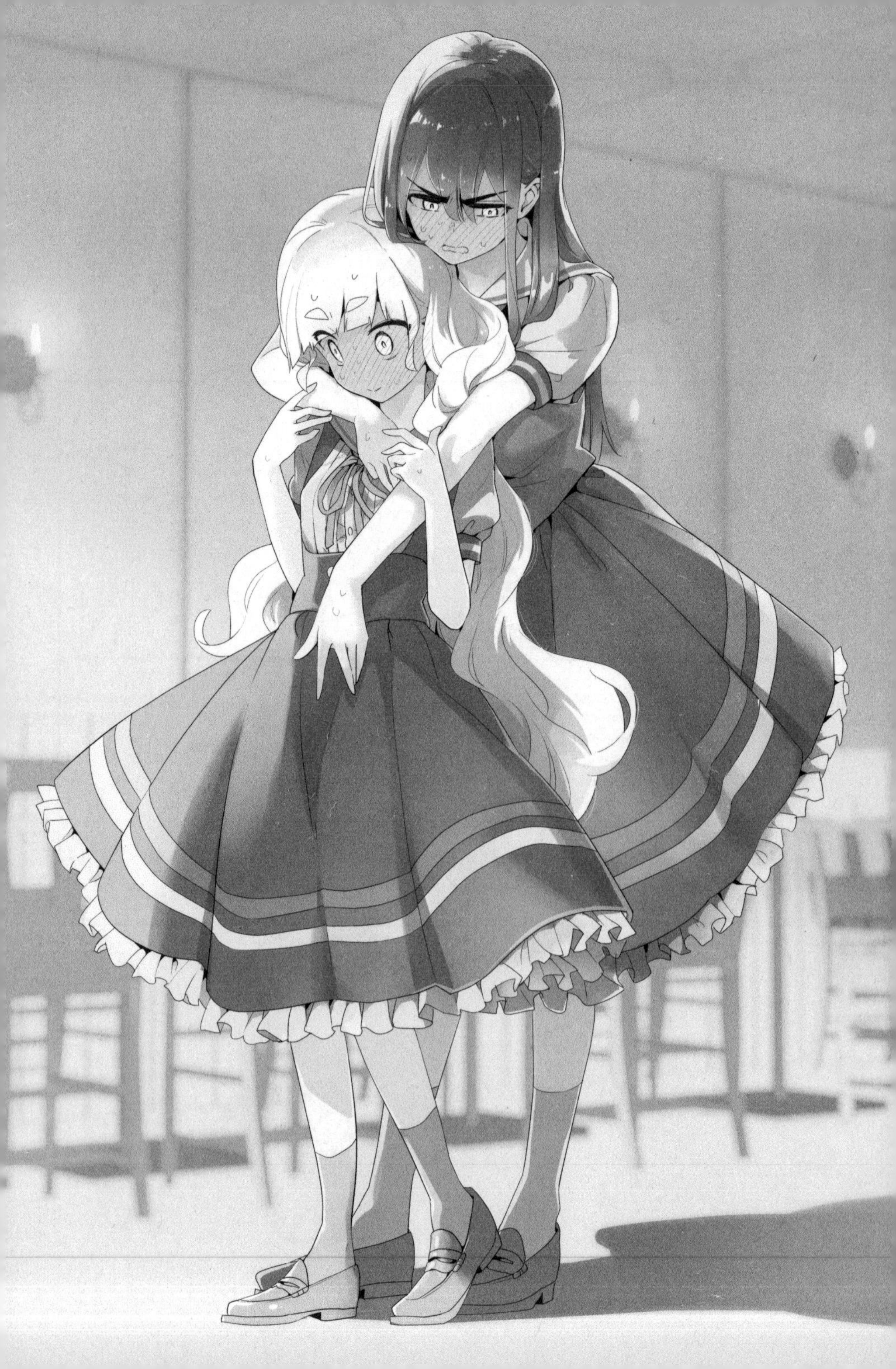

Hime-chan and Mitsuki-san's

Review! Café Liebe Operation Manual

Repaying Gifts

In the event that you receive a gift from a guest during your birthday period, you always thank them with a written reply known as a "*Dankeskarte.*" It's nice to write something in regards to the gift itself. Handwrite the note, and hand it to the guest when greeting them in the salon.

Now of course, this time we saw Mitsuki-san taking her presents home in one of the shop's trash bags, right? It would give a terrible impression if a guest saw that. Let's not do that anymore.

Danke Schön
Dear Mikoshiba-sama,
Thank you for the tea.
I think I'll use it for
my daily tea time.
I will give you
my impressions of
the tea later on.
-Mitsuki Ayanokouji
?
Waste Disppsal Bag

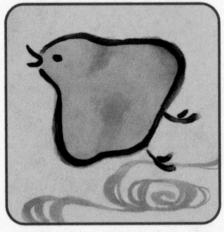

❧ miman ❧

Salutations.
Here, Hime and Mitsuki's relationship
grows complicated, for the two welcome
a birthday in twilit melancholy.
...Will the sun rise once more?

Yuri Is My Job!

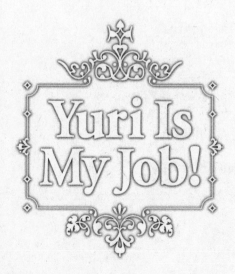

PERFECT WORLD

Rie Aruga

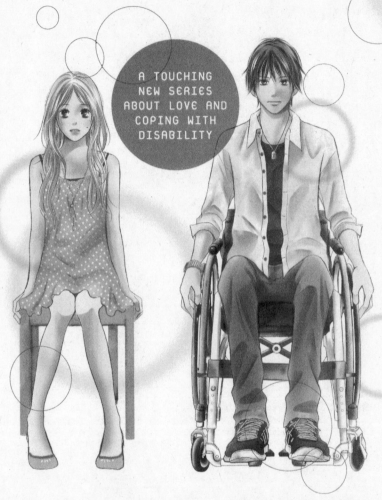

A TOUCHING NEW SERIES ABOUT LOVE AND COPING WITH DISABILITY

An office party reunites Tsugumi with her high school crush Itsuki. He's realized his dream of becoming an architect, but along the way, he experienced a spinal injury that put him in a wheelchair. Now Tsugumi's rekindled feelings will butt up against prejudices she never considered — and Itsuki will have to decide if he's ready to let someone into his heart...

"Depicts with great delicacy and courage the difficulties some with disabilities experience getting involved in romantic relationships... Rie Aruga refuses to romanticize, pushing her heroine to face the reality of disability. She invites her readers to the same tasks of empathy, knowledge and recognition."
—Slate.fr

"An important entry [in manga romance]... The emotional core of both plot and characters indicates thoughtfulness... [Aruga's] research is readily apparent in the text and artwork, making this feel like a real story."
—Anime News Network

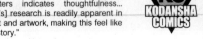

KC KODANSHA COMICS

Knight of the Ice ©Yayoi Ogawa/Kodansha Ltd.

SKATING THRILLS AND ICY CHILLS WITH THIS NEW TINGLY ROMANCE SERIES!

A rom-com on ice, perfect for fans of *Princess Jellyfish* and *Wotakoi*. Kokoro is the talk of the figure-skating world, winning trophies and hearts. But little do they know... he's actually a huge nerd! From the beloved creator of *You're My Pet* (*Tramps Like Us*).

Chitose is a serious young woman, working for the health magazine *SASSO*. Or at least, she would be, if she wasn't constantly getting distracted by her childhood friend, international figure skating star Kokoro Kijinami! In the public eye and on the ice, Kokoro is a gallant, flawless knight, but behind his glittery costumes and breathtaking spins lies a secret: He's actually a hopelessly romantic otaku, who can only land his quad jumps when Chitose is on hand to recite a spell from his favorite magical girl anime!

KC
KODANSHA COMICS

The art-deco cyberpunk classic from the creators of *xxxHOLiC* and *Cardcaptor Sakura*!

"Starred Review. This experimental sci-fi work from CLAMP reads like a romantic version of *AKIRA*."
—Publishers Weekly

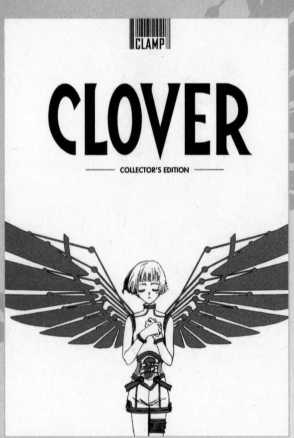

CLOVER © CLAMP-ShigatsuTsuitachi CO.,LTD./Kodansha Ltd.

Su was born into a bleak future, where the government keeps tight control over children with magical powers—codenamed "Clovers." With Su being the only "four-leaf" Clover in the world, she has been kept isolated nearly her whole life. Can ex-military agent Kazuhiko deliver her to the happiness she seeks? Experience the complete series in this hardcover edition, which also includes over twenty pages of ravishing color art!

KC/
KODANSHA COMICS

MAGIC ✦ KNIGHT RAYEARTH
25TH ANNIVERSARY EDITION
CLAMP

A BELOVED CLASSIC MAKES ITS STUNNING RETURN IN THIS GORGEOUS, LIMITED EDITION BOX SET!

This tale of three Tokyo teenagers who cross through a magical portal and become the champions of another world is a modern manga classic. The box set includes three volumes of manga covering the entire first series of *Magic Knight Rayearth*, plus the series's super-rare full-color art book companion, all printed at a larger size than ever before on premium paper, featuring a newly-revised translation and lettering, and exquisite foil-stamped covers.

A strictly limited edition, this will be gone in a flash!

KC/ KODANSHA COMICS

"Clever, sassy, and original....*xxxHOLiC* has the inherent hallmarks of a runaway hit."
—NewType magazine

Beautifully seductive artwork and uniquely Japanese depictions of the supernatural will hypnotize CLAMP fans!

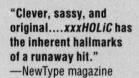

Kimihiro Watanuki is haunted by visions of ghosts and spirits. He seeks help from a mysterious woman named Yuko, who claims she can help. However, Watanuki must work for Yuko in order to pay for her aid. Soon Watanuki finds himself employed in Yuko's shop, where he sees things and meets customers that are stranger than anything he could have ever imagined.

The beloved characters from
Cardcaptor Sakura return in a brand new, reimagined fantasy adventure!

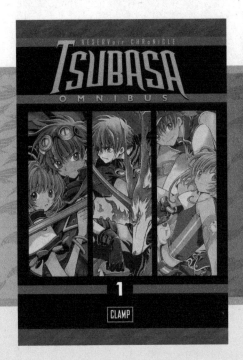

"[*Tsubasa*] takes readers on a fantastic ride that only gets more exhilarating with each successive chapter." —Anime News Network

In the Kingdom of Clow, an archaeological dig unleashes an incredible power, causing Princess Sakura to lose her memories. To save her, her childhood friend Syaoran must follow the orders of the Dimension Witch and travel alongside Kurogane, an unrivaled warrior; Fai, a powerful magician; and Mokona, a curiously strange creature, to retrieve Sakura's dispersed memories!

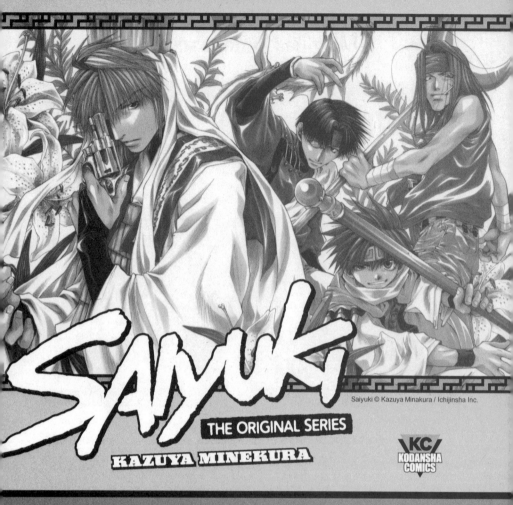

Young characters and steampunk setting, like *Howl's Moving Castle* and *Battle Angel Alita*

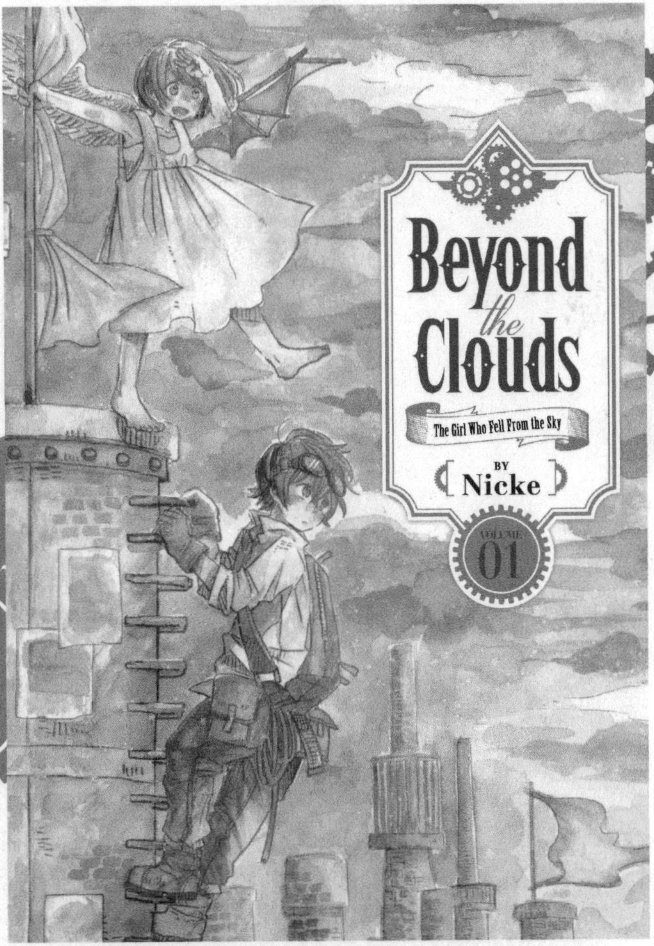
Beyond the Clouds
The Girl Who Fell From the Sky
BY
Nicke
VOLUME
01

Beyond the Clouds © 2018 Nicke / Ki-oon

A boy with a talent for machines and a mysterious girl whose wings he's fixed will take you beyond the clouds! In the tradition of the high-flying, resonant adventure stories of Studio Ghibli comes a gorgeous tale about the longing of young hearts for adventure and friendship!

KC KODANSHA COMICS

A SMART, NEW ROMANTIC COMEDY FOR FANS OF *SHORTCAKE CAKE* AND *TERRACE HOUSE*!

A romance manga starring high school girl Meeko, who learns to live on her own in a boarding house whose living room is home to the odd (but handsome) Matsunaga-san. She begins to adjust to her new life away from her parents, but Meeko soon learns that no matter how far away from home she is, she's still a young girl at heart — especially when she finds herself falling for Matsunaga-san.

Something's Wrong With Us

NATSUMI ANDO

The dark, psychological, sexy shojo series readers have been waiting for!

A spine-chilling and steamy romance between a Japanese sweets maker and the man who framed her mother for murder!

Following in her mother's footsteps, Nao became a traditional Japanese sweets maker, and with unparalleled artistry and a bright attitude, she gets an offer to work at a world-class confectionary company. But when she meets the young, handsome owner, she recognizes his cold stare...

KC
KODANSHA
COMICS

A Kodansha Comics Trade Paperback Original
Yuri Is My Job! 6 copyright © 2020 miman
English translation copyright © 2020 miman

Published in the United States by Kodansha Comics, an imprint of Kodansha USA Publishing, LLC, New York.

Publication rights for this English edition arranged through Kodansha Ltd., Tokyo.

First published in Japan in 2020 by Ichijinsha Inc., Tokyo as *Watashi no Yuri wa Oshigotodesu!*, volume 6.

ISBN 978-1-63236-930-7

Printed in the United States of America.

www.kodanshacomics.com

9 8 7 6 5 4 3 2
Translation: Diana Taylor
Lettering: Jennifer Skarupa
Editing: Haruko Hashimoto
Kodansha Comics edition logo design by Phil Balsman
Kodansha Comics edition cover design by My Truong

Publisher: Kiichiro Sugawara

Director of publishing services: Ben Applegate
Associate director of operations: Stephen Pakula
Publishing services managing editor: Noelle Webster
Assistant production manager: Emi Lotto, Angela Zurlo